Java™ Enterprise Design Patterns

Patterns in Java™, Volume 3

MARK GRAND

WILEY COMPUTER PUBLISHING

John Wiley & Sons, Inc.

New York • Chichester • Weinheim • Brisbane • Singapore • Toronto

Publisher: Robert Ipsen
Editor: Theresa Hudson
Developmental Editor: Kathryn A. Malm
Managing Editor: Angela Smith
New Media Editor: Brian Snapp
Text Design & Composition:

Designations used by companies to distinguish their products are often claimed as trademarks. In all instances where John Wiley & Sons, Inc., is aware of a claim, the product names appear in initial capital or ALL CAPITAL LETTERS. Readers, however, should contact the appropriate companies for more complete information regarding trademarks and registration.

This book is printed on acid-free paper. ∞

This publication is designed to provide accurate and authoritative information in regard to the subject matter covered. It is sold with the understanding that the publisher is not engaged in professional services. If professional advice or other expert assistance is required, the services of a competent professional person should be sought.

Library of Congress Cataloging-in-Publication Data:
Grand, Mark.
    Java Enterprise design patterns / Mark Grand.
        p.   cm.
    ISBN 0-471-33315-8 (pbk.: alk. paper)
    1. Java (Computer program language)   2. Web servers.   3. Object-oriented programming (Computer science)   I. Title.

QA76.73.J38 G72 2001
005. 13'3—dc21   2001045611

Printed in the United States of America.

10 9 8 7 6 5 4 3 2 1

C O N T E N T S

ACKNOWLEDGMENTS

This book would not have been possible without the inspiration, encouragement and assistance of others.

I want to thank Brad Appleton for his diligent reviews and concern with form.

Wolfgang W. Keller provided extensive feedback on the transaction patterns chapter.

Frank Sauer provided excellent feedback on the database patterns chapter.

I also want to thank the members of the pattern discussion group at University of Illinois, Champaign-Urbana, for their invaluable comments on my manuscript: Joe Yoder, Brian Foote, Hiroaki Nakamura, Roger Whitney, Ralph Johnson, Brian Marick, Wanghong Yuan, Paul Rubel, Frederico Balaguer, Alejandra Garrido, Don Roberts, Zhijiang "John" Han, Weerasak Witthawuskul, Peter Hatch, Dragos Malolescu, and Les Tyrrell.

Last, but not least, I would like to thank my wife Nicole for her support and encouragement through the most difficult of times. This book could not have been finished without her understanding and patience.

ABOUT THE AUTHOR

Mark Grand is a consultant specializing in distributed systems, object-oriented design, and Java. He is currently working on an open source framework for gluing components and programs into an application.

Mark Grand is the author of a series of books titled *Patterns in Java*. He is a consultant who specializes in Distributed Systems, Object Oriented Design, and Java. He was the architect of the first commercial B2B e-commerce product for the Internet.

1

Introduction
to Software Patterns

Software patterns are reusable solutions to recurring problems that occur during software development. For purposes in this book, we refer to software patterns simply as *patterns*.

What makes a bright, experienced programmer so much more productive than a bright but inexperienced programmer? Experience. Experience gives programmers wisdom. As programmers gain experience, they recognize the similarity between new problems and those problems that they have solved before. With even more experience, they recognize that the solutions for similar problems follow recurring patterns. Experienced programmers recognize the situations where these patterns apply and quickly draw on existing solutions without having to stop, analyze the problems, and then pose possible strategies.

When a programmer discovers a pattern, it's just an insight. In most cases, to go from a nonverbalized insight to a well-thought-out idea that the programmer can clearly articulate is surprisingly difficult. It's also an extremely valuable step. When we understand a pattern well enough to put it into words, we are able to intelligently combine it with other patterns. More important, once put into words, a pattern can be used in discussions among programmers who know the pattern. That allows programmers to more effectively collaborate and combine their wisdom. It can also help to avoid the situation where programmers argue over various solutions to a problem only to find out later that they were really thinking of the same solution but expressing it in different ways.

Putting a pattern into words has an additional benefit for less experienced programmers who have not yet discovered the pattern. Once a pattern has been put into words, more experienced programmers can teach it to programmers who are new to the pattern.

This book provides experienced programmers with a common vocabulary to discuss patterns. It also allows programmers who have not yet discovered a pattern to learn about the pattern.

Though this book includes a substantial breadth of patterns, additional patterns did not make it into this book. You, dear reader, may discover some of these patterns for yourself. Some patterns you discover may be highly specialized and of interest to only a small number of people. Other patterns may be of very broad interest and worthy of inclusion in a future volume of this book. If you wish to communicate such a pattern to me, my e-mail is mgrand@mindspring.com.

The patterns cataloged in this book convey constructive ways of organizing parts of the software development cycle. Other patterns that recur in programs are not constructive. These types of patterns are called *AntiPatterns*. Because AntiPatterns can cancel out the benefits of patterns, this book does not attempt to catalog them.

Description of Patterns

Patterns are usually described using a format that includes the following information:

- A description of the problem that includes a concrete example and a solution specific to the concrete problem
- A summary of the forces that lead to the formulation of a general solution
- A general solution
- The consequences, good and bad, of using the given solution to solve a problem
- A list of related patterns

Pattern books differ in how they document patterns. The format used in this book varies depending on which phase of the software life cycle the pattern addresses. The patterns in this book are related to a few different phases of the software life cycle. The pattern descriptions are organized into the section headings described here. Because the nature of the patterns varies, not every heading is used in every pattern.

Pattern Name

The Pattern Name section consists of the name of the pattern and a bibliography reference that indicates where the pattern originated. Most patterns don't have any additional text under this heading. For those that do, this section contains information about the derivation or general nature of the pattern.

The bibliography reference indicates where the ideas in the pattern were first written in the form of a pattern. Because patterns are based on established practices, in many cases there are other sources of the ideas in the pattern other than the bibliography reference. Usually, the author of a pattern is not the first person to discover the ideas that underlie the pattern. In particular, I do not claim to be the first person to discover the ideas presented in this book. Those patterns with a bibliographic reference to this book merely indicate that I know of no other place where that particular set of ideas has been documented as a pattern. The bibliography entry next to a pattern name is provided to help you trace the development of the pattern itself, not the underlying ideas.

Synopsis

The Synopsis section provides a brief summary of the pattern—both the essence of the problem that the pattern aims to solve and the solution provided by the pattern. The synopsis is primarily directed at experienced programmers who may recognize the pattern as one they already know, but may not have had a name for. After recognizing the pattern from its name and synopsis, it may be sufficient to skim over the rest of the pattern description.

Don't be discouraged if you don't recognize a pattern from its name and synopsis. Instead, read carefully through the rest of the pattern description to better understand it.

Context

The Context section describes the problem that the pattern addresses. For most patterns, the problem is introduced in terms of a concrete example. After presenting the problem in the example, the Context section suggests a design solution for that problem.

Forces

The Forces section summarizes the considerations that lead to the problem's general solution presented in the Solution section. The Forces section also summarizes considerations that would lead you to forgo the solution. The reasons for not using a solution are as important as the reasons for using a solution. Both are organized as bulleted points as follows:

☺ Reasons to use a solution are bulleted with a happy face.
☻ Reasons not to use a solution are bulleted with a sad face.

Solution

The Solution section is the core of the pattern. It describes a general-purpose solution to the problem that the pattern addresses.

Consequences

The Consequences section explains the implications—good, bad, and neutral—for using the solution. Most consequences are organized into bulleted points like this:

☺ Good consequences are bulleted with a happy face.
● Neutral consequences are bulleted with a dot.
☻ Bad consequences are bulleted with a sad face.

Implementation

The Implementation section describes the important considerations to be aware of when executing the solution. It may also describe some common variations or simplifications of the solution. Some patterns may not have an Implementation section because these concerns are not relevant.

Known Uses

The Known Uses section highlights some well-known uses for the pattern.

Code Example

The Code Example section contains a code example showing a sample implementation for a design that uses the pattern. For some patterns, such as Graphical User Interface (GUI) design patterns, a code example is not relevant.

Related Patterns

The Related Patterns section contains a list of patterns that are related to the pattern described.

A Very Brief History of Patterns

The idea of software patterns originally came from the field of architecture. An architect named Christopher Alexander wrote some revolutionary books that describe patterns in building architecture and urban planning:

- *A Pattern Language: Towns, Buildings, Construction* (Oxford University Press, 1977)
- *The Timeless Way of Building* (Oxford University Press, 1979)

The ideas presented in these books are applicable to a number of fields outside of architecture, including software.

In 1987, Ward Cunningham and Kent Beck used some of Alexander's ideas to develop five patterns for user-interface design. They published a paper on the UI patterns at OOPSLA-87: *Using Pattern Languages for Object-Oriented Programs.*

In the early 1990s, four authors—Erich Gamma, Richard Helm, John Vlissides, and Ralph Johnson—began work on one of the most influential computer books of this decade: *Design Patterns*. Published in 1994, the book popularized the idea of patterns. *Design Patterns* is often called the Gang of Four, or GoF, book.

This book you are reading represents an evolution of patterns and objects since the GoF book was published. The GoF book used C++ and SmallTalk for its examples. I use Java and take a rather Java-centric view of most things. When the GoF book was written, the Unified Modeling Language (UML) did not exist. It's now widely accepted as the preferred notation for object-oriented analysis and design. Therefore, that is the notation I use in this book.

Organization of This Book

This book follows my previous two works on *Patterns in Java*. The first volume focused exclusively on general-purpose design patterns. The second volume moved away from design patterns to include a variety of patterns used to assign responsibilities to classes, design GUIs, write code, and test software.

This third volume contains design and architectural patterns for use in distributed and enterprise applications. The topics include patterns related to transaction design, distributed computing, concurrency, time, and using databases with object-oriented programs.

As with my previous books on Java patterns, this one begins with a brief description of the UML subset used to document the patterns. Chapter

3, containing an overview of the software life cycle, provides the context in which the patterns are used. Chapter 3 also offers a case study that includes examples for using the patterns. The remaining chapters describe different types of patterns.

The CD-ROM that accompanies this book contains all of the code examples. In some cases, the examples on the CD-ROM are more complete than those that appear in this book. The CD-ROM also contains trial versions of software related to the patterns.

The Java examples that appear in this book are based on JDK 1.3.

2

Overview of UML

The Unified Modeling Language (UML) is a notation that you can use for object-oriented analysis and design. This chapter contains a brief introduction to the UML and to the subset and extensions of the UML that are used in this book. For a complete description of the UML, see www.omg.org.

Books on UML define the pieces of information stored in instances of a class as *attributes;* they define a class's encapsulations of behavior as *operations.* Those terms, like UML, are not specific to any implementation language. However, this book is not language neutral. It assumes that you are using Java as your implementation language. This book also uses mostly Java-specific terms rather than terms that are language neutral but less familiar to Java programmers. For example, I use the words *attribute* and *variable* interchangeably, preferring the Java-specific term, *variable*. I use the words *operation* and *method* interchangeably, preferring the Java-specific term, *method*.

UML defines a number of different kinds of diagrams. The rest of this chapter is organized into sections that describe each of those diagrams and the elements that appear in them.

If you are experienced with object-oriented design, you will find most of the concepts that underlie the UML notation to be familiar. If you find many of the concepts unfamiliar, read only as much of this chapter as you

7

feel comfortable with. In later chapters, if a UML diagram contains something you want explained, return to Chapter 2 and find a diagram that contains a similar UML element.

Class Diagram

A *class diagram* is a diagram that shows classes, interfaces, and their relationships. The most basic element of a class diagram is a class. Figure 2.1 shows many of the features that a class can have within a class diagram.

Classes are drawn as rectangles. The rectangles can be divided into two or three compartments. The class rectangle shown in Figure 2.1 has three compartments. The top compartment contains the name of the class. The middle compartment lists the class's variables. The bottom compartment lists the class's methods.

The symbols that precede each variable and method are *visibility indicators*. The possible visibility indicators and their meanings are as follows:

+ Public
# Protected
− Private

The variables in the middle compartment are shown as follows:

`visibilityIndicator name : type`

Therefore, the two variables shown in the class in Figure 2.1 are private variables. The name of the first variable is `instance` and its type is `AudioClipManager`. The name of the second variable is `prevClip` and its type is `AudioClip`.

```
            AudioClipManager

-instance:AudioClipManager
-prevClip:Audioclip

«constructor»
-AudioClipManager( )
«misc»
+getInstance( ):AudioClipManager
+play(:AudioClip)
+loop(:AudioClip)
+stop( )
...
```

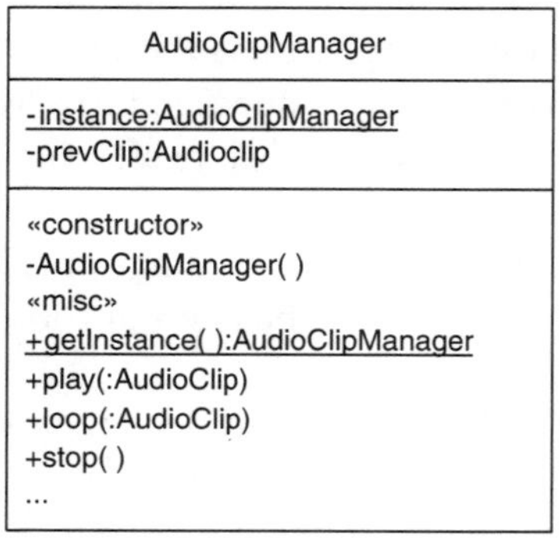

FIGURE 2.1 Basic class.

Though not shown in Figure 2.1, an initial value can be indicated for a variable by following the variable's type with an equal sign followed by the value like this:

```
ShutDown:boolean = false
```

You will notice that the first variable shown in the class is underlined. If a variable is underlined, that means it is a static variable. This applies to methods, too. Underlined methods are static methods.

The methods in the bottom compartment are shown as follows:

```
visibilityIndicator name ( formalParameters ) : returnType
```

The `getInstance` method shown in the class in Figure 2.1 returns an `AudioClipManager` object.

The UML indicates a void method by leaving out the `": returnType"` from a method to indicate that it does not return anything. Therefore, the `stop` method shown in the class in Figure 2.1 does not return any result.

A method's formal parameters consists of a name and type like this:

```
setLength(length:int)
```

If a method has multiple parameters, commas separate them:

```
setPosition(x:int, y:int)
```

Two of the methods in the class shown in Figure 2.1 are preceded by a word in guillemets:

```
<<constructor>>
```

In UML, drawing a word in guillemets is called a *stereotype*. A stereotype is used like an adjective to modify what comes after it. The `constructor` stereotype indicates that the methods that follow it are constructors. The `misc` stereotype indicates that the methods that come after it are regular methods. Additional uses for stereotypes are described later in this chapter.

One last element that appears in the class shown in Figure 2.1 is an ellipsis (. . .). If an ellipsis appears in the bottom compartment of a class, it means that the class has additional methods not shown in the diagram. If an ellipsis appears in the middle compartment of a class, the class has additional variables not shown in the diagram.

Often, it is not necessary or helpful to show as many details of a class as are shown in Figure 2.1. Figure 2.2 shows a class that is drawn with only two compartments:

When a class is drawn with only two compartments as shown in Figure 2.2, its top compartment contains its name and its bottom compart-

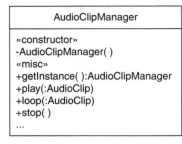

FIGURE 2.2 A two-compartment class.

ment shows its methods. If a class is drawn with only two compartments, it simply means that its variables are not shown. It does not mean that it has no variables.

The visibility indicators may be omitted from methods and variables. When a method or variable is shown without a visibility indicator, that means only that there is no indication of the method's or variable's visibility. It does not imply that the methods or variables are public, protected, or private.

A method's parameters may be omitted if their return values are also omitted. For example, the visibility indicators and method parameters are omitted from the class shown in Figure 2.3.

The simplest form of a class contains only one compartment with the class name, as shown in Figure 2.4.

A one-compartment representation of a class merely identifies the class. It provides no indication about what variables or methods the class has.

Interfaces are drawn in a manner similar to classes. The difference is that the name in the top compartment is preceded by an `interface` stereotype. Figure 2.5 is an example of an interface.

Classes and interfaces are important elements of class diagrams. The other elements of a class diagram show the relationships between classes and interfaces. Figure 2.6 is a typical class diagram.

The lines in Figure 2.6 indicate the relationship between the classes and interface. A solid line with a closed, hollow head such as the one in

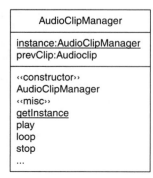

FIGURE 2.3 Simplified class.

AudioClipManager

FIGURE 2.4 A one-compartment class.

Figure 2.7 indicates the relationship of a subclass that inherits from a superclass.

The class diagram in Figure 2.6 shows the abstract class `Product` as the superclass of the `ConcreteProduct` class. You can tell that it is abstract because its name is italicized. You can tell that its methods are abstract because they are also italicized.

A similar sort of line is used to indicate that a class implements an interface. It is a dotted or dashed line with a closed head, as shown in Figure 2.8.

The class diagram in Figure 2.6 shows that the `Factory` class implements the `FactoryIF` interface.

The other lines show the other types of relationships between the classes and interface. UML calls these other types of relationships *associations*. A number of things can appear with associations to provide information about the nature of an association. The following items are optional, but this book consistently uses them wherever it makes sense.

Association name. Somewhere around the middle of an association there may be an *association name*. The name of an association is always capitalized. There may be a triangle at one end of the association name. The triangle indicates the direction in which you should read the association.

Looking at Figure 2.6, you will see that the association between the `Factory` and `ConcreteProduct` classes has the name `Creates`.

Navigation arrows. Arrowheads that may appear at the ends of an association are called *navigation arrows*. Navigation arrows indicate the direction in which you may navigate an association.

‹‹interface›› AddressIF
getAddress1 setAddress1 getAddress2 setAddress2 getCity setCity getState setState getPostalCode setPostalCode

FIGURE 2.5 Interface.

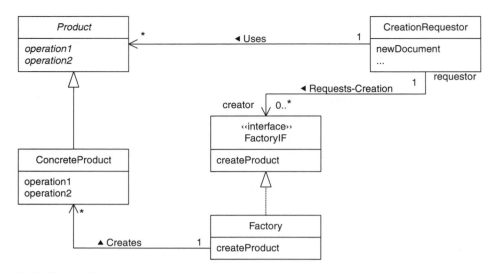

FIGURE 2.6 Class diagram.

Looking at the association named `Creates` in Figure 2.6, you will see that it has a navigation arrow pointing from the `Factory` class to the `ConcreteProduct` class. Because of the nature of creation, it seems clear that this means the `Factory` class is responsible for creating instances of the `ConcreteProduct` class.

The nature of some associations is less obvious. To make the nature of such associations clear, it may be necessary to supply additional information about the association. One common way to clarify the nature of an association is to name the role that each class plays in the association.

Role name.   To clarify the nature of an association, the name of the role that each class plays in the association can appear at each end of an association next to the corresponding class. Role names are always lowercase. That makes them easier to distinguish from association names, which are always capitalized.

In Figure 2.6, the `CreationRequestor` class and the `FactoryIF` interface participate in an association named `Requests-Creation`. The `CreationRequestor` class participates in that association in a role called `requestor`. The `FactoryIF` interface participates in that association in a role called `creator`.

FIGURE 2.7 Where a subclass inherits from a superclass.

◁······················· **FIGURE 2.8** Implements an interface.

Multiplicity indicator.   Another detail of an association that is usually supplied is how many instances of each class participate in an occurrence of an association. A multiplicity indicator may appear at each end of an association to provide that information. A multiplicity indicator can be a simple number like 0 or 1. It can be a range of numbers indicated like this:

`0..2`

An asterisk as the high value of a range means an unlimited number of occurrences. The multiplicity indicator `1..*` means at least one instance; `0..*` means any number of instances. A simple `*` is equivalent to `0..*`.

Looking at the multiplicity indicators in Figure 2.6, you will see that each one of the associations in the drawing is a one-to-many relationship.

Figure 2.9 is a class diagram that shows a class with multiple subclasses.

Although the drawing in Figure 2.9 is perfectly valid, the UML allows a more aesthetically pleasing way to draw a class with multiple subclasses. You can combine the arrowheads as shown in Figure 2.10. The diagram in Figure 2.10 is identical in meaning to the diagram in Figure 2.9.

Sometimes there is a need to convey more structure than is implied by a simple one-to-many relationship. The type of one-to-many relationship where one object contains a collection of other objects is called an *aggregation*. A hollow diamond at the end of the association indicates aggregation. The hollow diamond appears at the end of the association attached to the class that contains instances of the other class. The class diagram in Figure 2.11 shows an aggregation.

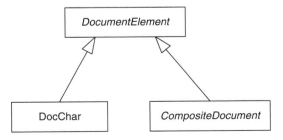

FIGURE 2.9 Multiple inheritance arrows.

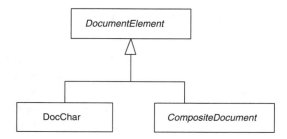

FIGURE 2.10 Single inheritance arrow.

The class diagram in Figure 2.11 shows a class named MessageManager. Each of its instances contains zero or more instances of a class named MIMEMsg.

UML has another notation to indicate a stronger relationship than aggregation. That relationship is called *composite aggregation*. For an aggregation to be composite, two conditions must be satisfied:

- Aggregated instances must belong to only one composite at a time.
- Some operations must propagate from the composite to its aggregated instances. For example, when a composite object is cloned, its clone method will typically clone the aggregated instances so that the cloned composite will own clones of the original aggregated instances.

Figure 2.12 is a class diagram that contains a composite aggregation.

The class diagram in Figure 2.12 shows a Document class. Document objects can contain Paragraph objects. Paragraph objects can contain DocChar objects. Because of the composite aggregation, you know that Paragraph objects do not share DocChar objects and Document objects do not share Paragraph objects.

Some associations are indirect. Instead of classes directly associated with each other, they are associated indirectly through a third class. Consider the class diagram in Figure 2.13. The association in Figure 2.13 shows that instances of the Cache class refer to instances of the Object class through an instance of the OjbectID class.

There is another use for ellipsis in a class diagram. Some class diagrams need to show that a class has a large or open-ended set of subclasses

FIGURE 2.11 Aggregation.

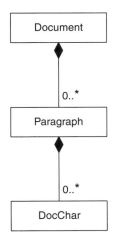

FIGURE 2.12 Composite aggregation.

while showing only a few subclasses as examples. The class diagram in Figure 2.14 shows how ellipsis can be used to show just that.

The class diagram in Figure 2.14 shows a class named DataQuery that has subclasses named JDBCQuery, OracleQuery, SybaseQuery, and an indefinite number of other classes that are indicated by the ellipsis.

An association between classes or interfaces implies a dependency that involves an object reference that connects two objects. Other types of dependencies are possible. A dashed line is used to indicate a dependency in the more general sense. Figure 2.15 shows an example of such a dependency.

The classes in a class diagram can be organized into *packages.* Packages are drawn as a large rectangle with a small rectangle above the large one. The small rectangle contains the name of the package. The small and large rectangles are arranged to have an overall shape similar to a manila folder. The class diagram in Figure 2.16 contains a package named ServicePackage. A visibility indicator can precede the name of classes and interfaces that appear within a package. Public classes are accessible to classes outside of the package; private classes are not.

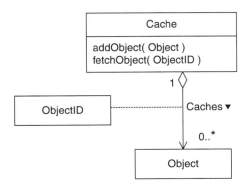

FIGURE 2.13 Association class.

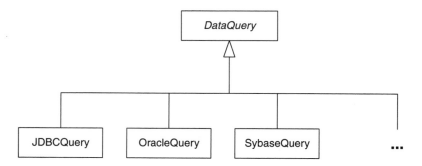

FIGURE 2.14 Open-ended subclasses.

There may be aspects of a design you cannot make sufficiently clear without adding a comment to a diagram. Comments in the UML are drawn as a rectangle with its upper right corner turned down. Comments are connected to the diagram element to which they relate by a dashed line. The class diagram in Figure 2.17 contains a comment.

Figure 2.17 shows the static class MilestoneMemento, which is a private member of the GameModel class. There is no standard way in the UML to represent a static private member class. The diagram uses a stereotype as an extension to the UML to indicate that the MilestoneMemento class is static. It uses an association to indicate that the MilestoneMemento is a private member of the GameModel class. To make the relationship even more clear, there is a comment about it in Figure 2.17.

Class diagrams can include objects. Most of the objects in the diagrams in this book are drawn as shown in Figure 2.18.

The object shown in Figure 2.18 is an instance of a class named Area. The underline tells you that it is an object. A name may appear to the left of the colon (:). The only significance of the name is that if you can use it to identify the individual object.

Some diagrams indicate an object as just an empty rectangle with nothing inside it. Obviously, blank objects cannot be used to identify any

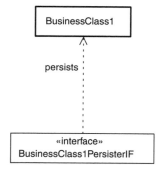

FIGURE 2.15 Dependency.

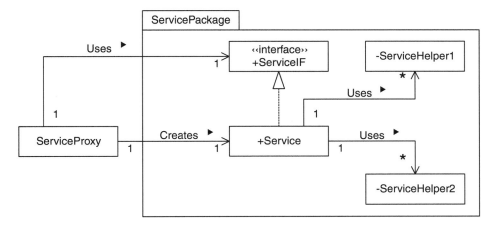

FIGURE 2.16 Package.

particular kind of object. However, they can be used in a diagram that shows a structure in which objects of unspecified type are connected. The class diagram in Figure 2.19 shows such a structure.

The lines that connect two objects are not associations. The lines that connect objects are called *links*. Links are connections between objects, whereas associations are relationships between classes. A link is

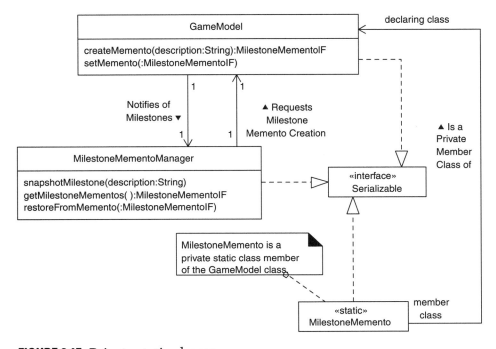

FIGURE 2.17 Private static classes.

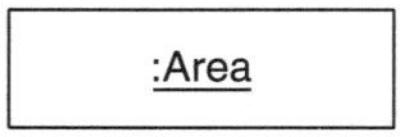

:Area

FIGURE 2.18 Object.

an occurrence of an association, just as an object is an instance of a class. Links can have association names, navigation arrows, and most of the other embellishments that associations can have. However, since a link is a connection between two objects, links may not have multiplicity indicators or aggregation diamonds.

Some diagrams consist only of objects and links. Such diagrams are considered a kind of class diagram. However, there is a special name for that kind of diagram—an *object diagram.* Figure 2.20 is an example of an object diagram.

Collaboration Diagram

Class and object diagrams show relationships between classes and objects. They also provide information about the interactions that occur between classes. They do not show the sequence in which the interactions occur or any concurrency that they may have.

Collaboration diagrams show objects, the links that connect them, and the interactions that occur over each link. They also show the sequence and concurrency requirements for each interaction. Figure 2.21 is a simple example of a collaboration diagram.

Any number of interactions can be associated with a link. Each interaction involves a method call. Next to each interaction or group of interactions is an arrow that points to the object whose method is called by the interaction. The entire set of objects and interactions shown in a collaboration diagram is collectively called a *collaboration.*

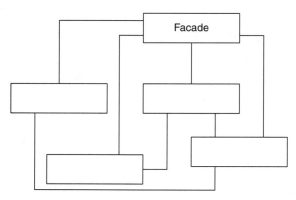

FIGURE 2.19 Blank objects.

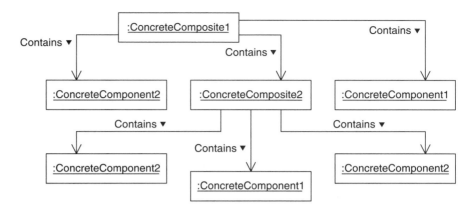

FIGURE 2.20 Object diagram.

Each of the interactions shown in Figure 2.21 begins with a sequence number and a colon. Sequence numbers indicate the order in which method calls occur. An interaction with the number 1 must come before an interaction with the number 2 and so on.

Multilevel sequence numbers consist of two or more numbers separated by a period. Notice that most of the sequence numbers in Figure 2.21

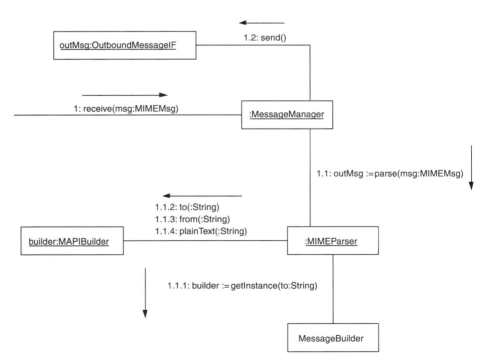

FIGURE 2.21 Collaboration diagram.

FIGURE 2.22 Multiobject.

are multilevel sequence numbers. Multilevel sequence numbers correspond to multiple levels of method calls. The portion of a multilevel sequence number to the left of its rightmost period is called its *prefix.* For example, the prefix of 1.3.4 is 1.3.

Interactions numbered with a multilevel sequence number occur during another interaction's method call. The other method call is determined by the interaction's prefix. The method calls of the interactions numbered 1.1 and 1.2 are made during the method call of interaction 1. Similarly, interactions numbered 1.1.1, 1.1.2, 1.1.3, . . . occur during the method call of interaction 1.1.

Among interactions numbered with the same prefix, their methods are called in the order determined by the last number in their sequence numbers. Therefore, the methods of interactions numbered 1.1.1, 1.1.2, 1.1.3, . . . are called in that order.

As mentioned earlier, links represent a connection between two objects. Because of that, links may not have any multiplicity indicators. That works well for links that represent an occurrence of an association between a definite number of objects. Associations that have a star multiplicity indicator on either end involve an indefinite number of objects. There is no way to draw an indefinite number of links to an indefinite number of objects. UML provides a symbol that allows us to draw links that connect an indefinite number of objects. That symbol is called a *multiobject.* It represents an indefinite number of objects. It looks like a rectangle behind a rectangle. The collaboration diagram in Figure 2.22 contains a multiobject.

The collaboration diagram in Figure 2.22 shows an `ObservableIF` object calling a `Multicaster` object's `notify` method. The `Multicaster` object's implementation of the `notify` method calls `notify` method of an indefinite number of `ObserverIF` objects linked to the `Multicaster` object.

Objects created as a result of a collaboration may be marked with the property `{new}`. Temporary objects that exist only during a collaboration may be marked with the property `{transient}`.* The collaboration diagram in Figure 2.23 shows a collaboration that creates an object.

---

* The UML and Java use the word *transient* in very different ways. Java uses *transient* to mean that a variable is not part of an object's persistent state. UML uses it to mean that an object has a bounded lifetime.

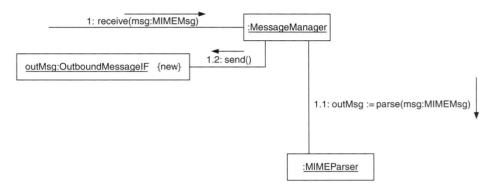

FIGURE 2.23 New object.

Some interactions occur concurrently rather than sequentially. A letter at the end of a sequence number indicates concurrent interactions. For example, the methods of interactions numbered 2.2a and 2.2b would be called concurrently and each call would run in a separate thread. Consider the collaboration diagram in Figure 2.24. The top-level interaction is numbered 1. During that interaction, first interaction 1.1 is invoked. Then interactions 1.2a and 1.2b are simultaneously invoked. After that, interactions 1.3 and 1.4 are invoked, in that order.

An asterisk after a sequence number indicates a repeated interaction. Consider the collaboration diagram in Figure 2.25.

The collaboration in Figure 2.25 begins by calling the `TollBooth` object's `start` method. That method repeatedly calls the object's `collectNextToll` method. The `collectNextToll` method calls the

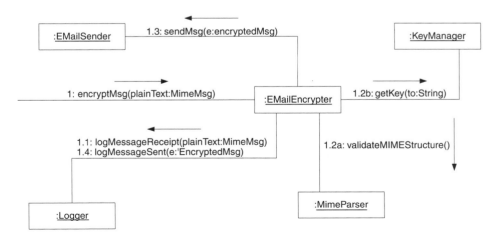

FIGURE 2.24 E-mail encrypter.

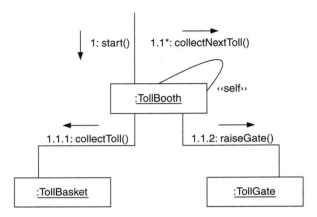

FIGURE 2.25 Tollbooth.

TollBasket object's collectToll method and the TollGate object's raiseGate method.

One other thing to notice about the collaboration diagram in Figure 2.25 is the <<self>> stereotype that appears next to the link for interaction 1.1. It serves to clarify the fact that the link is a self-reference.

Unlike the example in Figure 2.25, most repetitive interactions occur conditionally. UML allows a condition to be associated with a repetitive interaction by putting it after the asterisk inside of square brackets. The collaboration diagram in Figure 2.26 shows an example of a conditional repetitive interaction.

Figure 2.26 shows an Iterator object being passed to a DialogMediator object's refresh method. Its refresh method in turn calls a Widget object's reset method and then repeatedly calls its addData method while the Iterator object's hasNext method returns true.

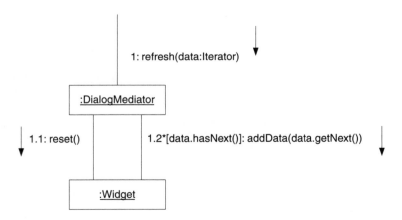

FIGURE 2.26 Refresh.

It is important to note that the UML specification does not define the meaning of conditions associated with repetitive interactions very precisely. In particular, the UML spec says that what appears between the square brackets can "be expressed in pseudocode or an actual programming language." This book consistently uses Java for that purpose.

When dealing with multiple threads, something that often needs to be specified about methods is what happens when two threads try to call the same method at the same time. UML allows that to be specified by placing one of the following constructs after a method:

{concurrency = sequential}. This means that only one thread at a time should call a method. No guarantee is made about the correctness of the method's behavior if the method is called by multiple threads at a time.

{concurrency = concurrent}. This means that if multiple threads call a method at the same time they will all execute it concurrently and correctly.

{concurrency = guarded}. This means that if multiple threads call a method at the same time, only one thread at a time will be allowed to execute the method. While one thread executes the method, other threads will be forced to wait until it is their turn. This is similar to the behavior of synchronized Java methods.

The collaboration diagram in Figure 2.27 shows an example of a synchronized method.

There are refinements to thread synchronization used in this book for which there is no standard representation in UML. This book uses some extensions to the {concurrency=guarded} construct to represent those refinements.

Sometimes the object that the threads need to synchronize on is not the same object whose method is called by an interaction. Consider the collaboration diagram in Figure 2.28.

FIGURE 2.27 Synchronized method call.

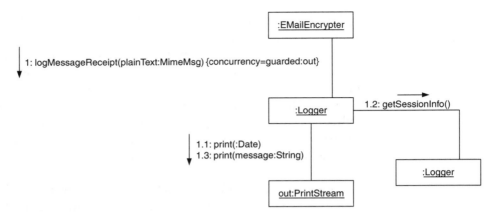

FIGURE 2.28 Synchronization using a third object.

In Figure 2.28, `{concurrency=guarded:out}` refers to the object labeled `out`. Before the method call can actually take place, the thread that controls the call must own the lock associated with the `out` object. This is identical to Java's semantics for a synchronized statement.

Sometimes there are preconditions beyond acquiring ownership of a lock that must be met before a thread may proceed with a method call. Such preconditions are indicated by a vertical bar followed by the precondition. The collaboration diagram in Figure 2.29 shows such preconditions following `guarded` and a vertical bar.

The collaboration diagram in Figure 2.29 shows two asynchronous interactions. One interaction calls a `PrintQueue` object's `addPrintJob` method to add a print job to the `PrintQueue` object. In the other interaction, a `PrintDriver` object calls the `PrintQueue` object's `getPrintJob` method to get a print job from the `PrintQueue` object. Both interactions have synchronization preconditions. If the print queue is full, then the interaction that calls the `addPrintJob` method will wait until the print queue is not full before proceeding to make the call to the `addPrintJob`

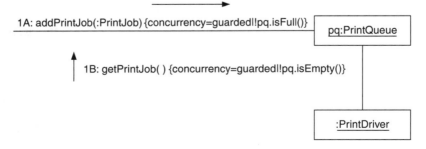

FIGURE 2.29 Print queue.

method. If the print queue is empty, then the interaction that calls the `getPrintJob` method will wait until the print queue is not empty before proceeding to make the call to the `getPrintJob` method.

A type of precondition that is not usually indicated with an expression is a requirement that an interaction not start until two or more other interactions finish. All interactions have an implicit precondition that they cannot start before the directly preceding interaction finishes. An interaction numbered 1.2.4 cannot start until the interaction numbered 1.2.3 completes.

Some interactions are required to wait for additional interactions to complete before they can start. Such additional predecessor interactions are indicated by listing them at the left side of the interaction followed by a slash (/) and the rest of the interaction. The collaboration diagram in Figure 2.30 contains an example.

In Figure 2.30, the interaction labeled 2.1a.1 cannot start until interaction 1.1.2 finishes. If an interaction must wait for more than one additional interaction to finish before it starts, they all appear before the slash, separated by commas.

The mechanisms discussed so far determine when the methods of a collaboration are called. They do not say anything about when method calls return. The arrows that point at the objects whose methods are called provide information about when the methods may return.

Most of the arrows in Figure 2.30 have a closed head, which indicates that the calls are synchronous. The method calls do not return until the method has completed doing whatever it does.

An open arrowhead indicates an *asynchronous method call*. An asynchronous method call returns to its caller immediately, while the method does its work asynchronously in a separate thread. The collaboration diagram in Figure 2.31 shows an asynchronous method call.

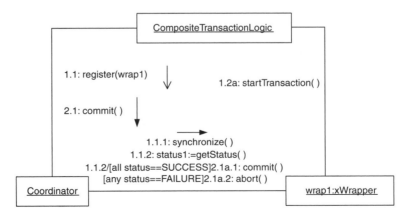

FIGURE 2.30 Additional predecessor interactions.

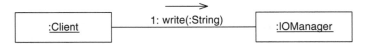

FIGURE 2.31 Asynchronous method call.

The UML defines arrowheads only for synchronous and asynchronous calls. As extensions to the UML, the UML allows other types of arrows to indicate different types of method calls. To indicate a balking call, this book uses a bent-back arrow, as shown in Figure 2.32.

When a balking call is made to an object's method and no other thread is executing that object's method, then the method returns when it is finished doing what it does. However, when a balking call is made and another thread is currently executing that object's method, the method returns immediately without doing anything.

You may have noticed that the object making the top-level call that initiates a collaboration is not shown in all of the preceding collaboration diagrams, which means the object that initiates the collaboration is not considered to be a part of the collaboration.

Up to this point, the objects you have seen how to model in the UML are passive in nature. They do nothing until one of their methods is called.

Some objects are active. A thread associated with them allows them to initiate operations asynchronously and independently of whatever else is going on in a program. Active objects are indicated with a thick border. Figure 2.33 contains an example of an active object.

Figure 2.33 shows an active `Sensor` object that calls a `Sensor-Observer` object's method without another object first calling one of its methods.

Statechart Diagram

Statechart diagrams are used to model a class's behavior as a state machine. Figure 2.34 is an example of a simple state diagram.

A statechart diagram shows each state as a rounded rectangle. All of the states in Figure 2.34 are divided into two compartments. The upper compartment contains the name of the state. The lower compartment contains a list of events to which the object responds while in that state without

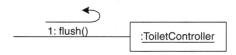

FIGURE 2.32 Balk.

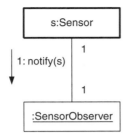

FIGURE 2.33 Active sensor.

changing state. Each event in the list is followed by a slash and the action it performs in response to the event. UML predefines two such events:

- The `enter` event occurs when an object enters a state.
- The `exit` event occurs when an object leaves a state.

If there are no events that a state responds to without changing state, then its rectangle is not divided into two compartments. Such a state is drawn as a simple rounded rectangle that contains only the state's name.

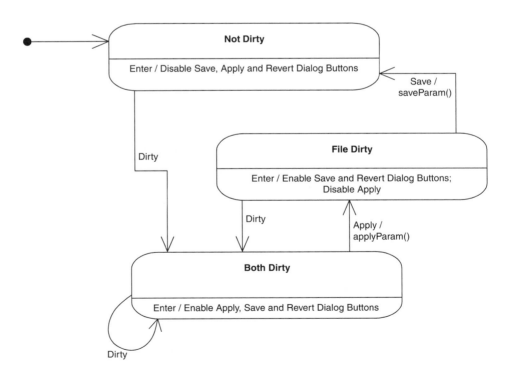

FIGURE 2.34 Statechart diagram.

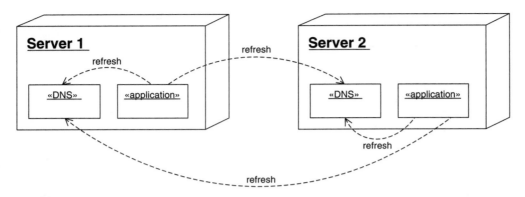

FIGURE 2.35 Deployment diagram.

Every state machine has an initial state that is the state an object is in before the first transition occurs. The initial state is drawn as a small solid circle.

Transitions between states are shown in statechart diagrams as lines between states. Normally, transition lines are required to have a label indicating the event that triggers the transition. The event may be followed by a slash and the action that occurs when the transition takes place.

If a statechart includes a final state, the final state is drawn as a small solid circle inside a larger circle.

Deployment Diagram

Deployment diagrams show how software is deployed onto computing elements. Figure 2.35 is an example of a deployment diagram.

Figure 2.35 shows two computing elements labeled Server1 and Server2. The UML terminology for computing element is *node*. Because this book uses *node* to mean other things, the term *computing element* is used instead.

The smaller boxes inside the computing elements are software components. A component is a collection of objects that are deployed together. Each of the computing elements in the diagram contains two components: a DNS component and an application component.

Communication between components is indicated by dashed lines. The dashed lines in Figure 2.35 indicate that the application components send messages to the DNS components. The dashed lines are labeled refresh.

CHAPTER

The Software Life Cycle

3

As stated previously, this book is devoted to patterns used during the object-oriented design phase of the software life cycle. In order to provide some perspective on how object-oriented design fits into the process of building and maintaining software systems, this chapter presents a very brief overview of the software life cycle.

A variety of activities take place during the lifetime of a piece of software. Figure 3.1 shows some of the activities that lead to software deployment.

Figure 3.1 is not intended to show all of the activities that occur during a software project, merely the more common ones. This is a typical context for using the patterns discussed in this work. Other books I've written on Java patterns describe recurring patterns that occur during the portion of the software life cycle labeled "Build" in Figure 3.1.

Figure 3.1 shows very clear boundaries between each activity. In practice, the boundaries are not so clear. Sometimes it is difficult to say if a particular activity belongs in one box or another. The precise boundaries are not important. What *is* important is to understand the relationships between these activities.

Earlier activities, such as defining requirements and object-oriented analysis, determine the course of activities that follow them, such as de-

Business planning: business case, budget			
Detailed planning	Define requirements: requirements specification		
	Define high-level essential use cases		
	Create prototype	Define high-level system architecture	
Build	Object-oriented analysis: low-level essential use cases, conceptual model, sequence diagrams		Write documentation and help
	Design user interface	Object-oriented design: class diagrams, collaboration diagrams, state diagrams	Logical database design	
	Usability testing	Coding	Physical database design	
	Testing		
Deployment			

FIGURE 3.1 Activities leading to software deployment.

fining essential use cases or object-oriented design. However, in the course of those later activities, deficiencies in the products of earlier activities emerge. For example, in the course of defining a use case, an ambiguous or conflicting requirement may become apparent. It may be necessary to modify existing use cases or to write new ones. You must expect such iterations. As long as the trend is for later iterations to produce fewer changes than earlier iterations, consider them part of the normal development process.

Following are brief descriptions of some of the activities shown in Figure 3.1. These descriptions provide only enough information to explain how the patterns discussed in this work apply to a relevant activity.

Business planning.   This typically starts with a proposal to build or modify a piece of software. The proposal evolves into a *business case*. A business case is a document that describes the pros and cons of the software project and includes estimates of the resources required to complete the project. If a decision is made to proceed with the project, then a preliminary schedule and budget are prepared.

Define requirements.   The purpose of this activity is to produce a requirements specification that says what the software produced by the project will and will not do. This typically begins with goals and high-level requirements from the business case. Additional requirements are obtained from appropriate sources to produce an initial requirements specification.

As the requirements specification is used in subsequent activities, necessary refinements to the requirements are discovered. The refinements are incorporated into the requirements specification. The products of subsequent activities are then modified to reflect the changes to the requirements specification.

Define essential use cases.   A *use case* describes the sequence of events that occurs in a specific circumstance between a system and other entities. The other entities are called *actors.* Developing use cases improves our understanding of the requirements, analysis, or design on which the use case is based. As we develop a better understanding of requirements, analysis, and design, we are able to refine them.

Essential use cases describe events in terms of the problem domain. Use cases that describe events in terms of the internal organization of software are called *real uses cases.*

The use cases most appropriate for refining requirements are high-level essential use cases. They are high level in that they explore the implications on which they are based on, but they do not try to add additional details.

Create prototype.   Create a prototype of the proposed software. A prototype can be used to get reactions to a proposed project. Reactions to a prototype can be used to refine requirements and essential use cases.

Define high-level system architecture.   Determine the major components of the system that are obvious from the original proposal. Also, determine their relationships.

Object-oriented analysis.   The purpose of this activity is to understand what the software produced by the project will do and how it will interact with other entities in its environment. The goal of analysis is to create a model of what the software is going to do, but not how to do it. The products of object-oriented analysis model the situation in which the software will operate from the perspective of an outside observer. The analysis does not concern itself with what goes on inside the software.

Object-oriented design.   The purpose of this activity is to determine the internal organization of the software. The products of the design effort identify the classes that will comprise the internal logic of the software. They also determine the internal structure of the classes and their interrelationships.

More decisions are made during object-oriented design than during any other activity. For that reason, this work includes more patterns that apply to object-oriented design than to any other activity.

Coding.   The purpose of this activity is to write the code that will make the software work.

Testing.   The purpose of this phase is to ensure that the software works as expected.

Transaction Patterns

A *transaction* is a sequence of operations that change the state of an object or collection of objects in a well-defined way that guarantees a consistent outcome. A transaction is useful because it satisfies constraints about the state of an object before, during, or after that transaction. For example, a particular type of transaction may satisfy a constraint that an object's attribute must be greater after the transaction than it was before the transaction. Sometimes, the constraints are unrelated to the objects that the transactions operate on. For example, a transaction may be required to take place in less than a certain amount of time.

Transactions play an important part in many different types of applications. Here are just a few examples:

- Transactions are important for automatic teller machines. They must never dispense money without deducting it from a customer's

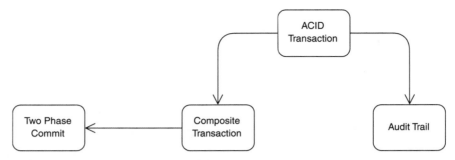

FIGURE 4.1 Transaction pattern map.

account or, conversely, deduct money from a customer's account without dispensing cash.

● A program that assigns network addresses to computers must never assign the same address to two different computers. A transaction can be used to ensure this.

● A number of computer manufacturers have programs that allow customers to order computers in custom configurations. When processing such an order, the program must generate a transaction that allocates exactly the right quantity of each part that is needed.

The patterns in this chapter provide guidance in selecting and combining constraints for common types of transactions. Figure 4.1 shows how the patterns in this chapter build on each other.*

The first and most fundamental pattern to read is the ACID Transaction pattern. It describes how to design transactions that never have inconsistent or unexpected outcomes. The Composite Transaction pattern describes how to compose a complex transaction from simpler transactions. The Two-Phase Commit pattern describes how to ensure that a composite transaction is atomic. The Audit Trail pattern describes how to maintain a historical record of ACID transactions.

In addition to being related to transactions, the patterns in this chapter also share the fact that they are usually implemented using software that you buy rather than build. For this reason, the focus of these patterns is the use of the solutions that they describe rather than their implementation.

You may notice the lack of code examples in this chapter. It is the author's opinion that the patterns in this chapter are too high level for concrete code examples to be useful. The application of these transaction-

---

* Figure 4.1 is not a UML diagram.

related patterns is readily understood at the design level. However, there is generally no clear relationship between individual pieces of code and the fact that they are part of a transaction. In many cases, objects are unaware of the transactions they participate in.

Throughout this chapter, what is done to a partially completed transaction that cannot complete is called *aborting*. Within the context of databases, it is more common to refer to this as *rolling back* a transaction. Because these patterns are presented in a broader context that includes application-level transactions, the term *abort* is used instead of *roll back*.

The topics discussed in this chapter are discussed in more detail in [Gray-Reuter93] and [Date94].

ACID Transaction

SYNOPSIS

Ensure that a transaction will never have an unexpected or inconsistent outcome. This is accomplished by ensuring that the transaction has the ACID properties: *a*tomicity, *c*onsistency, *i*solation, and *d*urability.

CONTEXT

Suppose you are developing software for a barter exchange business. It works as a clearinghouse for an indirect barter. For example, a hotel chain offers vouchers for a stay in one of its rooms in exchange for new mattresses. The clearinghouse matches the hotel with a mattress manufacturer that spends a lot of money on business trips. The clearinghouse also facilitates the exchange of the vouchers for the mattresses.

Every transaction that the system handles consists of an exchange of goods or services. Each transaction must correctly update the system's model of who is supposed to exchange what goods and services with whom. The system must not lose any transactions. The system must not duplicate any transactions. The system must ensure that two different clients do not make a deal for the same goods or service.

FORCES

☺ You want the result of a transaction to be well-defined and predictable. Given only the initial state of the objects in a transaction and the operations to perform on the objects, you should be able to determine the final state of the objects. For example, given an amount of money in a bank account and an amount of money to be deposited, the outcome of a transaction to deposit the money should result in the account balance being increased by the amount of the deposit. Even if the nature of the transaction is nondeterministic (that is a simulated roll of dice), given the initial state of the object involved you should be able to enumerate the possible outcomes.

☺ Once started, a transaction may succeed. It is also possible for a transaction to fail or abort. There are many possible causes for a transaction to fail. Many causes may be unanticipated. Even if a transaction fails, you don't want it to leave objects in an unpredictable state that compromises their integrity.

☺ A transaction can fail at any point. If there is a failure at a random point in the transaction, additional operations may be required to bring the objects involved into a predictable state. Determining what operations to perform may be difficult or impossible if a failed transaction can put objects in a state that violates their integrity.

☺ You want the outcome of transactions to depend only on two things:
  ● Initial state of the objects the transaction acts on
  ● Specific operations in the transaction
You do not want the outcome of a transaction to depend on anything else. In particular, if transactions are performed concurrently, you do not want their concurrency to affect the result of the transactions.

☺ If the results of a transaction are stored in volatile (nonpersistent) memory, then the observed results of the transaction are less predictable. The contents of volatile memory can change unpredictably. More generally, the observed results of a transaction are unpredictable if they do not persist as long as objects that are interested in the results or until another transaction changes the state of the affected objects.

☹ The requirements for some applications imply that the progress of some of their transactions can be observed by some other transactions. This is often true for long-lived transactions. For example, an inventory application for a chain of retail stores may support a transaction to order additional merchandise from a warehouse. The application may also require that users can query the state of the transaction:
  ● Does the warehouse have it in stock?
  ● Is it in transit?
  ● When will it be shipped?
  ● When will it arrive?

Satisfying all of the forces listed in this section may add complexity and overhead to the implementation of a transaction. The nature of some transactions ensures a satisfactory outcome without having to address all of the forces. For example, if there will be no concurrent transactions, then there is no need to address the possibility that concurrent transactions could interfere with each other. Also, if the outcome is the same whether a transaction is performed once or more than once, then recovery from catastrophic failure can be simplified.

It is not possible to take such shortcuts in the design of most transactions. If a transaction does not lend itself to the use of shortcuts, then there is a good justification for the complexity and overhead associated with satisfying all of the forces listed in this section.

SOLUTION

You can ensure that a transaction has a predictable result by ensuring that it has the ACID properties:

Atomic.   The changes a transaction makes to the state of objects on which it operates are atomic. This means that either all of the changes happen exactly once or none of the changes happen. These changes include internal state changes, database changes, transmission of messages, and visible side effects on other programs.

> If a transaction is not atomic, then the transaction's side effects could happen more than once. For example, an automatic teller machine (ATM) that does not process transactions atomically may sometimes process that same withdrawal twice. It would be possible for you to make a withdrawal, get your cash, and then a power surge could cause the ATM to process the withdrawal again after you were no longer there.

Consistent.   A transaction is a correct transformation of an object's state. At the beginning of a transaction, the objects on which a transaction operates are consistent with their integrity constraints. At the end of the transaction, regardless of whether it succeeds or fails, the objects are again in a state consistent with their integrity constraints. If all of the transaction's preconditions are met before the transaction begins, all of its postconditions are met after the transaction successfully completes.

> Suppose that the software that runs an ATM does not guarantee the consistency of its transactions. When you make a withdrawal, the amount of cash the machine dispenses might not be the same as the amount deducted from your account.

Isolated.   Even though transactions execute concurrently, it appears to each transaction, T, that other transactions execute either before T or after T but not both. That means that if an object that is involved in a transaction fetches an attribute of an object, it does not matter when it does so. Throughout the lifetime of a transaction, the objects on which the transaction operates will not notice any changes in the state of other objects as the result of concurrent transactions.

> If the software that processes transactions from ATMs does not enforce the isolation property, then two withdrawals from the same account at about the same time could produce wrong results. For example, both withdrawal transactions may fetch the same balance to compute the new account balance. The

result would be that the account balance would reflect one withdrawal or the other, but not both.

Durable. Once a transaction completes successfully (commits), the changes it has made to the state of the object(s) become relatively persistent. They will persist at least as long as any object can observe the changes.

If transactions from an ATM are not processed in a way that ensures that they are durable, then it might be possible for a withdrawal to be forgotten.

Because most database managers ensure that transactions performed under their control have these properties, many people think of ACID properties only in connection with database transactions. It is important to understand that the ACID properties are valuable for all kinds of transactions, including application-level transactions. For example, consider an application that is responsible for changing the price of gasoline at a gas station. When the price is changed it must be changed in three places: in the database that tells the cash registers how much to charge for gas, on the price displayed on the gas pumps, and on the electronic sign that advertises the price. If the price-change transaction does not exhibit the ACID properties, then the price can become inconsistent in all three places, subjecting the gas station to fines.

The point of this solution is to design transactions so that the transaction as a whole has the ACID properties. Use a transaction manager to manage as much of the transaction as you can. Database engines are the most common transaction managers in business applications.

Using a transaction manager is not enough if portions of a transaction are not under its control. For example, if an ATM does not function under the control of a transaction manager, it must be integrated with portions of a transaction that are under the control of a transaction manager to ensure that the actions of the ATM are atomic.

CONSEQUENCES

☺ Use of the ACID transaction pattern makes the outcome of transactions predictable.

☹ Use of the ACID transaction pattern can substantially increase that amount of storage required by a transaction. The additional storage requirement arises from a need to store the initial state of every object involved in a transaction so that if the transaction fails it is possible to restore the initial state of the objects it acted on. Maintaining the isolation of a transaction may require the copying of objects to allow a high level of concurrency. The purpose of the copies is to allow the original object to be modified while an unchanging copy of the original is visible to other transactions. Without the copies, it would be necessary to prevent transactions that need to see the original version of a row from running concurrently with transactions that update the row.

● ACID transactions are often implemented by transaction logic that manipulates objects indirectly through a mechanism that enforces ACID properties for transactions, such as a database manager. In cases where a transaction's logic is also responsible for maintaining the transaction's ACID properties, the complexity of the transaction logic may be greatly increased. Using a separate mechanism that enforces the ACID properties makes it much easier to correctly implement the logic that drives a transaction.

IMPLEMENTATION

The simplest way to ensure the ACID properties of a transaction is for the transaction logic to manipulate the state of objects through a tool such as a database manager that automatically enforces the ACID properties. If a program works with transactions that will not involve persistent data or objects, the performance penalty introduced by a database manager that persists data may be undesirable. Such applications may be able to take advantage of in-memory databases, which do not incur the overhead of saving data to disk.

Sometimes it is not possible to use any tool to enforce ACID properties. The common reasons for this are performance requirements and a need to keep the size of an embedded application small. Adding logic to an application to enforce the ACID properties for its transaction can introduce a lot of complexity into a design. When you use a separate tool to enforce the ACID properties, the complexity of enforcement is handled by the tool and is not part of the design. Also, tools that enforce ACID properties usually have had most of the bugs worked out of them. Getting all the bugs out of your own ACID enforcing code can be a lengthy process. It is usually better to buy rather than build ACID support whenever possible.

Here are strategies for explicitly supporting each of the ACID properties.

Atomicity

The primary issue to address when providing support for atomic transactions is that there must be a way to restore objects to their initial state if a transaction ends in failure.

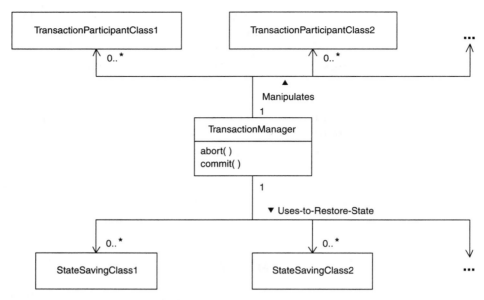

FIGURE 4.2 Saving state for future recovery.

The simplest way to be able to restore an object's state after a failed transaction is to save the object's initial state in a way that it can easily be restored. The Snapshot pattern (discussed in *Patterns in Java, Volume 1*) provides guidance for this strategy. Figure 4.2 is a class diagram that shows this general approach.

An object in the role of transaction manager manipulates instances of other classes that participate in a transaction. Before doing something that will change the state of an object that it manipulates, the transaction manager will use an instance of another class to save the initial state of the object. If the transaction manager's `commit` method is called to signal the successful completion of a transaction, then the objects that encapsulate the saved states are discarded. However, if the transaction manager detects a transaction failure, either from a call to its `abort` method or from the abnormal termination of the transaction logic, then it restores the objects that participate to their initial state.

If it is not necessary to save an object's state beyond the end of the current program execution, a simple way to save the object's state is to clone it. You can make a shallow copy* of an object by calling its `clone` method.

---

* A shallow copy of an object is another object whose instance variables have the same values as the original object. It refers to the same objects as the original object. The other objects that it refers to are not copied.

All classes inherit a `clone` method from the `Object` class. The `clone` method returns a shallow copy of an object if its class gives permission for its instances to be cloned by implementing the `Cloneable` interface. The `Cloneable` interface is a marker interface (see the Marker Interface pattern in Volume 1). It does not declare any methods or variables. Its only purpose is to indicate that a class's instances may be cloned.

In order to restore the state of an object from an old copy of itself, the object must have a method for that purpose. The following listing shows an example of a class whose instances can be cloned and then restored from the copy.*

```
class Line implements Cloneable {
    private double startX, startY;
    private double endX, endY;
    private Color myColor;
    ...
    public Object clone() { super.clone(); }

    public synchronized void restore(Line ln) {
        startX = ln.startX;
        startY = ln.startY;
        endX = ln.endX;
        endY = ln.endY;
        myColor = ln.myColor;
    } // restore(Line)
} // class Line
```

The class includes a `clone` method because the clone method that classes inherit from the Object class is protected. In order to provide public access to this method, you must override it with a public `clone` method.

If you need to save and restore instances of a class that does not have a public `clone` method and it is not possible for you to add a public `clone` method to its instances, then you will need an alternative approach. One such approach is to create a class whose instances are responsible for capturing and restoring the state of the objects lacking a clone method by using their publicly accessible methods.

For saving the state of an object whose state is needed indefinitely, a simple technique is to use Java's serialization facility. A brief explanation of how to use serialization is shown in the sidebar.

Saving the initial state of the objects a transaction manipulates is not always the best technique for allowing their initial state to be restored. If

---

* At the beginning of this chapter, I stated that there would be no code examples. The code examples that appear here are implementation examples and not examples of the pattern itself.

Serialization

Java's serialization facility can save and restore the entire state of an object if its class gives permission for its instances to be serialized. Classes give permission for their instances to be serialized by implementing the interface `java.io.Serializable`, like this:

```
Import Java.io.Serializable;
...
class Foo implements Serializable {
```

The `Serializable` interface is a marker interface (see the Marker Interface pattern in *Patterns in Java, Volume 1*). It does not declare any variables or methods. Declaring that a class implements the `Serializable` interface simply indicates that instances of the class may be serialized.

To save the state objects by serialization, you need an `ObjectOutputStream` object. You can use an `ObjectOutputStream` object to write a stream of bytes that contains an object's current state to a file or a byte array.

To create an `ObjectOutputStream` object that serializes that state of objects and writes the stream of bytes to a file, you would write code that looks like this:

```
FileOutputStream fout = new FileOutputStream("filename.ser");
ObjectOutputStream obOut = new ObjectOutputStream(fout);
```

The code creates an `OutputStream` to write a stream of bytes to a file. It then creates an `ObjectOutputStream` that will use the `OutputStream` to write a stream of bytes.

Once you have created an `OutputStream` object, you can serialize objects by passing them to the `OutputStream` object's `writeObject` method, like this:

```
ObOut.writeObject(foo);
```

transactions perform multiple operations on objects that contain a lot of state information, and the transaction modifies only some of the state information in the objects, saving the object's entire state information is wasteful.

In this situation, a more efficient implementation approach is based on the Decorator pattern described in *Volume 1*. The technique is to leave the original object's state unmodified until the end of the transaction and use wrapper objects to contain the new values. If the transaction is successful, the new values are copied into the original object and the wrapper objects are then discarded. If the transaction ends in failure, then the

The writeObject method discovers the instance variables of an object passed to it and accesses them. It writes the values of instance variables declared with a primitive type such as int or double directly to the byte stream. If the value of an instance variable is an object reference, the writeObject method recursively serializes the referenced object.

Creating an object from the contents of a serialized byte stream is called *deserialization*. To deserialize a byte stream, you need an ObjectInputStream object. You can use an ObjectInputStream object to reconstruct an object or restore an object's state from the state information stored in a serialized byte stream.

To create an ObjectInputStream object, you can write some code that looks like this:

```
FileInputStream fin = new FileInputSteam("filename.ser");
ObjectInputStream obIn = new ObjectInputStream(fin);
```

This code creates an InputStream to read a stream of bytes from a file. It then creates an ObjectInputStream object. You can use the ObjectInputStream object to create objects with instance information from the stream of bytes or restore an existing object to contain the instance information. You can get an ObjectInputStream object to do these things by calling its readObject method, like this:

```
Foo myFoo = (Foo)obIn.readObject();
```

The readObject method returns a new object whose state comes from the instance information in the byte stream. That is not quite what you need when restoring an object to its initial state. What you need is a way to use the instance information to set the state of an existing variable. You can arrange for that as you would for allowing an object's state to be restored from a clone. You ensure that the class of the objects to be restored has a method that allows instances of the class to copy their state from another instance of the class.

wrapper objects are simply discarded. The class diagram in Figure 4.3 shows this sort of design.

In this design, the objects that the transaction manipulates need not contain their own instance data. Nor do they need to implement the TransactionParticipantIF interface. Instead, a separate object contains their instance data. To ensure strong encapsulation, the class of the objects that contain instance data should be an inner class of the class of the manipulated objects.

When a transaction manager becomes aware than an object will be involved in a transaction, it calls the object's startTransaction method.

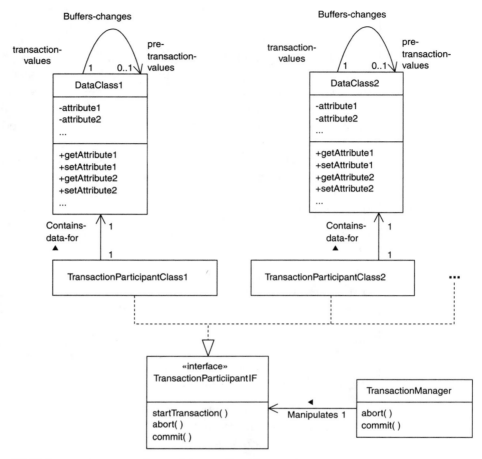

FIGURE 4.3 Atomicity through wrapper objects.

The `startTransaction` method causes the object to create and use a new data object. When the manipulated object calls one of the new data object's methods to fetch the value of an attribute, if the data object does not yet have a value for that attribute, it calls the corresponding method of the original data object to get the value.

If a transaction ends in failure, then the transaction manager object calls the `abort` method of each of the manipulated objects. Each object's abort method causes it to discard the new data object and any values that it may contain.

If a transaction ends in success, then the transaction manager object calls the `commit` method of each of the manipulated objects. Each object's `commit` method causes the new data object to merge its data values into the original data object. It then discards the data object.

This design requires data values to be copied only if they are altered by a transaction. It may be more efficient than saving an object's entire state if the object contains a lot of state information that is not involved in the transaction. The disadvantage of this design is that it is more complex.

Consistency

There are no implementation techniques specifically related to consistency. All implementation techniques that help to ensure the correctness of programs also help to ensure consistency.

The most important thing that you should do to ensure the consistency of a transaction is testing. The Unit Testing and System Testing patterns described in *Patterns in Java, Volume 2* are useful in designing appropriate tests. Using the Assertion Testing pattern, also described in *Volume 2*, to ensure that a transaction's postconditions are met can provide additional assurance of internal consistency.

Isolation

Isolation is an issue when an object may be involved in concurrent transactions and some of the transactions will change the state of the object. There are a few different possible implementation techniques for enforcing isolation. The nature of the transactions determines the most appropriate implementation technique.

If all of the transactions will modify the state of an object, then you must ensure that the transactions do not access the object concurrently. The only way to guarantee isolation is to ensure that they access the object's state one at a time by synchronizing the methods that modify the object's state. This technique is described in more detail by the Single Threaded Execution pattern described in *Volume 1*.

If some of the concurrent transactions modify an object's state, and others use the object but do not modify its state, you can improve on the performance of single-threaded execution. You can allow transactions that do not modify the object's state to access the object concurrently while allowing transactions that modify the object's state to access it in only a single-threaded manner. This technique is described in more detail by the Read/Write Lock pattern described in *Volume 1*.

If transactions are relatively long-lived, it may be possible to further improve the performance of transactions that use but do not modify the state of the object if it is not necessary for the objects to have a distinct object identity. You can accomplish this by arranging for transactions that use an object but do not modify the object's state to use a copy of the object. The following patterns can be helpful in doing this:

⊛ The Return New Objects from Accessor Method pattern (described in *Volume 2*)
⊛ The Copy Mutable Parameters pattern (described in *Volume 2*)
⊛ The Copy on Write Proxy pattern, which is used as an example in the description of the Proxy pattern in *Volume 1*

In those cases where it is not possible to do these things, a long-lived transaction may tie up resources for an unacceptably long time. This may necessitate using some alternative strategies. One possibility is to break the long-lived transaction into shorter-lived transactions. Other strategies involve giving up some of the ACID properties.

For example, you may allow other transactions that need a resource locked by a long-lived transaction to interrupt the transaction. This is reasonable when combined with another technique called *checkpoint/restart*. Checkpoint/restart involves saving that state of transaction object at strategic points when the transaction objects are in a consistent state. When the transaction is interrupted, the objects it manipulates are restored to their most recently saved state. Later on, the transaction is restarted from the point where the states were saved.

Using this combination of techniques solves the problem of a long-lived transaction locking resources for an unacceptably long time at the expense of losing the atomicity and isolation properties.

Durability

The basic consideration for ensuring the durability of a transaction is that its results must persist as long as there may be other objects that are concerned with the object's state. If the results of a transaction are not needed beyond a single execution of a program, it is usually sufficient to store the result of the transaction in the same memory as the objects that use those results.

If other objects may use the results of a transaction indefinitely, then the results should be stored on a nonvolatile medium such as a magnetic disk. This can be trickier than it at first seems. The writing of transaction results to a disk file must appear atomic to other threads and programs. There are a few issues to deal with in ensuring this:

⊛ A single write operation may be translated into multiple write operations by the object responsible for the write operation or the underlying operating system. That means that data written using a single write call may not appear in a file all at once.
⊛ Operating systems may cache write operations for a variety of efficiency reasons. That means data written by multiple write operations

may appear in a file at the same time or it may be written in a different sequence than the original write operations.

☹ When accessing remote files, additional timing issues arise. When a program writes information to a local file, the modified portion of the file may reside in the operating system's cache for some time before it is actually written to the disk. If another program tries to read the modified portion of a file while the modifications are still cached, most operating systems will be smart enough to create the illusion that the file has already been modified. If read operations on a file reflect write operations as soon as they occur, the system is said to have *read/write consistency*.

Read/write consistency is more difficult to achieve when accessing a remote file. That is partially because there can be unbounded delays between the time that a program performs a write operation and the time that the write arrives at the remote disk. If you take no measures to ensure that access to a remote file has read/write consistency, the following sequence of events is possible:

1. Program X reads the file.
2. Program X performs a write operation.
3. Program Y reads the unmodified but out-of-date file.
4. Program Y performs a write operation.
5. Program Y's write arrives at the file.
6. Program X's write arrives at the file.

Read/write consistency can be achieved through the use of locks, but that can seriously hurt performance.

☹ An object that may read the same data from a file multiple times will pay a performance penalty if it does not cache the data to avoid unnecessary read operations. When reading from a remote file, caching becomes more important because of the greater time required for read operations. However, caching introduces another problem.

If the data in a file is modified, then any cache that contains data read from the file is no longer consistent with the file. This is called the *cache consistency* problem.

The following paragraphs contain some suggestions on how to deal with the problems related to the timing of actual writes to local files. The Ephemeral Cache Item pattern explains how to handle cache consistency.

It is not generally possible to control exactly when the data from a write operation will actually be written to physical file. However, it is possible to force pending write operations to local file systems to complete. This guarantees that all pending write operations have completed at a known point in time. It is generally good enough for ensuring the durability of a transaction unless the transaction is subject to real-time constraints.

There are two steps to forcing write operations to local file systems to complete. The first step is to tell objects your program is using to perform write operations to flush their internal buffers. For example, all subclasses of `OutputStream` inherit a method named `flush`. A call to the flush method forces the `OutputStream` object to flush any internal buffers that it might have.

The second step to forcing write operations to local file systems to complete is to get the `FileDescriptor` object for the file your are writing. `FileDescriptor` objects have a method named `sync`. A call to a `FileDescriptor` object's `sync` method tells the operating system to flush any cached write operations for the associated file.

All ACID Properties

An implementation issue that affects all four ACID properties is how to handle a commit operation that is unable to successfully complete. In all cases, the objects manipulated by the transaction must be left in a consistent state that reflects either the success or failure of the transaction.

We are concerned about two failure modes. One is that the commit operation is unable to commit the changes made during the transaction, but the objects that are interested in the results of the transaction are alive and well. The other is a larger-scale failure that causes the commit operation not to complete and also causes all of the objects that are interested in the results of the transaction to die.

The problem is simplest when the failure is limited to the commit operation and the objects interested in the results of the transaction are still alive and well. In this case, since the commit could not succeed, the transaction must fail. All that is required is to restore the objects manipulated by the transaction to their state at the beginning of the transaction.

The larger-scale failure presents an additional challenge if the objects that were interested in the results of the transaction will persist after the failure. Before processes or threads are started that will allow objects to see an incomplete transaction, the incomplete transaction must be detected and its commit must be completed or backed out.

In summary, adding your own logic to an application to enforce ACID properties for transactions adds considerable complexity to the application. When possible, use an available tool that can manage the ACID properties for you.

If you must create your own support for the ACID properties of transactions, your design for each transaction will include some of the elements shown in the class diagram in Figure 4.4.

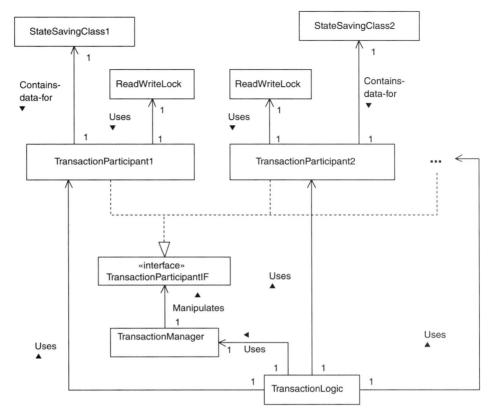

FIGURE 4.4 Generic transaction classes.

Here are descriptions of the roles classes play in ACID transactions as indicated in Figure 4.4:

Transaction Logic.   Though there are many ways to organize the logic of a transaction, the most common design is to have one class that encapsulates the core logic of a transaction. This class may encapsulate the core logic for multiple related transactions.

TransactionParticipant1, TransactionParticipant2, . . .   The logic encapsulated in a `TransactionLogic` class modifies the state of instances of these classes.

TransactionManager.   This class encapsulates reusable common logic to support atomicity. For distributed transactions, it may also encapsulate the logic to support durability. `TransactionLogic` objects use an instance of this class to manage a transaction.

TransactionParticipantIF. Each `TransactionParticipant` class implements this interface. The purpose of this interface is to allow a `TransactionManager` object to manipulate `TransactionParticipant` objects without having a dependency on any specific `TransactionParticipant` class.

StateSavingClass1, StateSavingClass2, . . . Classes in this role are responsible for saving and restoring the state of `TransactionParticipant` objects. These classes are usually specific to a single `TransactionParticipant` class or a small number of related `TransactionParticipant` classes.

ReadWriteLock. If concurrent transactions will be accessing `TransactionParticipant` objects, with some transactions modifying an object and other transactions just requiring read access, an instance of this class is used to coordinate shared read access and exclusive write access to the object. These classes are usually reusable.

To conclude this discussion of implementing the ACID properties, if it is at all possible to use an existing transaction manager, then do so. The details presented here for doing it yourself are complex and subtle. Using an existing transaction manager will generally produce better results.

KNOWN USES

Most Internet retail applications (i.e., www.amazon.com, www.walmart .com) use ACID transactions.

Database management systems guarantee ACID properties for transactions. Some use an implementation of atomicity based on keeping a copy of the initial state of each item involved in a transaction. For example, Interbase keeps the original and the modified version of every record involved in a transaction until the transaction completes. When the transaction completes, it discards one or the other, depending on whether the transaction succeeds or fails.

Oracle uses an implementation of atomicity that is analogous to the implementation using wrapper objects.

RELATED PATTERNS

Snapshot. The Snapshot pattern (described in *Volume 1*) describes techniques for saving and restoring the state of objects. This is the better way to recover from a transaction failure when a transaction involves a long sequence of operations that modify the state of a small number of simple objects.

Command.   The Command pattern (described in *Volume 1*) describes techniques for remembering and undoing a sequence of operations. This is the better way to recover from a transaction failure when a transaction involves a short sequence of operations that modify the state of a large number of complex objects.

Transaction State Stack.   The Transaction State Stack pattern may be used to make a transaction's changes to multiple objects atomic.

Audit Trail.   Logging a sequence of operations to support the Command pattern is structurally similar to maintaining an audit trail.

System Testing.   The System Testing pattern (described in *Volume 2*) should be used to ensure the consistency of transactions.

Unit Testing.   The Unit Testing pattern (described in *Volume 2*) may also help to ensure the consistency of transactions.

Single Threaded Execution.   The Single Threaded Execution pattern (described in *Volume 1*) can be used to keep transactions that modify the state of the same object isolated from each other.

Read/Write Lock.   The Read/Write Lock pattern (described in *Volume 1*) can be used to keep transactions that use the same object isolated from each other while allowing transactions that do not modify the object's state to execute concurrently.

Read/Write Consistency.   If you directly manage the storage of persistent distributed objects, you may need the Read/Write Consistency pattern to ensure that data and objects that are read from files are consistent with the most recent write operation.

Ephemeral Cache Item.   If you directly manage the storage of persistent distributed objects, you may need the Ephemeral Cache Item pattern to ensure that the result of a locally initiated read operation matches the current contents of a remote store.

Composite Transaction

SYNOPSIS

You want to design and implement transactions correctly and with a minimum of effort. Simple transactions are easier to implement and make correct than complex transactions. You should design and implement complex transactions from simpler ACID transactions.

CONTEXT

Sometimes, you want to design a complex ACID transaction using existing ACID transactions as building blocks. Using existing ACID transactions to build a more complex transaction does not automatically give it the ACID properties. Consider the following situation.

You work for the IT department of a supermarket chain. In addition to having a number of stores that sell food, the company has a central facility that produces bread, cakes, and other baked goods for the stores. The IT department provides systems to support these activities:

- There is manufacturing software for the bakery. Every evening it is fed the quantities of each item that each store will need for the following day. It produces reports telling the bakers how much of each item to produce and what ingredients to order for the following day.
- There is transportation scheduling software. Every evening it is fed the quantities of each item each store will need for the following day. It schedules trucks to transport baked goods to the stores. It produces reports telling the bakers how much of each item to put in each truck.

Currently, the amount of each product each store needs for the next day must be keyboarded into both software applications. This increases labor costs. It makes data entry errors more likely, since there are twice as many opportunities to make mistakes. The costs of data entry errors are higher because they can lead to baked goods being produced but not loaded onto a truck or too many trucks being scheduled.

You have the task of creating a mechanism that allows the data to be entered only once. You think of writing a data entry program that will put the data in the appropriate database table of each application. Though you know that you can make it work, you search for another way. Because the program would assume the internal structure of other applications, you are concerned about maintenance problems later on.

Reading each application's documentation, you find that they both have an application program interface (API) to programmatically present data to each application. Transactions initiated by the APIs have the ACID properties. This gives you a way to build the data entry mechanism using only supported features of the applications.

The fact that both APIs support the ACID properties greatly simplifies the task of building a composite data entry transaction with a predictable outcome. By creating a composite transaction that simply invokes each API, you get a transaction that is consistent and durable without doing anything else. However, you must carefully consider how to ensure that the composite transaction is atomic and isolated. They will generally not be atomic or isolated. You must either take additional steps to make them so or determine that a less stringent guarantee of their behavior is sufficient. Without proper attention to these details, transactions can be lost, they can be applied multiple times, or concurrent transactions may corrupt each other.

The composite transaction in the example is not automatically atomic. That is not a problem, for two reasons.

- Before the transaction runs, the quantity of all baked goods scheduled to be produced for a store is zero. For that reason, there is no need to save the old values before the transaction. You can back out the transaction by setting all of the values to zero.
- Both the component transactions are *idempotent*. Idempotent means that a transaction can happen once or more than once and still have the same outcome. For example setting the price that gas pumps charge for gas is an idempotent operation.

  If all of the component transactions are idempotent, it simplifies the task of recovery from a crash, because the only information that needs to be saved is the fact that the transaction was begun. It is not necessary to be certain that composite transaction has not completed.

The other area you will need to address is isolation. Though each component transaction has the isolation property, this sequence of events is possible:

Composite Transaction 1	*Composite Transaction 2*
Manufacturing Transaction 1	
	Manufacturing Transaction 2
	Transportation Transaction 2
Transportation Transaction 1	

If the composite transaction is isolated from other transactions, then neither transaction should be able to observe state changes made by the other. This is not the case in the preceding scenario. In this sequence of events, the first half of transaction 1 sees things as they were before transaction 2; the second half of transaction 1 sees things as they are after transaction 2. If you need only to isolate these transactions from each other, you can solve the crash recovery problem and the isolation problem the same way: Before the composite transaction invokes any of its component transactions, it can store the transaction data in a file. When the transaction is done, it deletes the file. If a crash prevents the completion of the transaction, then when the program restarts it can detect the existence of the file and restart the transaction.

The existence of the file can also be used to isolate transactions. Using the Lock File pattern, if the file exists when a composite transaction starts, it waits until the file no longer exists before it continues.

Figure 4.5 is a class diagram that shows your design.

Figure 4.5 adds a detail not previously discussed. Instead of using just one transaction file, it uses one transaction file per store. This is based on an assumption that each store enters data only for itself and for no other stores. This means concurrent transactions from different stores are isolated from each other simply because they are from different stores. You need the file only to isolate concurrent transactions from the same store. Forcing transactions for one store to wait for

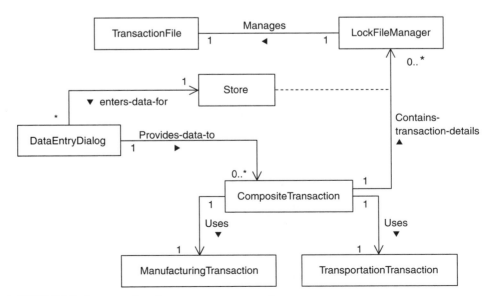

FIGURE 4.5 Composite data entry transaction.

transactions for another store to complete introduces an unnecessary delay.

In this example, it was possible to find a solution that did not require that the composite transaction was atomic and isolated. This is the exception rather than the rule. In most cases, it is necessary to take measures to ensure that a composite transaction has all of the ACID properties.

FORCES

☺ Building complex transactions with predictable outcomes from simpler transactions is greatly facilitated if the simpler transactions have the ACID properties.

☺ If the ACID properties of a set of transactions are implemented using a single mechanism that supports nested transactions, then implementing the ACID properties for a composite transaction composed of those transactions is very easy.

☹ If the ACID properties of a set of component transactions are implemented using a mechanism that does not support nested transactions, then implementing ACID properties for a composite transaction is more difficult. Implementing a composite transaction with component transactions whose ACID properties are implemented using incompatible mechanisms that do not work with each other is also difficult. In some cases, it is impossible.

☹ It is difficult for a maintenance programmer who must maintain a composite transaction to understand the full inner workings of a composite transaction, especially if there are multiple levels of composition.

SOLUTION

Design classes that implement complex transactions so that they delegate as much work as possible to classes that implement simpler transactions. When selecting classes that implement transactions for incorporation into more complex transactions, you should use classes that already exist and are known to be correct, or you should select classes that will have multiple uses.

The simpler transactions should have the ACID properties. That greatly simplifies the task of ensuring predicable properties for the composite transaction.

Carefully choose the granularity of the simpler transactions. When designing with existing transactions, you generally have to work with the transactions as they exist. If you are designing the simpler transactions along with the complex, the granularity of the simpler transaction should be a balance between the need to keep the simpler transactions simple and the need to keep the more complex transactions understandable.

Sometimes, circumstances make it complicated to ensure the ACID properties of a composite transaction. Figure 4.6 shows the structure of a simple composite transaction design when there are no such complicating circumstances.

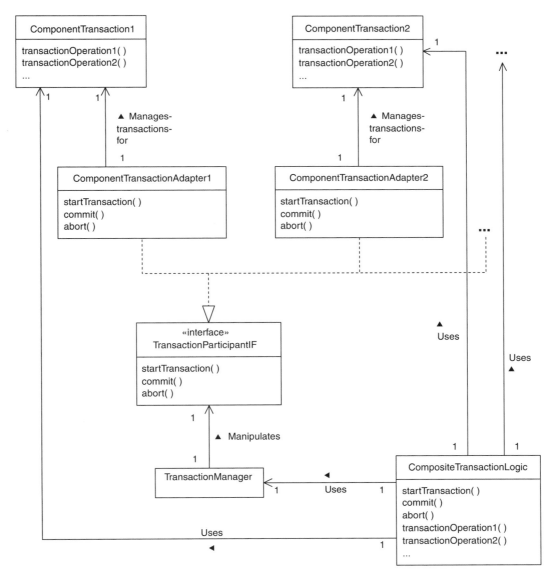

FIGURE 4.6 Composite transaction pattern.

The classes shown in Figure 4.6 play the following roles in the Composite Transaction pattern:

CompositeTransactionLogic.   Although there are many ways to organize the logic of a transaction, the most common design is to have one class that encapsulates the core logic of a transaction. This class can encapsulate the core logic for multiple related transactions.

ComponentTransaction1, ComponentTransaction2, . . .   Classes in this role encapsulate a component transaction that is part of the composite transaction. `CompositeTransactionLogic` classes delegate transaction operations directly to `ComponentTransaction` objects. However, transaction management operations that begin or end a transaction are delegated indirectly through a `TransactionManager` class.

TransactionManager.   This class encapsulates reusable common logic to support atomicity and isolation. For distributed transactions, it may also encapsulate the logic to support durability. `CompositeTransactionLogic` objects use an instance of this class to manage a transaction.

In order to be independent of the classes that it manages within a transaction, it interacts with these classes through a `TransactionParticipantIF` interface.

TransactionParticipantIF.   `TransactionManager` classes interact with `ComponentTransaction` classes through an interface in this role.

ComponentTransactionAdapter.   Unless `ComponentTransaction` classes are specifically designed to work with the `TransactionManager` class being used, they don't implement the `TransactionParticipantIF` interface that the `TransactionManager` class requires. Classes in the `ComponentTransactionAdapter` role are adapters that implement the `TransactionParticipantIF` interface with logic that delegates to a `ComponentTransaction` class and supplements its logic in whatever way is necessary.

There are two areas in which applications of this pattern most often vary from the organization shown in Figure 4.5. Both areas of variation usually add complexity.

The first area of variation is that some portions of the composite transaction's logic may not already be encapsulated as a self-contained transaction. In many cases, such logic is too specialized for you to have an expectation of reusing it. It may not be possible to justify encapsulating such specialized logic in this way. In these situations, the design usually looks like a hybrid of Figures 4.3 and 4.6, with some portions of the logic encapsulated in self-contained transactions and the unencapsulated portions having the additional details shown in Figure 4.3.

The other area of variation is managing the predictability of the composite transaction's outcome. The preferred strategy for doing that is to ensure that the composite transaction has the ACID properties. Extensive experience has shown this is to be a successful strategy. Though using component transactions that have the ACID properties may simplify the task of ensuring that the composite transaction has the ACID properties, it is not sufficient.

The simplest situation for ensuring the ACID properties of the composite transaction is when there is a single mechanism for ensuring the ACID properties of all of the component transactions and the mechanism supports nested transactions. Such a mechanism does not only allow individual component transactions to abort themselves, it also allows the composite transaction to abort and restore all objects modified by committed component transactions to the state they had at the beginning of the composite transaction.

The simplest possibility is that you are using a tool to manage transactions and the tool supports nested transactions. Alternatively, if you control the implementation of all of the component transaction classes that you are using, then it is relatively easy to modify the techniques described by the ACID Transaction pattern to support nested transactions.

If the component transactions are managed by a mechanism that does not support nested transactions, then you will need a different way to ensure the predictable outcomes of the composite transactions. If the component transactions are managed by different mechanisms, as is the case in the example under the "Context" heading, it is also necessary to find a different way to ensure the predictability of the outcome of the composite transaction.

The Two Phase Commit pattern describes a way to combine component transactions that have the ACID properties and are managed by different mechanisms into one composite transaction that has the ACID properties. However, you may not be able to use the Two Phase Commit pattern if all of the classes that encapsulate the component transactions have not been designed to participate in the Two Phase Commit pattern.

In some cases, it may be impractical or even impossible to ensure the ACID properties for the composite transaction. You will find descriptions of common alternatives and how to implement them under the "Implementation" heading.

CONSEQUENCES

☺ Writing classes that perform complex transactions by having them delegate to classes that perform simpler transactions is a good form of reuse, especially when the classes that implement the simpler transactions already exist or will have multiple uses.

☺ The core logic of a transaction implemented as a composite transaction is less likely to contain bugs than a monolithic implementation of the same transaction. That is because the component transactions you build on are usually already debugged. Since implementing transactions in this way simplifies the core logic of the transaction, there are fewer opportunities to introduce bugs into it.

☹ If you are not able to use nested transactions or the Two Phase Commit pattern to manage the ACID properties of a composite transaction, it may be difficult to implement the ACID properties for the composite transaction. It may even be impossible to implement the ACID properties for the composite transaction. In such situations, you are forced to compromise on the guarantees you can make about the predictability of the transaction's outcomes.

● If there are no dependencies between component transactions, then it is possible for them to execute concurrently.

IMPLEMENTATION

There are a number of lesser guarantees that you may try to implement when it is not possible to enforce the ACID properties for a composite transaction. Some of the more common ones are discussed in this section

When it is not possible to ensure that a transaction is atomic, it may be possible to ensure that it is idempotent. If you rely on idempotence rather than atomicity, then you must be able to ensure that a transaction will be completed at least once after it is begun.

In some situations, it is possible to ignore the issue of isolation. If the nature of the transaction ensures that no concurrent transactions will modify the same objects, then you do not need to anything to ensure that the transactions execute in isolation.

KNOWN USES

Sybase RDBMS and SQL Server support nested transactions and facilitate the construction of composite transactions.

JAVA API USAGE

The Java Transaction API has facilities to aid in the construction of composite transactions.

RELATED PATTERNS

ACID Transaction. The Composite Transaction pattern is built on the ACID transaction pattern.

Adapter. The Composite pattern uses the Adapter pattern, which is described in *Volume 1*.

Command. The Command Pattern (described in *Volume 1*) can be the basis for an undo mechanism used to undo operations and restore objects to the state they were in at the beginning of a transaction.

Composed Method. The Composed Method pattern (described in *Volume 2*) is a coding pattern that describes a way of composing methods from other methods and is structurally similar to the way the Composite Transaction pattern composes transactions.

Lock File. The Lock File pattern can be used to enforce the isolation property for a composite transaction.

Two Phase Commit. The Two Phase Commit pattern can be used to ensure the ACID properties of a composite transaction composed from simpler ACID transactions.

Mailbox. When there is a need to ensure the reliability a composite transaction, you will want to take steps to ensure the reliability of the component transactions that constitute it. If the composite transaction is distributed, you will also want to ensure the reliable transmission of messages between the objects that participate in the transaction by such means as the Mailbox pattern.

Two Phase Commit

This pattern is based on material that appears in [Gray-Reuter93].

SYNOPSIS

If a transaction is composed of simpler transactions distributed across multiple database managers, you want them to either all complete successfully or all abort, leaving all objects as they were before the transactions. You achieve this by making an object responsible for coordinating the transactions so that they all complete successfully or all abort.

CONTEXT

Suppose that you have developed software for a barter exchange business. The software is responsible for managing barter exchanges. It records offers of exchange, acceptances, and the consummation of each exchange.

The business has grown to the point where it has offices in a number of cities, each office facilitating barter exchanges among people local to its city. The business's management has decided that it is time to take the business to the next level and allow barter between people in different parts of the country. They want someone in one city to be able to swap theater tickets for balloon rides near a different city. Currently, that is not possible.

Each office runs its own computer that manages transactions for its clients. The offices run independently of each other. In order to support exchanges between clients of different offices, it must be possible to execute ACID transactions that are distributed between multiple offices.

To make this happen, there must be a mechanism that coordinates the portion of each transaction that executes in each office. It must be the case that every portion of each transaction successfully commits or every portion of each transaction aborts. It must never happen that one office thinks that a transaction completed successfully and another thinks that it aborted.

FORCES

☺ Otherwise-independent atomic transactions must participate in a composite atomic transaction.

☺ If any one of the component transactions participating in a composite atomic transaction fails, all must fail. This implies that the component transactions are coordinated in some way.

☺ Though it is possible to distribute the responsibility for coordinating transactions over multiple objects, it is an unusual design decision. Distributing coordination of self-contained transactions adds complexity. It is an area that is not as well understood as designs that make a single object responsible for the coordination. Distributed coordination of transactions remains a valid research topic.

☺ There is extensive industry experience with designs that make a single object responsible for coordinating transactions. Because of this experience, designs that make a single object responsible for coordinating transactions are well understood and widely written about.

☺ The results of a transaction should persist as long as any objects may be interested in the results or until another transaction changes the state of the affected objects. If the transactions being coordinated have the ACID properties, then their durability attribute implies that this will be true for the results of each of the coordinated transactions individually.

☹ The responsibility for coordinating component transactions persists until the composite transaction has completed. However, the object(s) responsible for coordinating a transaction may experience a catastrophic failure during a transaction.

☹ The requirements for some applications imply that some composite transactions should not be atomic. This is often true for long-lived transactions or application-level transactions. For example, an inventory application for a chain of retail stores may support a transaction to order additional merchandise from a warehouse. If the warehouse does not have all of the ordered merchandise, then the warehouse will need to backorder the merchandise and send the merchandise to the stores after the merchandise arrives. To allow store managers to effectively manage the display of their inventory, they will need to be aware of the status of orders they send to the warehouse. It must be possible for store managers to know when the merchandise that they ordered is backordered.

SOLUTION

Make a single object responsible for coordinating otherwise-independent ACID transactions participating in a composite transaction so that the composite transaction has the ACID properties. The object responsible for the coordination is called the *coordinator*. The coordinator coordinates the completion of the composite transaction in two phases. First, it determines whether each component transaction has completed its work successfully. If any of the component transactions complete unsuccessfully, then the coordinator causes all of the component transactions to abort. If all of the component transactions complete successfully, the coordinator causes all of the component transactions to commit their results.

The class diagram in Figure 4.7 shows the roles in which objects participate in the Two Phase Commit pattern.

Here are descriptions of the roles in which classes participate in the Two Phase Commit pattern:

CompositeTransactionLogic.   A class in this role is responsible for the top-level logic of a composite transaction.

Coordinator.   An instance of a class in this role is responsible for coordinating the component transactions of a composite transaction. It determines whether they are all successful and then either tells them all to commit or to all abort. Classes in this role are usually reusable and contain no application specific code.

ComponentTransaction1, ComponentTransaction2, . . .   Classes in this role encapsulate the component transactions that comprise the composite transaction.

TransactionWrapper1, TransactionWrapper2, . . .
`ComponentTransaction` objects can participate directly in the Two Phase Commit pattern only if they are designed to do so. That is usually not the case. `ComponentTransaction` objects that are not designed to directly participate in the Two Phase Commit pattern can do so through a wrapper object that provides the logic necessary to do so. Classes in this role are those wrapper objects. The details of the logic they need to provide are discussed later in this section.

TransactionWrapperIF.   Classes in the `TransactionWrapper` role must implement this interface, which is required by the `Coordinator` class.

The collaboration diagram in Figure 4.8 illustrates the way that these classes work together.

Here is a step-by-step description of the interactions shown in Figure 4.8:

1.   The composite transaction is started.

1.1, 1.2.   The composite transaction registers the objects that wrap the component transactions with the `Coordinator` object. This simplifies the logic of the composite transaction by allowing it to

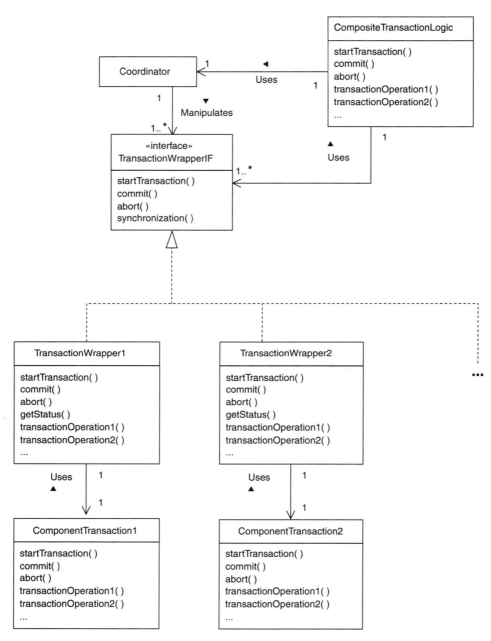

FIGURE 4.7 Two Phase Commit pattern.

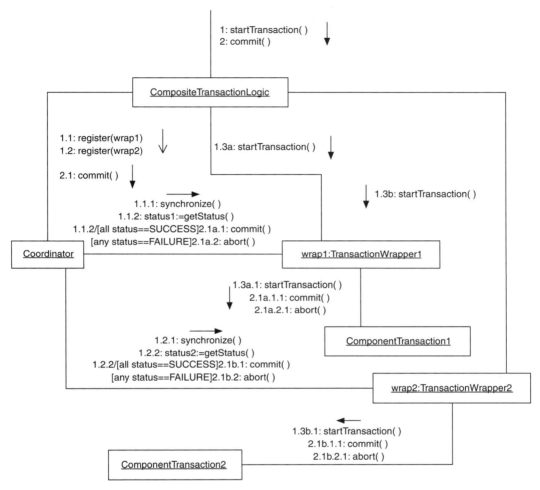

FIGURE 4.8 Two phase commit collaboration.

commit or abort the transaction with a single call to the `Coordinator` object. It also allows the `Coordinator` object to provide better handling of component transactions that fail. This is discussed in more detail under the "Implementation" heading.

These calls are asynchronous. They start another thread to do their work and then return immediately.

1.1.1, 1.2.1. The `Coordinator` object calls the `synchronize` method of the objects that wrap the component transactions. The purpose of these calls is to enable the `Coordinator` object to know when each of the component transactions has completed. Calls to the `synchronize` methods do not return until the component transaction they are associated with completes.

The call that precedes these calls is asynchronous. These calls made by the `Coordinator` object are made in a different thread than the calls to the `Coordinator` object. The objects that call the `Coordinator` object's `register` method are able to go about their business while the `Coordinator` object is waiting for its calls to `synchronize` methods to return.

1.1.2, 1.2.2. The `Coordinator` object calls the `getStatus` method of the objects that wrap the component transactions. The purpose of these calls is to determine whether each component transaction succeeded or failed.

If *any* of the component transactions failed, then instead of allowing this sequence of interactions to continue, the `Coordinator` object causes all of the other component transactions to abort and ends the transaction.

1.3a, 1.3b. The logic of the composite transactions starts each of the component transactions by calling the `startTransaction` method of the wrapper object for each component transaction. When possible and advantageous, the invocations of the component transactions are concurrent. In many cases, that is not possible. Sequential invocation of component transactions is more common than concurrent invocation.

1.3a.1, 1.3b.1. The wrapper objects start their corresponding component transaction.

2. The `CompositeTransactionLogic` object's `commit` method is called. A call to the `commit` method requests the object to commit the results of the composite transaction.

2.1. The `CompositeTransactionLogic` object delegates the work of committing the composite transaction to the `Coordinator` object by calling its `commit` method.

2.1a.1, 2.1b.1. For each component transaction, the `Coordinator` object waits for the transaction to complete. If the status of all of the component transactions indicate that they completed successfully and will be able to commit their results successfully, then the `Coordinator` object calls the `commit` method of each component transaction's wrapper object.

2.1a.1.1, 2.1b.1.1. If their `commit` method is called, the wrapper objects for the component transactions commit those transactions.

2.1a.2, 2.1b.2. If any component transactions did not complete successfully or their status indicates that some of them will not be able to successfully commit their results, then the `Coordinator` object calls the `abort` method of each component transaction's wrapper object.

2.1a.2.1, 2.1b.2.1.   If their `abort` method is called, the wrapper objects for the component transactions abort those transactions.

Based on this, the additional logic that wrapper objects for component transactions may be required to provide are as follows:

- The ability to tell whether a component transaction has completed its work successfully and will be able to successfully commit its results
- The ability to determine whether a component transaction will be unable to complete its work

When a Component Transaction Fails

A `Coordinator` object learns that a component transaction has failed when its wrapper's `getStatus` method returns failure. If any of the component transactions fail, the `Coordinator` object aborts them all.

When a Component Transaction Object Crashes

When a `Coordinator` object learns that a component transaction object has crashed, it also aborts all of the component transactions. `Coordinator` objects are generally not able to learn directly that a component transaction object has crashed. Instead, they generally learn indirectly of a crash. A `Coordinator` object may infer that a component transaction object has crashed by the amount of time it takes for the call to the component object's `getStatus` method to return. If the call takes too long to return, the `Coordinator` object may consider the call to have timed out and infer that the call will never return.

If the length of time that a component transaction takes is highly variable, then the amount of time that must elapse before the `Coordinator` object may consider the call to have timed out may be unreasonably long. In such cases, the `Coordinator` object can use the Heartbeat pattern to detect the crash of a `Coordinator` object.

When the Coordinator Crashes

One other aspect of this pattern to look at more closely is what happens when the `Coordinator` object crashes.

When a `Coordinator` object has a transaction pending, it records in a file the fact that there is a pending transaction and the identities of the transaction's participants. If the `Coordinator` object crashes, it is automatically restarted.

After the `Coordinator` object restarts, it checks the file for pending transactions. When the `Coordinator` object finds a transaction in the file, the transaction will be in one of three states:

The transaction may be open. In this case, the Coordinator object does not need to take any immediate action.

The transaction may be aborted. This will be the case if the Coordinator object received a request to abort the transaction, but had not informed all of the transaction's participants to abort before the crash. In this case, the Coordinator object calls the abort method of all the transaction's participants.

The transaction may be committed. This will be the case if the Coordinator object received a request to commit the transaction, but had not informed all of the participants to commit before the crash. This is the most interesting of the three cases.

If the `Coordinator` object had been asked to commit the transaction before it crashed, it has to find out the status of the participants before it can proceed. The `Coordinator` object proceeds by calling the `getStatus` method of all the transaction's participants. Each call to a participant's `getStatus` method tells the `Coordinator` object one of three things:

- The participant has committed the transaction.
- The participant is ready to commit the transaction.
- The participant is unable to commit the transaction.

Because of the way that Two Phase Commit works, it should never be the case that some participants have been committed and other participants are unable to commit. Once the `Coordinator` object knows the status of all the participants, it either asks all of the participants to commit or all of the participants to abort the transaction.

CONSEQUENCES

☺ The Two Phase Commit pattern ensures that all component transactions in a composite transaction either commit their results or abort.

☺ In most situations, the Two Phase Commit pattern adds only a modest amount of overhead.

☹ There is a situation in which a transaction implemented using the Two Phase Commit pattern can take an indefinite amount of time to complete.

The lifetime of a composite transaction is greater than the lifetime of its component transactions. In a distributed environment, it is possible for some components of the transaction to have some sort of catastrophic failure while the others are alive and well. If the object(s) coordinating a transaction experience a catastrophic failure, the Coordinator object can generally detect the failure within a bounded and predetermined amount of time. In such cases, the Coordinator object tells the rest of the component transactions to abort.

If the Coordinator object experiences a catastrophic failure, it is generally not possible to guarantee a maximum amount of time it will take for it to be restarted and complete the transaction. That means there is no definite guarantee on how long it can take for coordinated transactions to complete.

☹ Some transactions cannot participate in the Two Phase Commit pattern because there is no way for a wrapper object to get the information it needs about the transaction.

IMPLEMENTATION

It is possible to guarantee an upper bound on the amount of time it takes for coordinated transactions to complete by forcing them to abort after a predetermined amount of time has elapsed. This has the unfortunate consequence of creating a period of time in which it is possible for the outcome of the coordinated transactions to become inconsistent. The problem arises from the fact that when the object(s) that coordinates a transaction decides that the coordinated transactions should commit their results, the message does not reach the objects responsible for each transaction at the same time. This creates a window of vulnerability between the time that the message to commit reaches the first transaction and the time it reaches the last transaction. During that window, some of the transactions may time out, causing those transactions to abort while those that the message reaches in time commit their results.

In distributed environments, you should ensure that the Coordinator object becomes aware of the catastrophic failure of a component transaction within a bounded amount of time. The simplest solution is available if the component transaction takes about the same amount of time to complete every time it runs. In this situation, the Coordinator object can detect a catastrophic failure of a component transaction by placing a limit on how much time it will wait for it to complete before it decides that the component transaction has failed.

If the amount of time that a component transaction requires is not predictable, you can use the Heartbeat pattern to ensure that the Coordinator object detects a catastrophic failure within a set amount of time.

Another implementation issue for two phase commit is how to ensure that after a `TransactionWrapper` object has been asked to commit its transaction and agrees to commit its transaction that it actually does commit its transaction. This generally involves a flag indicating that a commit is pending and a commit mechanism that is idempotent (can be invoked more than once with the same result as invoking it only once). In normal circumstances, the commits proceeds, and the flag is set to indicate that no commit is pending. If the `TransactionWrapper` object is restarted after a crash, it will notice that there is a commit pending and invoke the commit mechanism. It doesn't know whether the commit was completed previously, but because the commit is idempotent, it does not matter whether the commit is being invoked a second time.

JAVA API USAGE

The Java Transaction API defines interfaces that are suitable for some of the roles of the Two Phase Commit pattern.

KNOWN USES

The CORBA transaction service supports the Two Phase Commit pattern. Databases such as Oracle and Sybase that support distributed transactions use the Two Phase Commit pattern.

RELATED PATTERNS

ACID Transaction.   The Two Phase Commit pattern is used to build composite transactions having the ACID properties from component transactions that have the ACID properties.

Composite Transaction.   The Two Phase Commit pattern is used with the Composite Transaction pattern.

Decorator.   The Decorator pattern (described in Volume 1) provides the basis for the organization of the wrapper objects used in the Two Phase Commit pattern.

Heartbeat.   The Heartbeat pattern may be used with the Two Phase Commit pattern to ensure that the `Coordinator` object is able to detect catastrophic failures of component transactions in a bounded amount of time.

Process Pair.   The Process Pair pattern may be used to restart a `Coordinator` object after it crashes.

Audit Trail

SYNOPSIS

You need to verify that transactions are being processed correctly and honestly. Maintain a historical record of transactions that have been applied to an object or a set of objects. The record should contain enough detail to determine how the objects affected by the transactions reached their current state.

CONTEXT

Suppose that you are designing software for a business that will serve as a clearinghouse for barter exchanges. Each transaction will involve the exchange of a combination of goods and services.

Each day, the clearinghouse's clients make deals. At the end of each day, all clients are expected to consummate their trades through the exchange of certificates promising the future delivery of goods or services. The clearinghouse provides its clients with the necessary digital certificates that it expects them to digitally sign and forward to the indicated recipient. Because of subsequent trades, the recipient of the certificate may be a different party than anyone with whom the client made any direct deal.

Clearinghouse clients must trust the clearinghouse to correctly identify the recipients of the goods or services that they have traded away. For this reason, there must be a way to verify the correctness and honesty of the clearinghouse. One way to do that is to keep an audit trail.

The audit trail will consist of a record of all trades. By reviewing randomly selected sequences of transactions, it is possible for auditors to verify that the transactions are handled correctly and honestly.

FORCES

☺ You need a record of the transactions that have modified the state of an object or set of objects in order to determine if the current state of the object(s) is correct.

☺ You need to account for the actions of an object. The need for accountability can come from the application domain. For example, in accounting and finance applications, real-world financial events drive the actions of objects. These applications generally have requirements that it be possible to audit the actions of these objects so that they can be compared with real-world events. Such audits provide an opportunity to detect human error and dishonesty in recording financial events.

☺ The need for object accountability may come from internal design considerations such as the need to review an object's actions for security or debugging purposes. A record of an object's actions may help detect patterns in a hacker's actions. When debugging a program, comparing a record of an object's actions with its expected actions can help in tracking down bugs.

☺ Once a record is made of a transaction, it must not be possible to alter that record. If it is possible to alter it, then you cannot be sure of what actually happened.

☹ The number of recorded transactions consistently grows, but the amount of available online storage does not.

☹ The purpose of keeping a historical record of transactions is to enable auditors or troubleshooters to verify that the transactions in the record satisfy a set of expectations or requirements. In many cases, the volume of transactions makes it impractical for people to examine every individual transaction. In such cases, people will need a way to examine samples or summaries of the transactions.

SOLUTION

Maintain a historical record of transactions. The record should include all transactions that affect the state of objects of interest. In order to use the historical record to determine whether the objects are currently in the correct state, it is necessary to determine the object's original state. For this purpose, you also store the original state of the object. Knowing the original state of an object makes it possible to determine whether or not the transactions applied to an object after it was in that state should have brought the object to its current state.

The record should also include transactions initiated by objects of interest. The purpose of such a historical record is to record the behavior of the object that initiates the transactions. In many cases it is necessary for the historical record to include information about the object's state at the time it initiated a transaction in order to evaluate the object's behavior.

To facilitate the analysis of transaction records, the transaction records should be under the control of a mechanism such as a database manager that allows people to extract samples or summaries of the transaction. For example, consider the situation described under the "Context" heading. It would be desirable to be able to pick an arbitrary clearinghouse client and review the sequence of trades that resulted in the client being told to send his or her trade goods to a particular recipient.

CONSEQUENCES

☺ If you use the Audit Trail pattern to keep track of the transactions that an object is given to process, then you can determine whether the object is in its correct state by auditing the transactions in the audit trail.

☺ If you used the Audit Trail pattern to keep track of the transactions an object initiates, you will have a way to validate its behavior or debug it.

☺ If an audit trail captures a complete transaction history along with the relevant object's initial state or historical states, then the audit trail can be used to reconstruct the relevant objects in the event of a catastrophic failure.

☹ The Audit Trail pattern adds complexity to designs.

☹ The storage requirements for maintaining an audit trail can be very large. As time goes on, an audit trail will continue to grow. If the audit trail is to be kept online, there is generally a constrained amount of space available for storing it. For that reason, it is common to transfer portions of an online audit trail that exceed a particular age to removable storage such as a tape.

IMPLEMENTATION

When an audit trail is mandated by application requirements, the collection of historical transactions that constitutes the audit trail is called a *journal*. As is the case with all audit trails, the transactions in a journal never change because they are a true and accurate record of history. If an application processes a transaction whose purpose is to correct the effects of a previous erroneous transaction, the transaction that corrects the problem is called an *adjustment transaction*.

There are many ways to implement the Audit Trail pattern. Figure 4.9 shows a sample design to implement the Audit Trail pattern.

In the design shown in Figure 4.9, `TransactionProcessor` objects process transactions encapsulated in `Transaction` objects, passing them to a `TransactionRecorder` object, which adds the transactions to the collection of `Transaction` objects it manages. `TransactionRecorder` objects

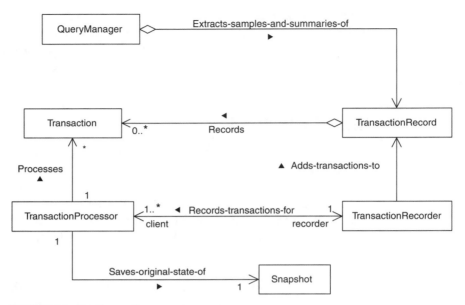

FIGURE 4.9 Audit trail pattern.

are responsible for adding information to the transactions that will be needed for the historical record. One such commonly needed piece of information is the time that a transaction was processed.

Figure 4.9 also includes a Snapshot object that encapsulates the original state of the TransactionProcessor object. The contents of the Snapshot object are used when analyzing the historical transaction record.

One other detail in Figure 4.9 is a QueryManager class. It is responsible for generating subsets and summaries of the historical transaction record as they are requested by auditors.

The historical record does not need to include failed transactions to be able to validate an object's current state from an historical record of transactions. However, there may be advantages to including failed transactions in the historical record. It can facilitate debugging and detection of security problems. Because those are not continuing needs, if there is support for failed transactions in the historical record it should be possible to turn off the inclusion of failed transactions. If it is possible to include failed transactions in a historical record some of the time, then all transactions in the record must include an indication of whether or not each transaction was successful.

The volume of transactions in some applications may make it impractical to store and manage a complete audit trail. If the number of transactions an application generates is too large, it becomes physically impossible for auditors to examine every item in an audit trail. In such cases, it may be possible to keep a partial audit trail that still allows valid audits to be performed.

When moving transactions offline, the object states that they gave rise to should be determined and stored online. This makes it possible to analyze the online portion of the historical record without having to access offline information.

For some applications, it is not possible to sufficiently limit the time historical transaction records are kept online to keep the online storage requirement small enough. If the application processes transactions for many objects, it may be sufficient to keep a historical transaction record only for randomly selected objects.

KNOWN USES

Accounting applications intended for medium to large applications support the Audit Trail pattern.

Workflow applications generally provide an audit trail that allows people to find out who did what with a work item.

Source code management systems such as CVS provide an audit trail describing what changes have been made to source code and who made them.

RELATED PATTERNS

ACID Transaction.   If the transactions in a historical record do not have the ACID properties, then it may not be possible to unambiguously determine the effect of each transaction on an object.

Snapshot.   The Snapshot pattern (described in *Volume 1*) provides advice on how to capture the state of an object.

C H A P T E R

5

Distributed
Architecture Patterns

The patterns in this chapter can be used to design the high-level architecture of distributed designs. Because some of these patterns involve infrastructure, the patterns can be incorporated into architectural designs using off-the-shelf reusable components.

There are a few recurring themes in these patterns. The most common and basic of these themes is multiple clients sharing the same object. For that reason, the Shared Object pattern is the first pattern in this chapter. It describes a centralized way of sharing objects. The Object Replication pattern describes a decentralized way of sharing objects.

Another recurring theme is handling failures. The Object Replication, Redundant Independent Objects, Prompt Repair, and Process Pair patterns describe ways to survive failures. The Demilitarized Zone pattern describes a way to avoid a type of security failure.

Because the patterns in this chapter are at the architectural level, code examples are of limited value. When reduced to code, the patterns tend to be diffused throughout the code. Examples tend to be excessively large and difficult to follow. For this reason, the patterns in this chapter do not have a "Code Example" section.

Shared Object

SYNOPSIS

You have some information or a limited quantity of a resource. You share objects among multiple clients in order to share encapsulated information or underlying resources. You centrally manage the object sharing with a separate object, so the sharing does not add to the complexity of the objects being shared or the objects sharing them.

CONTEXT

Suppose you are designing a point-of-sale system.* You are responsible for designing the part of the system that will process credit card payments. To process a credit card payment, the point-of-sale system must contact a credit card clearinghouse, verify that the credit card number is valid, and get approval for the transaction.

At the time of this writing, there is more than one way for point-of-sale systems to communicate with a credit card clearinghouse. The most common way for a point-of-sale system to connect is via telephone. If a point-of-sale system includes multiple cash registers but only one phone line, then sometimes one register must wait for another register to finish clearing a transaction before it can process its own transaction. To avoid delays caused by waiting for a telephone line, some multiple-register point-of-sale systems have multiple telephone lines. This allows them to simultaneously process as many credit card charges as there are telephone lines.

You design the point-of-sale system so that there is a `TelephoneLine` object responsible for each telephone line. Each `TelephoneLine` object is shared by all of the cash registers. Figure 5.1 shows these relationships.

In this design, cash registers work through a single `TelephoneLineManager` object to connect to the credit card clearinghouse. A `CashRegister` object calls the `TelephoneLineManager` object's `getPhoneConnection` method. If any `TelephoneLine` objects are not in use, the `TelephoneLineManager` object allocates one and returns the connection. Otherwise, the `TelephoneLineManager` object waits until a `TelephoneLine` object is available.

Point-of-sale system is the high-tech name for a cash register (with high-tech improvements).

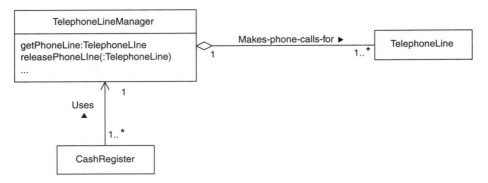

FIGURE 5.1 Shared telephone lines.

After the `CashRegister` object is finished using a telephone connection, it calls the `TelephoneLineManager` object's `releasePhoneConnection` method, which makes the `TelephoneLine` object available for other `CashRegister` objects.

FORCES

☺ Multiple client objects require access to an instance of the same class or an object that implements a particular interface.

☺ Client objects require access to a resource object that is unique or available only in limited quantities.

☺ Uncontrolled access by clients to resource objects will cause bad or unpredictable results. It is necessary to constrain access by client according to some policy such as exclusive access.

☺ You want the benefits that come from multiple objects sharing a resource. However, you don't want to burden the client objects that share the resource with the task of managing the resource. If there is a pool of resources to share, it is an even bigger burden for the client object to directly manage a pool of resources.

☺ It must be possible to administer some resource objects independently of their clients. This can involve an object responsible for administering multiple resource objects, or possibly all of the resource objects.

☺ Suppose multiple clients that reside on different computing elements share an object. The more clients the object has, the higher will be the demand for CPU cycles on the computing element on which the object resides.

☹ If a set of resource objects has many clients, you can reduce the likelihood that a client will have to wait for a resource by adding more resource objects. However, if all clients have to go through the same object to get a resource object allocated, then the object that allocates the resource becomes a bottleneck.

☹ If the clients of a set of resources are in remote locations and exchange a large volume of data with the resource objects, then having a set of resource objects all located in one place is undesirable. It can result in more communications or networking delay than is necessary. Having multiple sets of resources located in places closer to their clients can result in less or no communications or networking delay.

SOLUTION

Allow instances of a class to be shared by multiple objects. Put a single object in charge of allocating instances of the class to client objects. These relationships are illustrated in Figure 5.2.

Figure 5.2 shows multiple `Client` objects using shared `Resource` objects through a `Manager` object. The `Manager` object manages a collection of `Resource` objects. When a `Client` object needs a `Resource` object, the `Manager` object is responsible for centrally determining which `Resource` object a `Client` object will use. This must be governed by a policy, such as exclusive access, that ensures the correct use of the `Resource` object.

The `Manager` class must also implement a policy that determines what happens if no `Resource` objects are available. The most common policy is to simply wait until a `Resource` object becomes available.

CONSEQUENCES

☺ Sharing objects among multiple clients may be an effective way to manage limited resources.

FIGURE 5.2 Shared objects.

☺ If other objects share an object, then they indirectly share the resources used by the object.

☹ It is difficult to tune the performance of a system of objects in which the clients of a shared object reside on a different computer than the shared object and the objects used by the shared object also reside on different computers.

☹ If there are many clients, the Manager object can become a performance bottleneck. In such situations, if the clients are distributed over multiple computers, the Object Replication pattern may be a better way to manage the sharing of objects.

IMPLEMENTATION

If an object is shared by remote clients, they will access it asynchronously and sometimes concurrently. You need to take steps to ensure that the relevant methods of the shared object's class and the Manager class are thread safe in order to ensure their correct operation.

Manager Methods

The sort of methods a Manager class provides to its clients depends on the nature of the resource being managed. If operations on the resource are self-contained method calls, then the Manager class will typically be a proxy for the resource class. For example, consider a telemarketing application whose purpose is to call a telephone number, play a recorded message, and then hang up.

Suppose that a resource class named Spammer is responsible for this activity. Also suppose that the Spammer class has a method named spam that takes a telephone number and an AudioClip object as its parameters. When called, the spam method dials the telephone number, plays the AudioClip and then hangs up.

A Manager class for Spammer objects would have a spam method that would wait for a Spammer object to become available and then call its spam method.

If the client's interaction with a resource can involve a sequence of method calls, the Manager class methods shown in the example under the "Context" heading are typical. In this circumstance, the Manager class typically has a method that waits for a resource object to become available and then returns the resource object. The client then interacts directly with the resource object. When the client object is finished with the resource object, it passes the resource object to another of the Manager object's methods to make the resource object available to other clients.

If a `Manager` class is organized this way, it is possible for a client object to die before it releases a resource object. A `Manager` class can use the Heartbeat pattern to recognize the death or unreachability of a client object. Once it recognizes the problem, it must ask the resource object to abort whatever it was doing and make the resource object available for another client.

The Heartbeat pattern recognizes a high likelihood that an object has died. However, it cannot determine with certainty that a client has died. Therefore, the very first thing it must do when recognizing that a client has probably died is to ensure that if the client is still alive, any further attempts by it to interact with the resource object will fail. One way to accomplish this is to pass to clients a decorator object (the Decorator pattern is described in *Volume 1*) that has a method the `Manager` object can use to disable it.

The nature of some resources may require a `Manager` object to ask each resource object to put itself in a known state before the `Manager` object's method returns the resource object to a client.

Resource Allocation

A good way for the `Manager` class to allocate resources to clients is to use the Scheduler pattern, which is described in *Volume 1*. The Scheduler pattern describes a way to schedule single-threaded access to shared resources.

Multiple clients can access some resources concurrently if those clients only query the state of the resource and do nothing to change it. If changes to the state of a resource must be single-threaded, but queries of its state may be concurrent, then the Read/Write Lock pattern, also described in *Volume 1*, is a better way to implement the `Manager` class. It is better because it does not force queries of the state of a resource to wait for other queries of the resource's state to finish before they can start.

KNOWN USES

The architecture of many enterprise applications involves sharing objects:

- A long-distance telephone company has an object that resides on a mainframe that controls the routing of toll-free numbers. Many instances of a PC-based application share that object for the purpose of managing the routing of toll-free phone numbers.
- A food retailer uses a single shared data-collecting object to capture information from cash registers in all of its locations. This data-

collecting object is also used by a sales forecasting application and an inventory management application.

Shared objects also turn up in system software:

● Programs on multiple computers can share print queues.
● Multiple computers can share file systems.

RELATED PATTERNS

Static Locking Order. If `Client` objects work with multiple `Manager` objects to concurrently access multiple types of `Resource` objects, it is possible for two client objects to deadlock while waiting for different resources. `Client` objects should use the Static Locking Order pattern to avoid this sort of deadlock.

Object Replication. The Object Replication pattern provides a decentralized way for the clients of an object to share information. It also provides a way to use multiple manager objects so that a single manager object does not become a performance bottleneck.

Object Request Broker. The Object Request Broker pattern is used to share objects between remote clients.

Scheduler. The Scheduler pattern (found in *Volume 1*) describes a way to schedule access, one client at a time, to shared resources.

Read/Write Lock. The Read/Write Lock pattern (found in *Volume 1*) is a specialized form of the Scheduler pattern. It allows multiple clients to concurrently have read access to a resource, but allows exclusive access only for a client that modifies the resource.

Singleton. The Singleton pattern (found in *Volume 1*) describes classes that have a single instance that may or may not be shared. The Shared Object pattern describes objects that are shared and may have multiple instances.

Flyweight. If an object has no intrinsic state, then there is generally no need to impose concurrency restrictions on access to the object. The Shared Object pattern is inappropriate for sharing such objects because it adds unnecessary overhead. The Flyweight pattern (found in *Volume 1*) describes a way that local clients can share objects with no intrinsic state without any concurrency restrictions.

Object Request Broker

The Object Request Broker pattern is also known as *ORB* or Broker. It was previously published as the Broker pattern in [Buschman96].

This pattern description is intended to explain what object request brokers are and their use. It is not intended to provide enough detail to implement an object request broker.

SYNOPSIS

Objects in a distributed environment need to call methods of remote objects. For remote calls to work, many details must be just right. Provide an infrastructure that allows objects to make remote calls, with most of the details of the call hidden and handled automatically by the infrastructure.

CONTEXT

Suppose that you are designing an employee timekeeping system. The purpose of the system is to record when employees are working and when they are not. Figure 5.3 shows the system architecture.

The architecture consists of multiple timekeeping terminals that employees use to tell the system when they begin working and when they stop working. The terminals feed that information to a server. One or more

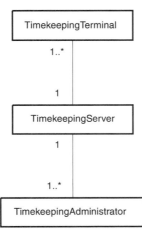

FIGURE 5.3 Employee timekeeping system architecture.

timekeeping administrators perform administrative tasks on the timekeeping data.

The components of this architecture contain objects that must call methods of objects in other components. You want to design an architecture that allows objects in different components to call each other's methods in a manner as simple and as easily maintainable as possible.

FORCES

A call from a method to another method in the same Java Virtual Machine (VM) is called a *local call*. A call from a method to a method in a different Java VM is called a *remote call*.

- ☺ You want to create distributed software in a way that minimizes the amount of programming time spent on interhost communication.
- ☺ A method should be able to make remote calls without knowing in which VM the called method resides, or even its physical location.
- ☺ When making a remote call, the parameters passed to a method, the method's result, or the exception it throws must be passed between the Java VMs. Neither the calling method nor the called method should be aware of the mechanism for passing the parameters, the result, or any exception.
- ☺ An environment that contains objects whose methods will be called remotely should be prepared to handle a remote call at any time, even if there are other active remote calls.
- ☺ An object that calls the methods of a remote object must have a way to identify that object.
- ☹ Mechanisms that hide programming details often add overhead. Some applications cannot tolerate the additional overhead.
- ☹ Many possible variations can occur on the basic semantics of method calls. They can involve such things as bulk data transfer, asynchronous method calls, or ensuring that the parameters of a call are transferred in a secure way. The more variations a mechanism that hides programming details can handle, the more difficult it is to learn to use.

SOLUTION

Hide the details of remote method calls by using a layered architecture. Use tools to automatically generate glue code to connect the methods or your code with a framework that supports the layered architecture. This layered architecture is shown in Figure 5.4.

The `Caller` and `Callee` roles constitute an application layer. Aside from the fact that `Caller` classes call `Callee` classes through an interface,

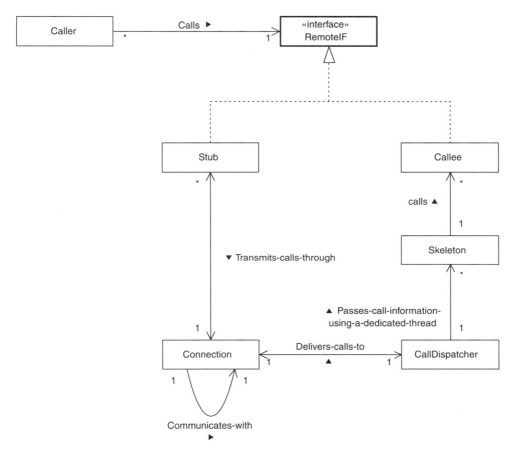

FIGURE 5.4 Object request broker pattern.

which is something they might do anyhow, nothing in this layer indicates that the Caller does not call the Callee directly.

The Stub, CallDispatcher, and Skeleton roles constitute a message layer. Stub classes turn a call into a message, which is interpreted by CallDispatcher and Skeleton classes. Skeleton classes are also responsible for generating response messages containing the outcome of the call.

The Connection role constitutes a transport layer that is responsible for transporting the messages and responses.

Here is a more detailed description of the roles that the classes and interfaces shown in Figure 5.4 play in the Object Request Broker pattern:

Caller. Classes in this role call methods of a proxy object* that implements the RemoteIF interface. Because they call methods

---

* The Proxy pattern is described in *Volume 1*.

through an interface, they need not be aware of the fact that they are calling the methods of a `Stub` object that is a proxy for the `Callee` object rather than the `Callee` object itself. The `Stub` object encapsulates the details of how calls to the `Callee` object are made and its location (e.g., direct calls to an object or calls through a remote proxy). These details are transparent to `Caller` objects.

RemoteIF. Objects that have methods that may be called by remote objects implement an interface that is in this role. A method can be called remotely if and only if it declared by a `RemoteIF` interface that its class implements.

Stub. Classes in this role implement a `RemoteIF` interface. Every `RemoteIF` interface has a corresponding `Stub` class. A `Stub` object is a remote proxy for an object in the `Callee` role whose methods can be called remotely. `Stub` classes implement the methods of a `RemoteIF` interface by passing on the fact that the method was called and the values of its parameters to a `Connection` object. They assemble information identifying the `Callee` object, the method being called, and the values of the arguments into a message. On the other end of the connection, part of the message is interpreted by a `CallDispatcher` object and the rest by a `Skeleton` object.

When the remote call returns, the `Skeleton` object sends a response back to the `Stub` object that contains the returned value or the exception thrown. The `Stub` object interprets the message by returning the value or throwing the exception.

Implementations of object request brokers include a mechanism for automatically creating `Stub` classes.

Connection. Classes in this role are responsible for the transport of messages between the environment of a remote caller and the environment of the callee.

CallDispatcher. Instances of classes in this role receive messages through a `Connection` object from a remote `Stub` object. They pass each message to an instance of an appropriate `Skeleton` class. Classes in this role may also be responsible for creating the instances of `Skeleton` classes.

`CallDispatcher` objects are responsible for identifying the `Callee` object whose method will be called by the `Skeleton` object. Typically, two ways of doing this are supported.

● The message identifies the specific `Callee` object whose method is to be called. In this case, the `CallDispatcher` object simply passes a reference to this `Callee` object to the `Skeleton` object.

- If the `CallDispatcher` object does not receive any information identifying a specific `Callee` object, then it can create one or reuse an existing one. Some object request broker (ORB) implementations make this configurable and call it an activation policy.

Skeleton. Classes in this role are responsible for calling the methods of `Callee` objects on behalf of remote `Caller` objects. For every `RemoteIF` interface there is at least one corresponding `Skeleton` class. Each `Skeleton` class is responsible for calling methods of objects that implement the corresponding `RemoteIF` interface.

A `CallDispatcher` object passes the message describing a method call to a `Skeleton` object. The `Skeleton` object extracts the argument values from the message and then calls the indicated method passing it the given argument values.

If the called method returns a result, then the `Skeleton` object is responsible for creating a message that contains the return value and sending it back to the `Stub` object so that the `Stub` object can return it.

If the called method throws an exception, the `Skeleton` object is responsible for creating an appropriate message. For object request broker implementations that are specifically designed for Java, such as RMI or Voyager, the message contains the actual exception thrown. This makes it possible for the `Stub` object that receives the message to rethrow the exception. Object request broker implementations not specifically designed for Java will generally provide some information about the exception.

Implementations of the Object Request Broker pattern include a mechanism for automatically generating `Skeleton` classes.

Callee. Classes in this role implement a `RemoteIF` interface. Instances of this class can be called locally through the `RemoteIF` interface, or remotely through a `Stub` object that also implements the same `RemoteIF` interface.

Figure 5.5 shows the interactions that occur when a remote call is made through an object request broker. Sometime before these interactions occur, at least two things must have happened.

- A call will have been made to initialize the object request broker.
- The method making the remote call will have obtained a `Stub` object to call the remote object. `Stub` objects are generally created in the following ways:

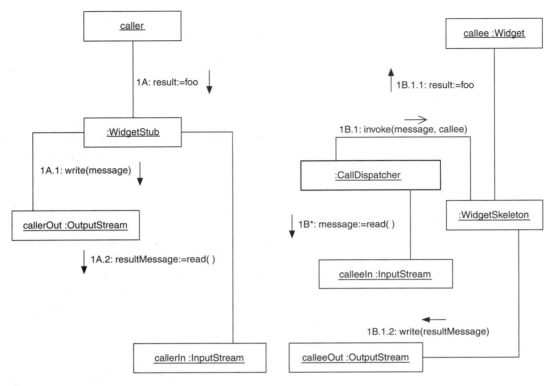

FIGURE 5.5 Object request broker Interactions.

- Object request brokers provide a mechanism that takes the logical name of an object and creates a Stub object in consultation with a mechanism that uses the Registry pattern to provide the location of the callee object.
- A stub is created from hard-wired information about the location and name of the callee object. This is generally to be avoided.
- A call to a remote method returns a Stub object to call another remote object.

Here are descriptions of the interactions shown in Figure 5.5:

1A. The caller object calls the WidgetStub object's foo method with the intention of calling the Widget object that may or may not be remote.

1A.1. The WidgetStub object asks the callerOut object to write a message that includes the class name Widget, the method name foo, and the arguments that the caller object passed to foo.

The `callerOut` object passes the message through a network connection to the `calleeIn` object.

1B.   The `CallDispatcher` object reads the message from the `calleeIn` object.

1B.1.   The `CallDispatcher` object extracts the class of the object to call from the message. It then obtains the actual object whose method is to be called.

   Using a different thread, the `CallDispatcher` object asynchronously calls the `invoke` method of a `WidgetSkeleton` object. It passes the message and the `callee` object whose method is to be called to the `invoke` method.

1B.1.1.   The `WidgetSkeleton` object extracts the name of the method to call and the arguments from the message. It then calls the `callee` object's `foo` method.

1B.1.2.   The `WidgetSkeleton` object constructs a message that contains the result produced by the call to the `Widget` object's `foo` method. This can be a returned value or a thrown exception. It then passes the message to the `calleeOut` object's `write` method, which passes the message through a network connection to the `callerIn` object.

1A.2.   The `CallerIn` object's `read` method returns the result message to the `WidgetStub` object.

1A (continued).   The `WidgetStub` object extracts the result from the message. If the result is a value, it returns it. If the result is an exception, it throws it.

There is usually a very direct relationship between the code that implements a stub method and the signature, return type, and declared exceptions of the corresponding interface method. This makes it possible to mechanically generate stubs from interfaces. Since hand-coding stub classes is much more time-consuming and error-prone than automatically generating stub classes with a program, implementations of the Object Request Broker pattern include a mechanism for automatically generating `Stub` classes from `RemoteIF` interfaces. For similar reasons, implementation of the Object Request Broker pattern also includes a mechanism to automatically generate `Skeleton` classes.

CONSEQUENCES

☺ Objects can call methods of other objects without knowing the location of the objects, or even whether the objects are remote.

☹ If you want the caller of a method to be unaware of whether a method call is local or remote, the caller will have to treat the call as if it is remote.

IMPLEMENTATION

Finding Remote Objects

The mechanisms for obtaining a stub for an object that will allow it to call the methods of a remote object vary with the implementation. However, they all involve identifying a remote object whose methods are called by the local object. Most implementations provide at least two modes of identification:

- One mode identifies only the machine on which the remote object will reside. Most implementations handle this mode of identification by creating an object on the remote machine. Objects created this way cannot be shared by remote clients. They exist only for the remote object for which they were created.
- The other common mode uniquely identifies the remote object. The Object Identifier pattern describes how to construct unique identifiers. Remote objects that know an object's unique identifier can share the object. The Registry pattern describes how objects may be found using a unique object identifier.

Administration

Implementations of the Object Request Broker pattern use the Strategy pattern (described in *Volume 1*) to instrument `Stub`, `Connection`, `CallDispatcher`, and `Skeleton` objects for such purposes as the following:

- Logging connections
- Tracing remote calls
- Modifying parameters to remote calls or their results
- Filtering calls to prevent some method calls from reaching their intended object

Return from a Call

Concurrency often plays a larger role in the design of remote procedure calls than in local procedure calls. This is because remote procedure calls always involve multiple processors, whereas most local procedure calls involve only one processor.

Some Object Request Broker implementations allow remote calls to be synchronous or asynchronous. Object Request Broker implementations that allow asynchronous method calls distinguish between those that return a result and those that return no result. If an asynchronous call is of the sort that returns a result, then the object request broker will provide a way to determine if the result has been returned and get its value.

Propagation of Exceptions

Object request brokers such as CORBA that are not specifically designed to work with Java do not propagate Java exceptions, although they may pass back values that indicate a remote exception occurred.

Implementations that are designed to work with Java, such as RMI and Voyager, pass remote exceptions back transparently if they are thrown during a synchronous call. If an exception is thrown out of a remote call, then the exception object is sent back to the caller and rethrown.

Distributed Reference Counting

Garbage collection is the mechanism Java normally uses to determine when the storage occupied by an object may be reclaimed. Garbage collection works by assuming an object is alive if and only if other objects that are alive have a reference to the object. If there are no references to an object from an alive object, then garbage collection will reclaim the object's storage.

For objects that are used only locally, garbage collection is a very transparent mechanism for reclaiming storage. Garbage collection does not work as transparently with objects that are referred to remotely. Garbage collectors are not aware of remote references to an object. To compensate for this, as long as there are any alive remote references to an object, you must ensure that there is a local reference to the object so that the garbage collector will not reclaim the object. All object request brokers create such a reference when an object first becomes remotely accessible.

Object request brokers, such as Voyager and RMI, that are specifically designed to work with Java implement some form of remote reference counting that automatically removes the local reference to an object when it has no remaining remote references. Object Request Broker implementations, such as CORBA, that are not specifically designed to work with Java do not automatically do this.

KNOWN USES

At the time of this writing, CORBA is the most widespread and mature implementation of the Object Request Broker pattern. A noteworthy aspect of CORBA is that it works with programs written in different languages. The fact that a method is written in C will be transparent to a caller written in COBOL, and vice versa. Because CORBA is language neutral, using it with some languages is less convenient than using an Object Request Broker implementation specifically designed to be used with a particular language. Java programs that use CORBA typically include code to bridge differences between CORBA's way of doing things and Java's way of doing things.

Remote Method Invocation (RMI) is a Java-based Object Request Broker implementation that is part of the core Java API. Because RMI is Java-based, it is well integrated with the semantics of Java. RMI has the capability of interoperating with CORBA.

Voyager is another Java-based Object Request Broker implementation.* It is a fuller featured Object Request Broker implementation that interoperates with CORBA, RMI, and DCOM.

RELATED PATTERNS

Object Identifier. The Object Identifier pattern provides additional guidance on uniquely identifying objects.

Proxy. Stub classes use the Proxy pattern, which is described in *Volume 1*.

Heartbeat. The Heartbeat pattern provides a general-purpose way to detect that a call to a remote method will never complete. Some object request brokers provide support for the Heartbeat pattern.

Registry. The Registry pattern describes a way for an Object Request Broker implementation to locate remote objects that have a known name or unique object identifier.

Thread Pool. `CallDispatcher` objects require a thread for each remote call they process. An implementation of the Object Request Broker pattern can use the Thread Pool pattern to recycle threads and avoid the expense of creating new threads.

Connection Multiplexing. Some Object Request Broker implementations use the Connection Multiplexing pattern to minimize the number of connections they use.

Layered Architecture. The Object Request Broker Architecture is an application of the Layered Architecture pattern discussed in [Buschman96].

---

* The Voyager home page is www.objectspace.com/Products/voyager1.htm.

Object Replication

The Object Replication pattern is based on [Fægri95].

SYNOPSIS

You need to improve the throughput or availability of a distributed computation. Distributed computations involve objects residing on multiple computing elements that are able to communicate with each other. In some circumstances, it is possible to improve the availability and throughput of a computation by replicating an object onto multiple computing elements while maintaining the illusion to the object's clients that there is only a single object.

CONTEXT

You are designing a knowledge base for a software vendor. It will be used by technical support technicians to provide worldwide customer support for a complex software product. When a customer calls with a problem, the knowledge base will guide a technician through a series of questions. The knowledge base will suggest possible resolutions based on the information provided by the customer. If the problem is beyond the ability of the technician or the knowledge base to solve, the problem devolves to an engineer who can solve the customer's problem. If appropriate, the engineer will add the problem and its resolution to the knowledge base. This extends the knowledge base so that the next time a customer calls with a similar problem, the technician on the case will be able to find its resolution in the knowledge base.

To provide worldwide, around-the-clock support, the company has four support centers located in different countries. The simplest way to set up the knowledge base is to run it in one central location. However, there are some problems with that. The knowledge base will be a mission-critical application. It is very important that it is available continuously to support staff. To avoid losing access to the knowledge base due to a communications or networking failure, your design calls for replicating the knowledge base in each support center. To ensure that the knowledge base is never unavailable because of a computer crash, you replicate the knowledge base on multiple computers in each support center.

You want the replication of the knowledge base to be transparent to the rest of the software system. That means other objects in the system must find an instance of the knowledge base without knowing the details of its replication. It also means that updates to the knowledge base must propagate from the instance to which they are applied to all other instances. The result should be that all the knowledge bases appear to contain all of the knowledge.

FORCES

☺ Replicating an object onto multiple computing elements can make a distributed system more fault-tolerant. If an object exists on only one computing element, the object becomes unavailable when that computing element is unavailable. If you replicate an object onto multiple computing elements, the object remains available when one of the computing elements is unavailable.

☺ In many cases, the closer an object is to its accessors, the more quickly they can access it. An object accessible through the local network can be accessed more quickly than an object in another city. Objects can access objects in the same computer's memory faster than they can access objects in another computer's memory. An object that is close to another object in a way that reduces the amount of time the other object needs to access it is said to have high *locality* with respect to the other object. If objects in multiple locations access the same object, you may be able to reduce their access time by replicating the object so that each of the object's replicas is close to its accessors.

☺ An extreme improvement in accessibility and performance through object replication occurs when objects reside on a computing element that is connected to other computing elements only some of the time. For example, a laptop computer can spend much of its time disconnected from any network. During these times, the objects on the laptop computer can access only those objects that are already on that computer.

☺ To promote the illusion that each client of a replicated object is a client of a single object, its mechanism for maintaining mutual consistency should be as transparent as possible.

☹ To achieve higher availability or increased throughput, replicated objects require redundant computing elements. The additional processors and memory add to the cost of a distributed system.

☹ The replicas of an object should be mutually consistent. They should all contain the same state information. Writing the code to keep them mutually consistent is difficult and error-prone.

☹ If all replicas of an object are subject to state modification, it may be necessary for them to pass a large number of messages between themselves to maintain mutual consistency. In some cases, the size of this communication requirement can be exponentially proportionate to the number of replicas. If the update operations must have the ACID properties in order to make the illusion of a single object perfect, the cost of making updates can be extremely expensive. In addition to the cost of message passing, many locks must be obtained and freed. The more replicas there are, the more time they spend managing locks.

SOLUTION

Replicate an object onto multiple computing elements while maintaining the illusion to the clients of the replicas that there is only a single object. Locate the replicas in a way that maximizes their locality to their clients.

Figure 5.6 shows the roles that classes and interfaces play in the Object Replication pattern.

Here are descriptions of the roles shown in Figure 5.6:

ReplicatedObject.   Classes in this role are replicated to be close to their clients.

ReplicationManagerIF.   `Client` objects interact with an interface in this role to get access to an instance of a class in the `ReplicatedObject` role.

ReplicationManager.   Classes in this role manage the creation and location of replicas of a replicated object. The intention is to provide client objects with a replica of a `ReplicatedObject` object that is local or relatively inexpensive for the client to com-

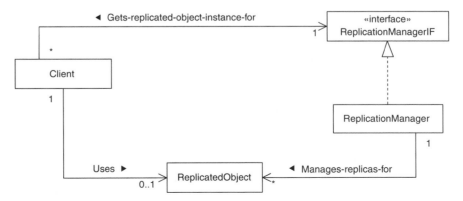

FIGURE 5.6 Object replication pattern.

municate with. A `ReplicationManager` finds the nearest replica of a replicated object. If the replica is too far away (which may simply mean that it is not local), then it creates a local replica and makes it available to the `Client` object. If there is a sufficiently close replica, the `ReplicationManager` makes it available to the `Client` object.

Client. Classes in this role use a class in the `ReplicatedObject` role. They gain access to a `ReplicatedObject` object by a call to a method of a `ReplicationManagerIF` object. If a `Client` object makes a call to a method of a `ReplicatedObject` and the call fails because the `ReplicatedObject` is no longer available, then the `Client` object just asks the `ReplicationManagerIF` object for another `ReplicatedObject` instance.

If the replicas are not immutable, then there must be a mechanism that propagates changes made to one replica to all other replicas. There is a discussion of change replication mechanisms under the "Implementation" heading.

Unless the class of a replicated object defines its `equals` method to be based on the information content of the object, it should be based on equality of the object's object identifiers. A replicated object's `equals` method should never be based on equality of object references.

CONSEQUENCES

☺ By having as many replicas of an object as the object has clients, you can maximize the replicas' locality to their clients and improve the performance of a system as a whole.

● Applying the Object Replication pattern results in multiple objects with an equal claim to the same identity. Replicated objects do not have a unique identity their clients can directly test with the `==` operator. However, one of their attributes may be an object identifier that is shared by all of the replicas.

☹ Enforcing the isolation property for transactions that modify a replicated object is problematic. Such enforcement is time-consuming, error-prone, and a valid research topic.

☹ Maintaining a consistent state among object replicas can be very time-consuming. This is especially true if the state of the objects is determined by remote objects.

● Most problems associated with replicated objects are related to their mutability. Replication of immutable objects does not have the problems associated with replicating mutable objects.

IMPLEMENTATION

Replication Management

Replication management begins when a client object calls a method of a `ReplicationManager` object to request the use of a replicated object. If there is a local replica, it is used. If there is no local replica, the `ReplicationManager` object finds some nearby replicas. If any of them are near enough, the `ReplicationManager` object selects one to be used. If no replicas are near enough, the `ReplicationManager` object creates a local replica.

The main variation between different schemes for replication management is the means by which the replication manager finds existing replicas. If just a few replicas are on the same local area network, then a good way to keep track of where they are is to keep their location in a central directory. The virtue of this strategy is its simplicity. However, if too many computers are trying to get the location of replicas simultaneously, then a central directory becomes a bottleneck. If computers wanting to find a replica are far away or have a very indirect network connection, then the network delays may have an unacceptable impact on throughput.

One way of overcoming these difficulties with a directory of replicas is to replicate the directory in known locations that are expected to be near the computers that will access them. This works well if you have a good idea of where the computer will be that will want to find replicas of replicated objects.

If you do not know in advance where replica directories will be needed, there is strategy you can use to compensate. It involves architecting `ReplicationManager` objects so that they can find each other over a network. It comes into play when the nearest replica directory is not in the same local network as a `ReplicationManager` object that wants to use it. Before the `ReplicationManager` object consults the directory, it sends a broadcast message through its local network asking any other `ReplicationManager` object that receives the message to send it the object replica it needs.

If all of the replicas are on the same local network and the network is highly reliable and has spare capacity, you may consider using broadcast messages to other `ReplicationManager` objects as the only mechanism for finding replica objects.

Change Replication

There are a few common types of change replication mechanisms. None is clearly superior to another; all have drawbacks. Choosing among them usually involves a compromise. In the following discussions of change replication schemes, the descriptions about their properties and implementation are vague. This is because change replication is an area in which programming practice is more developed than the computer science theory that describes it.

NAÏVE PESSIMISTIC CONCURRENCY

The easiest change replication mechanism to understand is *naïve pessimistic concurrency*. Before a change is accepted by one replica, it locks all of the other replicas to ensure that they all receive the same change at the same time without any other changes being made to them at the same time. The drawbacks to this mechanism include the following:

- It must take the time to lock every replica.
- It must take the time to communicate changes to every replica.
- Changes cannot occur concurrently.
- Simultaneous attempts to modify replicas require conflict resolution that can take time exponentially proportionate to the number of replicas to resolve.
- All replicas must be available to each other in order to be locked. If any of the replicas become unavailable to any other replica, then it is not possible to lock every replica, which makes it impossible to make changes to any of the replicas.

Naïve pessimistic change replication is generally the least attractive scheme. It is included here for purposes of comparison. If there will be more than two replicas, one of the other change replication schemes is a better choice.

Naïve pessimistic change replication is called *pessimistic* because it is based on the assumption that there will be concurrent changes. The two schemes that follow are considered less pessimistic because they assume only that concurrent changes are likely.

PRIMARY BACKUP

The *primary backup* approach is a good choice for change replication when it is not necessary to update all replicas simultaneously. In this scheme, one replica is chosen to be the primary replica. The other replicas are considered backups.

When a backup receives a request to change its state, it forwards the request to the primary. After changes are made to the primary replica, the primary replica forwards them to the backups. If the primary replica becomes unavailable, a backup is selected to be the new primary replica.

When implementing the primary backup scheme, an important design decision is how closely the state of backups must follow the primary. There is a range of possible policies.

At one end of the range is a policy that a call that changes the state of the primary does not return until it atomically changes the state of all of the backups to match the primary. Guaranteeing that the state of the backups matches the state of the primary ensures that every backup is ready to become the primary without requiring additional time to synchronize it with the state of the former primary.

The drawback to this extreme is that it is similar to the naïve pessimistic replication. Each call to a replica that changes its state does not return until it changes the state of every replica.

At the other end of the range is a policy requiring calls that change the state of a primary to return immediately. After the call returns, the primary asynchronously updates the backups without any limit on how long it will take to perform the updates. Without any limit on update time, there is no limit on how far the state of a backup can get behind the state of the primary. This is a problem when one of the backups must become the new primary. Without that limit, there is no limit on how long it can take to put a backup in the state it must be in to be the new primary.

A potentially more difficult problem to solve occurs when two replicas are both configured as primary. That situation can occur when a network is temporarily partitioned into two subnetworks. In this circumstance, the replicas in the subnetwork that does not have a primary select a replica as their primary. When the two subnetworks become one again, there are two primary replicas. When this happens, the state of the two primaries must somehow be reconciled. There is no general-purpose technique for doing this. In some cases, it is possible to devise an application-specific way of reconciling the state of multiple primaries.

MAJORITY VOTING

Majority voting is a change replication scheme that can more easily recover from a temporarily partitioned network. When one replica is changed, that change is atomically made to a majority of the replicas.

The majority voting scheme does not scale up very well. If there are 1000 replicas, then each change must atomically modify 501 of them. This results in a delay, but one that is only half as bad as the naïve scheme, which would need to modify all 1000 replicas before continuing.

There is also a limit to how small the majority voting scheme can be scaled, with three replicas being the lower limit. There is no majority if there are only two replicas.

TIMESTAMPING

A way of propagating changes that scales up well and is simple to implement is *timestamping*. In this scheme, attributes of a replicated object have a timestamp associated with them. Replicas propagate changes to other replicas in pairs. If one replica has an older timestamp for an attribute than another, it replaces the older value with the newer value and timestamp. If a replica is part of more than one pair, then when it is changed it propagates the change to all pairs it is part of.

There are two drawbacks to this scheme. One is that the clocks of all computers involved must be synchronized; otherwise, there is a risk that attribute values will become inconsistent. If only one source of changes exists for each attribute, this is not a problem, since all of the changes for an attribute will be timestamped by the same computer.

The other drawback to this scheme is that there is no limit to the amount of time it can take to propagate a change to all replicas. If replicas are hosted on computers that do not always have network connectivity, this can be a benefit rather than a drawback.

OPTIMISTIC REPLICATION

Optimistic replication gets its name from the assumption that concurrent changes will *not* be made to object replicas. Changes are replicated without first locking replicas. After the changes are made, they are checked to determine whether any concurrent conflicting changes were made. When there are no conflicting concurrent changes, optimistic replication proceeds rather quickly, without having to acquire any locks.

When a conflicting change is discovered, the time penalty can be severe. All of the replicas must be made consistent again. Though the details vary with the application, this typically involves locking all of the replicas and backing out all of the conflicting changes. If that happens very often, optimistic replication loses its speed advantage. Optimistic replication may be the optimal replication scheme when concurrent changes are rare and a larger variation in the time it takes to make changes can be tolerated.

KNOWN USES

Chat programs and other tools for collaboration among people generally use some form of object replication. Text and graphics objects that correspond to the work of the collaboration are replicated in each collaborator's instance of the software. As each collaborator modifies its local copy of an object, the changes are replicated in the other copies of the object.

Distributed file systems such as AFS or Coda replicate files for the purpose of increasing their locality and availability. Clients of such file systems simply access files through the most conveniently located server. The file system transparently finds and accesses the most conveniently located replica of a file. Such file systems also may create a replica of all or part of a file in a physical server when the file's usage justifies it.

Database managers also support replication to improve locality, throughput, and availability.

RELATED PATTERNS

Redundant Independent Objects.   The Redundant Independent Objects pattern is a more specialized pattern that describes the use of replication to increase the availability of objects.

Master-Slave.   The primary backup scheme for change replication is based on the Master-Slave pattern. The Master-Slave pattern is described in [Buschman96].

Optimistic Concurrency.   The Optimistic Concurrency pattern describes how to update data without the use of locks.

Immutable.   The Immutable pattern, described in *Volume 1*, explains the simplicity and safety that comes from designing objects to be immutable.

Object Request Broker.   The Object Request Broker pattern allows an object to be used in multiple places at the same time without it being in multiple places or replicated.

Redundant Independent Objects

The Redundant Independent Objects pattern is based on material from [Gray-Reuter93].

SYNOPSIS

You need to ensure the availability of an object even if it or the platform it is running on experiences a failure. You accomplish this by providing redundant objects that do not rely on any single common resource.

CONTEXT

Suppose you work for a company that makes money by buying mortgages and packaging them as pools of mortgages for which it sells bonds. This operation is currently automated. However, it averages over seven hours of downtime a year. Each hour of downtime causes the company to lose millions of dollars. Therefore, the company has decided to reimplement the automation as a highly available system with the goal of no more than five minutes of downtime a year. Achieving that level of availability is expensive, but the cost is only a fraction of the cost of the downtime.

There are a few strategies to follow in achieving this goal. One of the most basic is to ensure that no single point of failure can take the system down. There are a number of things to do at the hardware level to ensure that no single failure can make a system unavailable. Since this is a book about software design, this pattern ignores the hardware issues. It describes how to ensure that a single software failure will not make a system unavailable.

FORCES

☺ Two independent components of a system are much less likely to fail at the same time than they are at different times. For example, suppose that two components have a mean time between failure of 5000 hours (about 208 days). If the failures of the components are statistically independent events, the mean time between both components failing at the same time is $5000 \times 5000 = 25$ million hours (about 28.5 years).

☺ If the failures of redundant components are not independent events, then having a redundant component does not decrease the likelihood of failure.

☺ Components are called *redundant* if they perform the same task and if other components that depend on the task can function provided at least one of the components continues to perform the task. If redundant components are performing a task, then the products of that task are available as long as at least one of the redundant components continues to perform the task.

☺ The greater the expense of downtime, the easier it is to justify the cost of preventing downtime.

☹ Using redundant components increases the complexity of a system and the difficulty of designing, integrating, and configuring it.

☹ The use of redundant components increases the expense of building a system. The use of redundant components requires additional design time. Redundant software components take more time to code. The use of redundant hardware components requires the purchase of more hardware.

☹ There is no direct correlation between the availability of a system and its reliability or correctness. *Reliability* means that a system can be counted upon to consistently behave in a certain way. *Correctness* refers to how closely the actual behavior of a system conforms to its specification.

SOLUTION

Increase the availability of a system by building it with redundant independent components. The redundant components must be sufficiently independent so that the failure of one component does not increase the likelihood that another component will fail.

To ensure that multiple software components in the same redundant set do not fail as the result of a single hardware failure, the software components in a redundant set should all run on different hardware components. This is the minimum amount of independence needed to make redundant software components useful.

Running identical software components in a redundant set does not reduce the likelihood that all of the components will fail at the same time due to a bug. The components should be independently implemented, preferably by different teams. It is less likely that two independently implemented software components will share a particular bug. For this reason, redundant independently implemented software components are less likely to fail at the same time due to any one particular bug. Simply replicating the same implementation of a component makes it likely that both components will fail in the same way.

Here is an example of what can happen when the same implementation of a component is used on otherwise-independent computing elements: A rocket was launched. One of the processors that controlled the rocket failed due to a bug in its software causing an overflow error. The hardware on the rocket detected the failed software and tried to switch control to a redundant processor. The redundant processor was running identical software, so it also failed. The hardware was unable to switch control to the other processor, and it caused the rocket to self-destruct.

CONSEQUENCES

☺ The use of the Redundant Independent Objects pattern reduces, but does not eliminate, the likelihood that a system or service will be unavailable. Even if you consider the risk of unavailability acceptably low, you should consider developing contingency plans for handling the loss of availability.

● Accurately predicting the frequency with which a new or newly modified software component will fail is difficult in the most controlled of conditions. A record of actual failures should be kept to develop and fine-tune estimates of failure likelihood.

IMPLEMENTATION

The Redundant Independent Objects pattern is a specialized form of the Object Replication pattern. It has the same implementation issues as the Redundant Independent Objects pattern.

KNOWN USES

NASA uses triple redundancy for all onboard mission-critical computing components on space flights. Software used by stock exchanges to process stock trades use redundant software components. The software used to manage telephone networks uses redundant components.

DESIGN EXAMPLE

The deployment diagram in Figure 5.7 illustrates an application of the Redundant Independent Objects pattern.

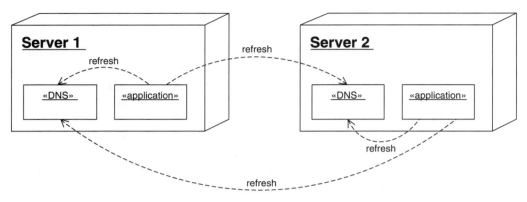

FIGURE 5.7 Highly available application.

Clients (not shown in Figure 5.7) want to use the application that runs as redundant components on both Server1 and Server2. Clients identify all instances of the application using a single logical name. To communicate with an application instance, a client must translate the logical name to the network address of an available application instance.

The components labeled DNS are redundant *name server* components. When a client wants to translate the logical application name to a network address, it queries the network name resolution mechanism on the computer on which the client is running. This mechanism directly or indirectly queries one of the DNS components shown in the diagram.* Other name servers know the address of both DNS components. If one of the DNS components does not respond to a request within a reasonable amount of time, the server will direct the request to the other DNS component. If either DNS component fails, the service they provide continues to be available.

When both application components are available, both DNS components have records that allow them to translate the logical application name to the network address for either application component. The records that the DNS components keep of the network addresses that correspond to the application components have an expiration time associated with them. While an application component is available, it periodically refreshes the record that each DNS component has for its network address. Because of the periodic refresh, the DNS components continue to have an unexpired record of the application component's network address.

If an application component ceases to be available, it will also cease to refresh its record in the DNS components. Shortly after that happens, the

---

* For readers familiar with the details of DNS, the address record for the application components is given a low time-to-live to ensure that only minimal caching of the application component's IP addresses takes place.

record that the DNS components have of the failed application component expires and clients are once again directed only to available application components.

RELATED PATTERNS

Prompt Repair. The Prompt Repair pattern is often used with the Redundant Independent Objects pattern to ensure the continued availability of a set of redundant independent objects even after a failure occurs.

Object Replication. The Redundant Independent Objects pattern is a specialized version of the Object Replication pattern.

Client-Dispatcher-Service. The Client-Dispatcher-Service pattern is often used with the Redundant Independent Objects pattern. The Client-Dispatcher-Service pattern is described in [Buschman96].

Prompt Repair

The Prompt Repair pattern is based on material from [Gray-Reuter93].

SYNOPSIS

When one of a set of redundant independent objects fails, one less failure must occur before the entire set of redundant objects becomes unavailable. To minimize the likelihood of a catastrophic failure, repair the failed object as soon as possible.

CONTEXT

Suppose you work for a company that has set the goal of making one of its critical systems highly available, with no more than five minutes of downtime a year. You have taken a first step toward that goal by ensuring that no single failure will make the system unavailable. You now need to ensure that after a failure occurs, the chance of a subsequent failure making the system unavailable is minimal.

FORCES

- ☺ Two independent components of a system are much less likely to fail at the same time than they are at different times. Though a system may be able to continue operating after one of the components has failed, it is at much greater risk of catastrophic failure caused by the other component failing.
- ☺ When some of the redundant components that perform a task have failed, there is less or no redundancy. The likelihood that the products of the task will become unavailable increases as redundancy decreases because fewer components must fail before there are none to perform the task. The shorter the time between the failure of a component and its repair, the less likely that task products will become unavailable.
- ☺ Components should be designed so that it is immediately obvious when a component fails. The more quickly a component failure can be detected, the sooner it can be repaired. The longer it takes to recognize that component has failed, the more time will elapse between a failure and its repair.
- ☹ Some systems must be highly available, but for only a limited amount of time. For example, the guidance system in a missile must be highly

available, but only until the missile reaches its target. In such systems, a higher level of redundancy may be a better way to ensure high availability than to plan for the repair of components.

☹ There is no direct correlation between the effort required to achieve the high availability of a system and its reliability or correctness. *Reliability* means that a system can be counted on to consistently behave in a certain way. *Correctness* refers to how closely the actual behavior of a system conforms to its specification.

SOLUTION

Ensure the continued high availability of redundant components by making them failfast and by promptly repairing failed components.

Failfast means that if a component fails, it fails in a way that allows the failure to be immediately detected by such means as throwing an exception or returning a special value from a method call. Detecting failures at the earliest possible time allows the failures to be repaired at the earliest possible time. Repairing failures at the earliest possible time minimizes the likelihood that additional components will fail before the repair is made.

In general, it is not possible for a program to fix its own bugs and continue functioning. Fortunately, that level of repair is not necessary, since the goal here is availability rather than reliability. The repair for an unavailable software component is to restart the component. Restart strategies are discussed later in the "Implementation" section.

CONSEQUENCES

☺ The use of the Prompt Repair pattern reduces, but does not eliminate, the likelihood that a system or service will be unavailable. Even if you consider the risk of unavailability acceptably low, you should also consider developing contingency plans for handling the loss of availability.

● Accurately predicting the frequency with which a new or newly modified software component will fail is difficult in the most controlled of conditions. A record of actual failures should be kept to develop and fine-tune estimates of failure likelihood.

IMPLEMENTATION

There are two common strategies for restart.

● The simplest restart strategy is *cold start*, which simply involves restarting the component so it is in a known initial state.

- The *checkpoint/restart* strategy is used to restart a component so that its state is closer to the state it had at the time of failure than to its initial state. The checkpoint/restart strategy saves the state of a component on persistent storage at strategic points in time. These saved states are called *checkpoints*. When the component is restarted, its state is restored to the most recent checkpoint.

To be confident that a component will always be failfast, you must test it very extensively. If it is not reasonable to assume that components will always be failfast, then you have to use additional strategies to detect failures, such as testing whether a component is performing incorrectly or not at all.

A simple way to detect whether a component has stopped performing is to set a maximum amount of time that a client will wait for a component to do something. After that amount of time has elapsed, the client considers the component to have *timed out* and assumes that it is no longer performing.

The time-out technique works best for components that usually take about the same amount of time to perform a given task. If the amount of time it takes a component to perform a task varies greatly, then you will need to set the time-out period to an unreasonably long amount of time. The Heartbeat pattern provides a more general way of detecting the failure of a component.

Voting is a general-purpose way to detect that some components in a set of redundant components are performing incorrectly. Voting works by observing the actions and outputs of all the components in a redundant set of components. Identical actions and outputs from the majority of components are considered correct. Actions and outputs that deviate from the majority are considered incorrect, and the components that produce them are considered to have failed.

One way to implement voting is to use a reusable voter object to perform the observations for a redundant set of components. This approach raises the problem of ensuring that the voter object is performing correctly. Because of this difficulty, when designing software components, the voter responsibility is generally given directly to the clients of a redundant set of objects.

KNOWN USES

Some Web sites use the Prompt Repair pattern to ensure the continued availability of a Web server. Solaris and other Unix-like operating systems can be configured to start a process when the system boots and automatically restart the process when it exits. Applications used by at least one stock exchange to process trades use the Prompt Repair pattern.

RELATED PATTERNS

Redundant Independent Objects.   The Prompt Repair pattern is used with the Redundant Independent Object pattern.

Process Pair.   The Process Pair pattern is used to ensure that software components on the same computing element are restarted when they fail.

Snapshot.   The Snapshot pattern (described in *Volume 1*) can be used to implement checkpoint/restart.

Mobile Agent

SYNOPSIS

An object needs to access very large volume of remote data. To conserve network bandwidth, instead of bringing data to an object, move the object to the data.

CONTEXT

You are developing an application that will allow people to construct custom mailing lists based on criteria that they specify. For example, someone may want a list of people whose ages range from 45 to 65, whose income is over $55,000 a year, who drive minivans, who spend at least $600 per year on recorded music, and who listen to jazz.

To construct these mailing lists, the application may have to consult many different databases, such as those from credit card companies, mail-order companies, motor vehicle bureaus, concert ticket-selling organizations, and others. To support the application, the company you work for arranges for the application to be allowed access to the databases of different companies.

The arrangements your company makes with database owners provide for a limited amount of network bandwidth for the application to communicate with their database. The arrangements also allow your company to colocate a computer at the same site as each database.

In some cases, the application will need to access a large volume of data in order to cross-check it against a smaller volume of data. Because the available bandwidth is limited, you want to use it as efficiently as possible. The conventional way for an application to use the bandwidth is to download the large volume of data to the customer's computer on which it is running. If this data is several times larger than the application and the data it has already captured combined, then the conventional way uses a lot more bandwidth than is necessary. It is a more efficient use of the bandwidth to move the application to the computer that is at the same site as the database and then move it back when it has finished using the large volume of data.

FORCES

☺ An object is smaller than the data that it accesses.
☺ An object accesses data that is in multiple locations.

☺ An object is launched from a nomadic platform, such as a laptop computer. You need the object to process data from remote data sources, even while the platform from which it was launched is disconnected from the network.

☺ An object is able to migrate from one computer to another at its own instigation.

☺ One computer is overloaded while another has resources to spare.

☺ In order for an object to migrate to another computer, the other computer must have a suitable environment to which the object can migrate.

☺ Clients of an object may still need to communicate with the object after it migrates to another computer.

☹ The migration of an object to another computer must happen in a way that limits the consequences of a loss of connectivity during the migration. If there is a failure, it must be impossible for the outcome to be that live objects on both computers claim to be the same object. The failure also must not cause the death of the object. A connectivity failure should either result in the failure or delay of a migration.

☹ A program is expected to promptly handle events sent to it from the computer it is running on. If the program migrates to another computer, then network delays over which it has no control may make its handling of events less prompt.

SOLUTION

An *agent* is a program that makes decisions and performs actions autonomously of its client in order to provide a service to the client. An example of an agent is a program that continuously searches the World Wide Web for pages that fit a description that you provide and alerts you as it finds them.

A *mobile agent* has an additional degree of freedom in that it can migrate from machine to machine in a heterogeneous network under its own control. Because a great deal of logic is common to all mobile agents, some of which is rather complex, mobile agents are usually implemented using a framework or other collection of reusable objects.

Mobile agents are able to initiate their own migration from one computer to another. To proceed with a migration, there must be an environment in the destination computer that facilitates the entry of the object into the new environment. The environment minimally must support the destination's side of a migration until it has progressed sufficiently for the mobile agent to take responsibility. Figure 5.8 shows the interactions involved in the migration of a mobile agent.

After a mobile agent has migrated to another computer, it has a different network address than it had before. The implementation of mobile

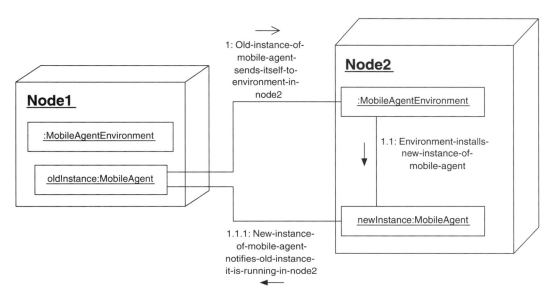

FIGURE 5.8 Mobile agent.

agents must include a mechanism to allow their clients to continue communicating with the mobile agent after it has migrated to a different computer. For the migration of mobile agents to happen in a truly autonomous manner and to minimize the consequences of network problems, this mechanism must not require mobile agents to register with a directory server every time it migrates.

CONSEQUENCES

☺ Mobile agents are able to migrate to the location where they are most easily able to obtain the resources that they require.

☹ If there is any concern about malicious mobile agents, an environment that hosts mobile agents should take measures to ensure that mobile agents that migrate to it belong there. It should also use Java's permission mechanism to verify that mobile agents are entitled to access the resources that they attempt to access.

☹ Centralized management of mobile agents is more complex than management of stationary objects. In addition to monitoring the state of the mobile agent itself, its location must be monitored, along with the state of its current environment.

☹ Maintaining communication with a mobile agent is another challenge for centralized management of mobile agents. Mobile agents may be unreachable from a centralized management object for indefinite periods.

- Having a globally unique object ID is more important for mobile agents than for other types of objects. This is because it must be possible to identify a mobile agent wherever it goes.
- ☹ Embedding sensitive data in mobile agents is risky if the mobile agents will be migrating to any environments that cannot be trusted.
- ☹ The use of mobile agents can change the way in which a design uses the notion of globally unique object IDs. When a mobile agent migrates, the same object ID will identify both the old and new instances, although they are physically different objects.

IMPLEMENTATION

The most essential implementation detail is the manner in which mobile agents are able to migrate from one computer to another. Figure 5.9 shows the basic interactions involved in the migration of a mobile agent. Descriptions of the interactions appear in Table 5.1.

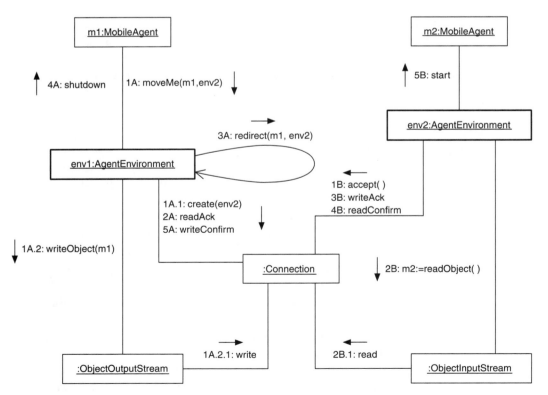

FIGURE 5.9 Migration of a mobile agent.

TABLE 5.1 Description of Interactions in Figure 5.9

Current Environment		*New Environment*	
1A	The mobile agent calls one of its environment's methods, requesting its migration to environment `env2`.		
	At this point, this instance of the mobile agent expects to shut down soon. It will continue to be active until told to shut down. Until then, the agent may modify its behavior to accommodate the circumstance.		
1A.1	The current environment creates a network connection with the new environment.	**1B**	The new environment accepts the network connection from the current environment.
1A.2	The current environment uses an `ObjectOutputStream` to serialize the mobile agent to a stream of bytes and send the stream to the new environment.	**2B**	The new environment calls the `readObject` method of an `ObjectInputStream`, so it can reconstruct the mobile agent from the byte stream.
1A.2.1	The `ObjectOutputStream` writes the stream of bytes to the network connection with the new environment.	**2B.1**	The `ObjectInputStream` reads the byte stream from the connection with the current environment.
			Once the byte stream is available from the network connection, the call to the `ObjectInputStream` object's `readObject` method returns the new copy of the mobile agent.
2A	The current environment receives an acknowledgment that the new environment received the mobile agent.	**3B**	The new environment sends an acknowledgment to the current environment that it received the mobile agent.
			At this point, the new copy of the mobile agent exists, but it is not active.
3A	The environment arranges for calls to the mobile agent to be sent to the new environment.		

TABLE 5.1 *(Continued)*

Current Environment		New Environment	
3A (cont.)	Since the instance of the mobile agent in the new environment is not yet active, the new environment will accept the calls on behalf of the new instance and make them wait until the new instance is active.		
4A	The environment tells the instance of the mobile agent to shut down. When this interaction is done, the environment should discard all references it has to the instance so that it can be garbage-collected.		
5A	The environment sends a confirmation to the new environment that the now old instance has shut down.	**4B**	The environment receives a confirmation that the older instance of the mobile agent is no longer active.
		5B	The environment notifies the new instance of the mobile agent that it should now become active. When this interaction is done, the environment allows calls to the mobile agent to proceed.

Some parts of this collaboration are worth examining in greater detail.

Completion of Pending Calls

It may be possible for the new instance to finish what the old instance started if everything it needs to finish is copied to the new environment as part of serialization/deserialization. Allowing the new instance to finish what the old instance started can reduce the amount of time it takes for the old instance to shut down and the migration to be complete. However, this must be done in a way that ensures that the old instance does not also attempt to finish the same work.

If the work in question concludes by returning a result, the fact that the result came from a different place than the original call must be transparent to the calling client. This means the handling of returned results must be based not on the physical origin of the result, but rather on the object ID of the object from which the result came.

Calls to a Mobile Agent during Migration

A mobile agent is still active after it has initiated a migration. At this point, there are two reasonable ways to handle new calls to the mobile agent from its clients. When it receives a call, it can process it in the old environment or forward it to the new environment. Processing the calls it receives after initiating a migration can delay the completion of the migration. Any calls that it starts processing must be finished before the new instance becomes active, since the new instance will know nothing about calls made to the old instance after the new instance was serialized. This may not be a consideration for mobile agents that expect few calls from clients and are able to process calls in a short amount of time.

If a mobile agent handles calls made to it in this period by forwarding them to the environment to which it is migrating, the migration is not delayed. However, this means it will be possible for the old instance to forward calls to the new environment before the new environment has received the new instance of the mobile agent. Allowing this can pose a denial-of-service security risk.

The problem is that this forces us to allow an environment to receive calls on behalf of mobile agents that it does not yet know are migrating to it. This leaves open the possibility that the environment will be waiting to pass calls on to mobile agents that never migrate to it. A malicious or buggy object that sends mobile agent calls to the wrong environment can cause it to queue up so many calls that it runs out of memory. To minimize the risk, you can require that calls to an environment for a mobile agent it does not yet know it is receiving come from a trusted source.

Calls Made after Migration from Old Environment

Another issue to consider is how future calls from existing clients of a mobile agent will be transparently directed to its new location. There are two reasonable ways to do this:

- The mobile agent can inform all of its clients of its new location at the time of the migration.
- The old environment can tell clients of the mobile agent's new location when they try to call the mobile agent at its old location.

At first glance, notifying all the clients at the time of migration may seem simpler, since all client notifications are done at once. However, it has a number of drawbacks that make notifying clients at the time of their next call the more attractive option. Some potential disadvantages are as follows:

- The mobile agent must be sufficiently aware of its clients to send a message to each one of them.
- The mobile agent may spend a lot of time trying to send messages to clients that no longer exist.
- It may also spend time sending messages to clients that will never try to communicate with the mobile agent again.

Unless, for other reasons, a reliable messaging mechanism is planned that will address these issues, notifying all of the clients at migration time is not a good choice.

Notifying clients of a mobile agent's new location when they attempt to call it at an old location avoids wasted effort. To implement this, the environment creates a forwarding object after a mobile agent has migrated. When the environment receives a message intended for a mobile agent that has migrated away, it delivers it to the corresponding forwarding object. The forwarding object forwards the call to the environment where the mobile agent migrated. It also sends a message back to the client, informing it of the mobile agent's new location. If the client is accessing the mobile agent through a proxy object, then the proxy object can encapsulate the mobile agent's current location and hide the mobility of the agent from other objects.

The lifetime of the forwarding object is controlled by the same mechanism that controlled the original object. This is typically some sort of distributed reference counting scheme.

Reusing Connections between Environments

Because environments use `ObjectOutputStream` objects and `ObjectInputStream` objects with many connections, they may have a mechanism that allows them to reuse rather than create `ObjectOutputStream` objects and `ObjectInputStream` objects. You can use the Connection Multiplexing pattern for this purpose.

KNOWN USES

Aglets is a framework developed by IBM for building mobile agents.*
Voyager is an ORB that supports mobile agents.†

---

* The Aglets home page is www.trl.ibm.co.jp/aglets/.

†The Voyager home page is www.objectspace.com/Products/voyager.

A *worm* is a specialized form of mobile agent that has been around longer than mobile agents. A worm is a program that moves from computer to computer on a network to perform a lengthy computation (e.g., the first few million digits of π). If a worm comes to a computer that is busy doing something, it moves on immediately. If the worm comes to a computer that has many spare cycles, the worm stays and uses those computing cycles until they are required for something else. Then the worm moves on.

At the time of this writing, the Object Management Group (OMG) is currently working on a specification for an agent framework to support mobile agents. It will be called Mobile Agent System Interoperability Facilities Specification (MASIF) and will work on top of the Common Object Request Broker Architecture (CORBA).

RELATED PATTERNS

Object Request Broker.   The Object Request Broker pattern is used with the Mobile Agent pattern to facilitate communications between mobile agents and other objects. Mobile agents can be implemented on top of the Object Request Broker pattern.

Object Replication.   One application of the Object Replication pattern is to ensure that an object is near its accessors. The Mobile Agent pattern provides a way for an object to be near different accessors at different times.

Layered Agent.   The Layered Agent pattern (described in [Kendall-Malkoun96]) describes agents from a broader perspective.

Demilitarized Zone

This pattern is also known as DMZ.

SYNOPSIS

There is a risk that hackers will compromise the security of a publicly accessible server. You do not want a consequence of that to be that they gain access to servers that are not publicly accessible and that contain sensitive information. Put servers that are accessible to the public Internet on a publicly accessible LAN located between your firewall and the public Internet.

CONTEXT

Suppose that you are planning the deployment of a system that will allow people to buy goods from your company through a publicly accessible Web server. You want to do this with minimal security risks. One of the ways to minimize security risks is to prevent anyone from outside of your organization from connecting directly to your inventory, accounting, or other internal systems.

The standard way to prevent unauthorized outsiders from accessing the computers on a private network while allowing them legitimate connections with computers on the public Internet is to use a device called a *firewall*. The firewall sits between a private network and the public Internet. It allows traffic from the public Internet to the private network only if it satisfies the security policies with which it has been configured. Figure 5.10 depicts this configuration.*

Figure 5.10 shows some servers connected together through an Ethernet-based local area network. Also shown are the Internet and a router. A *router* is a device that allows a local network to be connected to the Internet. Between the router and the Ethernet is a firewall. The firewall allows only network traffic that complies with the security policies for which it is configured to access the Ethernet.

Security policies for firewalls vary. They generally allow inbound traffic for connections that are initiated from the private network. They can

---

* Note that Figure 5.10 is not in the UML notation. The UML does not include any form of network diagram.

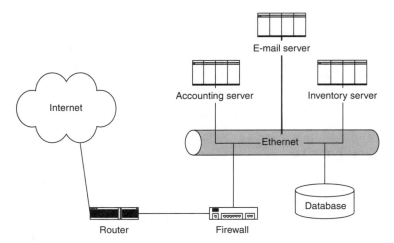

FIGURE 5.10 Firewall.

also allow connections from trusted network addresses to specific services on specific servers.

The system that you want to deploy will involve a publicly accessible Web server and a mail server. You need to deploy the servers in a manner that allows them to be accessed publicly without compromising the security of other servers that are not supposed to be publicly accessible.

FORCES

☺ If the security of a server is compromised, you don't want an intruder to have an easy time gaining access to other machines, especially other machines that contain sensitive data.

☺ If the security of a publicly accessible server behind the firewall is compromised, an intruder can gain access to other servers behind the firewall.

☺ If the security of a publicly accessible server in front of the firewall is compromised, an intruder does not gain any easier access to servers behind the firewall.

☹ Publicly accessible servers located in front of the firewall are exposed to greater security risks than servers located behind the firewall.

SOLUTION

Locate all publicly accessible servers on a network that is behind the router but in front of the firewall. We refer to this network as a *demilita-*

rized zone (DMZ). Only other machines behind the firewall and possibly in the DMZ know the network addresses of servers behind the firewall.

Machines that connect through the public Internet are able to connect only to servers in the DMZ. Machines coming in through the public Internet never communicate directly with the servers behind the firewall because the firewall will not allow it, with the possible exception of communications initiated from behind the firewall.

Servers in the DMZ are allowed to communicate with servers behind the firewall, but only in those ways that are known to be absolutely necessary.

CONSEQUENCES

☺ Clients communicating through the public Internet cannot communicate directly with servers behind the firewall, so they are unable to directly attack the security of servers behind the firewall.

☹ Communicating indirectly with servers behind the firewall increases the amount of time it takes for the communication to happen.

☹ For some applications, using the Demilitarized Zone pattern may add complexity to a server by forcing it to be split into two pieces.

IMPLEMENTATION

The correct and secure implementation of the Demilitarized Zone pattern requires a substantial knowledge of networking in general and the specific network on which it is deployed in particular. This pattern should be implemented in consultation with a network administrator familiar with the network in question and possibly also a security expert.

KNOWN USES

Many diverse organizations have used the Demilitarized Zone pattern to deploy publicly accessible applications. The author is aware of airlines, telephone companies, computer manufacturers, transportation companies, and financial institutions that have used it.

DESIGN EXAMPLE

Figure 5.11 shows an extended version of the network diagram from Figure 5.10 with a publicly accessible Web server and an e-mail server deployed.

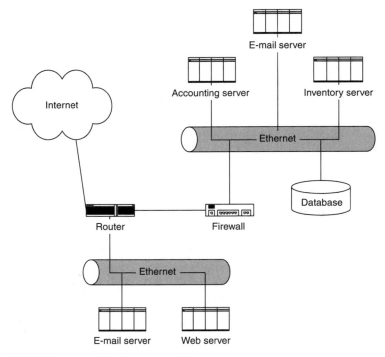

FIGURE 5.11 Publicly accessible servers.

Figure 5.11 includes two servers that are accessible from the public Internet. They are in a demilitarized zone on the network. The e-mail server in the demilitarized zone is the only e-mail server outside of the firewall with which e-mail servers inside the firewall communicate. All e-mail messages traveling between the Internet and e-mail servers behind the firewalls go through the e-mail server in the demilitarized zone.

The Web server accesses the accounting and inventory servers. It is the only machine outside of the firewall that is able to access them.

RELATED PATTERNS

Protection Proxy. The Protection Proxy pattern at the object level is structurally similar to the Demilitarized Zone pattern at the network level.

Process Pair

SYNOPSIS

To keep a process or software component highly available, you want it to be automatically restarted if it fails. Organize highly available software components in pairs, so that if one fails the other restarts it.

CONTEXT

Many years ago, when mainframes were the only type of computer you would find in a business, a security-conscious company owned a computer from a vendor whose initials were not IBM. The company's system programmers discovered a bug in the operating system that could allow an application program to execute with the same privileges as the operating system. The company repeatedly asked the vendor to fix the bug, but the vendor never got around to it. After making a number of requests, the company's system programmers came up with a scheme to get the vendor to take the bug seriously.

The system programmers wrote a program to demonstrate the bug to the vendor in a dramatic way. They put it on a tape and sent it to the vendor. After the tape arrived at the vendor, an operator put the tape on one of their mainframes and ran the program.

After the program finished running, the operator noticed that it left behind two processes, named Robin Hood and Friar Tuck. The operator waited a few minutes, but the processes did not go away. The operator tried to kill the process named Robin Hood. The operator expected the process to die quietly. Instead, these messages appeared on the operator's console:

```
Robin Hood: Friar Tuck help me! I'm under attack.
Friar Tuck: Never fear Robin Hood! I'll save you!
```

After reviewing the status of the processes, the operator found that the Robin Hood process had been restarted. The operator then tried killing the Friar Tuck process. These messages appeared on the operator's console:

```
Friar Tuck: Robin Hood help me! I'm under attack!
Robin Hood: Never fear Friar Tuck! I'll save you!
```

After reviewing the processes, the operator found that the Friar Tuck process had been restarted.

The operator tried killing these processes a few more times until it became clear that if he killed one the other would restart it. The only way the operator had of killing both processes at the same time was to reboot the computer. After the computer finished rebooting, the processes were back again. The operator tried another reboot and the same thing happened. Admitting defeat, the operator called for some programmers to figure out what was going on.

Eventually they determined that the program on the tape had taken advantage of the bug in the operating system's security. It had patched itself into the image of the operating system on the disk drive. To eradicate the program, they had to reinstall the operating system. Reinstalling that operating system took the better part of a day.

The vendor then fixed the bug.

FORCES

☺ If a software component fails, it must be restarted.
☺ A software component should not be restarted while it is still running.
☹ It may not always be possible to determine with certainty that a software component has stopped running. It may only be possible to determine that it is likely that a software component has stopped running.

SOLUTION

Make two software components responsible for restarting each other if one of them fails.

Keep each aware that the other is alive by having the components send each other a periodic notice that it is still alive. If the notice from a component is too late, the other component assumes that the component has failed and restarts it.

CONSEQUENCES

☺ Use of the Process Pair pattern boosts the availability of software components.
☹ It may be possible for a software component to be restarted when it has not actually failed.
☹ The process pair pattern increases the complexity of software components and makes them less cohesive.

IMPLEMENTATION

The Heartbeat pattern describes the details of one object inferring the failure of another based on the absence of a periodic signal.

If a software component that is part of a pair is aware of its impending failure, it should notify the other half of the pair so that it can be restarted sooner.

KNOWN USES

A number of transaction manager products use the Process Pair pattern, including Compaq's NonStop Transaction Manager/MP and BEA's Tuxedo transaction manager.

A telephone company used the Process Pair pattern on a project that involved providing a highly available service to the public.

RELATED PATTERNS

Heartbeat.   The Process Pair pattern uses the Heartbeat pattern.

Prompt Repair.   The Prompt Repair pattern deals with restarting software components replicated on independent computing elements.

C H A P T E R

6

Distributed Computing Patterns

The patterns in this chapter involve designs for computations that are performed in multiple computing environments or are structured as if they were performed in multiple computing environments. In this chapter, the phrase *computing environment* is used in a broad sense that includes databases as kind of computing environment.

Object Identifier

This pattern is also known as Primary Key. It was previously described in [Brown-Whitenack98].

SYNOPSIS

You need to uniquely identify an object that exists in multiple environments. Assign a globally unique identifier to the object, allowing it to have a unique identity when it is shared between programs or databases.

CONTEXT

Suppose you're designing a computer system for a business that operates a barter clearinghouse for the exchange of goods and services. The same goods and services may be involved in multiple trades during a business day. People who have agreed to a trade during the day need to know who should receive the goods or services that they have traded away. Since the other party in the trade may have traded the goods or services to others, at the end of the day the original parties to a trade cannot assume where they are supposed to send the goods or merchandise.

At the end of each business day, procedures are followed to settle all trades. These procedures include determining where each item involved in a trade should be sent.

To ensure that each item involved in a trade is properly tracked, the computer system assigns it a unique identifier. Assigning each item a unique identifier prevents it from being confused with similar items. This is important because similar items may differ in condition or in other ways. People will expect to receive the specific item they traded for.

The clearinghouse will have locations in different cities. To allow the computer system to scale up to many locations and clients, you decide to give it a distributed architecture. Each location will have its own computer system that works with the computer systems in the other locations.

It is expected that most barter exchanges will be between people who live in the same geographical area and work with the same clearinghouse location. However, some trades will involve multiple clearinghouse locations. To ensure that such trades are tracked properly, the identifier assigned to each item must be globally unique among all clearinghouse locations.

FORCES

☺ There is a need to determine whether two objects are the same object. You must be able to distinguish objects even if their attributes have identical values. For example, PCs may be identical in model, amount of memory, CPU type, and all other attributes. However, for security and accounting reasons it may be important for a company to keep track of the physical location of each PC and whose desk it is sitting on.

☺ If an object is common to multiple environments, such as databases or Java Virtual Machines, then you need a common way to uniquely identify the object in all of those environments.

☺ Most environments that manage objects use the physical location of the object as its unique identifier. A physical location is not generally unique between different environments. Over time, physical locations are not unique within the same environment. Over time, an environment may reuse the same location to store different objects.

☹ Some objects spend their entire lifetime in one environment. If such an object is visible only to other objects in the same environment, then there is generally no need to provide it with an identifier that will be unique outside its environment or lifetime.

☹ Associating an identifier with an object by storing it in the object increases the amount of storage that the object takes up. The larger the set of objects to be identified and the larger the set of environments that the object can exist in, the larger an object identifier must be to be globally unique. The larger an object identifier, the more storage it will consume.

☹ Some types of objects, such as strings and dates, are considered to be the same object if they contain the same values. Value objects such as these have no need for any sort of object identifier.

SOLUTION

If multiple environments share an object, generate a globally unique object identifier that identifies the object in all environments. To ensure uniqueness, the object identifier should combine an identifier unique within its environment and an identifier that uniquely identifies the environment. The environment ID should be combined with the object-specific identifier in a way that ensures that no two environments will generate the same object ID. The class diagram in Figure 6.1 shows this relationship.

Figure 6.1 shows an object environment containing many objects that can be shared with other environments. The environment also contains an

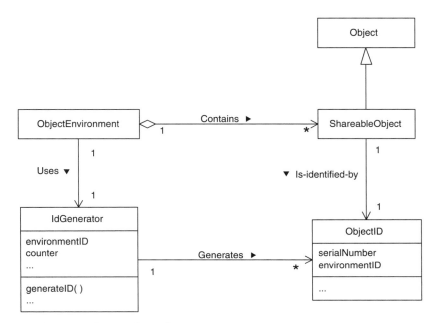

FIGURE 6.1 Object identifier.

unshared object that has the responsibility of generating object IDs for objects in its environment. Figure 6.1 shows this object as in instance of a class called IdGenerator. The object encapsulates a unique number that identifies the environment. It also encapsulates a counter whose value it combines with the environment identifier to form globally unique object identifiers. The environment uses the object identifiers it generates to create objects that can be shared with other environments.

Figure 6.1 shows the object identifier as a distinct object in order to present, as clearly as possible, the relationship between the object identifier and the other participants in the pattern. Some implementations do not actually realize object identifiers as separate objects.

Because a cost is involved in associating a globally unique object ID with an object, you should not create globally unique object IDs for objects that do not need them. If you know that an object will exist in only one environment and not be visible outside of that environment, then do not create a globally unique object ID for it.

CONSEQUENCES

☺ Each shareable object has a globally unique identifier that can be used to unambiguously determine the object's identity.

☺ Having a globally unique identifier allows an object to move between different environments and still retain its unique identity.

☺ Having a globally unique identifier allows objects in other environments to refer to that object.

☹ The Object Identifier pattern increases the time and memory required to create objects.

☹ Even if two different environments are designed using the object ID, they may not be able to share uniquely identified objects if the implementation details are different.

IMPLEMENTATION

Representation of Environment IDs

The representation for environment IDs must allow for a sufficiently large number of identifiers to allow every environment that needs a unique environment to have one. A variable-length representation, such as a string, has no practical limit to the number of environment IDs it can represent. However, variable-length representations take more time to compare and manipulate than fixed-length representations.

The drawback to fixed-length representations is that the total number of IDs they can represent is determined at design time. It cannot be easily changed later. An `int` may be sufficiently large for many applications. However, if it is possible that there will *ever* be a need for more environment IDs than can be represented by an `int`, you should use a larger representation.

Representing the Object-Specific Portion of an ID

The issues regarding the representation of an object ID are similar. The object-specific portion of an object ID must be able to represent as many IDs as there will ever be objects created in an environment. Because there is generally a need to generate the IDs frequently and cheaply, the usual representation is an integer that can be generated by a counter of the appropriate number of bits. Both the anticipated rate of object creation and the lifetime of the environment should be considered when deciding on the number of bits to represent the object-specific portion of an object ID. For a distributed game, a counter the size of an `int` may be sufficient. For longer-running programs, you may need to use a `long`. For a database or other environment where objects may persist indefinitely, you should use a counter with a representation such a `BigDecimal` that allows the size of the counter values to grow indefinitely.

Representing a Complete Unique Object Identifier

The number of bits required for the combined environment and object-specific portions of an object ID is generally more than can fit in a long. For that reason, it is common for object IDs to be represented as an array of bytes or an array of a larger integer type. An advantage of an array over a representation that defines fields to contain pieces of object IDs is that it makes increasing the length of object IDs less disruptive. It is a smaller change to increase the length of an array than to change the definition of a class. Using an array of `short` or larger type allows comparisons of IDs with fewer comparison operations. Using an array of bytes provides a smaller granularity of storage allocation and allocates fewer excess bits.

Assigning Unique Identifiers to Environments

Another implementation issue is how to assign identifiers to environments. If the set of environments will be stable and there will be only a small number of them, then manual assignment of environment identifiers is possible and in some cases preferable. For example, consider the case of a multiplayer game implemented as a distributed program. If there is a one-to-one correspondence between environments and players, then the player's names may be good environment IDs.

Another way to assign environment IDs is to have a server that provides environment IDs. Such a server can be centralized as the sole source of environment IDs. A server that is the sole source for environment IDs can be a performance bottleneck. The risk of server failure may also be of concern. If performance is a concern, then there should be multiple servers. There must be a scheme to ensure that the servers issue no duplicate IDs.

Embedding Location in the ID

Some applications have a need to use unique object identifiers to determine the location of the object so they can communicate with it. Incorporating a network address into an object identifier and providing a way to extract it can be a practical solution to the problem. It works well if network addresses are stable for the lifetime of an object and objects do not migrate to other environments. If these conditions do not hold, then a more general solution to the problem is to use proxies that encapsulate the knowledge of how to communicate with the underlying object and have the object's unique object ID as an attribute.

ID Server

Using a server to assign IDs to individual objects is usually not a practical implementation option. Most applications create objects too frequently to justify the expense of getting individual IDs from a server.

In some situations, it is undesirable or impossible to rely on a central server to provide environment IDs. In such situations, it is often acceptable for each environment to choose its own ID arbitrarily in a way that makes it unlikely for two environments to choose the same ID. For example, the exclusive OR of the current time in milliseconds and the environment's network address may be good enough.

KNOWN USES

Many proprietary applications have their own way of implementing the Object Identifier pattern. Reusable mechanisms that use the Object Identifier pattern generally do not provide their clients direct access to the object IDs that they generate and manage. Instead, they encapsulate them under another mechanism to keep their clients independent of the way they implement object IDs.

Voyager is an ORB that allows programs running in different Java VMs to share objects. Voyager's scheme for assigning object IDs does not involve a centralized name server, but still provides a high degree of confidence that the IDs it generates will be globally unique. Voyager provides support for a type of object called a *mobile agent*. Mobile agents are objects that can migrate from one Java VM to another.

Globally unique object IDs are especially important for mobile agents. It is important for objects that interact with a mobile agent to identify the mobile agent without knowing which VM is the mobile agent's current location. It is also important that mobile agents be able to communicate with objects they are interested in without the mobile agent having to be concerned with which VM it is currently in. The Mobile Agent pattern describes mobile agents in greater detail.

Object-oriented databases assign a unique object ID to every object stored in a database. Even if the database is distributed, objects will generally be identified by a single ID throughout the database. Most object database vendors have standardized on APIs defined by ODMG* as a means for clients' programs to work with their databases. One of the responsibilities of those APIs is to provide two-way mapping between the object IDs that the database uses and the object IDs that the client uses.

---

* The ODMG APIs are described in [ODMG97].

Because you use the Object Identifier pattern for objects that will be shared, you will be concerned with interactions between the Object Identifier pattern and serialization. Serialization is Java's mechanism for converting an object to a stream of bytes so that it can be sent through a network connection. Serialization is described in more detail in the description of the Snapshot pattern in Volume 1.

Serializing a sharable object and sending it to another environment through a byte stream has the effect of copying the object. If this happens, there will be more than one of these sharable objects that claims to be the same object. If not handled properly, this can be a serious problem. There are a few reasonable ways to handle the situation:

- You can avoid the situation by leaving the object where it is and using it remotely via the Object Request Broker pattern.
- You can handle the situation by ensuring that the original object is no longer used after it is copied to another VM, following the Mobile Agent pattern.
- You can also handle the situation by ensuring that changes to one copy of the object are propagated to all other copies of the object using the Object Replication pattern. This can be complicated and slow if not designed carefully. If you choose this option, you should take extra care in reviewing your design.

JAVA API USAGE

RMI includes a mechanism that generates object IDs that are highly likely to be globally unique. It uses a combination of the time and hash code of an object to identify an environment.

Java's core API does not include a provision for assigning true globally unique IDs to objects. The Java language provides every object with an object ID that is unique within a Java Virtual Machine at a point in time. These object IDs are `int` values. A program can explicitly access an object's ID through the API by using the `java.lang.System.identityHashCode` method.

Because Java garbage-collects objects that are no longer being used, object IDs can be recycled. Over time, it is possible for the same object ID to identify different objects. Garbage collection makes the use of fixed-length object IDs practical for long-running programs. Without garbage collection, if a program runs long enough to create enough objects, it will overflow any fixed-size object identifier. When an object is garbage-collected, its object ID can be assigned to a new object. With garbage collection, the set of object ID values will not be exhausted unless more objects are in use at one time than there are possible IDs.

CODE EXAMPLE

Here is a sample implementation of the classes shown in Figure 6.1. It begins with an implementation of the `ObjectID` class.

```
public class ObjectID {
    private long environmentID;
    private long serialNumber;

    /**
     * Constructor
     */
    ObjectID (long environmentID, long serialNumber) {
        this.environmentID = environmentID;
        this.serialNumber = serialNumber;
    } // constructor (long, long)
```

Notice that the constructor is not public. This is because instances of the `ObjectID` class are supposed to be created by the `IDGenerator` class so that the details of ID creation can be hidden from other classes.

```
    /**
     * Return true if the given object is an ObjectID object
     * with the same environmentID and serialNumber as this
     * object.
     */
    public boolean equals(Object obj) {
        if (obj instanceof ObjectID) {
            ObjectID that = (ObjectID)obj;
            return (this.environmentID == that.environmentID
                    && this.serialNumber == that.serialNumber);
        } // if instanceof ObjectID
        return false;
    } // equals(Object)

    /**
     * Return a hash code for this object.
     */
    public int hashCode() {
        return (int)environmentID & (int)(environmentID >>> 32)
                ^ (int)serialNumber ^ (int)(serialNumber >>> 32);
    } // hashCode()

    /**
     * Return a string representation of this object.
     */
    public String toString() {
        return getClass() .getName()
                + "[" + environmentID + "," + serialNumber + "]";
    } // toString()
} // class ObjectID
```

The `ObjectID` class overrides the `toString`, `equals`, and `hashCode` methods it inherits from the `Object` class so they return a result based on the contents of an `ObjectID` object.

Here is a listing of the `IDGenerator` class that generates object IDs. The IDs that its `generateID` method returns are based on the environment ID passed to its constructor. Where the environment IDs come from is outside the scope of this example.

```
class IDGenerator {
    private long environmentID;
    private long counter=0;

    /**
     * Constructor
     * @param id The id value for this environment
     */
    IDGenerator (int id) {
        environmentID = id;
    } // constructor (int)

    /**
     * Return a unique object ID represented as an array of short.
     */
    public ObjectID generateID() {
        counter++;
        return new ObjectID(environmentID, counter);
    } // generateID()
} // class IdGenerator
```

Notice that the `IDGenerator` class is not public. Since it is a detail of object creation, there is no need to access it outside the package that contains those details.

Here is a skeletal listing of the `ObjectEnvironment` class. It shows the support it provides for new objects getting an object ID.

```
public class ObjectEnvironment {
    private static IDGenerator myIDGenerator;
    ...
    static ObjectID generateID() {
        return my IDGenerator.generateID();
    } // generateID()
    ...
} // class ObjectEnvironment
```

Finally, here is the implementation of the `SharableObject` class. Its constructor gets its object ID. It overrides the `toString`, `equals`, and `hashCode` methods it inherits from the `Object` class so that those methods return a result based on the object's `ObjectID`.

```
public class SharableObject {
    private ObjectID myObjectID;
```

```
    public SharableObject() {
        myObjectID = ObjectEnvironment.generateID();
    } // constructor()

    /**
     * Produce a string representation of this SharableObject.
     */
    public String toString() {
        return "SharableObject[" + myObjectID + "]";
    } // toString()

    /**
     * Return true if the given object has the same id as this object.
     */
    public boolean equals(Object obj) {
        if ( !(obj instanceof SharableObject)) {
            return false;
        } // if instanceof
        SharableObject that = (SharableObject)obj;
        return this.myObjectID.equals(that.myObjectID);
    } // equals(Object)

    /**
     * Return a hash code based on this sharable object's id.
     */
    public int hashCode() {
        return myObjectID.hashCode();
    } // hashCode()
} // class SharableObject
```

RELATED PATTERNS

Most patterns related to distributed computing use the Object Identifier pattern implicitly or explicitly. Here are some of the more notable related patterns:

Object Request Broker and Registry.   You can use the Object Request Broker pattern with the Registry pattern to encapsulate an implementation of the Object Identifier pattern and minimize the number of classes that are dependent on it.

Mobile Agent.   The Mobile Agent pattern uses the Object ID pattern.

Object Replication.   The Object Replication pattern uses the Object ID pattern.

Registry

This pattern is also known as Name Service. It was previously described in [Sommerlad98].

SYNOPSIS

Objects need to contact other objects for which they know only the object's name or the name of the service it provides but not how to contact it. Provide a service that takes the name of an object, service, or role and returns a remote proxy that encapsulates the knowledge of how to contact the named object.

CONTEXT

You work for a telephone company that has been growing by acquiring other telephone companies. After it acquires another company, there is a corporate policy to make the newly acquired company's customer service systems available through your company's existing user interfaces.

The architecture the company uses for these integration projects is to create an adapter object for each of the acquired company's systems. These objects implement the interfaces with which your company's customer service applications expect to work. It implements the interfaces by interacting with the acquired system in a way that makes the acquired systems appear to behave in the same manner as your company's existing customer service systems.

To make the customer service client applications aware of the new objects, you add their name to a configuration file. The client applications need no other modification. What makes this possible is a shared registry object used by the client applications. The wrapper objects register their names with the registry object. When the client applications ask the registry object to look up a name, it returns a proxy object that they can use to communicate with the named wrapper object.

FORCES

- ☺ Instances of a class exist to provide a service to other objects.
- ☺ Instances of a service providing class must be shared by other objects because it is not feasible for there to be more than a very few instances of the class.

☺ Other objects cannot use the service-providing object if they do not know that it exists or do not have a way to refer to the object.

☺ From time to time, you may need to change the location of shared-service-providing objects. You do not want such configuration changes to require changes to the clients of the service-providing objects. If such a change occurs during the lifetime of an object that uses a service-providing object, you want it to be able to find the new service-providing object.

☹ Some applications involve a very large number of clients. For example, consider a Java applet that prepares income taxes and files them electronically. It may reasonably be expected to have tens of thousands of clients at one time near the filing deadline. At such times, network bandwidth is in short supply. You do not want the applets using network bandwidth to consult a server simply to find out which remote object the applet should contact to get tax instructions or file a return. You are better off passing that information to the applet as a parameter.

☹ Objects in a real-time application that has rigid timing requirements may not be able to afford the time it takes to consult an external service in order to get a way to refer to another external object.

SOLUTION

Register service-providing objects with a registry object that is widely known to other objects. The registration associates a name with a remote proxy that encapsulates the knowledge of how to call the methods of the names object. When presented with a name, the registry object produces the proxy. Figure 6.2 shows the organization of this design.

Here are the roles that classes play in the organization shown in Figure 6.2:

Client.   Objects in this role want to use a shared object that is in the ServiceObject role, but do not have any way to refer to it. What they do have is a name for the ServiceObject role and a way of referring to a registry object.

ServiceObject.   Client objects share objects in this role for the service that they provide. Client objects are able to find the same ServiceObject by presenting its name to a registry object.

ServiceIF.   Interfaces in this role are implemented by both ServiceObject objects and RemoteProxy objects.

RemoteProxy.   Instances of classes in this role are a proxy for a ServiceObject that implements the methods of the ServiceIF

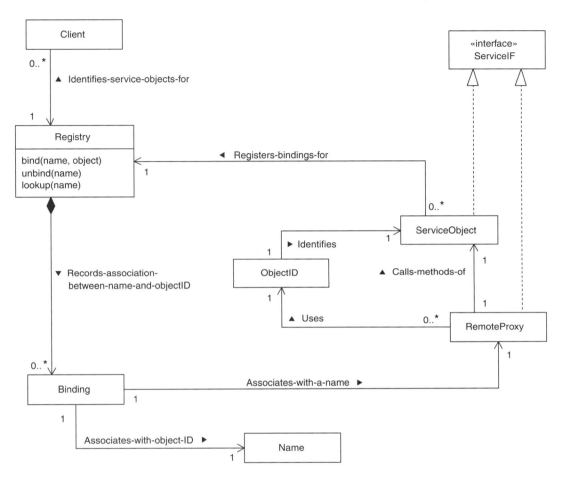

FIGURE 6.2 Registry object.

interface by remotely calling the corresponding method of a
`ServiceObject` object.

ObjectID.   Instances of a class in this role identify a `Service-`
`Object`. `RemoteProxy` objects use an `ObjectID` object to identify the `ServiceObject` that they are a proxy for.

Registry.   Objects in the `ServiceObject` role register themselves
with a `Registry` object. That registration consists of the object
passing its name and a `RemoteProxy` object to the `Registry`
object's `bind` method. The registration remains in effect until
the name of the object is passed to the `Registry` object's `unbind`
method. While the registration is in effect, the `Registry` object's
`lookup` method returns the proxy when it is passed the object's
name.

Binding. Registry objects use Binding objects internally to pair names with proxies.

Name. Objects in this role are used as a key to look up object IDs in a registry.

CONSEQUENCES

☺ Used in isolation, the Registry pattern simply provides a layer of indirection that determines which service object a client object will use.

☺ Client objects are able to access service objects without having any prior knowledge of where the service objects are. That means it is possible to change the location of service objects without having to make any changes to the client classes.

☹ Client and service objects are required to have prior knowledge of where the Registry object is.

IMPLEMENTATION

One of the simplest ways to implement the Registry pattern is to use a HashTable in the Registry object role. The drawback to this approach is that it works only for local objects. The Registry pattern is often combined with the Object Request Broker pattern to facilitate the distributed sharing of objects.

NAME SHARING

Sometimes multiple shared objects provide the same service or fill the same role. If an object needs to use one of them, you may want the choice to reflect a particular policy. An example of such a policy is to evenly balance the load on all of the service-providing objects.

The Registry pattern can be adapted to implement such policies by doing two things. The first is to allow Registry objects to associate multiple object IDs with the same name at the same time. The other is to apply some policy-driven logic when deciding which object ID to return when presented with a name.

DISTRIBUTED REGISTRY

A common architectural variation on the design discussed under the "Solution" heading is to make the registry a distributed service. There are two common ways of doing this, which can be combined.

One way of providing a distributed registry is to use the Object Replication pattern. When a registry is replicated in this way, the usual way to propagate changes between the registry replicas is to use the time-stamping technique discussed under the "Implementation" heading of the Object Replication pattern.

The other common way of providing a distributed registry is to organize `Registry` objects into a hierarchy. The `Registry` objects on the bottom of the hierarchy contain bindings for a limited set of objects. If one of these `Registry` objects is asked for a binding for a name it knows nothing about, it forwards the request to a `Registry` object one level higher in the hierarchy. `Registry` objects above the bottom of the hierarchy are able to tell from a prefix of the given object name whether one of the `Registry` objects under them will be the right place to look for a binding.

For example, suppose that a `Registry` object is asked to provide a remote proxy for an object named `ebox:custService`. If the `Registry` object does not have a binding for that name, it forwards the request to the `Registry` object above it in the hierarchy. That `Registry` object does not have a binding for the name, but it knows that one of the `Registry` objects under it is responsible for all names that begin with `ebox:`. It forwards the request to that `Registry` object, which finds a binding for the name and returns the proxy.

CORBA

CORBA is an ORB that is language neutral. It allows remote objects to pass data, but not behavior, to each other. In particular, it does not provide any way to pass proxy objects. The standard CORBA implementation of the Registry pattern is the CORBA naming service. Instead of binding names to proxies, it binds them to something called an Interoperable Object Reference (IOR). An IOR is a string that has, embedded in it, all of the information needed to contact an object.

OTHER

Other types of computing environments that are not object-oriented, such as relational databases, also use a pure value instead of a proxy to implement the Registry pattern.

KNOWN USES

Voyager has an implementation of the Registry pattern called the Federated Naming Service. It is also an example of a `Registry` object that is distributed using the Object Replication pattern.

The Registry pattern is used with the Object Request Broker pattern to allow clients of shared-service-providing objects to find the service-providing objects without having any foreknowledge of their object IDs. The CORBA naming service is an example.

The Registry pattern is also used in computer networks. Network naming services, such as DNS, are applications of the Registry pattern. DNS is organized into a hierarchy of `Registry` objects. DNS binds names to IP addresses rather than to proxies.

JAVAF API USAGE

RMI's `rmiregistry` program is an application of the Registry pattern.

Instances of the `java.util.ResourceBundle` class are another application of the Registry pattern. It differs from the basic Registry pattern in that all of the objects registered in a `ResourceBundle` are registered when the object is created rather than after its creation.

CODE EXAMPLE

The code example for the Registry pattern appears to be simpler than the class diagram in Figure 6.2 would suggest. This is because it `Registry` class delegates most of what it does to the `Hashtable` class. The `Hashtable` class handles the management of `Binding` objects.

```
public class Registry {
    private Hashtable hashTable = new Hashtable();

    public void bind(String name, Object obj) {
        hashTable.put(name, obj);
    } // bind(String, Object)

    public void unbind(String name) {
        hashTable.remove(name);
    } // unbind(String)

    public Object lookup(String name) {
        return hashTable.get(name);
    } // lookup(String)
} // class Registry
```

RELATED PATTERNS

Proxy.   The Registry pattern uses the Proxy pattern (described in *Volume 1*).

Object Request Broker.   The Registry pattern is often used with the Object Request Broker pattern.

Shared Object.   Registry objects are shared objects.

Protection Proxy

The Protection Proxy pattern is mentioned in [GoF95].

SYNOPSIS

Malicious objects may attempt to violate the integrity of other objects by using reflection or other means to access methods or variables they should not. You can prevent this by requiring other objects to access sensitive objects through a proxy that limits access based on security considerations. The proxy implements measures to ensure that other objects do not gain access to features of a sensitive object that they are not entitled to.

CONTEXT

You are writing software for a new kind of smart food processor that turns raw ingredients into cooked, ready-to-eat food by slicing, dicing, mixing, boiling, baking, frying, and/or stirring the ingredients. On a mechanical level, the new food processor is a very sophisticated piece of equipment. However, a crucial part of the food processor is a selection of programs to prepare different kinds of foods. A program that can turn flour, water, yeast, and other ingredients into different kinds of bread is very different from a program that can stir-fry shrimp to exactly the right texture. The food processor will be required to run a great variety of programs that allow it to produce a great variety of foods. Because of the large variety of programs that will be required, it is not possible to build all of the necessary programs into the food processor. Instead, the food processor will load its programs from a CD-ROM or similar media. Because it is not possible for you to produce all of the many programs that will be needed yourself, you publish the interfaces for these programs so that others will be able to produce programs for the food processor.

The food processor uses the Dynamic Linkage pattern (described in *Volume 1*) to allow these dynamically loaded programs to work with the software in the food processor environment. Figure 6.3 shows the basic organization of this.

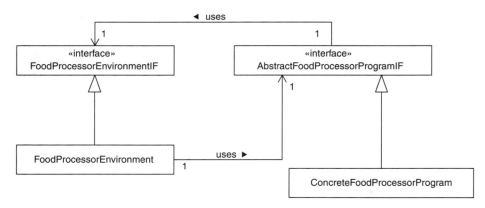

FIGURE 6.3 Basic food processor organization.

The top-level class of the dynamically loaded program is required to implement the `AbstractFoodProcessorProgram` interface. This requirement ensures that the program has certain methods that the environment can call to invoke it. When the food processor environment invokes the program, it passes it a reference to an object that implements the `Food-ProcessorEnvironmentIF` interface to allow the program to communicate with the environment.

Because the food processor is intended for consumers, safeguards are important to ensure that the device is safe to use. For example, its chopping and slicing mechanism should not be in motion unless the consumer has pushed the button that is supposed to start the action. For that reason, you want to ensure that a loaded program does not call any of the environment's methods other than those declared by the `FoodProcessor-EnvironmentIF` interface. No program is likely to violate the interface's encapsulation by mistake. However, you want to ensure that malicious programs do not cause bad things to happen. Just one such incident could result in a very expensive lawsuit that ruins your company's reputation and finances.

Malicious programs may try to discover and call methods of the environment object that are not part of the interface by using Java's reflection API. To prevent that and other undesirable actions, you design a security manager class that prevents a program from successfully calling any reflection methods and other parts of the Java API that it should not. However, it is possible for a motivated hacker to circumvent those precautions with a lower-level hack.

The Java VM does nothing at runtime to prevent any methods from being called, even if they are declared private. It is possible for a highly malicious hacker to obtain a food processor and reverse-engineer the classes of the software in the food processor. Once the hacker has identified the classes in the food processor and the methods, that person can create a program with the ability to call any method of any object to which the program can get a reference. Such a program can freely call private methods. It is also possible for such a program to access the private variables of objects to which it can get a reference. Clearly, to ensure that a malicious program cannot corrupt an object, you must prevent it from getting a reference to the object. At the same time, you must somehow allow legitimate calls to the object that implements the `FoodProcessorEnvironmentIF` interface.

One way to allow an object to call another object's methods without having a reference to it is through a proxy. Figure 6.4 shows the addition of a proxy to the food processor organization.

The class diagram in Figure 6.4 shows a proxy interposed between the program and the environment. The class labeled `FoodProcessorEnvironmentProxy` implements the `FoodProcessorEnvironmentIF` interface. When a program is invoked, it is passed a reference to an instance of the `FoodProcessorEnvironmentProxy` class. To communicate with the environment, the program calls methods declared by the `FoodProcessorEnvironmentIF` interface and implemented by the `FoodProcessorEnvironmentProxy` class. Those implementations simply call the corresponding method of a `FoodProcessorEnvironment` object.

The proxy allows the program to invoke the environment's methods without having a reference to the environment. In order for the proxy to do its job, it must have a reference to the environment. For the proxy to have any value, it must keep its reference to the environment in a place

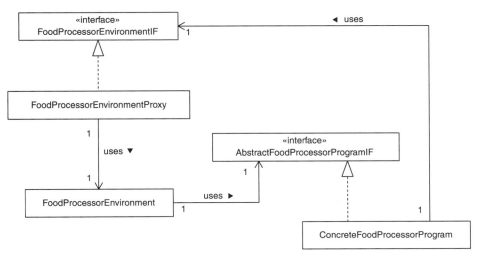

FIGURE 6.4 Food processor with proxy.

that its clients cannot get to. Clients can potentially take the reference if it is stored in an instance variable. Clients cannot take it out of a local variable. A technique for hiding the reference in a local variable is described in the "Solution" section.

FORCES

☺ A set of classes that act as a host environment for other classes may find itself hosting a malicious class. Examples of such hosting environments are servers that host servlets, browsers that host applets, and environments that host mobile agents.

☺ An object will have trusted and untrusted clients. An untrusted client should satisfy a security check before the object satisfies a request from it. The object should not burden trusted clients with the expense of security checks.

☺ You have a class that is part of a trusted protection domain that gives it access to highly sensitive services. Before an instance of the class satisfies a request from one of its clients that will cause it to access one of those sensitive services, the object requesting the service must satisfy a security check.

☺ You do not want the code that performs the security check to access any of the sensitive services, because the sensitive services must not be accessed until the security check is complete. To avoid any possibility that the code that implements the security check will inadvertently call a method that accesses a sensitive service, you do not want it to be in the trusted protection domain.

☺ You have a class that must remain highly secure from its clients. Untrusted objects that use the class's instances must not be able to get a direct reference to the class's instances.

☺ Malicious classes can call the private methods of other classes and access the private variables of other classes. However, malicious classes cannot access the local variables of other classes.

☺ You need to be able to limit the effectiveness of *denial-of-service attacks*. A denial-of-service attack is an attack on the availability of a service. It works by flooding a server with bogus or unnecessary requests for service. While the server's resources are tied up servicing the bogus requests, it may not have enough resources to properly service legitimate service requests.

☹ If an object is accessing another object remotely, it is not possible for it to bypass the interface of the object it is accessing remotely. However, it may still be possible for it to mount a denial-of-service attack.

SOLUTION

Restrict access to an object by local untrusted clients by forcing them to access the object through a proxy. The purpose of the proxy is to limit access to only those methods that are declared in a public interface. The proxy may further limit the access by determining whether the client should be allowed to call the method that it is calling.

Make the proxy an active object that handles method calls from clients by scheduling calls to methods of the object for which it is a proxy to be made in its own thread, one at a time.

The class diagram in Figure 6.5 shows the roles that classes play in the Protection Proxy pattern.

Here are descriptions of the roles that classes and interfaces play in the Protection Proxy pattern.

Client.   Instances of classes in this role have a reference to an object that implements the `ServiceIF` interface and use its methods.

ServiceIF.   An interface in this role is a public interface that declares methods `Client` objects call to access services provided by the `Service` class. Both the `ProtectionProxy` class and the `Service` class implement this interface. Untrusted `Client` objects are allowed to reference instances of `ProtectionProxy` class but not instances of the `Service` class. Trusted `Client` objects, if they are believed to be correctly behaved and not malicious, may be given a direct reference to an instance of the `Service` class.

ProtectionProxy.   Classes in this role implement the `ServiceIF` interface. Their implementations of the interface's methods work by calling corresponding methods of the `Service` class. Implementations of these classes must be able to prevent malicious client classes from gaining a direct reference to a `Service` object. They must also prevent denial-of-service attacks. The details of how it does these things are presented after this list of roles.

    `ProtectionProxy` classes may be required to determine if the callers of its methods are allowed to call them. I recommend that your designs use Java's permission classes to determine if an object in a particular context is allowed to do something. For designs that use permission classes, classes in the `Protection-Proxy` role should delegate the determination of whether to allow a method call to an object that implements the `java.security.Guard` interface.

Service.   Classes in this role implement the methods that the corresponding `ProtectionProxy` class covers.

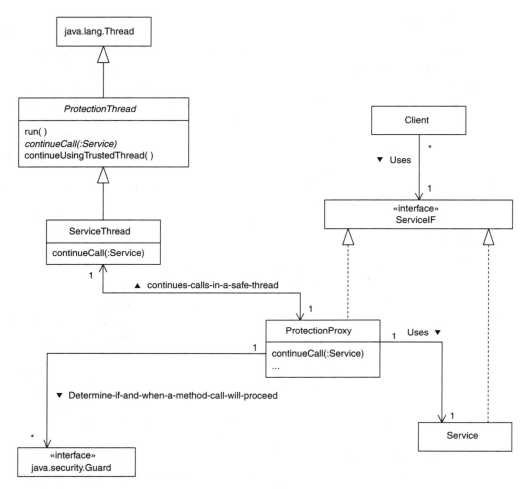

FIGURE 6.5 Protection proxy pattern.

java.security.Guard. This is not a role. It is an actual interface defined in the Java API. The ProtectionProxy class may have the responsibility of determining whether a caller of its methods is allowed to call its methods. If the ProtectionProxy class is required to make the determination, it delegates the decision to an object that implements the java.security.Guard interface. The java.security.Guard interface declares a method called checkGuard that is passed an object as an argument. The check-Guard method throws a SecurityException if methods of the object it is passed may not be called in the current context.

The Permission class implements the java.security .Guard interface. The Guard object that ServiceProxy objects use is usually an instance of a subclass of the Permission class.

ServiceThread.   An instance of a class in this role is responsible for hiding a reference to the `Service` object that a `Protection-Proxy` object will be using. It also limits the effectiveness of denial-of-service attacks by ensuring that method calls do not proceed until a minimum amount of time has elapsed since the previous method call. It inherits the reusable logic for doing these things from its superclass.

When a client object calls one of the `ProtectionProxy` object's methods, the method puts the values of its arguments in the object's instance variables. Putting the values of the arguments in instance variables makes the values visible to another thread. The method sets the value of another instance variable to indicate which method is being called. The current thread is unable to continue with the call any further, so it waits for the `ServiceThread` to execute the rest of the call. The current thread is forced to wait for the `ServiceThread` because neither it nor the `ProtectionProxy` object have a reference to the `Service` object.

Because its superclass is reusable, a `ServiceThread` class does not inherit any logic for supplying the `Service` object reference to the `ProtectionProxy`. When a `ProtectionProxy` object needs a `Service` object reference, its superclass passes a `Service` object reference to the abstract method `continue-Call`. The `ServiceThread` class provides an implementation of the `continueCall` method that passes the `Service` object reference to the `ProtectionProxy` object's `continueCall` method.

Protection Thread.   This abstract class contains the reusable logic used by `ServiceThread` classes. Its `run` method keeps a reference to a `Service` object in a local variable, where it is not visible to any other thread. When another thread calls a `ProtectionThread` object's `continueUsingTrustedThread` method, the `ProtectionThread` object's `run` method passes the `Service` object to the abstract method `continueCall`.

java.lang.Thread.   This is not a role. It is the class in the Java API responsible for controlling threads of execution. It is also the superclass of the `ProtectionThread` class.

To call the methods of a `Service` object, a `Protection-Proxy` object must have a reference to the `Service` class object. If a `ProtectionProxy` class is required to protect its associated `Service` class from malicious `Client` objects, `Protection-Proxy` objects cannot store their reference to a `Service` object in an instance variable. Malicious `Client` objects can access another object's private instance variables. However, malicious `Client` objects cannot access another object's local variables.

A `ProtectionProxy` class can keep references to a `Service` class in a local variable by having its own thread. Having its own thread also allows a local variable to be kept alive indefinitely. By making that thread sleep for a small period of time after each call, you can ensure that method calls to the `Service` object are not made any more frequently than the period of time the thread sleeps. A common type of denial-of-service is to call an object's methods so frequently and concurrently that few CPU cycles are left for more legitimate activities. Enforcing a minimum frequency for method calls and constraining them to be one-at-a-time calls can reduce the effectiveness of a denial-of-service attack.

Figure 6.6 is a collaboration diagram that shows some details of how the hiding of a reference and postponement of the next method call work. Here are descriptions of the interactions shown in Figure 6.6:

1. The `ServiceThread` object is created. References to the `ProtectionProxy` object and the `Service` object are passed to

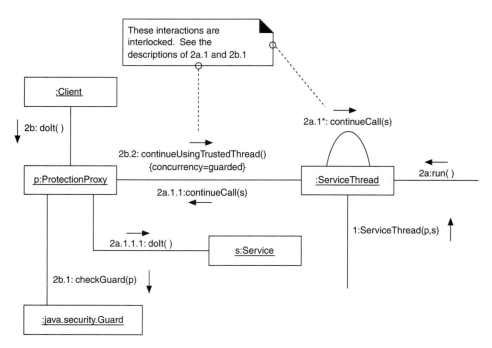

FIGURE 6.6 Protection proxy collaboration.

the `ServiceThread` object's constructor. The constructor puts these object references in the constructed object's instance variables. Since no other object can have a reference to the new `ServiceThread` object until the constructor returns, the reference in the instance variable is not a problem at this point.

After setting the instance variables, the constructor starts the thread of execution that the `ServiceThread` object will control. The thread copies the `Service` object reference to a local variable and sets the instance variable to null.

The constructor then waits for the other thread to set the instance variable to null. After the instance variable is set to null, the constructor returns. When the constructor returns, the instance variable is null and a local variable contains the `Service` object reference. At this point, the `Service` object reference is accessible only within the `ServiceThread` object's run method.

2a. The `ServiceThread` object's thread of execution begins by calling the object's `run` method. The `run` method begins by copying the `Service` object reference to a local variable. Then the `run` method sets the instance variable that contained the reference to null. It then notifies the thread that created the `ServiceThread` object that it can stop waiting for the instance variable to be set to null.

The `run` method then enters an infinite loop. At the beginning of each iteration, the `run` method waits for another thread to call the `continueUsingTrustedThread` method. Calls to the `continueUsingTrustedThread` method notify the run method that the `ProtectionProxy` object needs to call the `Service` object. When the run method receives this notification, it stops waiting and continues the current iteration.

The iteration then calls the `continueCall` method. The `continueCall` method allows the `ProtectionProxy` object to securely make a call to the `Service` object.

The iteration concludes by sleeping for a predetermined amount of time. The purpose of the sleep is to prevent the next call to a `ProtectionProxy` object's methods from calling the `Service` object during that time. This guarantees a minimum amount of time between calls from the `ProtectionProxy` object to the `Service` object. It also limits the effectiveness of a denial-of-service attack.

After the iteration concludes, the run method begins another iteration by waiting for the `continueUsingTrustedThread` method to be called.

2b. The `Client` object calls the `doIt` method of an object that implements the `ServiceIF` interface. In this situation, the object that implements the `ServiceIF` interface is a `ProtectionProxy` object. Its methods provide the functionality of the `Service` object by indirectly calling its methods.

2b.1. The `ProtectionProxy` object calls its `Guard` object's `checkGuard` method to find out whether the `Client` object is allowed to call the `ProtectionProxy` object's method. If the `Client` object is not allowed to make the call, the `checkGuard` method throws a `SecurityException`.

2b.2. At this point, the `ProtectionProxy` object cannot call the `doIt` method of the `Service` object because it does not have a reference to the `Service` object. However, the `Protection-Proxy` object does have a reference to the `ServiceThread` object. It calls the `ServiceThread` object's `continueUsing-TrustedThread` method.

The purpose of the `continueUsingTrustedThread` method is to notify the `ServiceThread` object that it should initiate a call to the `Service` object. The `continueUsingTrustedThread` method notifies the `run` method that it should continue with its current iteration and call the `continueCall` method. The `continueUsingTrustedThread` method then waits to be notified when the `run` method's call to the `continueCall` method has returned. After being notified, the `continueUsingTrustedThread` method returns.

2a.1. The `ServiceThread` object's `run` method is notified by the object's `continueUsingTrustedThread` method when the `ProtectionProxy` object needs to call one of the `Service` object's methods. When the `run` method receives the notification, it passes a reference to the `Service` object to the `continueCall` method.

The contribution of the `ServiceThread` object's `continueCall` method is that it knows how to pass a reference to the `Service` object to the `ProtectionProxy` object.

2a.1.1. The `ServiceThread` object's `continueCall` method calls the `ProtectionProxy` object's `continueCall` method. The purpose of this method is to call the `Service` object method that corresponds to the `ProtectionProxy` method originally called by the other thread. If any parameters need to be passed to the `Service` object's method, the original method passes them to the `continueCall` method through instance variables. If there is a result to return, this method passes it back to the original method through instance variables.

2a.1.1.1. The `ProtectionProxy` object's `continueCall` method calls the `Service` object's method that corresponds to the original `ProtectionProxy` method.

CONSEQUENCES

☺ Like other forms of proxy, use of the Protection Proxy pattern reduces the number of dependencies between classes and promotes reuse. It reduces the number of dependencies by hiding the class of the actual object being called from the calling object and by limiting the methods by which the client object can call to those declared by the `ServiceIF` interface. Because there are fewer dependencies between the client and service-providing class, there are more opportunities to reuse them.

☺ The Protection Proxy pattern forces even malicious clients of an object to limit themselves to working with the object through its declared interface.

☺ You can use the Protection Proxy pattern to control the priority of the threads that call an object's methods.

☹ Calling a method through a protection proxy takes longer than a direct call.

☹ Protection proxies add complexity to a design. It is always simpler, though less robust, for a client object to directly access the service object.

IMPLEMENTATION

If there is no need to determine whether client objects are permitted to access a `Service` object, you can leave the `Guard` object out of the design.

In some cases, there is a high degree of confidence that client objects will not be malicious. In such situations, the only motivation for using the Protection Proxy pattern is to protect `Service` objects from client objects that are not well behaved. If there is a belief that client objects will not be malicious, then the complexity and overhead that the `ProtectionThread` class adds may outweigh its benefits. If that is the case, you can simplify your design by leaving out the `ProtectionThread`.

If a `ProtectionThread` object catches an exception thrown from a call to one of the `Service` object's methods, it should rethrow the exceptions in the original calling thread.

The Protection Proxy pattern is noteworthy for using multiple threads without being a concurrency pattern. You can use the Thread Pool pattern with the Protection Proxy pattern to make it concurrent.

KNOWN USES

Some mobile agent frameworks, such as Voyager, use protection proxies to control access to objects.

The InfoBus 1.2 specification* defines an architecture that allows objects conforming to the specification to exchange data without having direct knowledge of each other. The InfoBus specification accomplishes this by defining a number of interfaces. Objects that implement the appropriate interfaces can participate in an InfoBus by simply attaching themselves to the InfoBus.

In the course of interacting with other objects through the InfoBus, an object will receive references to objects that implement some of the InfoBus interfaces. Objects are supposed to respect the interfaces and not try to access object features that are not part of the interface.

Objects attached to the same InfoBus may not have any reason to trust each other. For that reason, the InfoBus recommends that objects take precautions against objects that do not respect interfaces. Some of the interfaces an object passes to an InfoBus are accessible by other participating objects and others are not. The InfoBus specification recommends that if an InfoBus will pass an object reference to other participating objects, the reference be indirect. The recommendation is that the objects pass a proxy that implements the required interface. To support that recommendation, the InfoBus software includes a set of proxy classes that implement the interfaces. The InfoBus specification refers to these classes as *proxy listener classes*.

General-purpose operating systems, such as Unix or Linux, generally use a form of protection proxy to control application calls to sensitive operating system services.

Most network firewall products include a proxy feature that hides the network address of hosts on the private side of the firewall. It substitutes its own address so that hosts on the public side of the firewall see only that address of the firewall when communicating with hosts on the private side of the firewall.

JAVA API USAGE

The core Java API does not use the Protection Proxy pattern. However, the `java.security` package does provide a policy-based permission architecture. If that architecture is used in a design, it greatly reduces the security burden on other classes for determining whether a method call should be allowed to proceed.

All a class need do to determine whether the methods of a particular object may be called in a particular context is to call the `checkGuard`

---

* The InfoBus 1.2 specification can be found at http://java.sun.com/beans/infobus/spec12/ IB12Spec.htm.

method of an object that implements the `Guard` interface. Such objects are typically `Permission` objects. A call to the `checkGuard` method of a `Permission` object determines whether the current call context has that permission.

CODE EXAMPLE

Here is a sample implementation of the Protection Proxy pattern.

Any interface that declares at least one method is suitable for the `ServiceIF` interface role. The one in this example is as follows:

```
public interface ServiceIF {
    public int getInfo() ;
    public void setInfo(int x);
    public void doIt();
} // interface ServiceIF
```

`Client` objects are probably the least interesting kind of object in the pattern. Any instance of a class that calls a method through the `ServiceIF` interface can be a `Client` object.

Any class that implements the given `ServiceIF` interface can be a service class. Here is an example:

```
public class Service implements ServiceIF {
    ...
    public int getInfo() {
        int x = 0;
        ...
        return x;
    } // getInfo()

    public void setInfo(int x) {
    ...
    } // setInfo(int)

    public void doIt() {
        ...
    } // doIt()
} // interface ServiceIF
```

The `ProtectionProxy` class is more interesting because it encapsulates some logic. It begins by defining constants that it will use to dispatch calls to the correct `Service` object method. It also defines variables that it uses to pass parameter values to `Service` object methods and to pass results back to its method's callers.

```
class ProtectionProxy implements ServiceIF {
    private static final int GET_INFO = 1;
```

```
private static final int SET_INFO = 2;
private static final int DO_IT = 3;

private ServiceThread serviceThread;
private int whichMethod;
private int intResult;
private int intArg;

private Guard myGuard;

ProtectionProxy(Service service) {
    serviceThread = new ServiceThread(service, this);
    ...
} // constructor(Service)
```

Implementations of the methods declared by the ServiceIF interface all follow the same pattern.

- First, they call the guard object's checkGuard method to ensure that their caller should be permitted to make the call.
- Then they set the whichMethod variable to a constant that corresponds to the method. The value of the whichMethod variable is used later to dispatch a call to the corresponding method in the Service object.
- If the method has any parameters, it copies their values to instance variables.
- They call the serviceThread object's continueUsingTrustedThread method so that the appropriate method of the Service object will be called in a trusted thread by a method that has a reference to the Service object in a local variable.
- If the method is supposed to return a result, it will expect that result to be stored in an instance variable and will return the contents of the instance variable.

```
public int getInfo() {
    myGuard.checkGuard(this);
    whichMethod = GET_INFO;
    serviceThread.continueUsingTrustedThread();
    return intResult;
} // getInfo()

public void setInfo(int x) {
    myGuard.checkGuard(this);
    intArg = x;
    whichMethod = SET_INFO;
    serviceThread.continueUsingTrustedThread();
    return;
} // setInfo(int)

public void doIt() {
    myGuard.checkGuard(this);
```

```
        whichMethod = DO_IT;
        serviceThread.continueUsingTrustedThread();
    } // doIt()
```

The implementations of the `ServiceIF` methods call the `Service-Thread` object's `continueCall` method. That method arranges for another thread to call the `ProtectionProxy` object's `continueCall` method, passing it a reference to the `Service` object.

The purpose of the `ProtectionProxy` object's `continueCall` method is to call the `Service` object's method that corresponds to the `ServiceIF` implementing method that was originally called. The `continueCall` method uses the value of the `whichMethod` instance variable to determine which of the `Service` object's methods to call. If it has to pass any parameters to a method, it expects instance variables to contain the parameter values. If it calls a method that returns a result, it will set an instance variable to the returned value.

```
    void continueCall(Service service) {
        switch (whichMethod) {
          case GET_INFO:
            intResult = service.getInfo();
            break;

          case SET_INFO:
            service.setInfo(intArg);
            break;

          case DO_IT:
            service.doIt();
            break;
        } // switch
    } // continueCall(Service)
} // class ProtectionProxy
```

The `ServiceThread` class inherits much of its interesting behavior from the `ProtectionThread` class.

```
public abstract class ProtectionThread extends Thread {
    private static final long MIN_FREQUENCY = 2000;

    private Object service;
    private boolean pending = false;
    private boolean done = false;
    private Throwable thrownObject = null;
```

The `ProtectionThread` constructor is responsible for securely transferring the reference to the `Service` object from its argument to an instance variable to the new thread's local variable. It begins by setting the `myService` instance variable to refer to the `Service` object. It then starts the thread, which copies the `Service` object reference to a local variable and then sets the `myService` instance variable to null.

It must be the case that no other object can have a reference to the new `ProtectionThread` object until its constructor returns. For that reason, it is important that the constructor does not return until after `service` has been set to null.

As a practical matter, no other thread will get a reference to a `ProtectionThread` object until its constructor returns. The Java language specification does make it possible for another thread to get a reference to an object before it is fully constructed unless the constructor is `synchronized`. For this reason, the constructor is `synchronized`.

```
public synchronized ProtectionThread(Object myService) {
    service = myService;
    Thread t = new Thread(this);
    t.start();
    try {
        while (service!=null) {
            wait();
        } // while
    } catch (InterruptedException e) {
    } // try
} // constructor(Service)
```

When a `ProtectionThread` object's `start` method is called, it begins a new thread of execution that calls the `run` method. The `run` method begins by copying the reference to the `Service` object from an instance variable to a local variable. Then it sets the instance variable to null and notifies the thread that called the constructor.

After the notification, the run method enters the loop that is central to the purpose of the `ProtectionThread` class. The loop waits to be notified that there is a pending call to the `Service` object that it should complete on behalf of a `Client` object. When it is so notified, it passes the reference to the `Service` object to the `continueCall` method so that it can complete the call to the `Service` object.

```
public synchronized void run() {
    Object myService = service;
    service = null;
    notifyAll();
    try {
        while (true) {
            while (!pending) {
                wait();
            } // while !pending
            pending = false;
            try {
                continueCall(myService);
```

```
            } catch (ThreadDeath e) {
                throw e;
            } catch (Throwable e) {
                // Arrange for object to be rethrown in
                // client thread
                thrownObject = copyThrowable(e);
            } finally {
                done = true;
            } // try
            notifyAll();
            sleep(MIN_FREQUENCY);
        } // while
    } catch (InterruptedException e) {
    } // try
} // run()
```

The continueCall method is abstract because the ProtectionThread class is supposed to be reusable and the details of continuing the call will depend on the ProtectionProxy class and the Service class.

```
    public abstract void continueCall(Object myService) ;
...
```

The ProtectionProxy class calls the continueUsingTrustedThread to indicate that there is a pending call to the Service object.

```
    public synchronized void continueUsingTrustedThread()
                            throws RuntimeException,Error {
        try {
            pending = true;
            notifyAll();
            while(!done) {
                wait();
            } // while
        } catch (InterruptedException e) {
        } finally {
            done = false;
            if (thrownObject != null) {
                Throwable temp = thrownObject;
                thrownObject = null;
                if (temp instanceof RuntimeException)
                  throw (RuntimeException) temp;
                if (temp instanceof Error)
                  throw (Error) temp;
                // this should never happen
            } // if
        } // try
    } // continueUsingTrustedThread()
} // class ProtectionProxy
```

Finally, here is the ServiceThread class:

```
class ServiceThread extends ProtectionThread {
    private ProtectionProxy proxy;

    ServiceThread(Service service, ProtectionProxy proxy) {
        super(service);
        this.proxy = proxy;
    } // constructor
    public void continueCall(Object myService) {
        proxy.continueCall((Service)myService);
    } // continueCall(Object)
} // class ServiceThread
```

RELATED PATTERNS

Proxy.   The Protection Proxy pattern is a specialized version of the Proxy pattern, which is described in *Volume 1*.

Template Method.   The Protection Proxy pattern uses the Template Method pattern (described in *Volume 1*) to abstract out the reusable portion of the thread management logic.

Thread Pool.   You can use the Thread Pool pattern with the Protection Proxy pattern to create a multithreaded proxy.

Mobile Agent.   You can use the Protection Proxy pattern to keep the mobile agent environment safe from malicious mobile agents.

Publish-Subscribe

The Publish-Subscribe pattern was described in [Buschman96].

SYNOPSIS

You need to provide timely delivery of messages to one or more objects. Deliver messages to subscribed recipient objects by transmitting each message to each recipient. Ensure reliable delivery by repeating the transmission after an attempt fails until delivery is successful.

CONTEXT

Suppose you are designing a system to distribute the results of sporting events. The purpose of this system will be to support a business that will provide this information to subscribers. As soon as the results of an event are known, they must be sent to customers who subscribe to the service.

There are two common strategies for delivering messages. One strategy is to have potential recipients poll for messages. This strategy has two significant drawbacks:

- It does not provide immediate delivery. Once the result of a sporting event becomes available, recipients do not receive the result until the next time they poll for it.
- Because sporting event results become available on a sporadic basis, most of the time spent polling by potential recipients will produce no results. The fruitless polling is a waste of bandwidth. If there are many potential recipients, it can be a very big waste of bandwidth.

The other strategy is for the system to transmit results to recipients as the results become available. This strategy is a good fit for the problem.

FORCES

- ☺ Messages must be reliably delivered to their recipient(s) as soon as possible.

☺ Messages must be delivered to remote recipients.

☺ There is no available network infrastructure that allows you to multi-cast events to all recipients.*

☺ Messages are sent at sufficiently irregular intervals so that when the recipients poll for messages, much of the time the polling will find no messages.

☺ Communication between remote objects is less reliable than communication between local objects. There is usually less bandwidth available for communication between remote objects than between local objects.

☹ If multiple message sources send messages to the same recipient at the same time, the recipient may be overwhelmed and unable to properly handle the messages.

☹ Bandwidth is more efficiently used to deliver multiple messages to a recipient as a single batch than to deliver them individually.

☹ The effort required to send a message to multiple recipients may exceed the resources of the message source.

SOLUTION

Objects that want to receive messages register to receive them. Messages are transmitted as soon as they become available. Figure 6.7 shows the roles that classes and interface typically play in this.

Here are descriptions of the roles shown in Figure 6.7:

MessageSource.   Classes in this role create messages and pass them to an object that implements the `PublisherIF` interface. Any class that contains calls to `PublisherIF` methods fills this role.

PublisherIF.   Classes in the `Publisher` role implement this interface.

Publisher.   `Subscriber` objects register their interest in receiving messages with `Publisher` objects. When a `Publisher` object receives a message from a `MessageSource` object, it tries to deliver it to all of the `Subscriber` objects that have registered with the `Publisher` object to receive messages. The delivery mechanism is implemented in a way that allows messages to be delivered to remote objects.

Subscriber.   Classes in this role are responsible for receiving messages from `Publisher` objects on behalf of `Receiver` objects.

---

* Multicast is a network protocol that allows a network infrastructure to deliver the same message to multiple recipients.

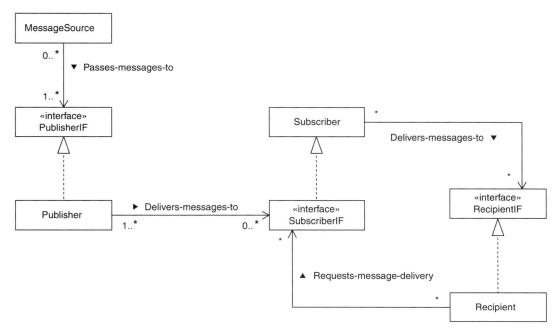

FIGURE 6.7 Publish-Subscribe pattern.

`Receiver` objects tell a `Subscriber` object that they are interested in receiving a certain sort of message. The `Subscriber` object registers the interest in messages with the appropriate `Publisher` object.

`Subscriber` objects also provide the reusable portion of the logic needed to receive messages. This may include such things as listening for network connections or datagrams from `Publisher` objects, or filtering messages. When a `Subscriber` object has a message to pass on to a `Recipient` object, it does so through the `RecipientIF` interface.

SubscriberIF. Classes in the `Subscriber` role implement this interface. `Recipient` objects use this interface to register their interest in receiving messages.

Recipient. Classes in this role are responsible for registering to receive messages and also receiving messages.

`Recipient` objects communicate their interest in receiving messages by calling a method declared by the `SubscriberIF` interface.

RecipientIF. Classes in the `Recipient` role implement this interface. `Subscriber` objects use this interface to pass messages to `Recipient` objects.

The collaboration between instances of these classes is illustrated by Figure 6.8. Here are descriptions of the interactions shown in Figure 6.8:

1.   A Recipient object tells a `Subscriber` object that it wants to receive messages.

1.1.   A `Subscriber` object registers with a possibly remote `Publisher` object to receive messages.

2A.   `MessageSource` objects send messages to a `Publisher` object for delivery to `Subscriber` objects.

2B.   In most cases, this will be a remote call.

The `Publisher` object delivers the messages it receives from `MessageSource` objects to `Subscriber` objects. Failed delivery attempts are repeated until successful. The `Subscriber` object performs any processing that is common to receiving all messages.

2B.1.   After it performs common processing for all messages, the `Subscriber` object passes the message on to the `Recipient` object.

CONSEQUENCES

☺ Use of the Publish-Subscribe pattern allows delivery of messages to recipients at the earliest possible time.

☺ Making message delivery the responsibility of an object dedicated to message delivery rather than the responsibility of the message source provides some important benefits. Even if it takes a long time to successfully deliver a message, the program that initiated a message is

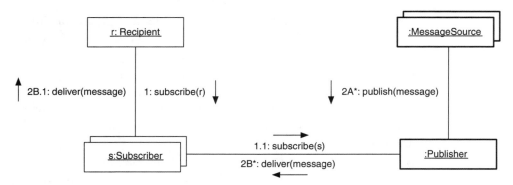

FIGURE 6.8 Publish-Subscribe collaboration.

free to terminate before the message is delivered. Also, the efforts to deliver the message do not take resources away from the program that was the message source. The message source does not even have to know the quantity or identity of its message's recipients.

☺ If the `Publisher` object receives messages from multiple message sources for some of the same recipients, it can combine them and reduce the amount of network traffic. However, most of the time, messages from different sources do not arrive at a `Publisher` object at the same time.

☺ Changing the actual `Publisher` and `Subscriber` classes used to provide the Publish-Subscribe functionality is transparent to `Message-Source` and `Recipient` objects because of the way the pattern uses interfaces.

IMPLEMENTATION

Usually, the Publish-Subscribe pattern is implemented by buying software for that purpose rather than writing an implementation from scratch. Implementing the pattern with all of the features you want is usually more expensive to do in-house than it is to buy.

For some applications, it may be desirable for `Publisher` objects to maintain a collection of old messages that are delivered to new subscribers when they subscribe. The purpose in delivering such messages to new subscribers is to help them get caught up.

The order in which messages are delivered is an issue for some implementations. Sometimes it is important to deliver messages in the same order that they were sent. In some cases, it is important to be able to prioritize messages so that higher-priority messages are delivered before lower-priority messages.

Most implementations of the Publish-Subscribe pattern include the ability to associate a topic or classification with each message. In such implementations, when a recipient object asks to receive messages, it includes a set of topics of interest. That results in messages associated with only those topics being sent to the recipient object.

KNOWN USES

Sybase's SQL Anywhere uses publish-subscribe for data replication. The Voyager ORB provides publish-subscribe distribution of events. IBM's MQSeries software includes a module for publish-subscribe distribution of messages.

JAVA API USAGE

Java Message Service API supports publish-subscribe based delivery of messages.

CODE EXAMPLE

The code example for this pattern is a limited and simple implementation of the `Publisher` and `Subscriber` classes. The various simplifications and limitations are explained along with the interfaces and classes involved. We begin with the `PublisherIF` interface.

```
public interface PublisherIF {
    /**
     * Deliver the given object associated with the given topic
     * to registered subscribers.
     */
    public void deliverMessage(Serializable message,
                              Serializable topic)
                                      throws RemoteException;
} // interface PublisherIF
```

The `PublisherIF` interface declares a method for objects to request delivery of a message to registered and appropriate recipients. In this sample implementation, messages may be any kind of `Serializable` object.* Implementations intended to deliver specific kinds of messages will generally use a more specialized type.

Though it is not a necessary part of the Publish-Subscribe pattern, this implementation provides a topic parameter to be passed along with each message. This implementation delivers messages only to recipients that registered to receive messages associated with the given topic. This is a very common feature of Publish-Subscribe implementations.

Publish-Subscribe implementations that support topics generally do so with a more specialized type. They may also recognize a hierarchy of topics so that a message is delivered to recipients who are registered for a message's specific topic or for a more general topic that includes the message's topic.

Here is a `Publisher` class that implements the `PublisherIF` interface:

```
public class Publisher extends UnicastRemoteObject
                implements PublisherIF, RemotePublisherIF {
```

---

* This sample implementation uses RMI as the basis of communication between `Publisher` and `Subscriber` objects. RMI is able to pass objects as parameters to remote methods only if their class implements the `java.io.Serializable` interface.

The `Publisher` class extends `java.rmi.server.UnicastRemote-Object`. This is necessitated by the fact that this implementation of Publish-Subscribe uses Java's RMI to allow the `Publisher` and `Subscriber` classes to communicate. The simplest way to allow RMI to make a class's methods remotely callable is to have the class extend `UnicastRemoteObject`.

The `Publisher` class also implements two interfaces. One is the `PublisherIF` interface that we have already examined. The other interface, `RemotePublisherIF`, is another artifact of using RMI. It declares all the methods of the `Publisher` class that can be called remotely.

Registrations of `Subscriber` objects are organized by topic using a `HashMap`. The topic is used as the `HashMap` key. The values are lists of `Subscriber` objects that want to receive messages related to the same topic.

```
private HashMap subscribers;

public Publisher() throws RemoteException,
                          MalformedURLException,
                          UnknownHostException {
    Naming.rebind(PUBLISHER_NAME, this);
    subscribers = new HashMap();
} // Constructor(String)
```

The constructor's call to `Naming.rebind` registers the name of the `Publisher` object with the RMI registry. This allows `Subscriber` objects to find the `Publisher` object by looking up their name in an RMI registry.

The name of the `Publisher` object is hard-coded (`PUBLISHER_NAME` is defined in `RemotePublisherIF`). This means only one `Publisher` object can exist on each host machine. A production quality implementation of the Publish-Subscribe pattern should allow each `Publisher` object to have a unique and well-known name.

The `Publisher` class has a method to allow `Subscriber` objects to register to receive messages associated with a given topic from a `Publisher` object.

```
public void addSubscriber(RemoteSubscriberIF subscriber,
                          Serializable topic) {
    ArrayList subscriberList;
    subscriberList = (ArrayList)subscribers.get(topic);
    if (subscriberList == null) {
        subscriberList = new ArrayList();
        subscribers.put(topic, subscriberList);
    } // if null
    subscriberList.add(subscriber);
} // addSubscriber(RemoteSubscriberIF, Serializable)
```

Multiple calls to this method can associate a `Subscriber` object with multiple topics. There is no checking to see if a `Subscriber` object is already subscribed to a given topic. Publisher objects trust Subscriber objects not to have multiple registrations for the same topic at the same time. You may want your implementation of the Publisher class to check for this.

Notice that there is no reference to the Subscriber class. The Publisher class references the Subscriber class indirectly through the RemoteSubscriberIF interface, which declares all of the Subscriber class methods that will be called remotely.

The Publisher class also has a method that a Subscriber object can call to tell a Publisher object to stop sending messages related to a given topic.

```
public void removeSubscriber(RemoteSubscriberIF subscriber,
                             Serializable topic) {
    ArrayList subscriberList;
    subscriberList = (ArrayList)subscribers.get(topic);
    if (subscriberList != null && subscriberList.size()>0) {
        int index = subscriberList.indexOf(subscriber);
        if (index >= 0) {
            subscriberList.remove(index);
        } // if
    } // if size>0
} // removeSubscriber
```

Finally, the Publisher class implements the deliverMessage method declared by the PublisherIF interface. Other objects call a Publisher object's deliverMessage method so it will deliver a message associated with a given topic.

```
public void deliverMessage(Serializable message,
                           Serializable topic)
                                    throws RemoteException {
    ArrayList subscriberList;
    subscriberList = (ArrayList)subscribers.get(topic);
    if (subscriberList != null) {
        int subscriberCount = subscriberList.size();
        for (int i=0; i<subscriberCount; i++) {
            RemoteSubscriberIF subscriber;
            subscriber
              = (RemoteSubscriberIF)subscriberList.get(i);
            subscriber.deliverMessage(message, topic);
        } // for
    } // if null
} // deliverMessage(Serializable, Serializable)
} // class Publisher
```

Here is the RemotePublisherIF interface that allows Subscriber objects to communicate with Publisher objects using RMI.

```
public interface RemotePublisherIF extends Remote {
    // The name of all publishers
    public static final String PUBLISHER_NAME = "publisher";
```

In this example, both the `Publisher` class and the `Subscriber` class use this constant for the name of all `Publisher` objects. Most real-world implementations require a more sophisticated naming scheme.

```
public void addSubscriber(RemoteSubscriberIF subscriber,
                          Serializable topic)
     throws RemoteException;

public void removeSubscriber(RemoteSubscriberIF subscriber,
                             Serializable topic)
     throws RemoteException;
} // interface RemotePublisherIF
```

The subscriber counterpart to this interface is the `RemoteSubscriberIF` interface. The `RemoteSubscriberIF` interface declares all of the methods of the `Subscriber` class that may be called remotely using RMI.

```
public interface RemoteSubscriberIF extends Remote {
   public void deliverMessage(Serializable message,
                              Serializable topic)
      throws RemoteException;
} // interface RemoteSubscriberIF
```

The `deliverMessage` method that the `RemoteSubscriberIF` interface declares is similar in nature to the `Publisher` class's `deliverMessage` method. When a message source object calls a `Publisher` object's `deliverMessage` method, it delivers the given message to `Subscriber` objects that have registered for the given topic. `Publisher` objects deliver messages to `Subscriber` objects by calling a `Subscriber` object's `deliverMessage` method. A `Subscriber` object's `deliverMessage` method in turn delivers messages to recipient objects that have registered to receive messages associated with the given topic.

Here is the Subscriber class:

```
public class Subscriber extends UnicastRemoteObject
                  implements SubscriberIF,
                             RemoteSubscriberIF {
```

This implementation of the `Subscriber` class is structurally similar to the preceding implementation of the `Publisher` class. It keeps track of objects that will receive messages using the same data structure. It uses a `HashMap` with the topic as the key and a list of recipient objects as the value.

```
     private HashMap listeners;
```

The reason that the name of this `HashMap` instance variable is `listeners` is that `Subscriber` objects communicate with message recipient objects using Java's delegation event model. `Subscriber` objects encapsulate message-topic pairs in event objects and deliver the event objects to the recipient objects. Using Java's event terminology, the recipient objects receive messages by listening for events.

The advantage to encapsulating messages in events is that it makes it easier to treat `Subscriber` objects as JavaBeans and use them with tools that manipulate beans.

```
/**
 * The publisher object's proxy.
 */
private RemotePublisherIF publisher;
```

This implementation of Publish-Subscribe allows each `Subscriber` object to work with only a single `Publisher` object. It works with the `Publisher` object through a proxy object that implements the `RemotePublisherIF` interface. The `Subscriber` object's constructor is responsible for creating the proxy for the `Publisher` object.

```
public Subscriber(String publisherHost)
                      throws RemoteException,
                             UnknownHostException,
                             NotBoundException,
                             MalformedURLException {
    listeners = new HashMap();
    String urlName = "//" + publisherHost
      + "/" + RemotePublisherIF.PUBLISHER_NAME;
    publisher = (RemotePublisherIF)Naming.lookup(urlName);
} // constructor()
```

The constructor identifies the `Publisher` object that the `Subscriber` object will work with by combining the name of the host on which the object resides with the name defined in the `RemotePublisherIF` interface. It combines these into a URL string that it passes to `java.rmi.Naming.lookup`, which consults the appropriate RMI registry to get the proxy to the `Publisher` object.

The event class that `Subscriber` objects use to encapsulate messages is called `MessageEvent` and is shown later in this section. Following the naming conventions of the event model, the name of the method that a recipient object calls to register to receive messages is `addMessageListener`.

```
synchronized
    public void addMessageListener(MessageListener listener,
                              Serializable topic)
                          throws RemoteException,
                                 NotBoundException {
    ArrayList listenerList;
    listenerList = (ArrayList)listeners.get(topic);
    if (listenerList == null) {
```

```
        listenerList = new ArrayList();
        listeners.put(topic, listenerList);
    } // if null
    if (listenerList.size()==0) {
        subscribe(topic);
    } // if size==0
    listenerList.add(listener);
} // addMessageListener(MessageListener, Serializable)
```

A listener object can make multiple calls to the `addMessageListener` method to register itself to receive messages on multiple topics. As implemented, multiple calls with the same listener and topic can result in the same message being delivered to the listener multiple times. This behavior can be avoided by adding appropriate checks.

```
// Add this subscriber and the given topic to the publisher.
private void subscribe(Serializable topic)
                            throws RemoteException,
                                    NotBoundException {
    publisher.addSubscriber(this, topic);
} // subscribe(Serializable)
```

Here is a method that recipient objects call when they no longer want to receive messages related to a given topic.

```
public void removeMessageListener(MessageListener listener,
                                    Serializable topic)
                            throws RemoteException,
                                    NotBoundException {
    ArrayList listenerList;
    listenerList = (ArrayList)listeners.get(topic);
    if (listenerList != null && listenerList.size()>0) {
        int index = listenerList.indexOf(listener);
        if (index >= 0) {
            listenerList.remove(index);
            if (listenerList.size() == 0) {
                unsubscribe(topic);
            } // if size
        } // if
    } // if size>0
} // removeMessageListener(MessageListener, Serializable)

// Add this subscriber and the given topic to the publisher.
private void unsubscribe(Serializable topic)
                            throws RemoteException,
                                    NotBoundException {
    publisher.removeSubscriber(this, topic);
} // subscribe(Serializable)
```

Publisher objects call this method remotely so that a `Subscriber` object will deliver a message to its listeners.

```
    public void deliverMessage(Serializable message,
                               Serializable topic) {
        ArrayList listenerList;
        listenerList = (ArrayList)listeners.get(topic);
        if (listenerList != null) {
            int listenerCount = listenerList.size();
            MessageEvent evt;
            evt = new MessageEvent(this, message, topic);
            for (int i=0; i<listenerCount; i++) {
                MessageListener listener;
                listener
                  = (MessageListener)listenerList.get(i);
                listener.receiveMessage(evt);
            } // for
        } // if null
    } // deliverMessage(Serializable, Serializable)
} // class Subscriber
```

This example concludes with the `SubscriberIF` interface that declares the methods of the `Subscriber` class that a recipient object can call.

```
public interface SubscriberIF {
    public void addMessageListener(MessageListener listener,
                                   Serializable topic)
                       throws RemoteException,
                               NotBoundException;
    public void removeMessageListener(MessageListener listener,
                                      Serializable topic)
                       throws RemoteException,
                               NotBoundException;
} // SubscriberIF
```

RELATED PATTERNS

Object Request Broker.   The Publish-Subscribe pattern is often used with the Object Request Broker pattern to deliver messages to remote objects.

Mailbox.   The Mailbox pattern provides an alternative solution for the delivery of messages.

Registry.   The registry pattern provides a way for `Subscriber` objects to find `Publisher` objects.

Retransmission.   The Retransmission pattern is often used with the Publish-Subscribe pattern to ensure reliable delivery of messages.

Retransmission

The pattern is based on material that is discussed in [Doeringer90].

SYNOPSIS

You need to ensure that an object can reliably send a message to a remote object. Following the maxim, "If at first you don't succeed, try again," you design the object to handle a failure to send a message by having it try again until the send is successful.

CONTEXT

Suppose you are designing a system to reliably transmit events to remote objects. Sometimes, an attempt to transmit an event to a client will fail. When it is not possible to deliver results to a subscriber immediately, the system must deliver the results to the subscriber at the earliest possible opportunity.

FORCES

- ☺ An object is required to reliably deliver a message to another object.
- ☺ Attempts to deliver a message sometimes fail.
- ☺ Using a server to ensure reliable delivery by repeating delivery attempts means that it is possible to deliver a message after the message source has stopped running. It also facilitates the gathering of delivery statistics.
- ☹ Some applications require events to be delivered immediately or not at all.

SOLUTION

Make a server object responsible for delivering messages to other objects. Have the server object handle failed attempts to deliver messages by repeating the attempt until it succeeds.

Figure 6.9 shows the roles that classes and interfaces play in the Retransmission pattern. Here are descriptions of the roles shown in Figure 6.9:

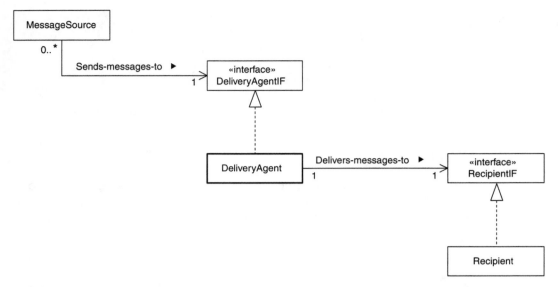

FIGURE 6.9 Retransmission pattern.

MessageSource.   Classes in this role create messages and pass them to an object that implements the `DeliveryAgentIF` interface. Any class that contains calls to `DeliveryAgentIF` methods fills this role.

DeliveryAgentIF.   Classes in the `DeliveryAgent` role implement this interface.

DeliveryAgent.   `MessageSource` objects pass messages to instances of classes in this role. When a message is passed to a `DeliveryAgent` object, it takes responsibility for delivering the message to a `RecipientIF` object. If its first attempt to deliver the message fails, it keeps repeating the attempt until it succeeds.

RecipientIF.   Classes in the `Recipient` role implement this interface.

Recipient.   Instances of classes in this role receive messages from `DeliveryAgent` objects.

CONSEQUENCES

☺ Use of the Retransmission pattern allows the reliable delivery of messages to recipients.

☺ Making message delivery the responsibility of an object dedicated to message delivery rather than the responsibility of the message source provides some important benefits. Even if it takes a long time to successfully deliver a message, the program that initiated a message is free to terminate before the message is delivered. Also, the efforts to deliver the message do not take resources away from the program that was the message source. The message source does not even have to know the quantity or identity of its message's recipients.

IMPLEMENTATION

The `DeliveryAgent` object bears the responsibility for ensuring the reliable delivery of messages. To be able to deliver a message after a crash, messages waiting to be delivered must be stored on disk or other nonvolatile medium. Another way of dealing with crashes is to make them very unlikely by using the High Availability pattern.

An implementation of the Retransmission pattern will be expected to deliver each message exactly once. One way to be certain that a delivery attempt succeeded is to have the `Recipient` object send an acknowledgment back to the `DeliveryAgent` object when it receives a message. If the `DeliveryAgent` object passes messages to the `Recipient` object with synchronous method calls, then the normal return of the method call serves as an implicit acknowledgment.

The Retransmission pattern is normally implemented using an ORB. If you implement the Retransmission pattern with RMI, you will always have an acknowledgment, since the only kind of call that RMI supports is a synchronous call. Some ORBs, such as CORBA and Voyager, in addition to supporting synchronous calls also support a type of asynchronous call that does not provide any sort of acknowledgment. This type of call is not usually appropriate for use with the Retransmission pattern.

To ensure that message delivery will continue if there is a crash, there must be a mechanism to automatically restart the `DeliveryAgent` object. You can use the Process Pair pattern to restart the `DeliveryAgent` object.

After a `DeliveryAgent` object delivers a message, it will typically discard the message or mark it delivered. If the `DeliveryAgent` object restarts between the time that a message is delivered and the time it discards or marks the message, then the `DeliveryAgent` object will not know that it delivered the message. It will try to deliver the message again.

`Recipient` objects can solve the problem of duplicate messages by recognizing and discarding them. `DeliveryAgent` objects can simplify the task of recognizing duplicate messages by ensuring that if a `Recipient` object receives duplicate messages they will be consecutive. This, in combination with assigning sequential message IDs, makes the recognition of duplicate messages very simple.

Over time, a `DeliveryAgent` object may accumulate undeliverable messages. For that reason, it may be necessary to place a time limit on how long a `DeliveryAgent` object will try to deliver a message before discarding it. Placing such a time limit on the lifetime of a message prevents the collection of undeliverable messages from growing indefinitely.

After a `DeliveryAgent` object fails to deliver a message, it attempts to redeliver the message. The more frequently it attempts redelivery, the less time is likely to elapse between when it becomes possible to successfully deliver the message and when it is actually delivered. However, the more frequently it attempts redelivery, the more bandwidth is wasted. If bandwidth is a concern, you must compromise between how quickly a failed-delivery message is delivered and wasting bandwidth.

This compromise is generally handled in one of two ways. The simpler of the two is to establish a fixed amount of time between delivery attempts. Another approach is to take advantage of the observation that the more time that has elapsed since the first attempt to deliver a message failed, the more time is likely to elapse until a delivery attempt can be successful. Based on this, a more sophisticated strategy that wastes less network bandwidth is to gradually increase the time between delivery attempts until it reaches a maximum.

KNOWN USES

A number of middleware packages use the Retransmission pattern for reliable distribution of messages. Simple Mail Transport Protocol (SMTP) servers (Internet mail servers) use the Retransmission pattern to forward mail to each other. The Transmission Control Protocol/Internet Protocol (TCP/IP) uses retransmission to ensure reliable delivery of data.

CODE EXAMPLE

The Retransmission pattern is usually used in combination with another pattern that involves the delivery of messages. The Retransmission pattern is commonly used with the Publish-Subscribe pattern. The code example for the Retransmission pattern is an extension to the Publish-Subscribe pattern that uses the Retransmission pattern. The example is a subclass of the `Publisher` class that overrides the `deliverMessage` method so that it will attempt to redeliver a message if the initial delivery attempt fails.

```
public class ReliablePublisher extends Publisher {
```

The following two constants determine the minimum amount of time that will elapse between redelivery attempts and how much time must elapse before attempts to redeliver a message are abandoned.

```
private static final long REDELIVERY_INTERVAL
    = 2*60*1000;                    // 2 minutes

private static final long EXPIRATION_INTERVAL
    =3*24*60*60*1000;               // 3 days
```

The `ReliablePublisher` class declares a private class named `RedeliveryAgent`. The `RedeliveryAgent` class is responsible for asynchronously making redelivery attempts for messages whose initial delivery attempt failed.

```
private RedeliveryAgent redeliverer = new RedeliveryAgent();
...
```

The `Deliver` method is responsible for the initial attempt to deliver a message.

```
public void deliverMessage(Serializable message,
                           Serializable topic) {
    ArrayList subscriberList;
    subscriberList = getSubscriberList(topic);
    if (subscriberList != null) {
        int subscriberCount = subscriberList.size();
        for (int i=0; i<subscriberCount; i++) {
            RemoteSubscriberIF subscriber;
            subscriber
              = (RemoteSubscriberIF)subscriberList.get(i);
            try {
                subscriber.deliverMessage(message, topic);
            } catch (RemoteException e) {
                Redelivery r;
                r = new Redelivery (subscriber,
                                    message,
                                    topic);
                redeliverer.scheduleRedelivery(r);
            } // try
        } // for
    } // if null
} // deliverMessage(Serializable, Serializable)
```

If an initial delivery attempt to a subscriber fails, the `delivery-Message` method calls the `redeliverer` object's `scheduleRedelivery` method. It schedules asynchronous redelivery attempts.

The `Redelivery` class is another private class. The `RedeliveryAgent` class requires that the information for a redelivery is contained in an instance of the `Redelivery` class.

```
private static class Redelivery {
    RemoteSubscriberIF subscriber;
    Serializable message;
    Serializable topic;
    long timeOfOriginalFailure;
    Date nextRedeliveryTime;

    Redelivery(RemoteSubscriberIF subscriber,
                Serializable message,
                Serializable topic) {
        this.subscriber = subscriber;
        this.message = message;
        this.topic = topic;
        this.timeOfOriginalFailure = System.currentTimeMillis();
        this.nextRedeliveryTime = new Date(timeOfOriginalFailure);
    } // constructor
} // class Redelivery
```

Here is the `RedeliveryAgent` class. In order to support asynchronous redelivery attempts, the `RedeliveryAgent` class implements the `Runnable` interface. This allows it to have its own thread.

```
private static class RedeliveryAgent implements Runnable {
    private TreeMap schedule = new TreeMap();
```

A `RedeliveryAgent` object uses a `TreeMap` to maintain a collection of redelivery objects in the order in which their redelivery is scheduled.

The `RedeliveryAgent` constructor starts the thread that will be responsible for redelivery attempts.

```
RedeliveryAgent() {

    new Thread(this).start();
} // constructor()
```

Here is the method that schedules redelivery attempts.

```
synchronized void scheduleRedelivery(Redelivery r) {
    long nextRedeliveryTime
      = System.currentTimeMillis()+REDELIVERY_INTERVAL;
    long elapsedTime
      = nextRedeliveryTime-r.timeOfOriginalFailure;
    if (elapsedTime>EXPIRATION_INTERVAL) {
        // Too much time has elapsed; give up.
        return;
    } // if
    r.nextRedeliveryTime.setTime(nextRedeliveryTime);
    schedule.put(r.nextRedeliveryTime, r);
    notify();
} // scheduleRedelivery(Redelivery)
```

The scheduleRedelivery method always schedules the next redelivery attempt into the future by a fixed amount of time. Many applications will run more efficiently with a more sophisticated policy for determining the time of the next redelivery. Such policies typically involved strategies such as randomization and using progressively longer intervals between redelivery attempts.

The run method contains the top-level logic for making redelivery attempts. It waits for the next scheduled redelivery attempt. When the time comes, it attempts to deliver the scheduled message. If the attempt fails, it calls scheduleRedelivery to schedule the next redelivery attempt.

```java
public void run() {
    while (!Thread.currentThread().isInterrupted()) {
        Redelivery r;
        try {
            r = waitForNextRedeliveryTime();
        } catch (InterruptedException e) {
            return;
        } // try
        try {
            r.subscriber.deliverMessage(r.message, r.topic);
        } catch (RemoteException e) {
            scheduleRedelivery(r);
        } // try
    } // while
} // run
```

The last method in this example is called to get the next scheduled redelivery. If no message is scheduled for redelivery, it waits until there is one. If a message is scheduled for redelivery and its time for redelivery has not come yet, it waits. Otherwise, it attempts a redelivery. If the redelivery is unsuccessful, it schedules the next redelivery for the message. Then it checks again for the next redelivery.

```java
private synchronized
  Redelivery waitForNextRedeliveryTime()
                        throws InterruptedException {
    while (true) {
        if (schedule.size()==0) {
            wait();
        } else {
            Date when = (Date)schedule.firstKey();
            long nextRedeliveryTime = when.getTime();
            long now = System.currentTimeMillis();
            if (nextRedeliveryTime>now) {
                return
                    (Redelivery)schedule.remove(when);
            } else {
                wait(nextRedeliveryTime-now);
            } // if
```

```
            } // if size
        } // while
    } // waitForNextRedeliveryTime()
  } // class RedeliveryAgent
} // class ReliablePublisher
```

RELATED PATTERNS

Object Request Broker.   The Retransmission pattern is often used with the Object Request Broker pattern to deliver messages to remote objects.

Mailbox.   The Mailbox pattern provides an alternate solution for the reliable delivery of messages.

High Availability.   You can use the High Availability pattern to minimize the likelihood that a `DeliveryAgent` object will crash or become otherwise unavailable.

Process Pair.   The Process Pair pattern describes a way to ensure that a `DeliveryAgent` object is automatically restarted after a crash.

Publish-Subscribe.   The Retransmission pattern is often used with the Publish-Subscribe pattern to ensure reliable delivery of messages.

Mailbox

SYNOPSIS

You need to provide reliable delivery of messages to objects. Facilitate the delivery of messages by storing messages for later retrieval by each recipient.

CONTEXT

Suppose that you work for an advertising agency. One way that the advertising agency makes money is by buying advertising time on TV, radio, and Web pages on behalf of its customers. The agency's customers prefer to buy advertising through the agency rather than directly for two reasons.

- The agency buys advertising time on behalf of many customers. Because of that, it buys advertising time in greater quantity than any one customer would. Because of the large volume of advertising time the agency buys, it is able to negotiate better prices than its customers can by negotiating individually.
- The value of advertising time to an advertiser is determined by how many people are expected to see the advertisement and how many of these people are the sort whom the advertiser expects to buy its product. For example, advertising time on a financial news TV show will be much more valuable to a manufacturer of luxury cars than to a toy manufacturer. By being able to accurately predict the quantity and type of people that will see an ad, the agency is able to get better results from ads than the advertisers themselves would be.

Advertising agencies use professional negotiators to negotiate the purchase of advertising time. They often do this working face-to-face with sellers of advertising. To get the best deal for the advertisers, they use a computer program running on a portable computer. The program determines the value of advertising time to each of their advertiser clients.

To make this determination of value, the program requires a great deal of information. To be as accurate as possible, the information must be as up-to-date as possible. Because the computer on which it runs is mobile, the program is not always able to connect to its source of information.

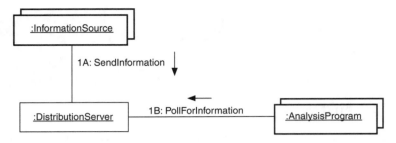

FIGURE 6.10 Reliable delivery of Information.

You must ensure that the program receives all information sent to it, whether or not the information source is able to connect to the program when it sends information. The architecture shown in Figure 6.10 is used to provide reliable delivery of the information to the program.

The way it works is that `InformationSource` objects send information to a `DistributionServer` object. Instances of the program poll the `DistributionServer` object for new information when they are able to connect to the `DistributionServer` object.

The negotiation process is specialized by advertising medium. Negotiations for TV, radio, print media, and Internet are conducted separately. For that reason, the set of information needed by each instance of the program depends on the specialization of the negotiator using it. For that reason, each piece of information is addressed only to the negotiators who will need it. When each instance of the program polls for new information, it receives only information that is addressed to the negotiator using it.

FORCES

☺ Asynchronous delivery of messages is desirable.

☺ It is not always possible to establish a connection with the intended recipient of a message.

☺ It is acceptable for messages to be delivered an indefinite amount of time after they are originally sent.

☺ Messages must be delivered to remote recipients.

☺ You want to minimize the resources required to send a message to multiple recipients.

☺ Messages are sent at sufficiently regular intervals that when the recipients poll for messages, much of the time there will be messages waiting for them.

☺ Communication between remote objects is less reliable than communication between local objects. There is usually less bandwidth available for communication between remote objects than between local objects. In the extreme case, remote objects may be able to communicate only a small portion of the time.

☺ It is more efficient of bandwidth to deliver multiple messages to a recipient as a single batch than it is to deliver them individually.

☺ Ensuring reliable delivery means that it should be possible for a message to be delivered after the message source has stopped running.

☹ If messages are sent at very irregular intervals, most of the time a potential recipient polls for messages there will be none, which is a waste of bandwidth.

☹ If a large number of potential recipients poll for messages at the same time, the server polled may be overwhelmed.

SOLUTION

Message sources send messages to a mailbox server along with a tag indicating the message's intended recipient. Potential message recipients poll the mailbox server for messages. Figure 6.11 shows the roles played by classes and interfaces in this pattern.

Here are descriptions of the roles in Figure 6.11 that classes and interfaces play in the Mailbox pattern:

MessageSource.   Classes in this role originate messages. They pass the messages to a possibly remote object that implements the MailboxIF interface along with a list of the message's intended recipients.

MailboxIF.   Classes in the MailboxServer role implement this interface. Such classes are responsible for storing messages until recipient objects poll for them.

MailboxServer.   Classes in this role implement the MailboxIF interface and are responsible for storing messages until a Recipient object polls for them.

RecipientID.   Objects in this role identify a unique Recipient object.

Mailbox.   MailboxServer objects maintain a collection of objects in this role. Each Mailbox is associated with a different RecipientID. Each Mailbox collects messages associated with its RecipientID. Messages associated with more than one RecipientID are collected in the mailbox associated with each of the RecipientID objects.

Message.   Classes in this role encapsulate messages.

Recipient.   Classes in this role are responsible for polling objects that implement the MailboxIF interface for messages.

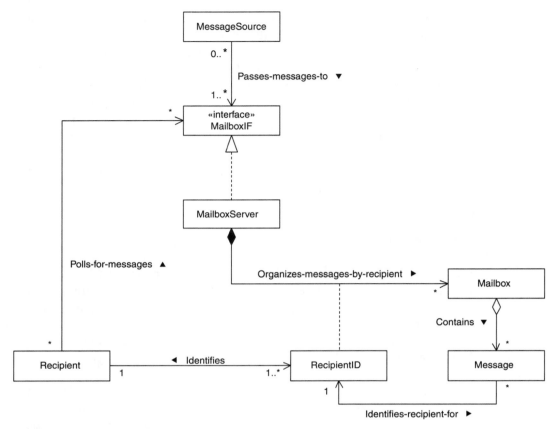

FIGURE 6.11 Mailbox pattern.

RecipientID objects identify instances of these classes. When Recipient objects poll a MailboxIF object for messages, they present it with the RecipientID objects that identify them.

CONSEQUENCES

☺ The Mailbox pattern provides reliable delivery of messages.

☺ Making message delivery the responsibility of an object dedicated to message delivery rather than the responsibility of the message source provides some important benefits. Even if it takes a long time to successfully deliver a message, the program that initiated a message is free to terminate before the message is delivered. Also, the efforts to deliver the message do not take resources away from the program that was the message source. The message source does not even have to know the quantity or identity of its message's recipients.

☺ The use of the Mailbox pattern may consume less network bandwidth than the Publish-Subscribe pattern. The Publish-Subscribe pattern uses network bandwidth for delivery attempts that fail. The Mailbox pattern does not have this overhead.

☺ When `Recipient` objects poll for messages, they may receive more than one message. By making it more likely that `Recipient` objects will receive multiple messages using a single connection, the use of network bandwidth is further reduced.

☺ Changing the actual `Mailbox` class used is transparent to `MessageSource` and `Recipient` objects because of the way the pattern uses interfaces.

☹ There is generally a delay between the time a message is sent and the time it is received. Most of the delay is attributable to the time between successful polling attempts by the recipient.

IMPLEMENTATION

Usually, the Mailbox pattern is implemented by buying software for that purpose rather than writing an implementation from scratch. Implementing the pattern reliably and with all of the features you want is usually more expensive to do in-house than it is to buy.

In order to provide reliable delivery of messages, a `MailboxServer` must store messages in a reliable way until a `Recipient` object polls for them. To do that, messages and `Mailbox` objects must be stored on non-volatile storage, such as a disk file.

`MailboxServer` classes may be implemented to accept only messages associated with `RecipientID` objects that it has prior knowledge of. Alternatively, `MailboxServer` classes may be implemented to accept messages associated with any `RecipientID` object. This is largely a trade-off between security and the needs of the application.

The security risk is that a `MailboxServer` object may become flooded with messages for a nonexistent `RecipientID` that is never polled for. There are other reasons messages may arrive at a `MailboxServer` object without being polled for. A common strategy to prevent such messages from becoming a problem is to delete such unpolled-for messages after a predetermined amount of time has passed.

Another security consideration may be authenticating `Recipient` objects. In some environments, there is a risk that malicious `Recipient` objects will poll for messages that are not intended for them. In such environments, you will need a way to verify that a `Recipient` object is entitled to receive messages associated with each `RecipientID` that it polls for.

KNOWN USES

E-mail is one of the oldest examples of the Mailbox pattern and also the source of the name. Most e-mail systems collect messages in mailboxes until people read them.

Electronic Data Interchange (EDI) messages are often sent using the Mailbox pattern.

IBM's MQSeries software supports message distribution using the Mailbox pattern.

CODE EXAMPLE

Here are some classes that provide a very basic implementation of the Mailbox pattern. They are designed to communicate with message sources and recipients using RMI. We begin with the MailboxIF interface:

```
public interface MailboxIF {
    public void sendMessage(Serializable msg, String[] recipients)
                throws RemoteException;

    public ArrayList receiveMessages(String[] recipients)
                                    throws RemoteException ;
} // interface MailboxIF
```

This MailboxIF interface has two methods. The sendMessage method is called by message sources. They pass it a message to send and an array of recipient IDs identifying the mailboxes to place the messages in. Recipient objects call the receiveMessages method and pass it an array of recipient IDs. The recipient IDs identify the mailboxes to poll for messages.

This implementation of the Mailbox pattern accepts any object as a message if its class implements the Serializable interface. More sophisticated implementations of the Mailbox pattern impose more structure on messages. This implementation of the Mailbox pattern uses strings as recipient IDs.

Here is an implementation of the MailboxServer class:

```
public class MailboxServer extends UnicastRemoteObject
                                    implements MailboxIF {
    private Hashtable mailboxes;
...
```

The implementation uses a Hashtable to organize its mailboxes.

```
    /**
     * Send a message to the given list of recipients.
     */
```

```
public void sendMessage(Serializable msg,
                        String[] recipients) {
    for (int i=0; i<recipients.length; i++) {
        Mailbox m = (Mailbox)mailboxes.get(recipients[i]);
        if (m!=null) {          // if recipient is registered
            m.addMessage(msg);
        } // if
    } // for
} // sendMessage(Serializable, String[])
```

This implementation ignores requests to send messages to recipients that do not already have mailboxes set up. Mailboxes are set up by separate methods for administering mailboxes.

Here is the method that recipients call to poll for messages.

```
/**
 * Receive messages intended for a given set of recipients.
 * @return An array of messages.
 */
public ArrayList receiveMessages(String[] recipients)
                                throws RemoteException {
    ArrayList outgoing = null;
    for (int i=0; i<recipients.length; i++) {
        Mailbox m = (Mailbox)mailboxes.get(recipients[i]);
        if (m!=null) {
            if (outgoing==null) {
                outgoing = m.getMessages();
            } else {
                outgoing.addAll(m.getMessages());
            } // if outgoing
        } // if m
    } // for
    if (outgoing==null) {
        return new ArrayList();
    } else {
        return outgoing;
    } // if
} // receiveMessages(String[])
```

Here are the administrative methods for adding and removing mailboxes. Note that these methods are not part of the `MailboxIF` interface, so message sources and recipients cannot call them.

```
/**
 * Register a recipient id so that it has a mailbox.
 */
public void registerRecipient(String recipient) {
    mailboxes.put(recipient, new Mailbox());
} // registerRecipient(String)

/**
 * Unregister a recipient so that it doesn't have a
```

```
    * mailbox.
    */
   public void unregisterRecipient(String recipient) {
       mailboxes.remove(recipient);
   } // unregisterRecipient(String)
} // class MailboxServer
```

Finally, here is the `Mailbox` class.

```
class Mailbox {
    private ArrayList messages = new ArrayList();

    /**
     * Add a message to this mailbox.
     */
    synchronized void addMessage(Serializable message) {
        messages.add(message);
    } // addMessage(Serializable)

    /**
     * Remove all of the messages from the mailbox and return them in an
     * array.
     */
    synchronized ArrayList getMessages() {
        ArrayList temp = (ArrayList)messages.clone();
        messages.clear();
        return temp;
    } // getMessages()
} // class Mailbox
```

RELATED PATTERNS

Publish-Subscribe. The Publish-Subscribe pattern provides an alternative solution for the reliable delivery of messages.

High Availability. The High Availability pattern can be used to ensure that a `MailboxServer` is highly available.

Object Request Broker. The Mailbox pattern is often used with the Object Request Broker pattern to deliver messages to remote objects.

Process Pair. The Process Pair pattern describes a way to ensure that a `MailboxServer` object is automatically restarted after a crash.

Registry. The registry pattern provides a way for `Subscriber` objects to find `MailboxServer` objects.

Heavyweight/Lightweight

SYNOPSIS

You are designing an application client that should be as small and thin as possible. The client must access some objects that have many attributes and/or attributes that are large objects. The client does not always need the attributes, so you arrange for the client to download the objects without the attributes and then lazily download the attributes as needed.

CONTEXT

Suppose you work for a company that operates a chain of superstores that sell building materials, hardware, floor coverings, appliances, and everything else you would need to build and furnish a house. To promote the sale of kitchen cabinets and appliances, you have been given the task of designing an application that customers will use to design a kitchen and then order everything in the design with the push of a button.

The system architecture calls for the client portion of the program to take the form of an applet. To minimize memory requirements and download times, the applet should be as small and thin as possible.

As the user selects cabinets, counter, appliances, and other things for the kitchen, the applet will need to display them as they will appear in the customer's kitchen. In order to do this in a fast and responsive way, the applet must download the objects that correspond to these things so that it has local access to these things.

The need to download these objects is at odds with the goal of keeping the applet as small as possible. All of these objects have another set of objects associated with them as attribute values. Some objects, especially appliances, have many attributes associated with them. Even without the appliances, the shear number of pieces that go into a kitchen can add up to a large number of attribute objects.

You observe that the applet does not usually use most of the attributes of the objects it downloads. Based on this observation, you decide to put attributes of objects that clients do not usually use into a separate object that is not downloaded unless needed. You organize the classes of objects the client will be downloading as shown in Figure 6.12.

Figure 6.12 shows how you organize the class for just one kind of item, a kitchen sink. A similar organization applies to many other kinds of

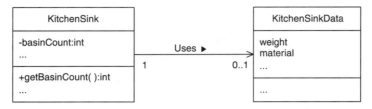

FIGURE 6.12 Class organization.

items. It includes a `KitchenSink` class that contains attributes that are always needed on both the client and the server.

Kitchen sink attributes that clients need only occasionally are in the `KitchenSinkData` class. On the server, instances of the `KitchenSink` class always have an associated instance of the `KitchenSinkData` class. On the client, instances of the `KitchenSink` class download an associated instance of the `KitchenSinkData` class only when they need it.

FORCES

☺ You want to keep the memory requirements for the client part of a program as small as possible.

☺ You want to minimize delays related to downloading data for the client part of a program.

☺ The client shares objects with the server. The client uses the shared objects occasionally or not at all.

☺ When the client does use the attributes of shared objects, it uses them enough so that it is much faster to copy them to the client in bulk than to access them remotely.

☹ If an operation initiated on the client requires access to a large amount of data on the server, it may be faster to perform the operation on the server than to copy the data to the client.

SOLUTION

Servers often need to share objects with their clients. A server may need to share an object that has much associated data that its client does not usually use. To reduce the client's memory requirements, create a lightweight version of the object for the client to use.

Figure 6.13 shows the roles that classes and interfaces play in the Heavyweight/Lightweight pattern.

SharedItem. Classes in this role are shared between a server and its client. They do not declare instance variables for data they

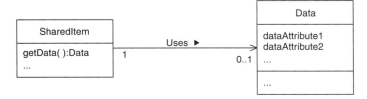

FIGURE 6.13 Heavyweight/lightweight pattern.

do not usually use, except for instance variables that refer to `Data` objects. When an instance of a `SharedItem` class is copied from a server to a client, its associated `Data` objects are not copied.

    `SharedItem` classes have a method that returns a reference to its instance's associated `Data` object. The client calls this when it wants to download the `Data` object.

Data. Instances of classes in this role contain instance data for a `SharedItem` object. A `Data` object is created for every `Shared-Item` object in a server environment. `SharedItem` objects are copied to a `client` environment without `Data` objects.

`Data` objects contain only instance data that is not usually used in the client environment. Instance data usually needed in the client environment is contained directly by `SharedItem` objects.

CONSEQUENCES

☺ If objects shared between a client and a server have data associated with them that is rarely used on the client, the use of a `Data` class is beneficial. In such a situation, putting data in a `Data` object that is copied from the server only when needed reduces the time spent downloading data and the amount of memory that data takes up on the client.

☹ If the assumption about the data being infrequently used on the client is wrong, then the use of `Data` objects will have the opposite effect. More time will be spent downloading data, and it will consume more memory on the client.

☹ The Heavyweight/Lightweight pattern increases the complexity of a design. It can result in your replacing one class with multiple classes. You may also need to add logic to manage the downloading of `Data` objects.

IMPLEMENTATION

It may be the case that not all of the data in a Data object is needed on the client at the same time. Because of the way the Heavyweight/Lightweight pattern works, all of the data in a Data object is downloaded together, whether or not it is needed at that time. If a large enough set of data attributes are not needed when the rest of the data is needed, then it may be advantageous to organize them into a second Data object.

An extreme situation is having a data attribute whose value involves so much data that it is worth managing its download individually. Individually managed attributes involve download logic similar to the logic for Data objects. The difference is that the client object has an instance variable that directly references the data rather than referencing a Data object that references the data.

A more fundamental issue for implementing the Heavyweight/Lightweight pattern is how to manage the download of Data objects. If you implement the pattern as shown under the "Solution" heading, you will be using a client-specific class to represent the shared object on the client. Because it is specific to the situation, it is a reasonable design decision for the class to manage the download of Data objects themselves using the Lazy Initialization pattern (described in *Volume 2*). This involves accessing the Data object through a private method that downloads the Data object if it has not already been downloaded. You will find an example of this under the "Code Example" heading later in this pattern description.

One final and essential detail is the way that Data objects are downloaded. A SharedItem object on the client downloads the Data object associated with the corresponding SharedItem object on the server by calling its getData method, either directly or indirectly. How the SharedItem object on the client is able to call the SharedItem object on the server varies with the structure of the application. The SharedItem object on the client may call the SharedItem object on the server indirectly through the same client object that downloaded it. It may make the call directly. There are many other possibilities.

KNOWN USES

The Heavyweight/Lightweight pattern has been used in independent proprietary projects in four different companies that the author knows of.

CODE EXAMPLE

Data classes usually declare only instance variables. The logic that manipulates their content is in the corresponding SharedItem class.

```
class Data implements Serializable {
    int dataAttribute1;
    String dataAttribute2;
    ...
} // class Data
```

Here is the corresponding `SharedItem` class. The instance variable it uses to refer to a data object is declared `transient` so that when a `SharedItem` object is serialized for downloading, the `Data` object is not copied with it.

```
class SharedItem implements Serializable {
    private transient Data myData;
    private Foo foo;
    ...
```

The `foo` object referred to is a client object that will know how to download the `Data` object.

```
    public SharedItem() {
        myData = new Data();
        //...
    } // constructor()

    Data getData() {
        return myData;
    } // getData()

    int getDataAttribute1() {
        checkData();
        return myData.dataAttribute1;
    } // getDataAttribute1()

    String getDataAttribute2() {
        checkData();
        return myData.dataAttribute2;
    } // getDataAttribute2()
    ...
    private void checkData() {
        if (myData==null) {
            myData = foo.getData();
        } // if
    } // checkData()
} // class SharedItem
```

The `checkData` method is called before every access to the `Data` object to ensure that the `Data` object has been downloaded. On the server, the `Data` object is created by the `SharedItem` constructor, so `checkData` never has anything to do on the server.

RELATED PATTERNS

Object Request Broker.   The Heavyweight/Lightweight pattern is usually implemented using the Object Request Broker pattern to facilitate communication between the client and the server.

Lazy Initialization.   The Lazy Initialization pattern can be used to manage the download of `Data` objects if client objects are responsible for the download of their own `Data` object. The Lazy Initialization pattern is described in *Volume 2.*

Virtual Proxy.   The Virtual Proxy pattern should be used to manage the download of `Data` objects if the same class is used to implement the client and server version of the shared object. The Virtual Proxy pattern is described in *Volume 1.*

Object Replication.   The Object Replication pattern addresses issues related to keeping the state of the client and server objects consistent.

Façade.   Like a façade object, a lightweight object hides the details of accessing objects behind it. The Façade pattern is described in *Volume 1.*

Heartbeat

SYNOPSIS

While a remote object is performing an operation on behalf of a client, periodically send a message back to the client indicating that the remote object is still alive.

CONTEXT

Suppose you work for a company that sells enterprise software applications. You are involved in design of a purchasing application. The company will sell it to customers who will run the software in their own computing environments. The details of these environments will vary considerably in such ways as architecture and performance.

The purchasing application will have a multitiered architecture. Some pieces of software that make up the application are required to detect the failure of other pieces. For example, the client piece that users interact with is required to tell users that an operation is unable to complete if the server piece that it works with crashes. That is so the users will not waste time waiting for something to finish that will never finish.

The simplest way to determine that a remote operation will not complete is to establish a time limit for the operation's completions. If the operation does not complete in that amount of time, you assume that it will not complete. To use this technique successfully, you must be sure that the operation in question will complete in some particular amount of time. Since the companies that will be buying the software will have very different computing environments, it is not possible to assume how long it will take the software to perform an operation in a customer environment.

FORCES

☺ You need a way to decide that a remote operation will not complete.
☺ The amount of time that the remote operation takes to complete is highly variable, or you have no idea how long it will take.
☺ Even when you do have a reasonable idea of how long a remote operation should take, you should allow for some variation due to such factors as high load on the remote host or network congestion.

☹ Network bandwidth is limited and you want to minimize network traffic.

SOLUTION

Have the remote object performing an operation periodically make a call back to the waiting client. These callbacks are called *heartbeat messages.* Receipt of a heartbeat message tells the client that the remote object is still alive. If too much time elapses between heartbeat messages, the client assumes that the remote object is dead or inaccessible. Figure 6.14 shows the roles that classes and interfaces play in the Heartbeat pattern.

Here are descriptions of the roles shown in Figure 6.14:

Client.   Instances of classes in this role make remote calls to Server objects. When making a remote call to a Server object, a Client object passes information to the Server object that allows it to call a method of an associated HeartbeatListener object.

Server.   Classes in this role respond to remote method calls from Client objects. While processing calls, they make periodic calls to a method of an object that implements the HeartbeatListenerIF interface.

HeartbeatListenerIF.   Classes in the HeartbeatListener role implement this interface. Server objects call a method of a remote HeartbeatListener object through an interface in this role.

HeartbeatListener.   Classes in this role receive heartbeat messages from a Server object on behalf of a Client object while the Server object is processing a remote call from the Client

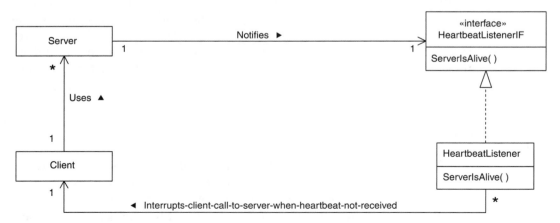

FIGURE 6.14 Heartbeat pattern.

object. If a `HeartbeatListener` object does not receive an expected heartbeat message within a certain amount of time, then the `HeartbeatListener` object is responsible for interrupting the `Client` object's call.

`HeartbeatListener` objects must be on the same physical host as their associated `Client` object.

The collaboration between the objects that participate in the Heartbeat pattern is shown in Figure 6.15.

Here are descriptions of the interactions shown in Figure 6.15:

1. A `Client` object calls its own `doIt` method. The method's implementation involves a call to the `Server` object's method `doIt` method.

1.1. Call a `HeartbeatListener` object's `startListening` method to tell it to start expecting to receive heartbeat messages.

1.2. The `Client` object calls the `Server` object's `doIt` method.

1.2.1A. The `Server` object does the things determined by its implementation of its `doIt` method.

1.2.1B. Between the time that the `Server` object's method is called and the time it returns, the `Server` object periodically sends heartbeat messages to the `HeartBeatListener` object so that it knows the `Server` object is still alive. The `Server` object sends these messages at regular and expected intervals.

1.2.1C. The `HeartBeatListener` object expects to receive heartbeat messages. It always expects to receive the next heartbeat message within a certain amount of time. This amount of time is called a *time-out interval*.

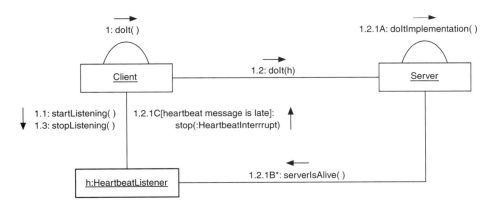

FIGURE 6.15 Heartbeat collaboration.

If the `HeartBeatListener` object does not receive the next heartbeat message before the time-out interval has elapsed, it interrupts the `Client` object's call to the `Server` object by forcing it to throw an exception. Since there may be some variation in the interval between the heartbeat messages, the selection of a time-out interval should account for such variations. It should be long enough to allow a high degree of certainty that something is wrong. It should be short enough to avoid wasting time. In many situations, the time-out is set to two to three times the expected interval between heartbeat messages.

CONSEQUENCES

☺ Use of the Heartbeat pattern allows client objects to determine that a remote object performing an operation is dead.

☺ The Heartbeat pattern also detects a loss of network connectivity with a remote object. However, it does not distinguish loss of network connectivity from the death of the remote object.

☹ The Heartbeat pattern does not detect situations where a remote object has experienced a failure that prevents it from completing an operation while still allowing it to send heartbeat messages as expected.

☹ The Heartbeat pattern also does not function well under heavy loads that interfere with a server's ability to send heartbeat messages on a timely basis. If the interval between heartbeat messages increases gradually, it may be possible for a clever implementation to notice the trend and adjust the time-out period. However, if a server or network is prone to sudden spikes in load, use of the Heartbeat pattern can result in the crash of a system due to a false alarm.

IMPLEMENTATION

The Heartbeat pattern is usually implemented within the context of the Object Request Broker pattern. The details of how you implement the Heartbeat pattern will vary with the ORB that you use. The variable part of the implementation is that you need to arrange for the server to be able to perform a callback to the client.

Some ORBs support one-way calls. One-way calls are invoked remotely and execute asynchronously, but the caller never gets any sort of notice that the call completed. This is the ideal call semantics for

Heartbeat calls, because it minimizes network traffic and does not require the caller to set aside resources to receive a call completion notice it does not need.

A second-best choice of call semantics is an asynchronous call. This does not require the server to wait for the heartbeat call to return. This works best when implemented by the ORB, since an ORB is generally able to handle asynchronous calls without needing any additional threads.

The RMI ORB that is used in the code example (as of the time this is being written) supports only synchronous calls. It does not support one-way or asynchronous calls.

The rest of the implementation involves arranging for the callbacks at periodic intervals. This is most straightforward when the ORB supports one-way or asynchronous call semantics. If the ORB supports one-way calls, then all that the Heartbeat implementation needs to be responsible for is making the heartbeat calls at a regular interval.

If the ORB does not support one-way calls but does support asynchronous calls, then before the Heartbeat implementation makes a heartbeat call, it should relieve the ORB of the results of previous calls. ORBs that support asynchronous calls cache the results of the calls until the results are fetched by the application.

ORBs that support only synchronous calls present an additional challenge. If the ORB supports one-way or asynchronous calls, an obvious and simple way for a server application to make periodic heartbeat calls is for it to have a thread dedicated to that purpose. If the ORB supports only synchronous calls, then it must either wait for each heartbeat call to return or use additional threads. Waiting for a heartbeat call to return can cause the next heartbeat call to be made too late. Using additional threads allows the next heartbeat call to be made before the previous one returns, but this adds complexity to the design.

KNOWN USES

The Heartbeat pattern is used by a number of independently developed applications.

CODE EXAMPLE

This section shows two sets of code examples. The first example is a straightforward implementation of the Heartbeat pattern. One of the points of the first example is that the implementation of the Heartbeat pattern can have some subtleties that are not obvious until you reduce it to code. For reasons that will be explained later, the straightforward implementation technique does not work with some ORBs.

The second example is a less direct implementation, but will work with some ORBs that the more direct approach will not. Both examples are written for RMI.

Here is the `Client` class for the first example:

```
class Client {
    private static final int TIMEOUT = 30000;
    private ServerIF server;
    private HeartbeatListener heartbeatListener;
...
```

The client begins operation by getting a remote reference to the server and creating a `HeartbeatListener` object. In this case, it does these things in its constructor.

```
Client(String serverHost) throws RemoteException,
                                 UnknownHostException,
                                 NotBoundException,
                                 MalformedURLException {
    String urlName = "//" + serverHost
      + "/" + ServerIF.SERVER_NAME;
    server = (ServerIF)Naming.lookup(urlName);
    heartbeatListener = new HeartbeatListener(TIMEOUT);
} // constructor(String)
```

The following method contains a call to one of the server's methods. The call to the server is preceded by a call to the `HeartbeatListener` to tell it to start listening for heartbeat messages. The call to the server passes a stub object to the server that allows the server to call the `Heartbeat-Listener` and pass it heartbeat messages.* After the call to the server returns, the client again calls the `HeartbeatListener` to tell it to stop listening for heartbeat messages.

If the `HeartbeatListener` does not receive any heartbeat messages within the time-out period specified to it, it throws a `HeartbeatException`. The actions discussed so far occur within a `try` statement that catches the `HeartbeatException` and handles the situation.

```
private void start() {
        ...
        try {
            heartbeatListener.startListening(TIMEOUT);
            server.doIt((HeartbeatListenerIF)heartbeatListener.getStub());
            heartbeatListener.stopListening();
```

---

* Stub classes are described in the Object Request Broker pattern section.

```
        } catch (HeartbeatException e) {
            ...
        } catch (RemoteException e) {
            ...
        } // try
        //...
    } // start
} // class Client
```

The stub object that the client passes to the server implements this interface.

```
public interface HeartbeatListenerIF extends Remote {
    /**
     * Server objects call this method periodically to announce
     * that they are still alive.
     */
    public void serverIsAlive() throws RemoteException ;
} // interface HeartbeatListenerIF
```

Here is the server class that goes with the client. It defines the period between heartbeat messages to be only one-third the time-out period that the client uses.

```
class Server extends UnicastRemoteObject implements ServerIF, Runnable {
    private HeartbeatListenerIF heartbeatListener = null;
    private static final int HEARTBEAT_PERIOD = 10000;
...
```

The server's constructor registers the server so that clients can find it (see the Registry pattern). Then it starts a thread that will be responsible for sending heartbeat messages at regular intervals while the client is waiting for a remote method call to return.

```
    public Server() throws RemoteException, MalformedURLException {
        Naming.rebind(SERVER_NAME, this);
        new Thread(this).start();
    } // constructor
```

Clients call the doIt method. While the doIt method is performing its function, it arranges for the server to send heartbeat messages to the client. It does this by assigning the stub object that the client passes to it to an instance variable. The stub is a proxy that allows the server to call the client's HeartbeatListener object's serverIsAlive method.

When the stub is accessible through an instance variable, the doIt method calls the notify method. The call to the notify method causes the thread responsible for sending the heartbeat messages to wake up and send a heartbeat message. It continues to do that until the Heartbeat-Listener instance variable is null.

```
    public synchronized void doIt(HeartbeatListenerIF stub) {
        try {
            heartbeatListener = stub;
            notify();
            ...
        } finally {
            heartbeatListener = null;
        } // try
    } // doIt(HeartbeatListenerIF)
```

The run method contains the logic for periodically calling the remoteHeartbeatListener.

```
    public synchronized void run() {
        while (!Thread.currentThread().isInterrupted()) {
            try {
                while (heartbeatListener==null) {
                    wait(HEARTBEAT_PERIOD);
                } // while heartbeatListener
                heartbeatListener.serverIsAlive();
            } catch (RemoteException e) {
                ...
            } catch (InterruptedException e) {
            } // try
        } // while true
    } // run()
} // class Server
```

The final class we will consider in this first example is the HeartbeatListener class. Other objects use the HeartbeatListener object to receive heartbeat messages on their behalf. A HeartbeatListener object is told to expect heartbeat messages no more than a certain number of milliseconds apart. If it does not receive a heartbeat message within the given time, it provides notification that the heartbeat message did not arrive.

```
public class HeartbeatListener extends RemoteObject
                                implements HeartbeatListenerIF,
                                           TimeOutListener {
    private TimeOutTimer timer;
    private int timeOutInterval;
    private Thread clientThread;
    private RemoteStub stub;
```

The HeartbeatListener class uses a class named TimeoutTimer that is not listed here. A TimeoutTimer object can be told to send an event to an object after a given number of milliseconds have elapsed.

```
    public HeartbeatListener() {
        timer = new TimeOutTimer(this, this);
    } // constructor()
```

After the startListening method is called, this object expects its serverIsAlive method to be called periodically, with the calls being no further apart than the number of milliseconds passed as a parameter. The way it works is that it asks the `TimeoutTimer` object to send it an event after the given amount of time has elapsed. It also saves a reference to the thread that called it; it may use the thread later to notify its caller if it does not receive an expected heartbeat message.

```
public void startListening(int interval) {
        timeOutInterval = interval;
        timer.start(interval);
        clientThread = Thread.currentThread();
    } // start(int)
```

Server objects call the `serverIsAlive` method periodically as a way of delivering a heartbeat message to announce that they are still alive. The `serverIsAlive` method postpones the time that the `TimeoutTimer` object will send an event to this `HeartbeatListener` object.

```
public void serverIsAlive() {
        timer.start(timeOutInterval);
    } // serverIsAlive()
```

After a call to its `stopListening` method, a `HeartbeatListener` object no longer expects its `serverIsAlive` method to be called. The `stopListening` method tells the `TimeoutTimer` object not to send it any event.

```
public void stopListening() {
        timer.cancel();
    } // stopListening()
...
```

The final method we will consider is the `timeOut` method that the `TimeOutTimer` object will call to pass a `TimeOutEvent` to a `HeartBeatListener`. When the method is called, it notifies the client of the time-out using the thread that last called the `HeartBeatListener` object's `startListening` method. It calls the thread's `stop` method. The `stop` method causes the thread to throw an exception from whatever code it is executing. After an exception is passed to its `stop` method, the next thing the thread does is to throw the exception.

```
public void timeOut(TimeOutEvent evt) {
        clientThread.stop(new HeartbeatException());
    } // timeOut(TimeOutEvent)
} // class HeartbeatListener
```

This implementation of the pattern follows the UML in a rather straightforward way. Though the implementation approach shown in this example will work with some ORB implementations, it will not work with RMI. The reason for that stems from the fact that RMI uses a dedicated socket for each remote call.* Because RMI creates a socket for each call, when the `timeOut` method calls the thread's `stop` method it will most likely be waiting for a read operation on the socket to return.

The call to the thread's `stop` method ensures that the next thing the thread does is to throw the given exception. However, the `stop` method cannot guarantee when the thread will do the next thing it does. In particular, the `stop` method cannot make a read operation return any sooner. If the thread is indeed waiting for a read to return, all that the call to the `stop` method accomplishes is to cause the thread to throw the exception if and when the read operation returns.

The fundamental purpose of the Heartbeat pattern is to determine within a fixed amount of time that a remote method call will not return. Because the thread does not throw the exception until the read operation returns, this purpose of the Heartbeat pattern is unfulfilled.

Though this approach to implementing the Heartbeat pattern does not work with ORBs that dedicate each connection to a single remote call, it will generally work with ORBs that use the Connection Multiplexing pattern. The Connection Multiplexing pattern involves the use of a single connection for multiple remote calls. When an ORB is implemented in this way, there is typically one thread responsible for receiving all the results of calls made over a connection. When this thread receives a response to a remote procedure call, it dispatches it to the thread that initiated the call. When the response to a remote procedure call arrives, the thread that initiated the remote call is typically waiting for an object's `wait` method to return.

This way of implementing the Heartbeat pattern works because the thread that initiated the remote call is typically waiting for something that its `stop` method can force to return immediately.

The straightforward implementation technique does not work with RMI because of the way it manages connections. It is possible to make the Heartbeat pattern work with RMI. To make it work, we will have to implement it at a lower level so that RMI does not get in the way. RMI has a mechanism that allows us to do just that.

RMI has a mechanism that allows you to provide objects that create sockets on behalf of RMI. The purpose of this mechanism is to allow you to provide instances of subclasses of `Socket` and `ServerSocket` that implement a communication protocol at a higher level than TCP/IP but lower than RMI. For example, you can use this mechanism to have RMI communicating over SSL.[†]

---

*Section 3.1 of the RMI specification for Java 1.2 says that the first thing a stub does when its method is invoked is that it "initiates a connection with the remote VM containing the remote object."

[†]Secure Sockets Layer (SSL) is a protocol that provides secure transmission of data. It is designed to be transparent to application protocol layers. SSL is defined by RFC 2246, available at www.alternic.com/rfcs/rfc2200/rfc2246.html.

We will use this mechanism to implement a protocol that allows a server to send heartbeat messages in a way that is transparent to RMI. The way it will work is that every time the server writes some bytes to the socket, the protocol will precede the bytes written with four bytes (an int) that is the number of bytes written. Heartbeat messages will be transmitted as zero-length writes.

It is possible to set a parameter that forces a read on a socket to time out if no bytes arrive to read within a specified amount of time. If no heartbeat messages or other data arrive within a specified amount of time, this mechanism will alert us.

Implementing the Heartbeat pattern in this way has the drawback that the server does not know exactly when a remote method call is in progress. This can result in the server sending unnecessary heartbeat messages.

We will begin the `Client2` class, which is the client portion of the example. The `Client2` class is similar to the `Client` class, so the listing leaves out some parts that are the same.

```
class Client2 {
    private static final int TIMEOUT_INTERVAL = 30000;
    private Server2IF server;
...
    private void start() {
        ...
        try {
            server.doIt();
        } catch (HeartbeatException e) {
            ...
        } catch (RemoteException e) {
            e.printStackTrace();
            ...
        } // try
        ...
    } // start
} // class Client2
```

The main difference between the `Client` class and the `Client2` class is that the `Client2` class does not bracket its call to the server's `doIt` method with method calls that announce the beginning and end of the remote call.

Since this implementation will send and receive heartbeat messages at the protocol level rather than as remote calls to a `HeartbeatListener` object, there is no need for the `HeartbeatListenerIF` interface that was used in the first example.

Here is the `Server2` class that works with the `Client2` class:

```
class Server2 extends UnicastRemoteObject implements Server2IF {
    private static final int TIME_OUT = 30000;
```

The `Server2` class uses a class named `HeartbeatSocketFactory` that appears in a later listing. The purpose of this class is to create `Socket` and `ServerSocket` objects on behalf of RMI that implement the protocol discussed previously and pass heartbeat messages from server to client.

The `main` method creates the `HeartbeatSocketFactory` object. This object will be used on both the server and the client. It passes into the constructor the maximum number of connections (50) that `ServerSocket` objects it creates should ask the operating system to accept and queue up for the server. It also passes to the constructor the number of milliseconds that the client should wait for a heartbeat message to arrive before deciding that it will not arrive.

```
public static void main(String[] argv) {
    try {
        HeartbeatSocketFactory hsf;
        hsf = new HeartbeatSocketFactory(50, TIME_OUT);
        new Server2(hsf);
    } catch (RemoteException e) {
        e.printStackTrace();
        e.detail.printStackTrace();
    } catch (Exception e) {
        e.printStackTrace();
    } // try
} // main(String[])
```

The constructor for the `Server2` class takes a `HeartbeatSocketFactory` argument. It passes the `HeartbeatSocketFactory` object to its superclass's constructor. It passes it twice. This is because RMI allows you to use a separate object for a `Socket` factory and a `ServerSocket` factory. Since the subclass of `Socket` and `ServerSocket` that we will be using will always be used in pairs to support the protocol discussed previously, we use a single object that does both.

```
public Server2(HeartbeatSocketFactory hsf)
                throws RemoteException,
                    MalformedURLException,
                    IOException {
    super(0, hsf, hsf);
    Naming.rebind(SERVER_NAME, this);
} // constructor
```

Like the `Client2` class's call to `doIt`, the `Server2` class's implementation of `doIt` is unencumbered with code to indicate when heartbeat messages should be sent.

```
public void doIt() {
    try {
```

```
            ...
       } catch (Exception e) {
          ...
       } // try
   } // doIt()
} // class Server2
```

The classes that we have examined so far in this example have been simpler than the corresponding classes in the first example. The reason is that we are moving the complexity to a lower level of the logic. This will become clear as we examine the HeartbeatSocketFactory class and the classes that it instantiates.

The purpose of the HeartbeatSocketFactory class is to instantiate subclasses of Socket and ServerSocket that implement the protocol to transmit and manage heartbeat messages. It implements the Serializable interface. This is so that RMI can send a copy of a HeartbeatSocketFactory object from the server to the client, where it is needed to create Socket objects.

```
public class HeartbeatSocketFactory extends RMISocketFactory
                                    implements Serializable {
    private int heartbeatTimeout;
    private int backlog;
public HeartbeatSocketFactory(int backlog, int timeout) {
        this.backlog = backlog;
        heartbeatTimeout = timeout;
    } // constructor(int)


    /**
     * Create a client socket connected to the specified host
     * and port.
     */
    public Socket createSocket(String host, int port)
                                        throws IOException {
        return new HeartbeatClientSocket(host,
                                         port,
                                         heartbeatTimeout);
    } // createSocket(String, int)


    /**
     * Create a server socket.
     */
    public ServerSocket createServerSocket(int port)
                                      throws IOException {
        return new HeartbeatServerSocket(port,
                                         backlog,
                                         heartbeatTimeout);
    } // createServerSocket(int)
} // class HeartbeatSocketFactory
```

The `HeartbeatServerSocket` class extends the `ServerSocket` class so that the `Socket` object it creates when it accepts a connection sends heartbeat messages to the client.

```
public class HeartbeatServerSocket extends ServerSocket {
    private int heartbeatTimeout;
```

In addition to the parameters it passes on to its superclass's constructor, the `HeartbeatServerSocket` class's constructor takes a parameter that is the maximum amount of time, in milliseconds, that the client will wait between heartbeat messages.

```
public HeartbeatServerSocket(int port,
                             int backlog,
                             int timeout)
                                    throws IOException {
    super(port, backlog);
    heartbeatTimeout = timeout;
} // constructor(int, int)
```

The `accept` method listens for a connection to be made, accepts it, and returns a `Socket` object that can be used to communicate with the connection. The `Socket` object it returns is actually an instance of `HeartbeatSocket`, a subclass of `Socket` that sends heartbeat messages to the client.

The `accept` method works by first creating a `HeartbeatSocket` object and then passing it to the `implAccept` method that the `Heartbeat-Socket` class inherits from the `Socket` class. It is the `implAccept` method that actually listens for a connection, accepts it, and associates the `HeartbeatSocket` object with the connection.

```
public Socket accept() throws IOException {
    Socket s = new HeartbeatSocket(heartbeatTimeout);
    implAccept(s);
    return s;
} // accept()
```

The `HeartbeatSocket` class is private to the `HeartbeatServer-Socket` class, since no other class needs to know it exists.

```
private static class HeartbeatSocket extends Socket {
    private int heartbeatTimeout;

    HeartbeatSocket(int timeout) {
        heartbeatTimeout = timeout;
    } // constructor
```

The implementation of the `HeartbeatSocket` class is very simple. It overrides the `getOutputStream` method so that it returns an instance of a subclass `OutputStream` that does the real work.

```
public OutputStream getOutputStream() throws IOException {
    OutputStream out = super.getOutputStream();
    return new HeartbeatOutputStream(out);
} // getOutputStream
```

The `HeartbeatOutputStream` class is private to the `Heartbeat-Socket` class. Instances of `HeartbeatOutputStream` function as wrappers for their underlying `OutputStream` that prefix the bytes sent by each write operation with the number of bytes written by the write operation. `HeartbeatOutputStream` objects have a thread associated with them that allows them to send heartbeat messages asynchronously.

```
private class HeartbeatOutputStream
        extends FilterOutputStream
            implements Runnable {
    HeartbeatOutputStream(OutputStream out) {
        super(out);
        Thread heartbeatThread = new Thread(this);
        heartbeatThread.setDaemon(true);
        heartbeatThread.start();
    } // constructor(OutputStream)
```

The `HeartbeatOutputStream` class overrides the write method in the obvious way to prefix each write with its length.

```
public synchronized void write(int b)
                        throws IOException {
    writeInt(1);
    out.write(b);
} // write(int)

public synchronized void write(byte b[],
                            int off,
                            int len)
                        throws IOException {
    writeInt(len);
    out.write(b, off, len);
} // write(byte[], int, int)
```

The thread that the `HeartbeatOutputStream` object's constructor starts calls the `run` method. It is responsible for sending heartbeat messages. It separates the heartbeat messages by only one-third of the time that the client will tolerate between messages. The purpose in doing that is to allow for fluctuations in the speed of the host the server is on and also in how loaded the network is. This is a somewhat conservative margin of safety for most environments. For production use, you may want to provide a mechanism to manually or automatically adjust it.

```
public synchronized void run() {
    Thread myThread = Thread.currentThread();
    while (!myThread.isInterrupted()) {
```

```
                    try {
                        wait(heartbeatTimeout/3);
                        writeInt(0); // write heartbeat message
                    } catch (InterruptedException e) {
                    } catch (IOException e) {
                    } // try
                } // while
            } // run()
```

The implementations of the `write` method call the `writeInt` method to write the number of data bytes that they are about to write.

```
        private void writeInt(int v) throws IOException {
            out.write((v >>> 24) & 0xFF);
            out.write((v >>> 16) & 0xFF);
            out.write((v >>> 8) & 0xFF);
            out.write((v >>> 0) & 0xFF);
        } // writeInt(int)
    } // class HeartbeatOutputStream
  } // class HeartbeatSocket
} // class HeartbeatServerSocket
```

Clients use an instance of the `HeartbeatClientSocket` class to manage their connection with the server. The `InputStream` object it provides to the client expects to receive heartbeat messages from the server. While `InputStream` object is waiting to receive data from the server, if it does not receive data or a heartbeat message within the specified time-out period, it throws a `HeartbeatException`.

```
class HeartbeatClientSocket extends Socket {
    /**
     * The maximum amount of time that should elapse before a
     * HeartbeatException should be thrown from a read.
     */
    private int heartbeatTimeout;

    /**
     * The last value passed to this object's setSoTimeout
     * method.
     */
    private int soTimeout = 0;
```

`Socket` objects have an attribute named `soTimeout`. The default value for `soTimeout` is zero. If the value of `soTimeout` is set to a value greater than zero and an attempt to read data from the socket takes more than that many milliseconds, the read throws an `InterruptedIO-Exception`. This class implements its behavior of timing out when no heartbeat message or data arrives by setting the value of its superclass's `soTimeout` attribute.

Even though the `HeartbeatClientSocket` class uses its superclass's `soTimeout` attribute for its own purpose, it still should behave appropriately when other objects set its instance's `soTimeout` attribute. If the attribute is set to a value greater than the value of the heartbeat time-out period, then no special measures are needed because a `HeartbeatException` will be thrown before the `InterruptedIOException` should be thrown. On the other hand, if the value of the `soTimeout` attribute is greater than zero but less than the value of the heartbeat time-out period, then the `Interrupted-IOException` will be thrown first. Since the value of the `soTimeout` attribute will vary over time, it is necessary to remember both the value of the heartbeat message time-out and the most recent `soTimeout` setting.

```java
private HeartbeatInputStream myInputStream;

/**
 * Creates a stream socket and connects it to the specified
 * port number on the named host.
 * @param host the host name.
 * @param port the port number.
 * @param timeout The amount of time in milliseconds that
 *                this socket should wait for a read
 *                operation to be satisfied or to receive a
 *                heartbeat message before throwing a
 *                HeartbeatException.
 */
public HeartbeatClientSocket(String host, int port, int timeout)
               throws UnknownHostException, IOException {
    super(host, port);
    heartbeatTimeout = timeout;
    super.setSoTimeout(timeout);
} // constructor(String, int)

public synchronized void setSoTimeout(int timeout)
                                throws SocketException {
    if (timeout>heartbeatTimeout || timeout==0) {
        super.setSoTimeout(heartbeatTimeout);
        soTimeout = 0;
    } else {
        super.setSoTimeout(timeout);
        soTimeout = timeout;
    } // if
} // setSoTimeout(int)

/**
 * Returns setting for SO_TIMEOUT. 0 returns implies that the
 * option is disabled.
 */
public synchronized int getSoTimeout()
                        throws SocketException {
    return soTimeout;
} // getSoTimeout()
```

The `getInputStream` method returns an `InputStream` object that can be used to read bytes from the socket's connection. This `InputStream` object is responsible for handling the private protocol that prefixes each write of bytes to the connection with the number of data bytes written.

The object that the `getInputStream` method returns is actually an instance of a subclass of `InputStream` named `HeartbeatInputStream`. In addition to handling the protocol, `HeartbeatInputStream` objects also monitor the arrival of heartbeat messages.

```
public InputStream getInputStream() throws IOException {
    if (myInputStream==null) {
        synchronized (this) {
            if (myInputStream==null) {
                InputStream superIn;
                superIn = super.getInputStream();
                myInputStream
                    = new HeartbeatInputStream(superIn);
            } // if
        } // synchronized
    } // if
    return myInputStream;
} // getInputStream()
```

The `HeartbeatInputStream` class is private to the `HeartbeatClientSocket` class because no other class has any reason to be aware of its existence.

A `HeartbeatInputStream` object's constructor starts a thread that the object uses internally to ensure that the socket's internal buffer does not become clogged with heartbeat messages. This is explained more fully later on.

```
private class HeartbeatInputStream extends FilterInputStream
                                   implements Runnable {
    HeartbeatInputStream(InputStream stream) {
        super(stream);
        Thread cleanupThread = new Thread(this);
        cleanupThread.setdaemon(true);
        cleanupThread.start();
} // constructor (InputStream)
```

The `read` method is where the `HeartbeatInputStream` class handles the private protocol and heartbeat messages. The zero-argument form of the `read` method simply delegates its work to the three-argument form of the `read` method.

```
private byte[] byteBuffer = new byte[1];

public int read() throws IOException {
    try {
        read(byteBuffer, 0, 1);
    } catch (EOFException e) {
        return -1;
    } // try
    return byteBuffer[0];
} // read()
```

If a call to this object's `read` method leaves some bytes of a server write operation unread, then the `bytesUnread` variable contains the number of bytes from that operation waiting to be read.

```
int bytesUnread;
```

```
    /**
     * Reads up to len bytes of data from this input stream
     * into an array of bytes. This method blocks until some input is
     * available.
     * @param       b     the buffer into which the data is read.
     * @param       off   the start offset of the data.
     * @param       len   the maximum number of bytes read.
     * @return      the total number of bytes read into the
     *              buffer, or -1 if there is
     *              no more data because the end of
     *              the stream has been reached.
     */
    public synchronized int read(byte b[],
                                 int off,
                                 int len)
                                     throws IOException {
        if (len==0) {
            return 0;
        } // if
        try {
            while (bytesUnread<=0) {
                bytesUnread = readInt();
            } // while
            int bytesToRead = Math.min(bytesUnread, len);
            int bytesRead = in.read(b, off, bytesToRead);
            bytesUnread -= bytesRead;
            return bytesRead;
        } catch (InterruptedIOException e) {
            if (soTimeout!=0) {
                throw e;      // Treat as a regular soTimeout
            } else {
                throw new HeartbeatException();
            } // if
        } // try
    } // read(byte[], int, int)
```

The `read` method uses the `readInt` method to read the byte counts that the server inserts into the data stream.

```
    private final int readInt() throws IOException {
        InputStream in = this.in;
        int c1 = in.read();
        int c2 = in.read();
        int c3 = in.read();
        int c4 = in.read();
        if ((c1 | c2 | c3 | c4) < 0)
          throw new EOFException();
```

```
        return ((c1 << 24) + (c2 << 16) + (c3 << 8) + (c4 << 0));
    } // readInt
```

Earlier we mentioned a thread that the `HeartbeatInputStream` object's constructor creates and promised to explain it in more detail.

Because the server side of this connection does not know when the client is waiting to receive bytes, it sends heartbeat messages whether or not the client is waiting. When the client does not have a read pending, the underlying socket implementation will buffer the heartbeat messages. If the client goes too long without reading the heartbeat messages, the underlying buffer will fill up and the server will find itself waiting for a write operation to complete.

The purpose of the thread and the `run` method that it calls is to read heartbeat messages internally when there are no external read requests.

```
        public void run() {
            Thread myThread = Thread.currentThread();
            while (!myThread.isInterrupted()) {
                try {
                    myThread.sleep(heartbeatTimeout*20);
                    // loop while where may be heartbeat
                    // messages to read and we are not reading
                    // something else.
                    while (true) {
                        synchronized(this) {
                            if ( bytesUnread>0
                                || available()<4) {
                              break;
                            } // if
                            bytesUnread = readInt();
                        } // synchronized
                    } // while true
                } catch (InterruptedException e) {
                } catch (IOException e) {
                } // try
            } // while !isInterrupted
        } // run()
    } // class HeartbeatInputStream
} // class HeartbeatClientSocket
```

RELATED PATTERNS

Object Request Broker. The Heartbeat pattern is used with the Object Request Broker pattern.

Connection Multiplexing. Whether or not the ORB being used with the Heartbeat pattern implements the Connection Multiplexing pattern can determine how you choose to implement the Heartbeat pattern.

Connection Multiplexing

SYNOPSIS

You are designing a distributed system in which, over time, one object may establish many connections with another object. To avoid the overhead of setting up and shutting down many connections between the same two objects, you arrange for one actual connection to carry the contents of multiple virtual connections.

CONTEXT

Suppose that you are designing software that backs up the files on a computer to a server over the Internet. The basic loop that it will execute while backing up files will consist of the following steps:

1. Fill a buffer with bytes from a file.
2. Write the contents of the buffer to the server.

To speed backups, you will want to have at least two threads executing this loop so that it will be possible for one buffer to be getting filled while the contents of another buffer are written to the server. Depending on the speed of the Internet connection relative to the speed of opening and reading files, you may achieve the best results with a higher number of threads.

The simplest way to organize such a multithreaded backup is to use one socket for each thread. Normally, there is one connection for each socket. However, increasing the number of concurrently open connections by a factor of two or higher may be a problem for the server. Each connection consumes memory and operating system resources. It would be ideal to have multiple sockets that share a single connection.

In the process of writing backup files to the server, you want to compress the files to minimize transmission time and the storage requirement on the server. To accomplish this you use the `java.util.zip.GZIPOutputStream` class. This is convenient, but you do not know how big the compressed form of the file will be until after it has been written to the server. Since you cannot tell the server how many bytes to expect before they are written, the client must be able to tell the server that it has read the end of the file. The simplest way to tell the server that it has reached the end of the file is to use a socket for each file. That way, you can simply close the socket after the entire file has been written, and when the server tries to read past that point, it sees the end of file.

The problem with using one socket per file is that normally there is a connection for each socket. If there are thousands of files to be backed up, then the time required to set up and shut down thousands of connections would add a noticeable amount of time to the backup operation. Having a way to create and close sockets without having to set up and shut down a connection each time would avoid this problem. Having each socket reuse the same connection accomplishes this.

FORCES

☺ An object wants to send multiple concurrent data flows to another object. The contents of the data flows are to be processed in like ways.

☺ An object wants to send multiple discrete data flows to another object. The simplest way to send multiple discrete data flows between two objects is to use a different connection for each data flow.

☺ Using multiple connections between the same two objects adds overhead. It takes time to set up and shut down each connection. Each connection takes up memory and uses operating system resources that may be limited in quantity. As objects share more connections, it becomes more important to minimize the resources required for each connection.

☹ Implementations of TCP/IP and similar protocols provide a buffer on the receiving end of a connection. The purpose of the buffer is so that when data is written to a connection, the data can be held in the buffer if there is no read operation waiting for the data. If the buffer is full, then the write operation to the connection will not complete until a read operation has made room for the data. The greater the volume of data being sent over a connection, the greater the likelihood that write operations will be forced to wait for read operations.

SOLUTION

Create subclasses of `Socket` and `ServerSocket` that support multiple virtual connections over a single actual connection. Figure 6.16 shows the roles that classes play in this pattern.

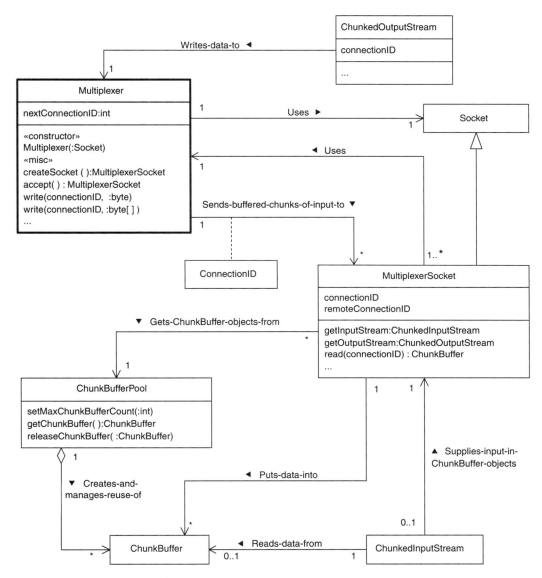

FIGURE 6.16 Connection multiplexing pattern.

Here are descriptions of the roles shown in Figure 6.16:

Socket.   Instances of classes in this role are associated with actual
connections. The class usually used in this role is
`java.net.Socket`.

Multiplexer.   This role is a central to the Connection Multiplexing
pattern. The pattern begins with the creation of a `Multiplexer`

object on each end of an actual connection. On each end of an actual connection, the `Socket` object responsible for that end of the connection is passed the `Multiplexer` class's constructor. After that, all interaction with the `Socket` objects and the underlying connection is through the `Multiplexer` objects.

`Multiplexer` objects manage virtual connections. The `Multiplexer` object on each side of an actual connection negotiates the creation of virtual connections with the other. To minimize the effort required, this generally involves one `Multiplexer` object sending the first piece of data associated with a virtual connection to the other `Multiplexer` object. The other `Multiplexer` object performs any needed internal bookkeeping, but generally does not need to send any additional messages because of the new virtual connection.

When bytes are written to a virtual connection, the `Multiplexer` object sends a message across the actual connection that consists of the virtual connection ID, the number of data bytes in the message, and the data bytes. The `Multiplexer` object at the other end of the actual connection reads messages using its own internal thread. It identifies the thread that is waiting to process a message based on the type of message and/or the virtual connection ID in the message. It takes appropriate action to make the message visible to the thread and wakes it up.

A `Multiplexer` object initiates a new virtual connection by creating a unique connection ID and simply sending a data message with the new connection ID to the other `Multiplexer` object. There is no assumption that a call to the remote `Multiplexer` object's `accept` method is pending. If there is no call waiting to accept a new connection, the connection is queued up to be accepted the next time the method is called.

ConnectionID. A `ConnectionID` contains a unique sequence of bytes that identifies a virtual connection to `Multiplexer` objects. `Multiplexer` objects use `ConnectionID` objects to associate each `MultiplexerSocket` object with a virtual connection.

MultiplexerSocket. Instances of a class in this role are used in place of `Socket` objects. Each `MultiplexerSocket` object is associated with one end of a virtual connection.

A `MultiplexerSocket` object for the server side of a connection is created and returned by a call to a `Multiplexer` object's `accept` method. A `Multiplexer` object's `accept` method listens for clients wanting to create a virtual connection. When it is able to accept a virtual connection, it returns a `Multiplexer-`

`Socket` object that is associated with the server side of the virtual connection.

A `MultiplexerSocket` object for the client side of a new virtual connection is created and returned by a call to a `Multiplexer` object's `createConnection` method.

When a `Multiplexer` object receives a data message for a virtual connection, it passes the data in the message to the `MultiplexerSocket` object associated with the virtual connection. The `MultiplexerSocket` object puts the data in a `ChunkBuffer` object, where it remains until the `ChunkBuffer` object is passed to a `ChunkedInputStream` object.

ChunkedOutputStream.   A class in this role is responsible for writing bytes to a virtual connection. The `MultiplexerSocket` object associated with the virtual connection creates a `ChunkedOutput-Stream` object. The `MultiplexerSocket` object's `getOutput-Stream` method returns the `ChunkedOutputStream` object.

The purpose of a `ChunkedOutputStream` object is to write bytes to a virtual connection. It passes the bytes passed to its `write` method to the associated `Multiplexer` object's `write` method. It handles the write of a large number of bytes by making writes to the `Multiplexer` object that are no larger than some predetermined size, typically a few thousand bytes. This has the effect of limiting the size of the messages that a `Multiplexer` object sends across an actual connection. The benefits of this are discussed under the "Consequences" heading.

ChunkBuffer.   Instances of classes in this role serve as buffers for bytes received by a `Multiplexer` object from a virtual connection.

When a `Multiplexer` object receives bytes through a virtual connection, it passes the bytes to the `MultiplexerSocket` object associated with the virtual connection. The `MultiplexerSocket` object puts the bytes in a `ChunkBuffer` object. If no `ChunkBuffer` object is associated with the `MultiplexerSocket` object, it uses a `ChunkBufferPool` object to allocate one. It allocates an additional `ChunkBuffer` object from the `ChunkBufferPool` object if there is not enough room in the `ChunkBuffer` object it was using.

ChunkedInputStream.   Instances of classes in this role are responsible for reading bytes from `ChunkBuffer` objects that they get from the `MultiplexerSocket` object they are associated with.

ChunkBufferPool.   Instances of classes in this role manage the creation and reuse of `ChunkBuffer` objects. When a `Chunked-`

InputStream object exhausts the bytes in a ChunkBuffer object, it passes the ChunkBuffer object to a ChunkBufferPool object's releaseChunkBuffer method. The releaseChunkBuffer method adds the ChunkBuffer object to a pool of ChunkBuffer objects waiting to be reused. When a MultiplexerSocket object calls a ChunkBufferPool object's getChunkBuffer method to allocate a ChunkBuffer object, it removes a ChunkBuffer object from the pool of ChunkBuffer objects and returns it. If there are no ChunkBuffer objects in the pool, the getChunkBuffer method creates and returns a ChunkBuffer object, unless the total number of ChunkBuffer objects it has created is equal to the configuration parameter.

The interactions between these classes are shown in greater detail in Figures 6.17 and 6.18.

Figure 6.17 shows these interactions related to writing data to a virtual connection:

1A. Create a Multiplexer object by passing to its constructor the Socket object that is associated with the actual connection that will transport the contents of virtual connections.

2A. Create a MultiplexerSocket object by calling the Multiplexer object's createSocket method. The creation of this object has the side effect of creating a new virtual connection associated with the MultiplexerSocket object. Because MultiplexerSocket is a subclass of Socket, the object can be passed to any method that expects a Socket.

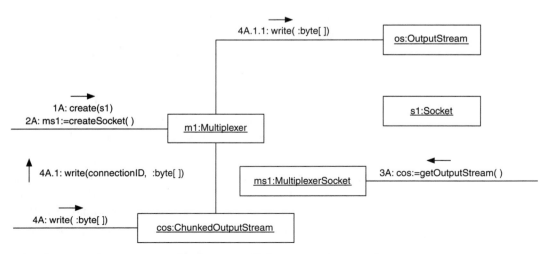

FIGURE 6.17 Connection multiplexing collaboration (writing).

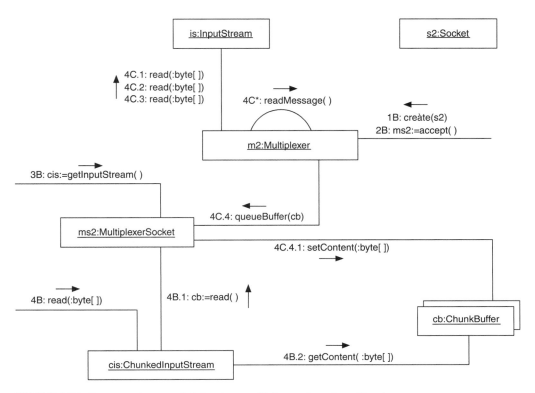

FIGURE 6.18 Connection multiplexing collaboration (reading).

3A. Call the `MultiplexerSocket` object's `getOutputStream` method to get the `ChunkedOutputStream` that writes to its associated virtual connection. Like any other socket, in order to write to the connection it encapsulates, you must first call its `getOutputStream` method to get the `OutputStream` that writes to the connection.

4A. Call the `ChunkedOutputStream` object's `write` method to write bytes to the virtual connection.

4A.1. The `ChunkedOutputStream` object calls the `Multiplexer` object's `write` method, passing it the connection ID that identifies the virtual connection it is associated with and the bytes that were passed to its `write` method.

If the number of bytes passed to the `ChunkedOutput-Stream` object in 4A is greater than a predetermined value, then this interaction occurs multiple times. Each time, the `Chunked-OutputStream` object passes to the `Multiplexer` object's `write` method a number of bytes no greater than the predetermined value.

4A.1.1. The `Multiplexer` object writes a message to the actual connection that consists of the virtual connection ID, the number of data bytes being written, and the data bytes.

Figure 6.18 shows the companion interactions for the interactions shown in Figure 6.17. In particular, it shows the interactions related to receiving bytes sent through a virtual connection.

Here is a detailed description of the interactions shown in Figure 6.18. The first three interactions are similar to the sending side.

1B. Create a `Multiplexer` object by passing to its constructor the `Socket` associated with the actual connection that will transport the contents of virtual connections.

2B. Create a `MultiplexerSocket` object by calling the `Multiplexer` object's `accept` method. This method accepts a waiting virtual connection or waits until there is a virtual connection to accept. It returns a `MultiplexerSocket` object that encapsulates the accepted virtual connection.

3B. Call the `MultiplexerSocket` object's `getInputStream` method to get the `ChunkedInputStream` that reads from its associated virtual connection.

4C. Once the creation interactions are done, the `Multiplexer` object starts a thread that repeatedly calls the `Multiplexer` object's `readMessage` method. The `readMessage` method repeatedly reads a message from the actual connection and dispatches the data it contains to the appropriate virtual connection.

4C.1. The `Multiplexer` object reads the connection ID of the virtual connection of the incoming message.

4C.2. The `Multiplexer` object reads the number of data bytes in the incoming message.

4C.3. The `Multiplexer` object reads the data bytes in the incoming message into an internal buffer.

4C.4. The `Multiplexer` object passes its internal buffer to the `queueBuffer` method of the `MultiplexerSocket` object associated with the virtual connection. This method copies the data bytes to a `ChunkBuffer` object. It places the `ChunkBuffer` object in a queue until it is taken out of it by interaction 4B.1.

The `MultiplexerSocket` object gets its `ChunkBuffer` objects from a `ChunkbufferPool` object. This interaction is not shown in the diagram.

If any threads are waiting to read data from the virtual connection, the thread that reads the message and puts its contents in the `ChunkBuffer` object notifies the waiting threads that they can stop waiting.

4C.4.1. The `Multiplexer` object calls the `setContent` method of allocated `ChunkBuffer` objects so that they contain the bytes from the incoming message. After this, the bytes remain in the `ChunkBuffer` objects until they are read by the `ChunkedInput-Stream` object.

4B. While the `Multiplexer` object is reading data bytes and putting them in `ChunkBuffer` objects, other objects not shown in the diagram are calling the `ChunkedInputStream` object's `read` method.

4B.1. The `ChunkedInputStream` object gets the next queued `ChunkBuffer` object from the `MultiplexerSocket` object.

4B.2. The `ChunkedInputStream` object's `read` method gets the bytes it returns from the `ChunkBuffer` object. When the `ChunkedInputStream` object empties a `ChunkBuffer` object of data bytes, it returns the `ChunkBuffer` object to the `Chunk-BufferPool` object to be recycled.

If the total number of allocated `ChunkBuffer` objects reaches a maximum value, the `Multiplexer` object stops reading messages from the actual connection until some `Chunk-Buffer` objects are released. If this situation occurs, it stalls all of the virtual connections.

If too many `ChunkBuffer` objects are allocated to a single virtual connection, the `Multiplexer` object treats it as a potential problem. It sends a message to the `Multiplexer` object at the other end of the actual connection to tell it to stop sending data to that virtual connection. When the number of `Chunk-Buffer` objects allocated to a virtual connection becomes low enough, the `Multiplexer` object considers the problem to be averted. It sends another message to the `Multiplexer` object on the other end of the actual connection telling it to resume sending data to the virtual connection.

CONSEQUENCES

☺ Multiple virtual connections can share a single actual connection with minimal impact to the code that uses the connections.

☺ If multiple virtual connections share a single actual connection, most of the overhead associated with creating and destroying connections is avoided while preserving the reliability of the underlying connection-oriented protocol.

By having the `Multiplexer` object on each side of an actual connect take responsibility for virtual connection IDs, the two sides are able to operate more independently and are less sensitive to defects in each other's operation. It allows for the possibility that two different versions of the `Multiplexer` class, which allocate connection IDs differently, are used on each side of an actual connection. The implementation section explains why this design decision may be advantageous when multiple actual connections are involved.

⊗ While a large number of data bytes are being written to a virtual connection, all other virtual connections may be prevented from sending data until the large write is finished. For some applications, this uneven access to the actual connection underlying the virtual connections may be a problem.

In some cases you can avoid this problem by ensuring that classes that use the virtual connection break large writes into reasonably sized chunks. Breaking writes of a large number of bytes into reasonably sized chunks allows virtual connections to share the actual connection more fairly.

If it is not practical for the objects using a virtual connection to limit the size of their writes, you can solve the problem by using the Scheduler pattern (described in *Volume 1*). The Scheduler pattern describes a way to explicitly enforce a policy that determines when a thread may have control of a resource, such as an actual connection. The Scheduler pattern can be implemented in a way that is transparent to classes that use the `Multiplexer` class. The drawback of using the Scheduler pattern is the complexity it adds to a design.

⊗ The main weakness of this pattern is that it is possible for the mishandling of one virtual connection to cause all virtual connections that share the same actual connection to stall. If enough bytes are received through a virtual connection and buffered without any read operations on that end of the virtual connection, the `Multiplexer` object will eventually be unable to allocate more `ChunkBuffer` objects. At that point, the `Multiplexer` object cannot read more data from the actual connection, because it has nowhere to put it. This condition persists until enough bytes have been read from the offending virtual connection to release some `ChunkBuffer` objects.

A `Multiplexer` object sends a message asking the other `Multiplexer` object to block writes to a virtual connection when the number of `ChunkBuffer` objects allocated to the virtual connection exceeds a predetermined threshold. This does not guarantee that the `Multiplexer` object won't run out of `ChunkBuffer` objects. When the `Multiplexer` object sends the message, it is the beginning of a race condition. When it sends the message, more data for the virtual connection may be on the way. By the time that the message gets to the other `Multiplexer` object, even more data may be on the way.

It is possible to use a more elaborate protocol to effectively limit the number of `ChunkBuffer` objects that a virtual connection will need. However, the overhead of using such a protocol is prohibitively expensive. It makes using actual connections more efficient than using virtual connections.

IMPLEMENTATION

For the sake of simplicity, this presentation of the Connection Multiplexing pattern assumes that there are just two remote objects passing multiple data streams between each other. Some situations involve objects that pass multiple data streams with multiple other objects. Though it is possible to use one `Multiplexer` object for each actual connection, it is more efficient to modify the pattern to use one `Multiplexer` object for multiple actual connections.

The operation of a `Multiplexer` object is driven by these parameters:

- The maximum number of bytes a `ChunkBuffer` object can contain.
- The maximum number of data bytes a `Multiplexer` object can send in a single message. This is generally less than or equal to the number of bytes that a `ChunkBuffer` object can contain.
- The maximum number of `ChunkBuffer` objects a `Multiplexer` object can allocate to virtual connections. If a `Multiplexer` object has this many `ChunkBuffer` objects allocated at one time and it needs another, it will stop reading messages from the actual connection until a `ChunkedInputStream` object's read operations release a `ChunkBuffer` object.

When the number of `ChunkBuffer` objects allocated to a single virtual connection reaches a predetermined number, the `Multiplexer` object requests that the `Multiplexer` object on the other end of the actual connection blocks write operations to that virtual connection. I will refer to this parameter as the *high-water mark*.

When the number of `ChunkBuffer` objects allocated to a single virtual connection drops below the high-water mark, a `Multiplexer` object will request that the `Multiplexer` object on the other end of the virtual connection stop blocking writes. It is not a good idea for the `Multiplexer` object to immediately request this.

Suppose that a `Multiplexer` object requested that writes to a virtual connection become unblocked as soon as the number of `ChunkBuffer` objects allocated to a virtual connection drops below the high-water mark. There is a good chance that it would immediately receive the contents of a previously blocked write to the virtual connection. There is also a good chance that the data it receives from that write would cause the `Multiplexer` object to allocate another `ChunkBuffer` object, which would cause it to request that writes to the virtual connection become blocked again. While a virtual connection is operating in this mode, every data message sent across the virtual connection results in sending three messages across the actual connection. Waiting for the number of `ChunkBuffer` objects allocated to a virtual connection to drop further below the high-water mark may reduce the number of messages that are sent to block and unblock writes to a virtual connection.

When the number of `ChunkBuffer` objects allocated to a virtual connection reaches the high-water mark, it indicates that at least one of two things has been happening: Writes to the virtual connection have been very frequent or reads of the virtual connection have been infrequent. If writes to the virtual connection have been very frequent, then it may have been using more than its fair share of the actual connection's capacity. Waiting until the number of `Chunk-Buffer` objects allocated to the virtual connection to reach a lower value gives other virtual connections greater access to the actual connection for a longer amount of time. If reads from the virtual connection have been infrequent, then waiting longer to unblock writes may postpone or prevent the total number of `ChunkBuffer` objects that the `Multiplexer` object has allocated reaching the maximum.

The point of this bullet is that the `Multiplexer` object needs a parameter other than the high-water mark to tell it when to request the unblocking of writes to a virtual connection. I will refer to this parameter as the *low-water mark*. When the number of `ChunkBuffer` objects allocated to a virtual connection drops to the low-water mark, the `Multiplexer` object requests the unblocking of writes to the virtual connection.

Determining a good value for these parameters usually requires some experimentation. Though it is not generally possible to recommend specific values, here are some guidelines:

● The number of bytes that a `ChunkBuffer` object should be able to hold should be large enough to hold most of the data bytes in most data messages.

- The maximum number of bytes that may be sent in a single message should be less than or equal to the number of bytes that a `ChunkBuffer` object can hold.

  You should consider two factors for a first estimate of the maximum number of `ChunkBuffer` objects that a `Multiplexer` object may allocate. The number of virtual connections that can be effectively supported at once is limited by the maximum number of `ChunkBuffer` objects that a `Multiplexer` object may allocate. Unless you are sure there will never be data to read from all connections at once, the number of virtual connections to be supported is an absolute minimum for the number of `ChunkBuffer` objects a `Multiplexer` object may allocate. However, that is too low for many applications. One `ChunkBuffer` object per connection makes the high- and low-water-mark parameters meaningless. Allowing `Multiplexer` objects to allocate twice as many `ChunkBuffer` objects as the number of virtual connections to support is a practical minimum.

The other factor to consider in arriving at a first estimate for the number of `ChunkBuffer` objects a `Multiplexer` object may allocate is how far writes to a virtual connection may get ahead of reads.

- Your first estimate for the high-water mark should be based on how far writes will get ahead of reads.
- The low-water-mark parameter should be at least two less than the high-water-mark parameter to avoid frequent messages to block and unblock write. One is often a good first estimate for this parameter.

KNOWN USES

The Voyager ORB uses the Connection Multiplexing pattern.

A proprietary program that backs up files over the Internet uses the Connection Multiplexing pattern to concurrently back up multiple files to a server over a single actual connection.

A number of proprietary CORBA programs use the Connection Multiplexing program.

CODE EXAMPLE

The code example for this pattern is an implementation of the Connection Multiplexing pattern for use with RMI. The RMI specification says that the first thing that happens to invoke a remote method when a stub's method is called is that it creates a new connection. This can add significant overhead to applications that make frequent remote method calls. It can be a bottleneck that limits the number of clients a server can handle concurrently. Virtualizing the connections eliminates most of the overhead.

First we will look at the `Multiplexer` class.

```
public class Multiplexer {
    private Socket actualSocket; // The actual connection.
    private DataOutputStream actualOut; // actual output stream
    private DataInputStream actualIn; // actual input stream
    private Hashtable socketTable; // key is connection id
    private ChunkBufferPool bufferPool;
```

`ChunkBufferPool` objects keep a collection of `ChunkBuffer` objects that are awaiting reuse. A `Multiplexer` object asks its `ChunkBufferPool` object for a `ChunkBuffer` object when it needs one. If the `ChunkBufferPool` object has any `ChunkBuffer` objects in its collection, it takes one out of the collection and gives it to the `Multiplexer` object. If the `ChunkBufferPool` object does not have any `ChunkBuffer` objects in its collection, then it creates a new one. When a `ChunkBuffer` object is no longer needed, it is returned to the `ChunkBufferPool` object. This is an application of the Object Pool pattern described in *Volume 1*.

```
private Queue connectionQueue = new Queue();
```

When a `Multiplexer` object receives data associated with a new virtual connection, it creates a `Socket` object and places it in a `Queue` object. It stays in the `Queue` until a call to the `Multiplexer` object's `accept` method takes it out of the `Queue` object and passes it to its caller.

```
private ConnectionIDFactory idFactory;
```

This `Multiplexer` implementation delegates the creation of `ConnectionID` objects to a class called `ConnectionIDFactory`.

```
private int connectionIDLength;
```

`Multiplexer` objects transmit `ConnectionID` objects as a sequence of bytes. The `Multiplexer` object on one end of an actual connection may create `ConnectionID` objects that are represented as a longer sequence of bytes than the other. This may be due to environmental differences or because the programs on each end of the actual connection are using different versions of the `Multiplexer` class.

`Multiplexer` objects must exchange connection IDs without regard to which `Multiplexer` object created the connection ID. To accomplish this, when two `Multiplexer` objects begin working with each other, they exchange the lengths of the connection IDs that they produce. They set the value of their `connectionIDLength` instance variable to the larger of the two lengths. They then force all of the connection IDs that they create to be that length. If the natural length of a connection ID is less than this, it is padded with zeros.

```java
// This array of bytes is used to read bytes directly from
// the actual connection.
private byte[] inputBuffer;
```

The next three variables contain some of the parameters discussed under the "Implementation" heading.

```java
private int maxMessageLength; // Maximum number of data
                             // bytes to put in a message.
private int highWaterMark;
private int lowWaterMark;
```

`Multiplexer` objects communicate with each other by sending messages over the actual connection. Each message begins with an `int` value that identifies the type of the message. If the value is a positive number, the message contains data for a virtual connection and the value is the number of data bytes in the message. The following negative values are used to indicate other types of messages.

```java
private static final int CLOSE_CONNECTION = -1;
private static final int BLOCK_WRITES = -2;
private static final int UNBLOCK_WRITES = -3;

private static final int MESSAGE_HEADER_LENGTH = 6;
```

The constructor for the `Multiplexer` class takes two arguments: The first argument is the socket for the actual connection. The second argument is an object that encapsulates the parameters discussed in the "Implementation" section that control the operation of the `Multiplexer` object.

```java
public Multiplexer(Socket actualSocket,
                   MultiplexerParameters parameters)
                                        throws IOException {
    this.actualSocket = actualSocket;
    maxMessageLength = parameters.maxMessageLength;
    highWaterMark = parameters.highWaterMark;
    lowWaterMark = parameters.lowWaterMark;
    actualSocket.setTcpNoDelay(false);

    // Create a DataOutputStream to write to the actual
    // connection
    int myBufferSize
      = MESSAGE_HEADER_LENGTH+maxMessageLength;
```

```
        OutputStream out = actualSocket.getOutputStream();
        BufferedOutputStream bout;
        bout = new BufferedOutputStream(out, myBufferSize);
        actualOut = new DataOutputStream(bout);

        // Send the buffer size we are using to the Multiplexer
        // object on the other side of the connection.
        actualOut.writeInt(myBufferSize);
        actualOut.flush();

        // Create a DataInputStream to read from the actual
        // connection. Use the buffer size sent by the other
        // Multiplexer object.
        InputStream in = actualSocket.getInputStream();
        int otherBufferSize
          = new DataInputStream(in).readInt();
        BufferedInputStream bin;
        bin = new BufferedInputStream(in);
        actualIn = new DataInputStream(bin);

        // Create a buffer for reading from the actual
        // connection.
        inputBuffer = new byte[otherBufferSize];

        // Negotiate the length of a connection ID with the
        // other Multiplexer object
        idFactory = new ConnectionIDFactory(actualSocket);
        actualOut.writeShort(idFactory.getByteSize());
        actualOut.flush();
        connectionIDLength = Math.max(idFactory.getByteSize(),
                                      actualIn.readShort());
        idFactory.setByteSize(connectionIDLength);

        // Create a ChunkBufferPool object to
        // manage ChunkBuffer objects.
        bufferPool
          = new ChunkBufferPool(parameters.maxBuffers,
                                maxMessageLength);
    } // constructor(Socket)

    /**
     * Return the address of the remote host that the actual
     * connection connects to.
     */
    public InetAddress getRemoteAddress() {
        return actualSocket.getInetAddress();
    } // getRemoteAddress

    /**
     * Return the local address that the actual connection is
     * connected to.
     */
    public InetAddress getLocalAddress() {
        return actualSocket.getLocalAddress();
    } // getLocalAddress()
```

```
/**
 * Create a virtual connection and return a socket object
 * that encapsulates it.
 */
public Socket createConnection() throws IOException {
    ConnectionID  id = idFactory.createConnectionID();
    MultiplexerSocket vsocket;
    vsocket = new MultiplexerSocket(id, actualSocket,
                                    this, bufferPool,
                                    highWaterMark,
                                    lowWaterMark);

    socketTable.put(id, vsocket);
    return vsocket;
} // createConnection()


/**
 * Write a byte to the given virtual connection.
 * @param connectionID The ConnectionID of the virtual
 *                     connection to write to.
 * @param b The byte to write to the virtual connection.
 */
void write(ConnectionID id, int b) throws IOException {
    synchronized (actualOut) {
        writeMessageHeader(1);
        id.write(actualOut);
        actualOut.write(b);
    } // synchronized
} // write(ConnectionID, int)


/**
 * Send a message to the Multiplexer sobject on
 * the other end of the given virtual connection telling it
 * to stop sending any more data messages.
 */
void startMoratorium(ConnectionID id) throws IOException {
    synchronized (actualOut) {
        writeMessageHeader(BLOCK_WRITES);
        id.write(actualOut);
    } // synchronized
} // startMoratorium(ConnectionID)


/**
 * Send a message to the Multiplexer object on
 * the other end of the given virtual connection telling it
 * to resume sending data messages.
 */
void endMoratorium(ConnectionID id) throws IOException {
    synchronized (actualOut) {
        writeMessageHeader(UNBLOCK_WRITES);
        id.write(actualOut);
    } // synchronized
} // endMoratorium(ConnectionID)
```

```
/**
 * Send a message to the Multiplexer object on
 * the other end of the given virtual connection telling it
 * that the virtual connection is closed.
 */
void endConnection(ConnectionID id) throws IOException {
    // If this is being called in response to a
    // CLOSE_CONNECTION message, the ConnectionID will
    // already have been removed from socketTable
    if (socketTable.get(id)!=null) {
        synchronized (actualOut) {
            socketTable.remove(id);
            writeMessageHeader(CLOSE_CONNECTION);
            id.write(actualOut);
        } // synchronized
    } // if
} // endConnection(ConnectionID)

/**
 * Close this object and free its resources.
 */
void close() {
    // close all of the sockets that depend on this object.
    Enumeration ids = socketTable.keys();
    while (ids.hasMoreElements()) {
        try {
            endConnection((ConnectionID)ids.nextElement());
        } catch (Exception e) {
        } // try
    } // while

    // Close the resources that this object uses.
    try {
        actualOut.close();
        actualIn.close();
        actualSocket.close();
    } catch (Exception e) {
    } // try
} // close

/**
 * Write len bytes from the specified array,
 * starting at index ndx to this output stream.
 * @param connectionID The connectionID to write to.
 * @param     b     the data.
 * @param     ndx   the start offset in the data.
 * @param     len   the number of bytes to write.
 */
void write(ConnectionID id,
           byte b[],
           int ndx,
           int len) throws IOException {
    synchronized (actualOut) {
```

```
            writeMessageHeader(len);
            id.write(actualOut);
            actualOut.write(b, ndx, len);
        } // synchronized
    } // write(ConnectionID, byte[], int, int)


    /**
     * Flush output buffers associated with the given
     * virtual connection.
     */
    void flush(ConnectionID id) throws IOException {
        // For now, there are no connectionID specific buffers.
        actualOut.flush();
    } // flush(int)
    private void writeMessageHeader(int messageHeader)
                                        throws IOException {
        actualOut.writeInt(messageHeader);
    } // writeMessageHeader(int)


    private int readMessageHeader() throws IOException {
        return actualIn.readInt();
    } // readMessageHeader()


    /**
     * Create a socket for a virtual connection created at the
     * other end of the actual connection. Put it in a queue
     * where it will stay until it is accepted.
     * @param id The ConnectionID for the new virtual
     *           connection.
     * @return The queued socket
     */
    private
    MultiplexerSocket queueNewConnection(ConnectionID id)
                                throws SocketException {
        MultiplexerSocket ms;
        ms = new MultiplexerSocket(id, actualSocket,
                                   this, bufferPool,
                                   highWaterMark,
                                   lowWaterMark);
        socketTable.put(id, ms);
        connectionQueue.put(ms);
        return ms;
    } // queueNewConnection(ConnectionID)


    /**
     * Accept a virtual connection. If there are no
     * connections waiting to be accepted, then this method
     * does not return until there is a connection to
     * accept.
     * @return The socket that encapsulates the accepted
     *         virtual connection.
     */
    public Socket accept() throws InterruptedException {
```

```
        return (Socket)connectionQueue.get();
    } // accept()

    /**
     * Accept a virtual connection.  If there are no
     * connections waiting to be accepted then this method does
     * not return until there is a connection to be accepted.
     * @param t The number of milliseconds this method should
     *          wait for virtual connection before throwing an
     *          InterruptedException
     * @return The socket that encapsulates the accepted
     *          virtual connection.
     * @exception InterruptedException If the given number of
     *          milliseconds elapse without a connection
     *          being accepted or the current thread is
     *          interrupted.
     */
    public Socket accept(int t) throws InterruptedException {
        return (Socket)connectionQueue.get(t);
    } // accept()
```

An instance of the private class, MessageDispatcher, is responsible for reading messages from an actual connection and dispatching them to the thread that will process them.

```
private class MessageDispatcher implements Runnable {
    private Thread dispatcherThread;
    private static final String THREAD_NAME
      = "MultiplexerDispatcher";

    MessageDispatcher() {
        dispatcherThread = new Thread(this, THREAD_NAME);
        dispatcherThread.start();
    } // constructor()

    /**
     * Top-level message dispatching logic.
     */
    public void run() {
        Thread myThread = Thread.currentThread();
        try {
            while (!myThread.isInterrupted()) {
                int messageHeader = readMessageHeader();
                if (messageHeader>0) {
                    readDataMessage(messageHeader);
                } else {
                    switch (messageHeader) {
                      case CLOSE_CONNECTION:
                          readCloseConnection();
                          break;
                      case BLOCK_WRITES:
                          readBlock();
                          break;
```

```
                        case UNBLOCK_WRITES:
                            readUnblock();
                            break;
                    } // switch
                } // if
            } // while
        } catch (IOException e) {
            // This Multiplexer object can no longer
            // function, so close it.
            close();
        } // try
} // run()


/**
 * Read the body of a data message, put the data in a
 * ChunkBuffer object and associate the ChunkBuffer
 * object with the virtual connection.
 * @param length The number of data bytes that the
 *               message header says the message
 *               contains.
 */
private void readDataMessage(int length)
                                    throws IOException {
    ConnectionID id;
    id = ConnectionID.read(actualIn,
                            connectionIDLength);
    MultiplexerSocket vsocket;
    vsocket = (MultiplexerSocket)socketTable.get(id);
    if (vsocket==null) {
        vsocket = queueNewConnection(id);
    } // if
    int messageLength = actualIn.readInt();

    // The message length should not exceed the
    // promised length, but allow for the possibility
    // that it may be longer.
    while (messageLength>inputBuffer.length) {
        actualIn.readFully(inputBuffer, 0,
                            inputBuffer.length);
        vsocket.queueBuffer(inputBuffer.length,
                            inputBuffer);
        messageLength -= inputBuffer.length;
    } // while
    actualIn.readFully(inputBuffer, 0, messageLength);
    vsocket.queueBuffer(messageLength, inputBuffer);
} // readMessageHeader()


/**
 * Read and process a CLOSE_CONNECTION message.
 */
private void readCloseConnection() throws IOException {
    ConnectionID id;
    id = ConnectionID.read(actualIn,
```

```
                                    connectionIDLength);
        MultiplexerSocket vsocket;
        vsocket =(MultiplexerSocket)socketTable.remove(id);
        if (vsocket!=null) {
            vsocket.close()
        } // if
    } // readCloseConnection()

    /**
     * Read and process a BLOCK_WRITES message.
     */
    private void readBlock() throws IOException {
        ConnectionID id;
        id = ConnectionID.read(actualIn,
                               connectionIDLength);
        MultiplexerSocket vsocket;
        vsocket =(MultiplexerSocket)socketTable.get(id);
        if (vsocket!=null) {
            vsocket.blockWrites();
        } // if
    } // readBlock()

    /**
     * Read and process a UNBLOCK_WRITES message.
     */
    private void readUnblock() throws IOException {
        ConnectionID id;
        id = ConnectionID.read(actualIn,
                               connectionIDLength);
        MultiplexerSocket vsocket;
        vsocket =(MultiplexerSocket)socketTable.get(id);
        if (vsocket!=null) {
            vsocket.unblockWrites();
        } // if
    } // readUnblock()
    } // class MessageDispatcher
...
} // class Multiplexer
```

An instance of the `ConnectionIDFactory` class is responsible for creating instances of the `ConnectionID` class. The information used to create a `ConnectionID` object depends on the actual connection that the `ConnectionID` is used with. A `ConnectionIDFactory` object encapsulates that information.

```
class ConnectionIDFactory {
    // Array of information common to all ConnectionID objects
    // associated with the same actual connection
    private byte[] commonInfo;
    private static final int PORT_NUMBER_LENGTH = 2;
    static final int SERIAL_NUMBER_LENGTH = 4;

    private int counter = 0;
    private int byteSize = -1;
```

```java
/**
 * constructor.
 * @param socket The socket that encapsulates the actual
 *               connection this object will produce
 *               ConnectionID objects for.
 */
ConnectionIDFactory(Socket socket) {
    InetAddress inetAddress = socket.getLocalAddress();
    byte[] address = inetAddress.getAddress();

    // We include port number to allow for the possibility
    // of one Multiplexer object working with multiple
    // actual connections from the same host.
    int port = socket.getLocalPort();

    // Assume only 2 significant bytes in a port number and
    // four bytes four bytes for a serial number
    commonInfo
      = new byte[address.length + PORT_NUMBER_LENGTH];

    System.arraycopy(address, 0, commonInfo, 0,
                     address.length);
    int portOffset = address.length;
    commonInfo[portOffset] = (byte)port;
    commonInfo[portOffset+1] = (byte)(port>>8);
} // constructor(Socket)

/**
 * Return the number of bytes that will be used to read or
 * write a ConnectionID created by this object.
 */
int getByteSize() {
    if (byteSize == -1) {
        return commonInfo.length+SERIAL_NUMBER_LENGTH;
    } // if
    return byteSize;
} // getByteSize()

/**
 * Set the number of bytes that will be used to read or
 * write a ConnectionID created by this object.
 */
void setByteSize(int newValue) {
    byteSize = newValue;
} // setByteSize(int)

/**
 * Create a new ConnectionID object.
 */
ConnectionID createConnectionID() {
    synchronized (this) {
        counter++;
    } // synchronized
    return new ConnectionID(commonInfo, counter);
```

```
    } // createConnectionID()
} // class ConnectionIDFactory
```

ConnectionID objects identify virtual connections with information
passed to their constructor by the ConnectionIDFactory object that creates them. The identifying information is unique for at least the lifetime of
the actual connection.

```
class ConnectionID {
    private byte[] id;

    /**
     * This constructor is intended to be called by a
     * ConnectionIDFactory object that creates
     * unique identifying information
     * @param myId An array of bytes with content that uniquely
     *              identifies the local end of the actual
     *              connection.
     * @param serialNum A value that uniquely identifies a
     *                   virtual connection created on this end
     *                   of the actual connection.
     */
    ConnectionID(byte[] myId, int serialNum) {
        int idLength = myId.length
                     + ConnectionIDFactory.SERIAL_NUMBER_LENGTH;
        id = new byte[idLength];
        int serialNumberOffset = myId.length;
        System.arraycopy(myId, 0, id, 0, serialNumberOffset);
        switch (ConnectionIDFactory.SERIAL_NUMBER_LENGTH ) {
          case 4:
              id[serialNumberOffset+3] = (byte)(serialNum>>24);
          case 3:
              id[serialNumberOffset+2] = (byte)(serialNum>>16);
          case 2:
              id[serialNumberOffset+1] = (byte)(serialNum>>8);
          case 1:
              id[serialNumberOffset] = (byte)serialNum;
        } // switch
    } // constructor(byte[], int)

    /**
     * The constructor is called internally by the
     * readConnectionID method to create ConnectionID objects
     * from data in an input stream.
     * @param myId An array of bytes with content that uniquely
     *              identifies the local end of the actual
     *              connection. This array is used directly by
     *              the new object and is not copied.
     */
    private ConnectionID(byte[] myId) {
        this.id = myId;
    } // constructor(byte[])
```

```
/**
 * Read a ConnectionID from the given InputStream.
 * @param in The InputStream to read from.
 * @param byteSize The number of bytes of id information to
 *                 read. This is needed because each end of
 *                 an actual connection may use a different
 *                 number of bytes.
 */
static ConnectionID read(InputStream in,
                         int size) throws IOException {
    byte[] id = new byte[size];
    if (in.read(id, 0, size) != size) {
        throw new IOException();
    } // if
    return new ConnectionID(id);
} // readConnectionID(InputStream)

/**
 * Write the bytes of identifying information in this
 * ConnectionID to the given OutputStream.
 */
void write(OutputStream out) throws IOException {
    out.write(id);
} // writeConnectionId(OutputStream)
```

The ConnectionID class overrides the equals and hashCode methods it inherits from the Object class so that the identifying information in ConnectionID objects can be used as the key in a Hashtable.

```
/**
 * Return true if this method's argument is a ConnectionID
 * that contains the same byte values as this ConnectionID
 * object.
 */
public boolean equals(Object obj) {
    if (obj instanceof ConnectionID) {
        ConnectionID other = (ConnectionID)obj;
        if (id.length == other.id.length) {
            for (int i=0; i<id.length; i++) {
                if (id[i]!=other.id[i]) {
                    return false;
                } // if
            } // for
            return true;
        } // if length
    } // if
    return false;
} // equals(Object)

/**
 * Return a hashcode based on the contents of this object.
 */
public int hashCode() {
```

```
            long h = 1234;
            for (int i = id.length; --i >= 0; )
                h ^= id[i] * (i + 1);

            return (int)((h >> 32) ^ h);
        } // hashCode()
...
} // class ConnectionID
```

ChunkBuffer objects are used to buffer input from a virtual connection until it is read by a ChunkedInputStream object.

```
class ChunkBuffer {
    private byte[] buffer;      // The actual buffer
    private int firstFree;      // Index of next byte to put
                                // content in.
    private int firstContent;   // Index of first byte content.

    /**
     * constructor
     * @param capacity The number of bytes this object should
     * be able to hold
     */
    ChunkBuffer(int capacity) {
        buffer = new byte[capacity];
    } // constructor(int)

    /**
     * Return the capacity of this object.
     */
    int getCapicity() { return buffer.length; }

    /**
     * Set the contents of this buffer.
     * @param bytes Array of bytes to store in this object.
     * @param offset The number of bytes before the content.
     * @param length The number of content bytes.
     * @return The number of bytes copied into this object.
     */
    synchronized int setContent(byte[] bytes, int offset, int length) {
        int freeByteCount = buffer.length - firstFree;
        int copyCount = Math.min(freeByteCount, length);
        System.arraycopy(bytes, offset,
                          buffer, firstFree,
                          copyCount);
        firstFree += copyCount;
        return copyCount;
    } // setContent(byte[], int, int)

    /**
     * Retrieve some bytes of content from this object.
     * @param bytes An array to copy the content into.
```

```
       * @param offset The first position to copy content into.
       * @param length The number of bytes of content requested.
       * @return The actual number of bytes of content retrieved.
       */
      synchronized int getContent(byte[] bytes, int offset, int length) {
          int availableBytes = firstFree - firstContent;
          int copyCount = Math.min(availableBytes, length);
          System.arraycopy(buffer, firstContent,
                            bytes, offset,
                            copyCount);
          firstContent += copyCount;
          return copyCount;
      } // getContent(byte[], int, int)

      /**
       * Return the number of data bytes available in this
       * object.
       */
      int available() {
          return firstFree - firstContent;
      } // available()

      /**
       * Force this ChunkBuffer object to be empty. This method
       * is intended to be called for ChunkBuffer objects that were
       * associated with a virtual connection that was closed.
       *
       * Since this method is intended to be called when no
       * threads will be trying to get or set its content, the
       * method is not synchronized.
       */
      void makeEmpty() {
          firstContent = 0;
          firstFree = 0;
      } // makeEmpty()
  } // class ChunkBuffer
```

The `MultiplexerSocket` class is a subclass of `Socket`. It provides access to the virtual connection it encapsulates that is transparent to objects expecting to work with a `Socket` object. `MultiplexerSocket` objects also provide a convenient place to queue `ChunkBuffer` objects until their content can be read by a `ChunkedInputStream` object.

```
class MultiplexerSocket extends Socket {
    private ArrayList chunkBufferQueue = new ArrayList();
    private ChunkBufferPool bufferPool;
    private int highWaterMark;
    private int lowWaterMark;
    private boolean moratoriumRequested = false;
    private ConnectionID id;
    private Multiplexer mux;
    private MultiplexerSocketImpl impl;
```

```
/**
 * This constructor is intended to be called only by
 * Multiplexer objects.
 *
 * @param id The ConnectionID that identifies the virtual
 *           connection this socket is associated with to the
 *           local Multiplexer object.
 * @param actual The socket that encapsulates the actual
 *                connection.
 * @param mux The multiplexer object that owns this
 *            object.
 * @param bufferPool The ChunkBufferPool that this object
 *                   will get ChunkBuffer objects from.
 * @param highWaterMark If the number of queued ChunkBuffer
 *                      objects reaches this value, request
 *                      the other end of the virtual
 *                      connection to stop sending input.
 * @param lowWaterMark After the number of queued
 *                     ChunkBuffer objects reaches the
 *                     highWaterMark value, request that
 *                     the other end of the virtual
 *                     connection resume sending input.
 */
MultiplexerSocket(ConnectionID id,
                  Socket actual,
                  Multiplexer mux,
                  ChunkBufferPool bufferPool,
                  int highWaterMark,
                  int lowWaterMark)
                            throws SocketException {
    this(id, mux, bufferPool,
        highWaterMark, lowWaterMark,
        new MultiplexerSocketImpl(id, actual, mux));
} // constructor
```

The design of the `java.net` package calls for the `Socket` class and its subclasses to delegate to a subclass of `SocketImpl` responsibility for interfacing with an actual transport mechanism. This `MultiplexerSocket` class follows that architecture by delegating responsibility for transport to the `MultiplexerSocketImpl` class.

```
/**
 * This constructor is intended to be called only by
 * the non-private constructor.
 * @param id The ConnectionID that identifies the virtual
 *           connection this socket is associated with to the
 *           local Multiplexer object.
 * @param mux The multiplexer object that owns this
 *            object.
 * @param bufferPool The ChunkBufferPool that this object
 *                    will get ChunkBuffer objects from.
 * @param highWaterMark If the number of queued ChunkBuffer
```

```
 *                            objects reaches this value, request
 *                            the other end of the virtual
 *                            connection to stop sending input.
 * @param lowWaterMark After the number of queued
 *                            ChunkBuffer objects reaches the
 *                            highWaterMark value, request that
 *                            the other end of the virtual
 *                            connection resume sending input.
 * @param impl The implementation object for this socket.
 */
MultiplexerSocket(ConnectionID id,
                  Multiplexer mux,
                  ChunkBufferPool bufferPool,
                  int highWaterMark,
                  int lowWaterMark,
                  MultiplexerSocketImpl impl)
                            throws SocketException {
    super(impl);
    this.id = id;
    this.mux = mux;
    this.bufferPool = bufferPool;
    this.highWaterMark = highWaterMark;
    this.lowWaterMark = lowWaterMark;
    this.impl = impl;
    impl.setMultiplexerSocket(this);
} // constructor(ConnectionID)


/**
 * Put some buffered input bytes in a ChunkBuffer.
 * @param byteCount The number of input bytes.
 * @param buffer A byte array that contains the input
 * @exception IOException if there is a problem
 */
synchronized void queueBuffer(int byteCount, byte[] buffer)
                                    throws IOException {
    // Before allocating a ChunkBuffer object for the
    // input, check for an already queued ChunkBuffer
    // object that has enough free space.
    int queueSize = chunkBufferQueue.size();
    int offset = 0;
    if (queueSize>0) {
        ChunkBuffer cb
          = (ChunkBuffer)chunkBufferQueue.get(queueSize-1);
        if (cb.available()>0) {
            int size = Math.min(byteCount, cb.available());
            cb.setContent(buffer, 0, size);
            byteCount -= size;
            offset = size;
        } // if available
    } // if queueSize
    if (byteCount>0) {
        ChunkBuffer cb = bufferPool.allocateChunkBuffer();
        cb.setContent(buffer, offset, byteCount);
```

```
                    chunkBufferQueue.add(cb);
                    notify();
                    if (moratoriumRequested) {
                        if (chunkBufferQueue.size()<=lowWaterMark) {
                            mux.endMoratorium(id);
                            moratoriumRequested = false;
                        } // if lowWaterMark
                    } else {
                        if (chunkBufferQueue.size()>=highWaterMark) {
                            mux.startMoratorium(id);
                            moratoriumRequested = true;
                        } // if highWaterMark
                    } // if moratoriumRequested
                } // if byteCount
        } // queueBuffer(int, byte[])


        /**
         * Release a ChunkBuffer object to a pool of unallocated
         * ChunkBuffer objects.
         */
        void releaseChunkBuffer(ChunkBuffer cb) {
            bufferPool.releaseChunkBuffer(cb);
        } // releaseChunkBuffer(ChunkBuffer)


        /**
         * Return the next queued ChunkBuffer.
         */
        synchronized ChunkBuffer getChunkBuffer()
                                        throws IOException {
            return bufferPool.allocateChunkBuffer();
        } // getChunkBuffer()


        /**
         * block writes to this virtual connection.
         */
        void blockWrites() {
            impl.blockWrites();
        } // blockWrites


        /**
         * Unblock writes to this virtual connection.
         */
        void unblockWrites() {
            impl.unblockWrites();
        } // unblockWrites()
} // class MultiplexerSocket
```

Here is the `MultiplexerSocketImpl` class to which the `Multi-plexerSocket` class delegates the responsibility for transporting data.

```
public class MultiplexerSocketImpl extends SocketImpl {
    // This ConnectionID identifies the virtual connection
    // associated with this object.
    private ConnectionID id;
```

```
        // The Socket that encapsulates the actual connection.
        private Socket actual;

        // The Multiplexer object this object is working with.
        private Multiplexer mux;

        // The InputStream that is returned by getInputStream().
        private ChunkedInputStream in;

        // The OutputStream that is returned by getOutputStream().
        private ChunkedOutputStream out;

        // This is true after this Socket has been closed.
        private boolean closed = false;

        // The MultiplexerSocket this object is working for.
        private MultiplexerSocket theSocket;

        // This is true after a request to block writes has been
        // received, until a request to unblock is received.
        private boolean outputMoratorium = false;

        // Read operations time out after this many milliseconds.
        // If zero there is no time out.
        private int timeout = 0;

        /**
         * constructor
         * @param id The connection ID that identifies the virtual
         *           connection this socket is associated with to the
         *           local Multiplexer object.
         * @param actual The socket that encapsulates the actual
         *               connection.
         * @param mux The multiplexer object that owns this
         *           object.
         * @param theSocket The socket that uses this object.
         */
        MultiplexerSocketImpl(ConnectionID id,
                              Socket actual,
                              Multiplexer mux) {
           this.id = id;
           this.actual = actual;
        } // constructor(ConnectionID, Socket)

        /**
         * Set the MultiplexerSocket that this object will work
         * with.
         */
        void setMultiplexerSocket(MultiplexerSocket theSocket) {
            this.theSocket = theSocket;
        } // setMultiplexerSocket(MultiplexerSocket)
...
        /**
         * Returns an input stream for this socket.
```

```
         * @exception SocketException if the socket is closed
         * @exception SocketException if optID is unknown.
         */
        public Object getOption(int optID) throws SocketException {
            switch (optID) {
              case SO_BINDADDR:
                  return actual.getLocalAddress();
              case SO_TIMEOUT:
                  return new Integer(timeout);
              default:
                  throw new SocketException();
            } // switch
        } // getOption(int)
...
    /**
     * Thrown a SocketException if this socket is closed.
     */
    private void checkClosed() throws SocketException {
        if (closed) {
            throw new SocketException("closed");
        } // if
    } // checkClosed()


    /**
     * block writes to this virtual connection.
     */
    void blockWrites() {
        outputMoratorium = true;
        if (out!=null) {
            out.blockWrites();
        } // if
    } // blockWrites


    /**
     * Unblock writes to this virtual connection.
     */
    void unblockWrites() {
        outputMoratorium = false;
        if (out!=null) {
            out.unblockWrites();
        } // if
    } // unblockWrites()
} // class MultiplexerSocketImpl
```

Here is the `InputStream` class that reads input by getting `Chunk-Buffer` objects containing input bytes from a `MultiplexerSocket` object.

```
class ChunkedInputStream extends InputStream {
    // This is true after this InputStream has been closed.
    boolean closed = false;
```

```
// The MultiplexerSocket object this object gets
// ChunkBuffer objects from.
private MultiplexerSocket mSocket;


// The current ChunkBuffer object.
private ChunkBuffer buffer = null;


// Buffer used for a single byte read.
private byte[] byteBuffer = new byte[1];


/**
 * constructor
 * @param mSocket The MultiplexerSocket object this object
 *                will work with.
 */
ChunkedInputStream(MultiplexerSocket mSocket) {
    this.mSocket = mSocket;
} // constructor(Multiplexer)


/**
 * Reads the next byte of data from the input stream. The
 * value byte is returned as an int in the
 * range 0 to 255. If no byte is available because the end
 * of the stream has been reached, the value -1 is
 * returned. This method blocks until input data is
 * available, the end of the stream is detected, or an
 * exception is thrown.
 * @return the next byte of data, or -1 if the end of the
 *                stream is reached.
 */
public int read() throws IOException {
    checkOpen();
    if (buffer==null || buffer.available()<1) {
        buffer = mSocket.getChunkBuffer();
        if (buffer==null) {
            return -1;
        } // if
    } // if
    if (buffer.getContent(byteBuffer, 0, 1) <1) {
        return -1;
    } // if
    return byteBuffer[0];
} // read()


/**
 * Reads up to len bytes of data from the input stream
 * into an array of bytes. An attempt is made to read as
 * many as len bytes, but a smaller number may be read,
 * possibly zero. The number of bytes actually read is
 * returned as an integer.
 *
```

```
 * This method blocks until input data is available, end
 * of file is detected, or an exception is thrown.
 * @param    b   The buffer into which the data is read.
 * @param    off The start offset in array b at which the
 *           data is written.
 * @param    len  the maximum number of bytes to read.
 * @return   the total number of bytes read into the
 *           buffer, or -1 if there is no
 *           more data because the end of the stream has
 *           been reached.
 */
public int read(byte b[], int off, int len)
                                           throws IOException {
    checkOpen();
    if (buffer==null || buffer.available()<1) {
        buffer = mSocket.getChunkBuffer();
        if (buffer==null) {
            return -1;
        } // if
    } // if
    return buffer.getContent(byteBuffer, 0, 1);
} // read(byte[], int, int)


/**
 * Returns the minimum number of bytes that can be read
 * (or skipped over) from this input stream without
 * blocking by the next caller of a method for this input
 * stream. The next caller might be the same thread or
 * another thread.
 *
 * The available method for class InputStream always
 * returns 0.
 */
public int available() throws IOException {
    checkOpen();
    if (buffer==null) {
        return 0;
    } // if
    return buffer.available();
} // available()


/**
 * Closes this input stream and releases any system
 * resources associated with the stream.
 */
public void close() {
    if (buffer!=null) {
        mSocket.releaseChunkBuffer(buffer);
    } // if
    closed = true;
} // close()


/**
 * Throw an IOException if this InputStream is closed.
```

```
         */
      private void checkOpen() throws IOException {
          if (closed) {
              throw new IOException("closed");
          } // if
      } // checkOpen()
...
} // class ChunkedInputStream
```

Here is the OutputStream class that is used to write bytes to virtual connections.

```
class ChunkedOutputStream extends OutputStream {
    private ConnectionID id;
    private Multiplexer multiplexer;
    private boolean closed = false; // True after being closed
    private boolean outputMoratorium = false;

    /**
     * constructor
     * @param multiplexer The multiplexer object this object
     *                    will write to.
     * @param id The ConnectionID of the virtual connection
     *           this object will write to.
     */
    ChunkedOutputStream(Multiplexer multiplexer,
                        ConnectionID id) {
       this.multiplexer = multiplexer;
       this.id = id;
    } // constructor(Multiplexer, int)

    /**
     * Writes the given byte to this output stream. The byte
     * to write is the eight low-order bits of the argument b.
     * The 24 high-order bits of b are ignored.
     * @param      b    The byte to write.
     */
    public void write(int b) throws IOException {
        checkClosed();
        multiplexer.write(id, b);
    } // write(int)

    /**
     * Write len bytes from the specified array
     * starting at index ndx to this output stream.
     * @param      b      the data.
     * @param      ndx    the start offset in the data.
     * @param      len    the number of bytes to write.
     */
    public void write(byte b[], int ndx, int len)
                                        throws IOException {
        checkClosed();
        multiplexer.write(id, b, ndx, len);
    } // write(byte[], int, int)
```

```
/**
 * Flushes this output stream, forcing any buffered output
 * bytes to be written.
 */
public void flush() throws IOException {
    checkClosed();
    multiplexer.flush(id);
} // flush()

/**
 * Closes this output stream and releases any resources
 * associated with it.
 * <p>
 * The close method of OutputStream does nothing.
 */
public void close() throws IOException {
    if (!closed) {
        flush();
    } //if
    closed = true;
} // close()

/**
 * Throw an IOException if this OutputStream is closed.
 */
private void checkClosed() throws IOException {
    if (closed) {
        throw new IOException("closed");
    } // if closed
    if (outputMoratorium) {
        synchronized (this) {
            try {
                do {
                    wait();
                } while (outputMoratorium);
            } catch (InterruptedException e) {
                throw new IOException();
            } // try
            if (closed) {
                throw new IOException("closed");
            } // if closed
        } // synchronized
    } // if outputMoratorium
} // checkClosed()

/**
 * Return true if this output stream is closed.
 */
boolean isClosed() {
    return closed;
} // isClosed()

/**
 * Block writes to this virtual connection.
```

```
    */
    synchronized void blockWrites() {
        outputMoratorium = true;
    } // blockWrites

    /**
     * Unblock writes to this virtual connection.
     */
    synchronized void unblockWrites() {
        outputMoratorium = false;
        notifyAll();
    } // unblockWrites()
} // class ChunkedOutputStream
```

Next, we look at classes that have something to do with RMI. RMI allows programs to alter the way that it creates `Socket` and `Server-Socket` objects by providing objects to which it can delegate those responsibilities.

To create `ServerSocket` objects on behalf of RMI, an object must implement the `RMIServerSocketFactory` interface. Here is a class that creates, on behalf of RMI, `ServerSocket` objects that accept virtual connections from `Multiplexer` objects.

```
public class VirtualServerSocketFactory
                        implements RMIServerSocketFactory {
    private Queue acceptQueue;
```

A `VirtualServerSocketFactory` object accepts connections from `Multiplexer` objects that have been registered with it. It works by creating a thread for each `Multiplexer` object and having that thread call the `Multiplexer` object's accept method. The thread does not return from the `accept` method until there is a new virtual connection for it to accept and return. When the thread returns, it puts the `Socket` object that encapsulates the new virtual connection in the `acceptQueue` queue. It stays there until a call to the `accept` method of the `ServerSocket` object that the `VirtualServerSocketFactory` object creates removes it from the queue.

```
    private Hashtable muxTable;
```

When a `Multiplexer` object is registered with a `VirtualServer-SocketFactory` object, the thread it creates is actually an instance of a subclass of `Thread` called `ConnectionAcceptor`. When a `Multiplexer` object is unregistered, the `VirtualServerSocketFactory` object must tell the thread to stop accepting connections on its behalf. To do this, it must keep track of the thread associated with each `Multiplexer` object. It keeps track of these associations by storing `ConnectionAcceptor` objects in the `muxTable Hashtable` with the `Multiplexer` object that they poll as their key.

```
private RMIVirtualServerSocket serverSocketInstance;
```

A `VirtualServerSocketFactory` object creates just one `ServerSocket` object. If asked multiple times to create a `ServerSocket` object, it will return the same `ServerSocket` object each time. The `VirtualServerSocketFactory` object uses its `ServerSocketInstance` variable to refer to this `ServerSocket` object.

```
public VirtualServerSocketFactory() {
    muxTable = new Hashtable();
    acceptQueue = new Queue();
} // constructor(int)

/**
 * Register a Multiplexer object so that this
 * object will use it.
 * @param mux The Multiplexer object to register.
 */
public void registerMultiplexer(Multiplexer mux) {
    muxTable.put(mux, new ConnectionAcceptor(mux));
} // registerMultiplexer(Multiplexer)

/**
 * Unregister a Multiplexer object so that this
 * object will stop using it.
 * @param mux The Multiplexer object to unregister.
 */
public void unregisterMultiplexer(Multiplexer mux) {
    ConnectionAcceptor acceptor;
    acceptor = (ConnectionAcceptor)muxTable.remove(mux);
    if (acceptor!=null) {
        acceptor.interrupt();
    } // if
} // unregisterMultiplexer(Multiplexer)
```

The `createServerSocket` method returns a server socket that accepts connections at the given port. If the given port number is −1, then it creates a server socket that accepts virtual connections from registered `Multiplexer` objects. Otherwise, it creates a standard `ServerSocket` object that accepts actual connections. This use of an otherwise illegal port number makes it possible for RMI to work with actual and virtual connections at the same time.

```
public ServerSocket createServerSocket(int port)
                                throws IOException {
    if (port==-1) {
        if (serverSocketInstance==null) {
            serverSocketInstance
                = new RMIVirtualServerSocket();
        } // if
```

```
            return serverSocketInstance;
        } // if
        RMISocketFactory defaultFactory;
        defaultFactory
            = RMISocketFactory.getDefaultSocketFactory();
        return defaultFactory.createServerSocket(port);
    } // createServerSocket(int)
...
```

Instances of the private class `ConnectionAcceptor` poll the `Multiplexer` object passed to their constructor for new connections.

```
    private class ConnectionAcceptor extends Thread {
        private Multiplexer mux;

        /**
         * Constructor
         * @param mux The Multiplexer object this object
         *            accepts connections from.
         */
        private ConnectionAcceptor(Multiplexer mux) {
            this.mux = mux;
            start();
        } // constructor(Multiplexer)

        public void run() {
            try {
                while (!isInterrupted()) {
                    acceptQueue.put(mux.accept());
                } // while
            } catch (InterruptedException e) {
            } // try
        } // run()
    } // class ConnectionAcceptor
```

The `ServerSocket` object that a `VirtualServerSocketFactory` creates is actually an instance of this private subclass of `ServerSocket`.

```
    /**
     * This subclass of ServerSocket accepts virtual
     * connections through a multiplexer object
     */
    private class RMIVirtualServerSocket extends ServerSocket {
        private int soTimeout = 0;

        /**
         * Constructor.
         * @param mux The multiplexer object this object will
         *            work with.
         * @exception  IOException  if an I/O error occurs
         *             when opening the socket.
         */
```

```
RMIVirtualServerSocket() throws IOException {
    // The superclass has no constructor that does not
    // bind a port. So we call the simplest
    // constructor and then immediately call the
    // superclass's close.
    super(0);
    super.close();
} // constructor

/**
 * Returns the local address of this server socket.
 * @return The address to which this socket is
 *         connected, or null if the socket is not
 *         connected.
 */
public InetAddress getInetAddress() {
    try {
        return InetAddress.getLocalHost();
    } catch (UnknownHostException e) {
        return null;
    } // try
} // getInetAddress()

/**
 * Returns the port on which this socket is listening.
 * @return -1
 */
public int getLocalPort() {
    return -1;
} // getLocalPort()

/**
 * Listen for a new virtual connection and accept it.
 * If there are no virtual connections waiting to be
 * accepted, this method does not return until there
 * is a virtual connection to be accepted.
 */
public Socket accept() throws IOException {
    try {
        return (Socket)acceptQueue.get(soTimeout);
    } catch (InterruptedException e) {
        throw new InterruptedIOException();
    } // try
} // accept()

/**
 * Closes this socket.
 */
public void close() {
    // Nothing to do.
} // close()

/**
 * Set SO_TIMEOUT to the specified timeout in
```

```
         * milliseconds. When this option is non-zero,
         * a call to accept() blocks for only this number of
         * milliseconds. If the timeout expires, a call to
         * accept throws a java.io.InterruptedIOException.
         * This must be set prior to a call to accept to have
         * an effect. The value must be greater than 0.
         * A timeout of zero is treated as an infinite timeout.
         */
        public void setSoTimeout(int timeout) throws SocketException {
            soTimeout = timeout;
        } // setSoTimeout(int)
...
    } // class RMIVirtualServerSocket
} // class VirtualServerSocketFactory
```

To create `Socket` objects on behalf of RMI, an object must implement the `RMIClientSocketFactory` interface. Here is a class that creates, on behalf of RMI, `Socket` objects for virtual connections.

```
public class VirtualClientSocketFactory
                        implements RMIClientSocketFactory {
    private Hashtable muxTable;

    /**
     * Constructor
     */
    public VirtualClientSocketFactory() {
        muxTable = new Hashtable();
    } // constructor(int)

    /**
     * Register a Multiplexer object so that this
     * object will use it.
     */
    public void registerMultiplexer(Multiplexer mux) {
        muxTable.put(mux.getRemoteAddress(), mux);
    } // registerMultiplexer(Multiplexer)

    /**
     * Unregister a Multiplexer object so that this
     * object will stop using it.
     */
    public void unregisterMultiplexer(Multiplexer mux) {
        muxTable.remove(mux.getRemoteAddress());
    } // unregisterMultiplexer(Multiplexer)
```

The `createSocket` method creates a client socket connected to the specified host and port. If the port number is –1 and the host's address matches one of the registered `Multiplexer` objects, then it ignores the port number passed to it and uses the `Multiplexer` object to create a virtual connection. Otherwise, it creates a real connection using RMI's default mechanism. Using an otherwise illegal port number in this way allows RMI to work with both actual and virtual connections.

```
public Socket createSocket(String host, int port)
                                       throws IOException {
    if (port==-1) {
        InetAddress remoteAddress;
        remoteAddress = InetAddress.getByName(host);
        Multiplexer mux;
        mux = (Multiplexer)muxTable.get(remoteAddress);
        if (mux !=null) {
            return mux.createConnection();
        } else {
            String msg;
            msg = "No Multiplexer registered for " +host;
            throw new IOException(msg);
        } // if mux
    } // if port
    RMISocketFactory factory;
    factory = RMISocketFactory.getDefaultSocketFactory();
    return factory.createSocket(host, port);
} // createSocket(String, int)
} // class VirtualClientSocketFactory
```

The final class that we will look at in this example is a convenience class. To have RMI use VirtualClientSocketFactory and Virtual-ServerSocketFactory objects by default, you need a class that is a sub-class of java.rmi.server.RMISocketFactory. RMISocketFactory is an abstract class that implements both the RMIClientSocketFactory and the RMIServerSocketFactory interface. The way to set defaults is to pass an instance of a subclass of RMISocketFactory to the RMISocketFactory class's static setSocketFactory method.

The VirtualSocketFactory class is a subclass of RMISocket-Factory that delegates to VirtualClientSocketFactory and Virtual-ServerSocketFactory.

```
public class VirtualSocketFactory extends RMISocketFactory {
    private VirtualClientSocketFactory clientFactory;
    private VirtualServerSocketFactory serverFactory;

    /**
     * Constructor
     */
    public VirtualSocketFactory() {
        clientFactory = new VirtualClientSocketFactory();
        serverFactory = new VirtualServerSocketFactory();
    } // constructor

    /**
     * Register a Multiplexer that can be used to
```

```
     * create Socket objects.
     */
    public void registerClientMultiplexer(Multiplexer mux) {
        clientFactory.registerMultiplexer(mux);
    } // registerMultiplexer(Multiplexer)

    /**
     * Unregister a Multiplexer object so that this
     * object will stop using it to create
     * Socket objects.
     */
    public void unregisterClientMultiplexer(Multiplexer mux) {
        clientFactory.unregisterMultiplexer(mux);
    } // unregisterMultiplexer(Multiplexer)

    /**
     * Create a client socket connected to the specified host
     * and port.
     *
     * If the port number is -1 and host name resolves to a
     * network address that matches one of the registered
     * Multiplexer object, then this method ignores the
     * port number passed to it and uses the
     * Multiplexer to create a virtual connection.
     * Otherwise it create a real connection using RMI's
     * default mechanism.
     */
    public Socket createSocket(String host, int port)
                                        throws IOException {
        return clientFactory.createSocket(host, port);
    } // createSocket(String, int)

    /**
     * Register a Multiplexer object so that this
     * object will use it to create
     * ServerSocket objects.
     */
    public void registerServerMultiplexer(Multiplexer mux) {
        serverFactory.registerMultiplexer(mux);
    } // registerMultiplexer(Multiplexer)

    /**
     * Unregister a Multiplexer object so that this
     * object will stop using it to create
     * ServerSocket objects.
     */
    public void unregisterServerMultiplexer(Multiplexer mux) {
        serverFactory.unregisterMultiplexer(mux);
    } // unregisterMultiplexer(Multiplexer)

    /**
     * Create a server socket. If the given port number is -1,
     * then it creats a server socket that accepts connections
```

```
 * from registered Multiplexer objects.
 * Otherwise, it creates a standard
 * ServerSocket that accepts actual connections.
 */
public ServerSocket createServerSocket(int port)
                                    throws IOException {
    return serverFactory.createServerSocket(port);
} // createServerSocket(int)

/**
 * Use the given name to a string of the form
 * //host:-1/name
 * This string can be used to register an object with a
 * name registry.
 */
public String makeRegistryString(String name)
                            throws UnknownHostException {
    return serverFactory.makeRegistryString(name);
} // makeRegistryString(String)
} // class VirtualSocketFactory
```

RELATED PATTERNS

Object Pool. The Connection Multiplexing pattern uses the Object Pool pattern (described in *Volume 1*) to manage data buffers.

Object Identifier. The `ConnectionID` objects used by the Connection Multiplexing pattern are an application of the Object Identifier pattern.

Layered Architecture. The Connection Multiplexing pattern uses the Layered Architecture pattern described in [Buschman96].

Scheduler. The Scheduler pattern can be used to ensure that all virtual connections get their fair share of the actual connection's bandwidth. The Scheduling pattern describes how to enforce a policy that determines when a thread is scheduled to use a resource.

Proactor. The Connection Multiplexing pattern uses the Proactor pattern which is described in [Schmidt97].

Concurrency Patterns

Session Object

This pattern was previously described in [Yoder-Barcalow98].

SYNOPSIS

There is a possibly large number of objects that determine the state of each session that a server has with its clients. Use a single object to contain all the state information needed during a session by the server. Make the object accessible to all objects that need state information for the current session.

CONTEXT

You are designing a client/server application to allow people to analyze a company's sales data. During the course of a session with this application, the server needs to know who is logged into each client for security reasons. It also needs to keep track of the client's previous requests to provide context.

One way to allow the server to keep track of each session's state is to create an instance of the entire server for each session. Creating an instance of most of the classes in the server for each session seems wasteful. You look for a better way.

FORCES

- ☺ A server needs to be aware of the state of each session.
- ☺ A server communicates with its clients through a stateless protocol. This makes it impossible for the server to manage the state of a session without some assistance from the client.
- ☺ You want to minimize the number of objects it takes for a server to be aware of each session's state.
- ☺ Some sessions are designed so there will always be an event that clearly signals the end of the session. For example, a session may end when a server loses its connection with a client or when the client issues a logout command. Other sessions are designed so there is no event that signals the end of a session. Without knowing when a ses-

sion ends, a server does not know when it can discard the state information associated with the session.

☹ If a server is required to handle a large number of concurrent sessions, the memory required by the state information may become problematically large.

SOLUTION

Encapsulate all of the state information associated with a session in a single object. Make that object visible to all objects that need access to state information. Figure 7.1 shows the role that classes play in this solution.

As shown in Figure 7.1, Server objects have a collection of Session objects. Each Session object in the collection is identified by its associated Client. The Implementation section describes a few different ways to organize the collection of Session objects and associate them with Client objects.

CONSEQUENCES

☺ The number of objects used to maintain the state of sessions is minimized.

☺ Session objects provide a common interface for accessing values shared by different parts of a program.

☹ Implementations of the Session Object pattern typically involve many methods that have a reference to a session object in their signature. They may also involve multiple classes with instance variables that refer to a session object through a ThreadLocal object (ThreadLocal objects are described at the end of the "Implementation" section). Because an implementation of the Session Object involves many classes and methods, it can be very time consuming to retrofit the use of session objects to a program that is well along in its development.

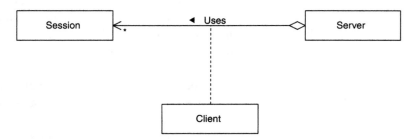

FIGURE 7.1 Session object.

IMPLEMENTATION

The first implementation issue we will examine is how to associate session objects with sessions. There are a few common ways of doing this.

Some application designs call for the client to maintain a network connection with the server for the entire duration of a session. For such applications, a session ends when the connection ends. A natural way to manage session objects in this situation is to associate each session object with the corresponding connection.

Figure 7.2 shows an organization that associates a connection with a session object. When a server accepts a connection from a client, it passes the connection to a session object that processes it in its own thread.

The design of some applications calls for a client and server to carry on a session without maintaining a connection for the duration of the session. In such applications, the server may not always know when a session is over. For such situations, it is usually best if the client keeps and manages the session objects. This arrangement avoids the difficulty of the server accumulating session objects for sessions that have ended without the server being aware of it. This way of managing session objects is especially good for situations in which sessions are over when a client dies. Figure 7.3 shows how this scheme works.

In this scheme, the client tells the server it wants to start a new session. The server then creates a session object and sends the session object to the client. Every time a client sends a message to the server, the message includes the session object. Another aspect of this is that the server does not use any session specific resources, such as files or locks, unless it is processing a call from a session's client. The advantage of this scheme is that the server has no session specific state. The server does not care what the lifetime of a session is. This scheme makes the lifetime of a session the responsibility of the client.

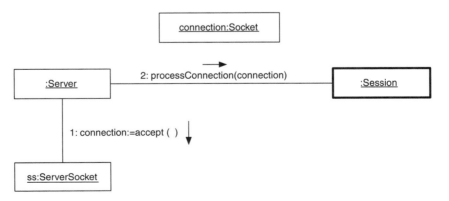

FIGURE 7.2 Session associated with a connection.

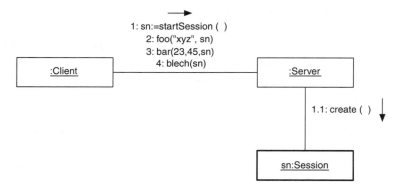

FIGURE 7.3 Client-managed connection.

If the duration of a session may exceed the lifetime of the client or the server, then you must use a different scheme for associating session objects with sessions. One such scheme is a variation of the one illustrated in Figure 7.3. The idea is to have the client store the session object in a disk file. This allows future clients to use the same session object. The drawback to this scheme is that it ties the future use of the session object to the same computer, or at least a computer that shares the file system that the session object is stored on. In many cases, the session is associated with a user rather than a computer or file system. In such cases, it is usually desirable for users to be able to continue a session with a server from a different computer than the one they started the session with.

A way to persistently associate a user with a session is to use a database. Even if there are multiple servers, they will be able to fetch the session currently associated with a user from the database. If sessions are persisted in this way, eventually there will be sessions in the database that are never continued. If you do nothing to handle such session objects, the number of these abandoned sessions in the database will increase indefinitely. To prevent the number of abandoned sessions in the database from getting too large, you can delete session objects from the database if their session has not been continued within a certain amount of time.

Another implementation issue to consider has to do with multithreaded servers. Most servers are multithreaded so they can handle multiple sessions concurrently. In a multithreaded server, you can't use instance variables to make session object visible to methods. The problem is that session objects must be visible only to method invocations that are involved with the corresponding session. A different thread or threads process each session. Instance variables are shared by all threads. Session objects must be visible only to the thread that is processing the corresponding session.

One way to make the session object visible to only one thread is to pass it as a parameter, as illustrated in Figure 7.4.

In this scheme, most method calls within a server include an argument to pass a reference to a session object. The disadvantages to this are that it makes method declarations and calls more verbose. It also adds to the time that it takes to call methods.

An alternative way to make session objects visible to only one thread is to use a `ThreadLocal` object to associate a session object with a thread. A `ThreadLocal` object associates a thread with an object. A `ThreadLocal` object is typically referenced by an instance variable like this:

```
ThreadLocal sessionContainer = new ThreadLocal();
```

You can associate an object with a `ThreadLocal` object like this:

```
sessionContainer.set(session);
```

You fetch an object from a `ThreadLocal` object like this:

```
session = (Session)sessionContainer.get();
```

What makes it interesting is that when you fetch an object from a `ThreadLocal` object, what you get is the last object that was associated with the `ThreadLocal` object by the thread that does the fetch. Two threads may access or modify values in a `ThreadLocal` object at the same time without interfering with each other.

KNOWN USES

A company that sells integrated application software sells a purchasing application with a client server architecture that associates session objects with connections between client and server.

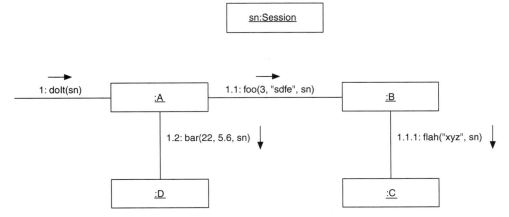

FIGURE 7.4 Session object visible as a parameter.

Web-based applications use cookies as a way of getting their clients (browsers) to store session objects.

There is an application that allows people to apply for life insurance on-line. People often do not have all of the required information when they first try to apply for insurance. For this reason, the application allows users to log off and finish later. The application implements this feature by saving a session object in a database.

CODE EXAMPLE

The code example is a skeletal implementation of a session class. It includes two pieces of information that most applications will need to know about sessions. One of these is the identity of the user. The example uses a numeric value that internally identifies a user. It is also common to use a string to identify the user.

The other piece of information is the user's locale setting. A server will typically use this information when generating messages for the user. If the server will use the locale information infrequently, it may make more sense to leave the locale out of the session class and have it be looked up in a database as needed.

```
public class Session implements Serializable {
    private long userID;
    private Locale locale;
    ...

    Session(long userID) {
        this.userID = userID;
    } // constructor

    public Locale getLocale() { return locale; }

    public void setLocale(Locale newValue) {
        locale = newValue;
    } // setLocale(Locale)

    ...
} // class Session
```

One other detail to notice about session class is that its constructor is not public. The reason for this is that servers will construct session objects but clients will not. This is based on the assumption that clients will receive session objects through a Java-based mechanism, such as RMI, that uses Java's serialization facility to copy the session object from the server to the client. Serialization does not use constructors.

RELATED PATTERNS

Singleton.   The Singleton pattern (described in *Volume 1*) uses a single instance of a class for an entire program. The Session pattern uses a single instance of a class per session.

Thread Pool.   You can use the Thread Pool pattern to manage the association between threads and sessions over time.

Lock File

SYNOPSIS

A program will need to have exclusive access to an external resource. You design the program to check for the existence of a lock file prior to accessing the resource. If the lock file exists, the program does not use the resource. If the lock file does not exist, the program creates the file and then uses the resource.

CONTEXT

Suppose you are designing a class whose purpose is to manage the contents of a file. To ensure its correct operation, instances of this class must avoid using a file while another instance of the class is using the same file. You want the class to use a mechanism that guarantees that a file is used by only one object at a time. You would like to use a locking mechanism that allows an object holding the lock to access a file, while preventing other objects from accessing the file at the same time.

Many operating systems have a file-locking feature that guarantees exclusive access to a file. Unfortunately, Java does not provide support for this sort of file locking. You could use the Java native code interface (JNI) to access an operating system feature. However, there are a number of negative consequences to using JNI that lead you to look for a different solution.

The solution you settle on is to create a *lock file*. A lock file is a file whose existence is a signal to other objects. If it exists, then other objects will know that the resource the lock file is associated with is in use. They will be expected to cooperate with the object that created the lock file by not using the resource while the lock file exists. When an object is finished using a resource, it deletes the lock file.

FORCES

☺ No more than one object at a time may access a resource.
☺ There is no available locking mechanism that guarantees exclusive access to a resource.
☺ An object performing an operation needs exclusive access to a resource. If it discovers that the resource is being used by another

object, an acceptable way for the object to handle the situation is to abort the operation.

☺ You need a way to coordinate access to a resource that will work the same way everywhere that Java runs. This is the most common reason for using the Lock File pattern.

☺ You are designing a distributed application that must coordinate the use of resources among multiple computers. The computer that coordinates the use of a particular resource can crash. When it comes back up, it is important that any locks that objects on other computers held before the crash are still intact.

☹ If an object discovers that a resource it needs is being used by another object, the object must wait until the resource is not being used by any other object before it uses the object. It is important that the object start using the resource as soon as it is available.

☹ Some schemes that arrange for objects to have exclusive access to a resource are based on cooperation. Such schemes rely on objects' voluntarily coordinating their use of a resource with each other. Such cooperative schemes do not work if there are any objects that access the resource without following the scheme and cooperating with other objects.

SOLUTION

Allow cooperating objects to have exclusive access to a resource by having each object first test for the existence of a lock file. A lock file is a file that generally contains either information to identify its creator or no data at all. Its existence simply indicates that the resource it is associated with is in use.

Before an object attempts to use a resource it needs, it checks for the existence of a lock file. If the lock file already exists, the object either aborts the operation it is performing or waits until the lock file no longer exists. If the file does not exist, the object creates the lock file. When the object is finished with the resource, it deletes the lock file. Figure 7.5 shows these interactions.

One important detail not shown in Figure 7.5 is that the test for the lock file's existence and the lock file's creation must be one atomic operation. If two objects simply test for the existence of a lock file at the same time and both conclude that they can proceed because no lock file exists, then they will both be accessing the resource at the same time.

The details of how to ensure that the test for the existence of a lock file and its creation are a single atomic operation are discussed under the "Implementation" heading.

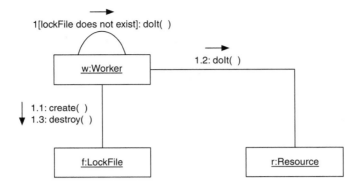

FIGURE 7.5 Lock file interactions.

CONSEQUENCES

☺ Objects that use the lock file pattern are able to coordinate the use of a resource among themselves.

☺ Lock files continue to exist after the computer they are on crashes. The locks that remote objects hold in the form of lock files are still intact after the computer they are on restarts.

☹ It is possible that an object will fail to delete a lock file after is it finished using a resource. This can happen because of a bug in the object, because the VM that an object is running crashes, or for other reasons. This situation may be detected by using a time-out strategy.

The object that created a lock file can periodically open the file, update its contents, and close the file. This forces the timestamp returned by the `lastModified` method of the `java.io.File` class to be updated. If the modification time is too far in the past, other objects can assume that the old lock file may be deleted. The main caution to observe is not to set the time-out period to be too short. Delays introduced by caching or remote file systems may cause other objects not to see an updated modification time immediately.

IMPLEMENTATION

The `java.io.File` class has a method that is specifically intended for use with the lock file pattern. The `createNewFile` method atomically checks for the existence of a file and creates it, if it does not already exist.

Lock File Naming

An implementation issue is the name of a lock file. To properly coordinate with each other, all objects participating in the Lock File pattern must agree on the name of the lock file. If the name of the lock file is always the same, then agreement on its name is trivial. However, if there are many different resources to coordinate access to, then there will be equally many lock files, each with its own name.

The usual way to manage the names of lock files, when there may be multiple lock files, is to derive the name of the lock file from the resource. For example, if the resources to be coordinated are files, then the name of the lock file corresponding to a file can be the name of the file followed by `.lock`. Using this scheme, if an object wants to modify a file named `foo.bar`, it will create a lock file named `foo.bar.lock`.

What to Do When There Is Already a Lock File for the Desired Resource

If an object wants to access a resource for which a lock file currently exists, the Lock File pattern calls for it to either wait until the file no longer exists or to abort whatever operation needs the resource. Waiting may be impractical if the object currently using the resources may hold it for a long period of time.

Hybrid policies are sometimes used. You could have an object wait for up to a predetermined amount of time for a lock file to be deleted. If the lock file still exists after that amount of time has elapsed, then it would abort what it is doing. Another way of dealing with the situation is having the object ask the client it is acting on behalf of how to resolve the situation.

KNOWN USES

FrameMaker is a program for creating large technical documents. It uses the Lock File pattern to prevent two people from accidentally editing the same file at the same time.

There are configuration management systems for source code that use the Lock File pattern to ensure that only one person is modifying the state of a source code file at any given time.

There are communication programs that coordinate access to serial ports using the Lock File pattern.

CODE EXAMPLE

The code example for this pattern is a subclass of `java.io.RandomAccess-File` that ensures exclusive access to files that it opens through the use of lock files.

```
public class ExclusiveRandomAccessFile
                                    extends RandomAccessFile {
    private static final String LOCK_FILE_SUFFIX = ".lck";
    private File lockFile;
```

This class forms the name of a lock file by appending `LOCK_FILE_SUFFIX` to the name of the file to open. After the lock file is created, its name is kept in a `File` object that is referenced by the `lockFile` instance variable until the lock file is deleted.

Because the superclass's constructor opens the file, this class must check for the existence of and create the lock file before it calls its superclass's constructor. For this purpose, the `ExclusiveRandomAccessFile` class provides the static method `openExclusive`. This method handles the details of the lock file and then creates an instance of the class that calls its superclass's constructor, which opens the file.

```
/**
 * Open the named file using a lock file to ensure
 * exclusive access.
 * @param fileName The name of the file to open.
 * @param mode This should either be "r" for read-only
 * access or "rw" for read-write access.
 * @exception FileSharingException
 * If there is already a lock file for the named
 * file.
 */
public static
ExclusiveRandomAccessFile openExclusive(String fileName,
                                        String mode)
                                throws IOException {
    File lockFile = new File(fileName+LOCK_FILE_SUFFIX);
    if (!lockFile.createNewFile()) {
        // lock file already exists
        throw new FileSharingException(fileName);
    } // if
    return new ExclusiveRandomAccessFile(fileName,
                                         mode,
                                         lockFile);
} // openExclusive(String)
```

The constructor simply calls the superclass's constructor and set the `lockFile` instance variable.

```
private ExclusiveRandomAccessFile(String fileName,
                                  String mode,
```

```
                                        File lockFile)
                                        throws IOException {
        super(fileName, mode);
        this.lockFile = lockFile;
} // constructor(String, String)
```

If the file is still open, the `close` method deletes the lock file before it closes the file.

```
public synchronized void close() throws IOException {
    if (lockFile!=null) { // If file is still open
        lockFile.delete();
        lockFile = null;
        super.close();
    } // if
} // close()
```

To make this class more robust, it overrides the `finalize` method to call its own `close` method. The `finalize` method is called by the garbage collector before it reclaims the storage that an object occupies. So if an `ExclusiveRandomAccessFile` object is garbage collected, its underlying file will be closed and the lock file deleted even if the application did not explicitly close the file. There is no guarantee that any specific object will ever be garbage collected, so this merely provides a chance that the file will be closed.

```
/**
 * Ensure that the underlying file is closed before this
 * object is garbage collected.
 */
protected void finalize() throws IOException {
    close();
} // finalize()
} // class ExclusiveRandomAccessFile
```

RELATED PATTERNS

Static Locking Order.   The Static Locking Order pattern is used with the Lock File pattern when there are multiple resources to be coordinated, in order to avoid deadlocks.

ACID Transaction.   The lock file pattern may be used in the implementation of the ACID Transaction pattern.

Static Locking Order

This pattern was described previously in [Heaney99].

SYNOPSIS

If two objects need exclusive access to the same set of resources, they can become deadlocked with each holding a lock on one resource and waiting for the other to release its resource. You avoid such deadlocks by ensuring that all objects acquire locks on resources in the same order.

CONTEXT

Suppose that you work for a company that provides field service for computers. You have been asked to solve a problem that has recently started happening.

Two of your company's applications occasionally hang. The problem is intermittent and only occurs in the evening. One of the applications is a program that field technicians use to enter information about what they did at a particular site, so that the appropriate parties can be billed and inventory levels adjusted. The other program runs at a scheduled time every evening. It goes through the inventory transactions of the day and, when appropriate, sends messages to parts vendors to register warranty information.

Most of the time, these programs work perfectly. Occasionally, a field technician working the evening shift will be entering information about a completed repair and both the warranty registration program and the technician's session hang.

Upon investigation, you find that the problem is a deadlock between the two programs. The program that the technician uses gets a lock on records in the customer database when the technician indicates which customer(s) that last job was for. As the technician enters the parts that were used in the repair job, the program also locks records in the inventory database. The warranty registration program obtains lock on records in the inventory database and then tries to access the customer database to complete the warranty information for a part. The problem is that occasionally the technician's program will have a customer record locked and want access to an inventory record. But the inventory program already has a lock on that inventory record and is trying to access the customer record that the other program already has locked. The two programs wait indefinitely to access the record that the other program has locked.

You solve the problem by modifying the warranty registration program so that it locks customer records before it locks the corresponding inventory record.

FORCES

☺ Multiple objects need to access a set of resources. The operations they perform on these resources require that some or all other objects be prevented from concurrently accessing the resources.

☺ Dynamically determining at runtime whether granting an object access to a resource will result in a deadlock can be a very expensive operation.

☺ Some transaction management mechanisms automatically detect deadlocks among the transactions that they manage. It will generally take them a while to detect the deadlock after it occurs. The way that most of these transaction managers handle a deadlock is to cause some or all of the transactions involved to fail. From the viewpoint of an application, such failures appear to be intermittent failures of the application. If it is important that the transaction behaves in a reliable and predictable way, then it is important for it to avoid such deadlocks.

☺ Objects access a set of resources that either is static or always fills a static set of roles.

☹ If resources can fill multiple roles, then it may take a prohibitively long amount of time to determine, in advance, whether a particular pattern of accessing resources can result in a deadlock.

SOLUTION

If objects lock multiple shared resources, then ensure that the resources are always locked in the same relative order. For example, if there are four resources, A, B, C, and D, then you could require all objects to lock them in that order. So one object may lock B, C, and D, in that order. Another object may lock A and C, in that order. However, no object may lock C and B, in that order.

The same strategy applies to situations where the specific resources that objects use vary, but the objects always fill the same roles. In this sort of situation, you apply the relative ordering to the roles rather than the resources. In the example under the "Context" heading, the specific database records that the programs use vary with the transaction.

CONSEQUENCES

☺ Use of the Static Locking order pattern allows you to ensure that objects will be able to lock resources without deadlocking.

☹ Forcing all objects to lock resources in a predetermined order can sometimes increase the amount of time it takes some objects to perform an operation. For an example, consider the case of the warranty registration program discussed under the "Context" heading.

In its original implementation, it only needed to fetch an inventory record once. Forcing it to lock a customer record before locking an inventory record requires it to fetch the inventory record twice. The first time it fetches an inventory record, it may discover that there is a warranty to register and which customer is involved. It then locks the appropriate customer record. It must then fetch the inventory record a second time after locking it.

IMPLEMENTATION

There are no special implementation considerations related to the Static Locking Order pattern.

KNOWN USES

The author has seen the Static locking order pattern used in a number of proprietary applications.

CODE EXAMPLE

The code example for the static locking pattern is an extension to the example for the Lock File pattern. It is an additional method whose arguments are an array of file names and an array of file mode strings ("r" or "rw"). It opens the files in sorted order. It returns an array of `ExclusiveRandomAccessFile` objects that correspond to the given file names.

If there is a problem opening any of the files, any files opened up to that point are closed and an exception is thrown.

```
public static ExclusiveRandomAccessFile[]
  openExclusive(String[] fileNames, String[] modes)
                                  throws IOException {
    int[] ndx = new int[fileNames.length];
    InsertionSort.sort(fileNames, ndx);
```

```
        ExclusiveRandomAccessFile[] opened
          = new ExclusiveRandomAccessFile[fileNames.length];
        try {
            for (int i=0; i<fileNames.length; i++) {
                opened[ndx[i]]
                    = openExclusive(fileNames[ndx[i]],
                                    modes[ndx[i]]);
            } // for
        } catch (IOException e) {
            // close any opened files
            for (int i=0; i<opened.length; i++) {
                if (opened[i]!=null) {
                    try {
                        opened[i].close();
                    } catch (IOException ee) {
                    } // try
                } // if
            } // for
            throw e;
        } // try
        return opened;
    } // openExclusive(String)
```

Here is the sort method that the openExclusive method calls:

```
/**
 * Fill the given <code>int</code> array with indices that can
 * be used to put the array of <code>Comparable</code> objects in
 * sorted order. If the array is
 * { "gh", "ab", "zz", "mm" }
 * then the <code>indices</code> array will be
 * { 1, 0, 3, 2 }
 * @exception IllegalArgumentException
 * If the two arrays are not the same length.
 */
public static void sort(Comparable[] a, int[] indices) {
    if (a.length!=indices.length) {
        String msg = "Different length arrays";
        throw new IllegalArgumentException(msg);
    } // if
    for (int i=0; i<indices.length; i++) {
        indices[i]=i;
    } // for
    for (int i=1; i<a.length; i++) {
        Comparable temp = a[i];
        int j = i-1;
        while (j>=0 && a[indices[j]].compareTo(temp)>0) {
            indices[j+1] = indices[j];
            j--;
        } // while
        indices[j+1] = i;
    } // for i
} // sort(Comparable[])
```

RELATED PATTERNS

ACID Transaction.   The Static Locking Order pattern can be used in the design of ACID transactions.

Lock File.   The Static Locking Order pattern can be used with the Lock File pattern to avoid deadlocks.

Optimistic Concurrency

SYNOPSIS

Improve throughput of transaction processing by not waiting for locks that a transaction may need. Instead, be optimistic and perform the transaction logic on private copies of the records or objects involved. Do insist that the locks be granted before the updates can be committed, but abort the transaction if conflicting updates were made prior to the granting of the locks.

CONTEXT

You are designing a student records system. One characteristic of a student records system is that most of the time it has a relatively low number of transactions to process. However, at certain times, such as the beginning of a semester, there is a very high level of activity. Your design must accommodate peak levels of activity while keeping the cost of the infrastructure low.

When there is a need to keep costs down, there are usually compromises to make. After analyzing the requirements, you decide that the most import guarantee to make is the level of throughput that the system will provide. It must be able to process a certain number of transactions per hour. Since the transactions that drive the peak periods will be submitted directly by students, the throughput requirement translates into a requirement to guarantee a maximum average response time. It will be acceptable if a small percentage of the transactions take noticeably longer than the average.

With these goals in mind, you begin examining the problem at hand to see if it has any attributes that you can exploit. You notice that it will be very unusual for two concurrent transactions to update information about the same student. Another thing you notice is that although the database manager you are using can handle concurrent transactions, its mechanism for granting locks is single-threaded. This means it is possible for lock management to become a bottleneck.

You decide that you can lessen the impact of single-threaded lock management by processing transactions in a way that does not require a transaction to obtain locks on records until the transaction is ready to commit changes to the records. Delays in granting locks will not have an impact on the completion of a transaction unless the delays are longer than the transaction takes to get to the point of committing its results. If the transaction is delayed in committing its results, the commitment of the results is all that will be delayed. The rest of the transaction will already be done.

FORCES

☺ Concurrent attempts to modify the state of an object or record are very rare. This is often the case when there are few concurrent transactions. It is also often the case when there are a very large number of records or objects and transactions only modify a small number of records or objects.

☺ Locks are granted centrally by a single-threaded mechanism and it is possible to update the contents of objects or records while waiting to find out if a requested lock will be granted.

☺ The available locking mechanism is coarse-grained. Its locks apply to an entire file or table or to a large set of objects. Such coarse-grained locks can cause multiple transactions to wait for a lock when the changes that they will make will not conflict with each other.

☹ Aborting a transaction because it could not obtain a lock and then starting the transaction over again can take a significant amount of time. It may take a lot more time than getting locks beforehand to ensure that the transaction has exclusive access to the resources that it will modify.

SOLUTION

Coordinate changes that transactions make to the state of records or objects by assuming that concurrent updates to the same record or object are very unlikely. Based on this assumption, proceed optimistically without first obtaining any locks. Instead, you rely on a field of the records or attribute of the objects to recognize when a conflicting update has occurred. This field or attribute will contain a version number or timestamp that contains a different value after each time the record or object is updated.

Organize the transaction processing into three phases:

1. **Read/Fetch.** Make a private copy of the state of each record or object that the transaction will update.
2. **Perform transaction logic.** Have the transaction work with its private copy of the records or states, using them as its source of data and updating them.
3. **Commit the updates.** After obtaining locks on all of the records or objects that the transaction has updated, verify that no other transactions have modified them. This is usually done by comparing their version number or timestamp with the private copies.

If any records or objects have been modified, abort the transaction. Otherwise, store the values in the private copies into the records or objects.

When implementing this pattern, it is *crucial* that no updates occur until after all of the locks that a transaction will need have been obtained.

CONSEQUENCES

- ☺ The Optimistic Concurrency pattern allows transactions to be more effectively multithreaded under heavy loads than more pessimistic ways of coordinating concurrent updates.
- ☹ When there are concurrent transactions that will modify the same records or objects, there is a bigger performance penalty with optimistic concurrency than with more pessimistic policies. Pessimistic policies can cause otherwise concurrent transactions to be performed serially. Optimistic concurrency can result in transactions' having to be aborted and restarted. It is possible for a transaction to be aborted multiple times before it is finally able to finish.

IMPLEMENTATION

Sometimes you may want to use optimistic concurrency with records or objects that do not have version numbers or timestamps. There are some strategies to work around this deficiency.

One strategy is to use the timestamp or version number of one record or object to control updates to another. This requires the cooperation of all transactions. If the record or object with the version number or timestamp is not naturally part of a transaction, then including it in a transaction adds overhead.

Another strategy is to compare the contents of a record or object with its original contents. This avoids the overhead of adding extraneous records or objects to a transaction. However, in some cases this can be at the expense of transactions' losing their guarantees of consistency and durability.

Consider the following sequence of events:

Transaction 1 reads record X.	Transaction 2 reads record X.
	Transaction 2 commits changes to record X.
	Transaction 3 reads records X and Y.
	Transaction 3 commits changes to records X and Y that cause record X to contain what it contained before.
Transaction 1 sees that record X contains the same as it did before, so it commits its changes to record X.	

In this sequence of events, a lengthy transaction begins by reading record X. While that transaction is processing, another transaction changes the contents of record X. A third transaction comes along and sets the contents of record X to what they were when the first transaction started. Because the lengthy transaction relies on the contents of record X to determine if another transaction has modified it, it modifies the record since it cannot tell that there have been intervening transactions.

KNOWN USES

SQL server and Sybase allow optimistic concurrency to be specified as the means of concurrency control.

Some groupware applications that allow people to collaborate on tasks use optimistic concurrency. In such applications, response time is improved by not having to wait for locks. Because these types of applications have user interfaces that are designed around the principle of direct manipulation, it is generally obvious to all users when there is a conflict between what users are doing. This usually causes users to avoid conflicting changes. When conflicts result in pauses in actions and actions' being aborted, the results are generally understood and acceptable.

CODE EXAMPLE

The code example updates a row in a database table using optimistic concurrency.

```
class Updater {
    ...
    private boolean gotLock = false;
```

After this example fetches the row to be updated, it asynchronously attempts to get a lock on the row. After the thread that gets the lock is finished, the value of the gotLock variable is true if it was successful in getting a lock on the row.

```
void update(Connection conn, String id)
                                throws SQLException {
    try {
```

Here is where this example gets the row to be updated without locking the row.

```
        Statement myStatement = conn.createStatement();
        String query;
```

```
query = "SELECT tot_a, tot_b, version, ROWID"
  + " FROM summary_tb"
  + " WHERE unit_id=" + id;
ResultSet result;
result = myStatement.executeQuery(query);
result.next();
BigDecimal totA = result.getBigDecimal(1);
BigDecimal totB = result.getBigDecmial(2);
long version = result.getLong(3);
String rowID = result.getString(4);
result.close();
```

At this point, the values from the row in question have been fetched, including the values for a lengthy computation and the row's version number.

The call to getLock returns immediately while it asynchronously gets a lock on the row in question. While getLock is getting the lock, a call to the doIt method performs a lengthy computation to produce a value that will be used to update the row.

```
Thread locker;
locker = getLock(myStatement, rowID, version);
totB = doIt(totA, totB);
locker.join();
```

The call to getLock returns the thread that is responsible for asynchronously getting the lock on the row in question. After getLock returns, a call to doIt computes a value that will be used to update the row in question. After the value is computed, a call to the thread's join method ensures that the update will not proceed until after the attempt to lock the row is complete.

The value of the gotLock variable will be true if the attempt to lock the row in question succeeded. If the lock attempt succeeded, the update proceeds and the transaction is committed.

```
if (gotLock) {
    String update;
    update = "UPDATE summary_tb"
      + " SET tot_b='" + totB + "'"
      + " WHERE ROWID='" + rowID + "'";
    myStatement.executeUpdate(update);
    conn.commit();
} else {
    conn.rollback();
} // if
myStatement.close();
} catch (InterruptedException e) {
    conn.rollback();
    return;
```

```
        } // try
    } // update()
```

Finally, here is the `getLock` method that asynchronously gets a lock.

```
    private Thread getLock(final Statement myStatement,
                           final String rowID,
                           final long version) {
      Thread lockThread = new Thread() {
            public void run() {
                String query;
                query = "SELECT version FROM summary_tb"
                  + " WHERE ROWID='" + rowID + "'"
                  + " FOR UPDDATE";
                ResultSet r;
                try {
                    r = myStatement.executeQuery(query);
                    gotLock = (version==r.getLong(1));
                    r.close();
                } catch (SQLException e) {
                    gotLock = false;
                } // try
            } // run()
        };
      lockThread.start();
      return lockThread;
    } // getLock(String)
    ...
} // class Updater
```

RELATED PATTERNS

ACID Transaction.   The Optimistic Concurrency pattern can be used in the implementation of the ACID Transaction pattern.

Static Locking Order.   The Static Locking Order pattern may be used with the Optimistic concurrency pattern to avoid dead-locks.

Object Replication.   The Optimistic Concurrency pattern can be used in the implementation of the Object Replication pattern.

Thread Pool

This pattern is partially based on material that appears at [Lea99], though not in the form of a pattern.

SYNOPSIS

By nature, many servers are presented with a steady stream of tasks to perform that must each be performed in their own thread. Creating a thread is a relatively expensive operation. Avoid the expense of creating a thread for each task by reusing threads. Manage the threads in a way that ensures that the total number of threads never exceeds a predetermined maximum.

CONTEXT

You are designing the server portion of an application for backing up files over a network. The way the application will work is that each computer schedules the client portion of the program to run once a day. When the client portion of the program runs, it sends the contents of files that need to be backed up to the server.

If the server can only receive one file at a time and more than one computer is trying to send a file to the server at the same time, then all but one computer will be waiting for their turn. In most situations, there is a limited window of time in which all backups must be done. Because the amount of time for finishing all backups is limited, designing the server to only receive one backup file at a time may prevent the backups from finishing in time. You need a design that allows the server to use time more efficiently.

One way for the server to use time more efficiently is to allow it to receive more than one backup file at a time. To make that happen, you design the server to use a different thread for each backup file it is receiving at the same time.

Once the server program is able to receive multiple files, the next performance improvement you make is to tune the server program to take advantage of the multiple file systems of the host on which it resides.

You find that you need to make yet another performance improvement. After analyzing the performance of the server software, you decide that improving the way that it manages threads would result in a significant performance boost. Your analysis indicates that there are two main problems with the way that threads are currently being used:

- Sometimes, there are more active threads than the environment can efficiently support.
- A disproportionately large amount of time is spent in creating threads.

You solve both of these problems by using a thread pool. A thread pool allows threads that have completed a task to be reused for other tasks. A thread pool can be used to limit the number of threads that are being used at one time.

FORCES

- ☺ A program, such as a server, is presented with an open-ended set of concurrent tasks to perform. Each task is independent of the other tasks. Each task should be performed in its own thread.
- ☺ The cost of creating threads is relatively high, both in terms of time and memory.
- ☺ There is an optimal number of threads that a server should be running at one time. If too many threads are running at the same time, the overall throughput of a program goes down. If too few threads are running, resources are underutilized.
- ☹ Threads that run tasks that last indefinitely are bad candidates for reuse, since the tasks that they run may never terminate.

SOLUTION

Keep a pool of idle threads. When a thread finishes a task, add it to the pool of idle threads. The next time a thread is needed to run a task, if there are any threads in the pool, use one of those threads instead of creating a new one. If there are no idle threads in the pool, create a new thread unless the number of threads managed by the thread pool equals a predetermined maximum. If the thread pool has already created its maximum number of threads, then tasks that need threads to run will wait until an existing thread managed by the thread pool becomes idle.

Figure 7.6 shows the roles that classes and interfaces play in the Thread Pool pattern. Here are descriptions of these roles:

Executor.   An interface in this role defines a method that can be passed a `Runnable` object for the purpose of executing it. The

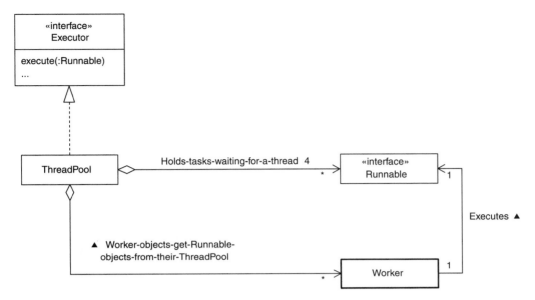

FIGURE 7.6 Thread Pool pattern.

Executor interface is implemented by classes that are responsible for controlling the execution of tasks.

ThreadPool.   Classes in this role implement the Executor interface. They manage a pool of threads used to execute tasks passed to them.

Runnable.   In order for its instances to contain logic that can be executed in its own task, classes must implement the interface java.lang.Runnable. Runnable objects are passed to a ThreadPool object's execute method which places them in a queue or similar data structure. Runnable objects stay in the queue until an idle Worker object takes them out of the queue and executes them.

Worker.   Worker objects have a thread associated with them. Their purpose is to run the tasks encapsulated by the Runnable objects passed to the ThreadPool. When a Worker object is not running a task, it is waiting to get its next Runnable object from the ThreadPool.

ThreadPool objects generally limit the number of Worker objects that exist at any one time. By limiting the number of Worker objects, they limit the number of threads that they use which keeps the machine that they are running on from being swamped with too many threads.

CONSEQUENCES

☺ Using the Thread Pool pattern may reduce the amount of time a program spends creating threads by allowing threads to be reused.

☹ Some Java virtual machines perform thread pooling behind the scenes. In such environments, the Thread Pool pattern will not generally reduce the amount of time a program spends creating threads. The only notable exception is when a thread pool object implements an application-specific policy to more intelligently allocate threads to tasks than the environment's thread pooling.

☺ The Thread Pool pattern provides a way of controlling the maximum number of threads that are running at one time. This can ensure that the number of concurrently running threads does not exceed the scheduling or memory resources of the host a program is running on. If demand exceeds the availability of these resources, throughput goes way down.

☹ If tasks need more threads than the one that performs the top-level logic of the task, managing the additional threads with the same thread pool as the top level thread can lead to deadlock. This can happen when all of a thread pool's threads are busy and all of the tasks its threads are running are waiting for the thread pool to allocate another thread to them. In this situation, all tasks are waiting for the thread pool to allocate a thread to them and the thread pool is waiting for one of them to finish so it can reuse its thread.

There are measures you can take to handle some of these situations. You can have the thread pool run a task with the same thread that requested the task rather than running it in its own thread. Though this avoids an immediate deadlock, it also avoids the concurrency of using a separate thread. For many applications, this is unacceptable.

Another way to avoid deadlock is to allocate all the threads a task will need at the same time. This is practical only if it is possible for the thread pool to know in advance how many threads the task will need.

IMPLEMENTATION

Some JVMs internally pool threads. When a Java program is running on such a JVM, the Thread Pool pattern may not reduce the amount of time spent creating threads. Use of the Thread Pool pattern may even increase the amount of time spent on thread creation by making the JVM's internal thread pooling less effective.

When Tasks Must Wait for a Thread

One reason to use a thread pool is to smooth out the load on a server over time by limiting the number of threads it uses to perform tasks. This implies that if tasks arrive when there are no idle threads to run them, they must wait for an idle thread. Managing tasks waiting for a thread is an important implementation issue. It can be especially important when tasks arrive at a consistently faster rate than they are processed.

One way to manage waiting tasks is to put them in a queue. Putting waiting tasks in a queue ensures that they are run in the order in which they arrive. You can choose other scheduling policies by choosing another data structure, such as a priority queue.

If it is possible for tasks to arrive at a faster rate than they are processed, it is possible for a queue to grow indefinitely. If a queue gets too large, then the amount of storage it takes up can be a problem, causing a shortage of available storage. You can avoid the queue's getting too long by placing a limit on the length of the queue.

If there are no idle threads available to process a task and the queue is at its maximum length, then it will not be possible to process the task in the normal way. The most reasonable alternatives are to either reject the task or use the thread that presents the task to the thread pool to perform the task.

Another possibility is to allow the length of the queue to grow beyond its normal maximum under exceptional circumstances. For a policy like this to work, you need to present the thread pool with enough information about each task for it to make this sort of decision.

The Thread Pool pattern assumes that tasks to be run are independent of each other, so they can be run in an arbitrary order without any problems. This can cause tasks that depend on other tasks to fail. It may be possible to accommodate tasks with dependencies by replacing the queue with a data structure that reflects the dependencies.

Managing the Number of Threads in a Thread Pool

To promote reasonable and predictable performance, you use the Thread Pool pattern to maintain a stable number of threads. However, rigidly enforcing a strict number of threads at all times can be wasteful. The only situation in which always maintaining a constant number of threads is the best policy is one where the tasks arrive at regular intervals and all involve about the same amount of work. In such situations, providing a fixed level of resources to service a fixed workload can be a very efficient design.

For most servers, the rate at which tasks arrive varies over time and the tasks vary in the amount of work they involve. For this reason, it is usually best if a thread pool does not create a thread until it is needed. Once a thread pool has as many threads as it has been configured for, it normally does not create more threads.

If tasks arrive faster than they can be processed, the thread pool will queue the tasks. Thread pool implementations may impose a maximum queue length. When a new task is presented to a thread pool and the queue is at its maximum length, then a thread pool may create a limited number of additional threads before resorting to other ways to dispose of the task.

At the other extreme, if there are sometimes big gaps of time between the arrival of tasks, most or all of the threads controlled by a thread pool may be idle. If idle threads consume memory or CPU cycles that could be put to better use, then when idle threads are unlikely to be needed they should be killed and made eligible for garbage collection. A reasonable heuristic for predicting if an idle thread will soon be needed is that the longer the thread has been idle, the longer it is likely to continue being idle. A simple way to implement this is to establish a maximum idle time. If a thread in a thread pool is idle longer than the maximum idle time, then the thread pool kills the thread and allows it to be garbage collected.

Thread Creation

Some applications may require a thread pool to create and use instances of a specialized subclass of `java.lang.Thread`. For example, it may need priorities to be handled specially or it may need threads to work differently than normal with `ThreadLocal` objects.

You can use the Factory Method pattern (described in Volume 1) to design a thread pool implementation that can be easily configured by its clients to create instances of an arbitrary subclass of `Thread`. This typically works by designing the `ThreadPool` class to have a method that can be passed a factory object; the `ThreadPool` object delegates the responsibility of creating `Thread` objects to the factory object.

Shutting Down a Thread Pool

There are a few different approaches to consider when organizing the orderly shutdown of a Thread Pool. The most conservative approach is to simply not allow the Thread Pool to accept any new tasks. When all of the previously accepted tasks are finished, the Thread Pool can shut down. This is a conservative approach. It assumes that the tasks will all eventually terminate without any intervention. It places no upper bound on how long it will take to shut a thread pool down.

A somewhat more aggressive approach is to discard any queued tasks waiting to be run. There should be a provision for sending notification of the tasks' being discarded to any interested objects.

An even more aggressive approach to shutting down a thread pool is to perform an intervention on the running tasks that hastens their termination. You may want the thread pool to wait a certain amount of time before it intervenes, to allow tasks to come to their normal completion.

When the thread pool does intervene, there are two tactics for it to try. The first is to call the `interrupt` method of the `Thread` object that is running a task that it wants to terminate. If the task is well behaved, it will detect that its thread has been interrupted and terminate itself in a reasonable amount of time.

There is no good way to tell how long a reasonable amount of time should be. Therefore, after an arbitrary amount of time, if a task has not terminated after its thread has been interrupted, the thread pool should assume that the task will not terminate itself. In this situation, there are no good options. The simplest option is to do nothing. If the resources the task is using need to be recycled, then doing nothing is unsatisfactory.

A thread pool can attempt to force the termination of a task by calling the `Thread` object's `stop` method. The `stop` method will succeed in terminating a task in many cases, when an `interrupt` fails. In order for `interrupt` to succeed, a task must periodically check to see if its `interrupted` flag is set and, if it is, take appropriate action. On the other hand, the `stop` method requires no cooperation from a task in order to terminate it. To succeed, the `stop` method simply requires that a task does not catch `ThreadDeath`, `Error`, or `Throwable`. Alternatively, if it does catch such objects, it must rethrow them.

The problem with using the `stop` method to terminate a task is that it works by causing a thread to throw an exception from *wherever* a task is executing. Unless code is carefully crafted to account for this possibility, it is possible for an unplanned exception thrown by the `stop` method to cause a method to exit in a way that leaves objects in an inconsistent state.

ThreadLocal Objects

The use of `java.lang.ThreadLocal` objects in an environment that uses the Thread Pool pattern to manage threads makes possible a rather difficult-to-diagnose bug. An assumption that underlies the use of `ThreadLocal` objects is that a given thread is always associated with the same task. If the association in a `ThreadLocal` object between a thread and a value may persist beyond the life of a task, then the value may be inappropriately used for the next task that the thread runs.

KNOWN USES

The Thread Pool pattern is used by a great variety of server programs to allow their concurrency properties to be tuned to match their environment and workload. The WebLogic application server uses a thread pool to manage the threads it uses to run servlets. The Voyager ORB uses a thread pool to manage the threads that service remote object calls. Multithreaded database managers such as Oracle use a thread pool internally to manage concurrent database requests.

CODE EXAMPLE

The code example for this pattern is a sample implementation of a thread pool.

A thread pool should be able to queue tasks. Before looking at the `ThreadPool` class, we will first look at a Queue class that it uses.

```
public class Queue {
    private ArrayList data = new ArrayList();
    private int maxQueueSize = Integer.MAX_VALUE;
```

This `Queue` delegates the storage of objects to an `ArrayList` object. It also imposes a maximum length on queues. When the length of a queue is greater than or equal to the maximum length, any attempts to put another object in the queue will wait until the length of the queue is less than the maximum value. The default maximum length is the largest value that can be represented by an `int`. For practical purposes, this places no real constraint on the length of a queue, because Java limits the length of an array to that value.

The first method listed below puts an object at the end of the queue. If the size of the queue is equal to or greater than the current value of `maxQueueSize`, then this method will wait until the size of the queue shrinks to less than `maxQueueSize`.

```
synchronized public void put(Object obj)
                        throws InterruptedException {
    if (Thread.currentThread().isInterrupted()) {
       throw new InterruptedException();
    } // if isInterrupted
    if (obj==null) {
       throw new IllegalArgumentException("null");
    } //if null
    while (data.size()>=maxQueueSize) {
        try {
            wait();
        } catch (InterruptedException e) {
```

```
            return;
        } // try
    } // while
    data.add(obj);
    notify();
} // put(Object)
```

The next `put` method is similar to the previous one. The difference is that it takes a second argument, which is the maximum number of milliseconds it should wait if the queue is at its maximum size. After waiting that long, it simply returns without adding the object to the queue. The method's caller can tell if the object was added to the queue because it returns true if is was able to add the object.

Something else both `put` methods have in common is that if they are called in a thread that has been interrupted, they both throw an `InterruptedException`.

```
synchronized public boolean put(Object obj, long msecs)
                                throws InterruptedException {
    if (Thread.currentThread().isInterrupted()) {
        throw new InterruptedException();
    } // if isInterrupted
    if (obj==null) {
        throw new IllegalArgumentException("null");
    } //if null
    long startTime = System.currentTimeMillis();
    long waitTime = msecs;
    while (data.size()>=maxQueueSize) {
        waitTime = msecs - (System.currentTimeMillis()
                            - startTime);
        if (waitTime <= 0) {
            return false;
        } // if waitTime
        wait(waitTime);
    } // while
    data.add(obj);
    notify();
    return true;
} // put(Object, long)
```

The next `get` method removes the object from the front of the queue and returns it. If the queue is empty, it waits until there is an object in the queue.

```
synchronized public Object get()
                    throws InterruptedException {
    while (data.size() == 0){
        wait();
    } // while
    Object obj = data.remove(0);
    notify();
```

```
      return obj;
   } // get()
```

The next `get` method is similar to the previous one. The difference is that it takes an argument that limits the length of time that the method will wait when the queue is empty. When the queue is empty and it has already waited the given number of milliseconds, the method stops waiting and returns null.

```
synchronized public Object get(long msecs)
                        throws InterruptedException {
    long startTime = System.currentTimeMillis();
    long waitTime = msecs;

    if (data.size()>0) {
        return data.remove(0);
    } // if data.size()
    while (true) {
        waitTime = msecs - (System.currentTimeMillis()
                        - startTime);
        if (waitTime <= 0) {
            return null;
        } // if waitTime
        wait(waitTime);
        if (data.size()>0) {
            Object obj = data.remove(0);
            notify();
            return obj;
        } // if data.size()
    } // while
} // get(long)
```

Concluding the `Queue` class, here is the method for setting the maximum queue length:

```
public void setMaxQueueSize(int newValue) {
    maxQueueSize = newValue;
} // setMaxQueueSize(int)
} // class Queue
```

Here is the class that is responsible for managing thread pools:

```
public class ThreadPool implements Executor {
```

This constant is the default value for the maximum pool size. For practical purposes, this value `Integer.MAX_VALUE` is the same as infinity.

```
public static final int DEFAULT_MAXIMUMPOOLSIZE
   = Integer.MAX_VALUE;
```

This constant is the default value for the normal pool size. For most applications, the normal pool size should be set to a value greater than one.

```
public static final int DEFAULT_NORMALPOOLSIZE = 1;
```

This constant is the default maximum time to keep worker threads alive while waiting for new tasks. Its value is one minute.

```
public static final long DEFAULT_MAXIDLETIME = 60 * 1000;
```

The variables that contain the maximum pool size and normal pool size are declared `volatile` to avoid having to explicitly make all of the code that references them `synchronized`.

```
protected volatile int maximumPoolSize
  = DEFAULT_MAXIMUMPOOLSIZE;
protected volatile int normalPoolSize
  = DEFAULT_NORMALPOOLSIZE;
```

`maximumPoolSize` is the maximum number of threads that the thread pool will have in the pool at any one time. The pool does not automatically preallocate threads. Instead, it creates a thread only when a task is passed to the `ThreadPool` object's `execute` method, a thread is needed to run it, the task cannot immediately be queued, and there are fewer threads than the maximum. The default value is very large, so you should set the maximum pool size with the constructor or the set method unless you are just using the thread pool to minimize thread construction overhead.

Handing off tasks to idle threads requires synchronization that in turn relies on JVM scheduling policies to ensure progress. Because of this, it is possible that a new thread will be created even though an existing worker thread has just become idle because it has not progressed to the point at which it can accept a new task. This phenomenon tends to occur on some JVMs when bursts of short tasks are executed.

`normalPoolSize` is the normal number of threads to be in the pool, when needed. When a new task is received, and fewer than the normal number of threads are in the pool, then a new thread is always created to handle the task, even if other threads are idly waiting for work. Otherwise, a new thread is created only if there are fewer than the maximum and the task cannot immediately be queued.

```
protected long maxIdleTime = DEFAULT_MAXIDLETIME;
```

If once in a pool a thread stayed in the pool forever, it would impede garbage collection of otherwise idle threads. This would defeat the resource-management benefits of pools.

One solution would be to use soft references. However, this would impose costly and difficult synchronization issues. Instead, threads are simply allowed to terminate and thus be eligible for garbage collection if they have been idle for the maximum idle time. The value of this parameter represents a trade-off between the effectiveness of garbage collection and the overhead of construction time. In most current Java VMs, thread construction and cleanup overhead is on the order of milliseconds. The default maximum idle value is one minute, which means that the time needed to construct and then garbage collect a thread is expended at most once per minute.

To establish worker threads permanently, pass a negative argument to `setMaxIdleTime`.

While tasks are waiting for a thread to perform them, they are in this queue:

```
protected final Queue handOff;
/** Lock object for protecting poolSize and threads map */
protected Object poolLock = new Object();

/**
 * Current pool size. Relies on poolLock for all locking.
 * But is also volatile to allow simpler checking inside
 * worker thread runloop.
 */
protected volatile int poolSize = 0;

/**
 * An object to map active worker objects to their active
 * thread. This is used by the interruptAll method.
 * It may also be useful in subclasses that need to
 * perform other thread management chores.
 * All operations on the Map should be done holding
 * a synchronization lock on poolLock.
 */
protected final Map threads;

/**
 * This object delegates the creation of threads to the
 * factory object referenced by this variable.
 */
private ThreadFactoryIF threadFactory
  = new DefaultThreadFactory();

/**
 * Construct a new pool with all default settings
 */
public ThreadPool() {
    this (new Queue(), DEFAULT_MAXIMUMPOOLSIZE);
} // constructor()

/**
 * Construct a new pool with all default settings except
 * for maximum pool size.
 */
```

```
    public ThreadPool(int maxPoolSize) {
        this(new Queue(), maxPoolSize);
    } // constructor(int)

    /**
     * Construct a new pool that uses the supplied Queue for
     * queuing, and with all default parameter settings.
     */
    public ThreadPool(Queue queue) {
        this(queue, DEFAULT_MAXIMUMPOOLSIZE);
    } // constructor(Queue)

    /**
     * Construct a new pool that uses the supplied Queue for
     * queuing, with all default parameter settings except
     * for maximum pool size.
     */
    public ThreadPool(Queue queue, int maxPoolSize) {
        maximumPoolSize = maxPoolSize;
        handOff = queue;
        runWhenBlocked();
        threads = new HashMap();
    } // constructor(Queue, int)

    /**
     * Return the maximum number of threads that may
     * simultaneously execute. New tasks are handled
     * according to the current blocking policy once this
     * limit is exceeded.
     */
    public int getMaximumPoolSize() {
        return maximumPoolSize;
    } // getMaximumPoolSize

    /**
     * Set the maximum number of threads that the pool should
     * have. Decreasing this value does not immediately kill
     * existing threads; they may later die when idle.
     * @exception IllegalArgumentException
     *             if less or equal to zero. (It is not
     *             considered an error for the maximum pool
     *             size to be less than the normal pool
     *             size. However, in this case there are no
     *             guarantees about behavior.)
     */
    public void setMaximumPoolSize(int newMaximum) {
        if (newMaximum <= 0) throw new IllegalArgumentException();
        maximumPoolSize = newMaximum;
    } // setMaximumPoolSize(int)

    /**
     * Return the normal number of threads to be in the pool.
     * (Default value is 1). If pool size is smaller than
```

```
         * this when a new task is received, a new thread is
         * started to handle the task.
         */
        public int getNormalPoolSize() {
            return normalPoolSize;
        } // getNormalPoolSize()

        /**
         * Set the normal number of threads to use.
         * @exception IllegalArgumentException if less than zero.
         *            (It is not considered an error to set the
         *            normal to be greater than the maximum.
         *            However, in this case there are no
         *            guarantees about behavior.)
         */
        public void setNormalPoolSize(int newNormal) {
            if (newNormal < 0) {
                throw new IllegalArgumentException();
            } // if
            normalPoolSize = newNormal;
        } // setNormalPoolSize(int)

        /**
         * Return the current number of threads in the pool.
         * This number is just a snapshot, and may change immediately.
         */
        public int getPoolSize() {
            return poolSize;
        } // getPoolSize()

        /**
         * Set the object that will be used to create threads.
         */
        public void setThreadFactory(ThreadFactoryIF newValue) {
            threadFactory = newValue;
        } // setThreadFactory(ThreadFactoryIF)
        /**
         * Return the current thread factory object.
         */
        protected ThreadFactoryIF getThreadFactory() {
            return threadFactory;
        } // getThreadFactory()

        /**
         * Create and start a thread to handle a new task.
         * Call only when holding poolLock.
         */
        protected void addThread(Runnable task) {
            ++poolSize;
            Worker worker = new Worker(task);
            Thread thread = getThreadFactory().createThread(worker);
            threads.put(worker, thread);
            thread.start();
        } // addThread(Runnable)
```

A `ThreadPool` object does not normally create threads until there is a task that needs it (and not always then). If you know in advance that there will be a need for a certain number of threads, creating the threads in advance of their need may result in a more consistent demand for CPU cycles and better throughput. This will generally be the case if you create the threads when there would otherwise be a lower demand for CPU cycles.

There is an interaction between creating threads in advance and the maximum idle time setting. When a thread is created in advance of its need, it may be idle for some time after it is created. If a thread is created so far in advance that it is idle for longer than the current setting of `maxIdleTime`, then the thread will be removed from the thread pool without ever being used. This defeats the whole purpose of creating threads in advance.

The `createThreads` method creates threads and adds them to the thread pool. Its argument is the number of threads that it is requested to create. If creating the requested number of threads would cause the size of the pool to exceed the maximum pool size, then the `createThreads` method creates fewer than the requested number of threads. The `createThreads` method returns the actual number of threads that it created, which may be as few as zero.

```java
public int createThreads(int numberOfThreads) {
    int ncreated = 0;
    for (int i = 0; i < numberOfThreads; ++i) {
        synchronized(poolLock) {
            if (getPoolSize() < getMaximumPoolSize()) {
                ++ncreated;
                addThread(null);
            } else {
                break;
            } // if
        } // synchronized
    } // for
    return ncreated;
} // createThreads
```

The next method, `interruptAll`, requests all threads in the pool to terminate by interrupting them. The `Worker` objects that provide the top-level logic for threads check for interruption after each task executed by their thread finishes. They terminate the thread if it has been interrupted. If the logic of the task checks for its thread's being interrupted, then the thread will terminate sooner. When new tasks are presented to the thread pool, new threads are created to replace the terminated threads, if needed.

Unfinished tasks are never dropped upon interruption. It is simple to clear interruption between tasks, but implementation characteristics of interruption-based methods are uncertain enough to warrant this conservative strategy. It is a good idea to be equally conservative in the way you code the tasks that run within pools.

```
public void interruptAll() {
    // Synchronized to avoid concurrentModification exceptions
    synchronized (poolLock) {
        for (Iterator it = threads.values().iterator();
                it.hasNext(); ) {
            Thread t = (Thread)(it.next());
            t.interrupt();
        } // for
    } // synchronized
} // interruptAll()
```

Normally, before shutting down a pool by a call to the `interruptAll` method, you should be sure that all clients of the pool are themselves terminated, in order to avoid hanging or losing commands. Additionally, you may wish to call the `drain` method to remove (and return) unprocessed tasks from the queue after shutting down the pool and its clients. If you need to be sure these tasks are processed, then you can explicitly call the `run` method of each task in the list returned by the `drain` method.

The `drain` method removes all unprocessed tasks from pool's queue, and returns them in a `java.util.List`. This should be used only when the pool has no active clients; otherwise, it is possible that the method will loop, removing tasks as clients put them in. This method can be useful after shutting down a `threadPool` (by a call to `interruptAll`) to determine if there are any pending tasks waiting to be processed. You can then, for example, execute all unprocessed tasks via code along the lines of:

```
List tasks = pool.drain();
for (Iterator it = tasks.iterator(); it.hasNext();) {
    ( (Runnable)(it.next()) ).run();
} // for
```

Here is a listing of the `drain` method:

```
public List drain() {
    boolean wasInterrupted = false;
    Vector tasks = new Vector();
    for (;;) {
        try {
            Object x = handOff.get(0);
            if (x == null)
                break;
            else
                tasks.addElement(x);
        } catch (InterruptedException ex) {
            // postpone re-interrupt until drained
            wasInterrupted = true;
        } // try
    } // for
    if (wasInterrupted) Thread.currentThread().interrupt();
    return tasks;
} // drain()
```

```
/**
 * Return the number of milliseconds to keep threads
 * alive waiting for new tasks. A negative value
 * means to wait forever. A zero value means not to wait
 * at all.
 **/
public synchronized long getMaxIdleTime() {
    return maxIdleTime;
} // getMaxIdleTime()

/**
 * Set the number of milliseconds to keep threads
 * alive waiting for new tasks. A negative value
 * means to wait forever. A zero value means not to wait
 * at all.
 */
public synchronized void setMaxIdleTime(long msecs) {
    maxIdleTime = msecs;
} // setMaxIdleTime(long)
/**
 * This method is called when a thread terminates.
 */
protected void workerDone(Worker w) {
    synchronized(poolLock) {
        --poolSize;
        threads.remove(w);
    } // synchronized
} // sooner

/**
 * Get a task from the queue
 */
protected Runnable getTask() throws InterruptedException {
    long waitTime = getMaxIdleTime();
    if (waitTime >= 0) {
        return (Runnable)(handOff.get(waitTime));
    } else {
        return (Runnable)(handOff.get());
    } // if
} // getTask()

/**
 * Private class that encapsulates the top-level logic for
 * pooled threads that runs tasks.
 */
protected class Worker implements Runnable {
    protected Runnable firstTask;

    Worker(Runnable firstTask) {
        this.firstTask = firstTask;
    } // constructor(Runnable)

    public void run() {
        try {
```

```
                  Runnable task = firstTask;
                  firstTask = null;
                  if (task != null) {
                     task.run();
                  } // if
                  // Continue working until max lowered
                  while (getPoolSize() <= getMaximumPoolSize()) {
                     task = getTask();
                     if (task != null) {
                        task.run();
                     } else {
                        break;
                     } // if
                  } // while
               } catch (InterruptedException e) {
                  // let this just fall through so the thread
                  // dies a quiet death.
               } finally {
                  workerDone(this);
               } // try
         } // run()
   } // class Worker
```

When a task is passed to a thread pool's `execute` method, normally either it gets a thread to run the task or it is put in the queue of tasks waiting for a thread. However, neither of those actions is possible if the number of threads in the pool is already the maximum, and the queue of waiting tasks is at its maximum length.

When it is not possible either to run a task or to queue it, then some less desirable strategy must be followed. This implementation of the Thread Pool pattern uses the Strategy pattern to manage and remember the currently selected strategy. There is a protected interface named `BlockedExecutionStrategy`. This interface defines a method called `blockedAction` that takes an argument that is a task. There are also protected classes that implement the `BlockedExecutionStrategy` interface. The current strategy for handling tasks that cannot be run or queued is represented as an instance of a class that implements the `BlockedExecutionStrategy` interface. Tasks that cannot be run or queued are passed to the `BlockedExecutionStrategy` object's `blockedAction` method, which is expected to take appropriate action.

This `ThreadPool` class defines three private classes that implement the `BlockedExecutionStrategy` interface. You can subclass the `ThreadPool` class to add more subclasses, and/or create subclasses of these strategy classes. If so, you will also want to add or modify the corresponding methods that set the current `BlockedExectionStrategy`.

```
protected interface BlockedExecutionStrategy {
   /**
```

```
     * Return true if successfully handled so, execute
     * should terminate; else return false if execute loop
     * should be retried.
     */
    public boolean blockedAction(Runnable task);
} // class BlockedExecutionStrategy
```

The next class implements the BlockedExecutionStrategy interface with logic that uses the thread that calls the ThreadPool object's execute method to synchronously run the given task. This is the default strategy for handling tasks that cannot be run or queued.

```
protected class RunWhenBlocked
                    implements BlockedExecutionStrategy {
    public boolean blockedAction(Runnable task) {
        task.run();
        return true;
    } // blockedAction(Runnable)
} // class RunWhenBlocked
```

The next class implements the BlockedExecutionStrategy interface with logic that causes the thread that calls the ThreadPool object's execute method to wait until the given task can be queued.

```
protected class WaitWhenBlocked
                    implements BlockedExecutionStrategy {
    public boolean blockedAction(Runnable task) {
        try {
            handOff.put(task);
        } catch(InterruptedException ex) {
            // Propagate interrupts
            Thread.currentThread().interrupt();
        } // try
        return true;
    } // blockedAction(Runnable)
} // class WaitWhenBlocked
```

The next class is the last of the BlockedExecutionStrategy classes. It implements the BlockedExecutionStrategy interface with logic that quietly discards the given task, so that the task will not be performed.

```
protected class DiscardWhenBlocked
                    implements BlockedExecutionStrategy {
    public boolean blockedAction(Runnable task) {
        return true;
    } // blockedAction(Runnable)
} // class DiscardWhenBlocked
```

The blockedExecutionStrategy instance variable refers to the current BlockedExecutionStrategy strategy object.

```
protected BlockedExecutionStrategy blockedExecutionStrategy;

/**
 * Return the strategy object for blocked execution
 */
protected synchronized
BlockedExecutionStrategy getBlockedExecutionStrategy() {
    return blockedExecutionStrategy;
} // getBlockedExecutionStrategy()
```

Because the classes that implement the BlockedExecutionStrategy interface are protected, it does not make any sense to have a set method for the current strategy. To use such a method, other classes would need visibility to the BlockedExecutionStrategy interface and the classes that implement it. Instead, the ThreadPool class has a public method that corresponds to each strategy.

```
/**
 * Set the policy for blocked execution to be that
 * the current thread executes the task if
 * there are no available threads in the pool.
 */
public synchronized void runWhenBlocked() {
    blockedExecutionStrategy = new RunWhenBlocked();
} // runWhenBlocked()

/**
 * Set the policy for blocked execution to be to
 * wait until a thread is available.
 */
public synchronized void waitWhenBlocked() {
    blockedExecutionStrategy = new WaitWhenBlocked();
} // WaitWhenBlocked()

/**
 * Set the policy for blocked execution to be to
 * return without executing the request
 */
public synchronized void discardWhenBlocked() {
    blockedExecutionStrategy = new DiscardWhenBlocked();
} // discardWhenBlocked()
```

Finally, here is the execute method that other classes call to have a ThreadPool object perform a task in a pool-supplied thread. The method normally returns when the task has been handed off for (possibly later) execution.

```
public void execute(Runnable task)
                              throws InterruptedException {
    while (true) {
        synchronized(poolLock) {
```

```
                            // Ensure normal number of threads
                            if (getPoolSize() < getNormalPoolSize()) {
                                addThread(task);
                                return;
                            } // if

                            // Try to give to existing thread
                            if (handOff.put(task, 0)) {
                                return;
                            } // if put
                                // There was no immediately available thread,
                                // so try to add a new thread to pool.
                                if (getPoolSize() < getMaximumPoolSize()) {
                                    addThread(task);
                                    return;
                                } // if maximumPoolSize
                        } // synchronized
                        // Cannot hand off and cannot create -- ask for help
                        if
  (getBlockedExecutionStrategy().blockedAction(task)) {
                                return;
                            } // if blockedAction
                    } // while
            } // execute(Runnable)
} // class ThreadPool
```

The `ThreadPool` class delegates the creation of new threads to objects that implement the `ThreadFactoryIF` interface.

```
public interface ThreadFactoryIF {
    /**
     * Return a Thread that runs the given Runnable object.
     */
    public Thread createThread(Runnable r);
  } // interface ThreadFactoryIF
```

If no `ThreadFactoryIF` object is explicitly given to a `ThreadPool` object to use, then by default it uses an instance of the `DefaultThreadFactory` class to create threads.

```
public class DefaultThreadFactory implements ThreadFactoryIF {
    public Thread createThread(Runnable r) {
        return new Thread(r);
    } // createThread(Runnable)
} // class DefaultThreadFactory
```

Finally, here is the `Executor` interface:

```
public interface Executor {
    public void execute(Runnable task)
        throws InterruptedException ;
} // interface Executor
```

RELATED PATTERNS

Object Pool. The Thread Pool pattern is a specialized form of the Object Pool pattern described in *Volume 1*.

Factory Method. Implementations of the Thread Pool pattern may use the Factory Method pattern (described in *Volume 1*) to allow greater flexibility in how they create new threads.

Singleton. The Singleton pattern (described in *Volume 1*) is often used with the Thread Pool pattern to ensure that all classes that want to use a `ThreadPool` object use the same `ThreadPool` object.

Guarded Suspension. Implementations of the Thread Pool pattern directly or indirectly use the Guarded Suspension pattern to manage the queuing of tasks.

Ephemeral Cache Item

SYNOPSIS

A cache can be used to keep a local copy of data from a remote data source. From time to time, the content of the data in the remote data source may change. You want a local cache to reflect such changes in a remote data source. Ensure that the data in the local cache matches the remote data source within a bounded amount of time by considering data in a cache to have a maximum useful lifetime.

CONTEXT

Suppose you work for a company whose business is to facilitate barter exchanges. People tell the barter exchange system what they are interested in offering for trade or trading for. The system matches up people who are parties to a potential trade. At that point, some negotiation may occur.

To arrive at a successful negotiation, it can be helpful to the parties involved to have information about recent trades that involved similar goods or services. To provide this information, the barter exchange system maintains a database of recent trades. Because people most commonly trade with others in the same geographical area, the barter exchange system is organized as a distributed system with a database and transaction processing system in each of its geographically distributed offices. Transaction histories, like the rest of the database, are geographically distributed.

Though most transactions are between people in the same geographical area, when people want to look at recent trades to help determine their negotiating strategy, they tend to be interested in other geographic areas. However, the time spent gathering transaction histories across geographical areas noticeably increases the time these queries take. You want to enhance the software for the barter exchange system to reduce the amount of time spent gathering remote transaction histories. With this goal in mind, you analyze usage statistics. You discover that some types of queries are more popular than others. You also discover that the popularity of some queries varies with the time of day or with the season. The approach that you choose to reduce the time spent gathering remote transaction histories is to cache the results of such queries locally, using the Cache Management pattern described in *Volume 1*.

When people ask for transaction histories, they want histories to include the most recent transactions. One of the drawbacks to using a cache is that without taking any special measures, the contents of a cache do not reflect updates to the data source that the contents came from. Simply caching transaction histories will result in the cache's accumulating old histories that are of diminishing interest as they get older. One way to keep a cache up-to-date would be to have data sources push updates to all caches as they occur. This makes sense if all or even most of the changes will be useful in the cache. However, after analyzing usage statistics, you find that the majority of transactions are never queried. Pushing all updates to every cache would be a big waste of resources.

It may be possible, using statistical techniques, to build a model that predicts which updates should be sent to the caches. However, the effort involved in creating and maintaining such a model is significant. It can be difficult to be certain of the ongoing quality of the result of such a model. To the extent that the future reflects the past, a statistical model can be very effective. However, conditions sometimes change, so the model will need to be reworked whenever its success in predicting which transaction will be needed by caches goes down. Instead of creating a statistical model, you decide on another technique that provides a good result with little up-front effort and negligible maintenance. The technique you select is based on the observation that the need for transaction histories to be recent is not absolute. It is sufficient that there be a guarantee that transaction histories in caches are no older that some predetermined amount of time, such as 20 minutes. All that is needed to provide such a guarantee is for transaction histories older than the guaranteed time to be automatically removed from the cache. Because of the way it is usually implemented, this guaranteed maximum age of objects in a cache is called the *time-to-live*.

FORCES

- ☺ A program needs read access to objects that are expensive to access or fetch. Such objects typically come from an external or remote source, such as a database.
- ☺ To reduce the amount of time it takes to access or fetch the most commonly accessed or fetched objects, you can place them in a local cache that takes little time to access.
- ☺ You need to ensure that the state of the objects in the cache is *relatively* current. It is sufficient to guarantee that the state of the objects in the cache is current within some specified amount of time.
- ☹ If there is a need to ensure that the state of the objects in the cache is *absolutely* current, then you must send updates from their sources to

the caches. If objects in the cache are updated more frequently than they are accessed, then you are better off not having a cache.

SOLUTION

Keep objects that may take a long time to fetch, such as those from remote or external sources, in a local cache that can be accessed quickly. Ensure that the states of objects in the cache are relatively current by associating a predetermined time-to-live with each object in the cache. After an object's time-to-live has elapsed, the object is removed from the cache. By assigning and enforcing the time-to-live, you guarantee that the states of the objects in the cache are current within the predetermined amount of time. Figure 7.7 shows the roles that classes play in the Ephemeral Cache Item pattern. Here are descriptions of the roles shown in Figure 7.7:

Client. Instances of classes in this role delegate the responsibility of obtaining access to specified objects to a CacheManager object.

ObjectKey. Instances of the ObjectKey class identify the object to be fetched.

CacheManager. Client objects request objects from a Cache-Manager by calling its fetchObject method. The argument to the fetchObject method is an ObjectKey that identifies the object to fetch. The fetchObject method works by first calling the Cache object's fetchObject method. If that fails, it calls the ObjectFetcher object's fetchObject method and passes the object to the Cache. The next time that the CacheManager is asked to produce the same object, it may be able to get it back from the Cache. The point of this is that getting the object back from the Cache object is faster than getting the object from the ObjectFetcher.

ObjectFetcher. ObjectFetcher objects are responsible for fetching or creating objects that are not in the cache.

Cache. A Cache object is responsible for managing the collection of cached objects so that, given an ObjectKey object, it quickly finds the corresponding object. The CacheManager object passes an ObjectKey to the Cache object's fetchObject method to get an object from the cache. If the CacheManager object does not get the requested object from the fetchObject method, then it requests the object from the ObjectFetcher object. If the ObjectFetcher object returns the requested object, then it will pass the fetched object to this object's

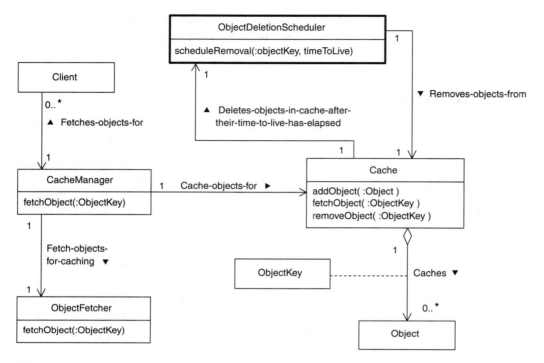

FIGURE 7.7 Ephemeral Cache Item pattern.

addObject method. The addObject method adds the object to the cache. If the cache is full, the addObject method may remove an object from the cache to make room for the object that it is adding to the cache.

ObjectDeletionScheduler.   After an object is added to a Cache, it passes that object and its time-to-live to the ObjectDeletionScheduler object's scheduleRemoval method. After the given time-to-live has elapsed, the ObjectDeletionScheduler object removes the object from the Cache by calling the Cache object's removeObject method.

CONSEQUENCES

☺ Removing objects from a cache after their time-to-live has elapsed is an effective way of limiting the number of objects in a cache. It prevents the cache from becoming excessively large.

☹ Removing objects from a cache after their time-to-live has elapsed generally lowers the hit rate for the cache. The shorter the time-to-live, the lower the hit rate drops.

IMPLEMENTATION

The most direct measure of a cache's effectiveness is its *hit rate*. The hit rate is the percentage of object fetch requests that the cache manager satisfies with objects stored in the cache. If every request is satisfied with an object from the cache, then the hit rate is 100 percent. If no request is satisfied, then the hit rate is 0 percent. Instrumenting the cache to measure its own hit rate can be helpful in empirically determining a good value for the cache contents' time-to-live.

The simplest way to assign a time-to-live value to objects in the cache is to assign the same value to all objects. If there is some way to predict how soon individual objects are likely to be updated, then it may be best to use the prediction to individually determine the time-to-live for each object. For example, consider the situation described under the "Context" heading.

Each historical transaction placed in the cache comes from a database that is dedicated to a geographical region. Some regions have predictably high transaction volumes and others have predictably low transaction volumes. In databases for high-volume regions, transaction histories are likely to become out-of-date sooner than in databases for low volume regions. For this reason, making the time-to-live longer for transaction histories from low-volume regions than for transaction histories from high-volume regions will result in a higher hit rate, while minimally impacting the currency of the cache's contents.

There are a number of other considerations related to the performance-tuning of caches in general. These are discussed in the "Implementation" section of the Cache Management pattern in Volume 1.

KNOWN USES

Most database managers that support distributed databases implement some form of the Ephemeral Cache Item pattern. For example, Oracle supports something called a snapshot, which is a local copy of a table that is updated periodically.

Distributed file systems such as NFS use the Ephemeral Cache Item pattern.

CODE EXAMPLE

The code example for this pattern is based on the transaction history problem under the "Context" heading. We will assume the existence of a `TransactionHistory` class. Each `TransactionHistory` object contains a historical transaction for a kind of goods or service. We will also assume that an `ItemID` object identifies the kind of goods or service. This brings us to the interesting portion of the example: the classes in the `Cache` and `ObjectDeletionScheduler` roles.

The code listing begins with the `TransactionHistoryCache` class, which is responsible for caching `TransactionHistory` objects. The class in the `ObjectDeletionScheduler` role is an inner class in the `TransactionHistoryCache` class.

```
class TransactionHistoryCache {
    private static final int TIME_TO_LIVE
        = 15*60*1000; // 15 Minutes
```

`TransactionHistory` objects are always assigned the same time-to-live, which is 15 minutes.

```
    /**
     * We use a linked list to determine the least recently
     * used TransactionHistory. The cache itself is implemented
     * by a Hashtable object. The Hashtable values are linked
     * list objects that refer to the actual TransactionHistory
     * object.
     */
    private Hashtable cache = new Hashtable();

    /**
     * This is the head of the linked list that refers to the
     * most recently used TransactionHistory.
     */
    LinkedList mru = null;

    /**
     * This is the tail of the linked list that refers to the
     * least recently used TransactionHistory.
     */
    LinkedList lru = null;

    /**
     * The maximum number of TransactionHistory objects that
     * may be in the cache.
     */
    private final int MAX_CACHE_SIZE = 80;

    /**
     * The number of TransactionHistory objects currently in
     * the cache.
     */
    private int currentCacheSize = 0;
```

This instance variable references the object that schedules and performs the removal of transaction histories from the cache.

```
private HistoryDeletionScheduler deletionScheduler
  = new HistoryDeletionScheduler();

/**
 * Objects are passed to this method for addition to the
 * cache. However, this method is not required to
 * actually add an object to the cache if the addition is
 * contrary to its policy for which objects should be
 * added. This method may also remove objects already in
 * the cache in order to make room for new objects.
 * @param history The TransactionHistory that is being
 * proposed as an addition to the cache.
 */
public void addHistory(TransactionHistory history) {
    ItemID id = history.getID();
    if (cache.get(id) == null) { // if history not in cache
        // Add history to cache, making it the most
        // recently used.
        if (currentCacheSize == 0) {
            // treat empty cache as a special case
            lru = mru = new LinkedList();
            mru.profile = history;
        } else {                  // currentCacheSize > 0
            LinkedList newLink;
            if (currentCacheSize >= MAX_CACHE_SIZE) {
                // remove least recently used
                // TransactionHistory from the cache.
                newLink = lru;
                lru = newLink.previous;
                cache.remove(id);
                currentCacheSize--;
                lru.next = null;
            } else {
                newLink = new LinkedList();
            } // if >= MAX_CACHE_SIZE
            newLink.profile = history;
            newLink.next = mru;
            mru.previous = newLink;
            newLink.previous = null;
            mru = newLink;
        } // if 0
        // put the now most recently used history in the
        // cache.
        mru.expirationTime
          = System.currentTimeMillis()+TIME_TO_LIVE;
        cache.put(id, mru);
        currentCacheSize++;
        deletionScheduler.scheduleRemoval(mru);
    } else {                    // history already in cache
        // addEmployee shouldn't be called when the object
        // is already in the cache. Since that has
        // happened, do a fetch so that the object becomes
        // the most recently used.
```

```
                fetchHistory(id);
        } // if cache.get(id)
    } // addHistory(TransactionHistory)

    private void remove(LinkedList node) {
        if (mru==node) {
            mru = node.next;
        } // if mru
        if (lru==node) {
            lru = node.previous;
        } // if
        if (node.next!=null) {
            node.next.previous = node.previous;
        } // if node.next
        if (node.previous!=null) {
            node.previous.next = node.next;
        } // if node.previous
        cache.remove(node.profile.getID());
    } // remove(LinkedList)

    /**
     * Return the TransactionHistory associated with the given
     * ItemID in the cache or null if no TransactionHistory is
     * associated with the given ItemID.
     * @param id the ItemID to retrieve a transaction history
     * for.
     */
    public TransactionHistory fetchHistory(ItemID id) {
        LinkedList foundLink = (LinkedList)cache.get(id);
        if (foundLink == null)
          return null;
        if (mru != foundLink) {
            if ( foundLink == lru ) {
                lru = foundLink.previous;
                lru.next = null;
            } // if lru
            if (foundLink.previous != null)
              foundLink.previous.next = foundLink.next;
            if (foundLink.next != null)
              foundLink.next.previous = foundLink.previous;
            mru.previous = foundLink;
            foundLink.previous = null;
            foundLink.next = mru;
            mru = foundLink;
        } // if currentCacheSize > 1
        return foundLink.profile;
    } // fetchHistory(ItemID)

    /**
     * private doublely linked list class for managing list of
     * most recently used transaction histories.
     */
    private class LinkedList {
        TransactionHistory profile;
```

```
    LinkedList previous;
    LinkedList next;
    long expirationTime;
} // class LinkedList
```

This private class is responsible for removing objects from the cache when their time comes.

```
private class HistoryDeletionScheduler extends Thread {
    /**
     * ArrayList to keep histories in order of expiration
     * time.
     */
    private ArrayList expirations = new ArrayList(100);

    HistoryDeletionScheduler() {
        start();
    } // constructor()

    /**
     * Schedule the removal of a TransactionHistory by
     * putting its LinkedList object in an ArrayList that
     * is sorted by expiration time.
     */
    synchronized void scheduleRemoval(LinkedList node) {
        int insertionIndex = findInsertionIndex(node);
        expirations.add(insertionIndex, node);
    } // scheduleRemoval(LinkedList)

    /**
     * Determine where in a LinkedList an object belongs
     * based on expiration times.
     */
    private int findInsertionIndex(LinkedList node) {
        long thisExpiration = node.expirationTime;
        int upperBound = expirations.size()-1;

        // Check common cases first
        if (upperBound<0) {
            return 0;
        } // if 0
        if (getExpiration(upperBound-1)<=thisExpiration) {
            return upperBound;
        } // if

        // use binary search to find correct index.
        int lowerBound = 0;
        while (upperBound>=lowerBound) {
            int midpoint
                = (upperBound-lowerBound)/2 + lowerBound;
            long midpointExpiration;
            midpointExpiration = getExpiration(midpoint);
            if (midpointExpiration==thisExpiration) {
                // For the equals case, midpoint or
```

```
                    // midpoint+1 will do. midpoint+1 may be
                    // faster to insert in an ArrayList.
                    return midpoint+1;
                } // if
                if (midpointExpiration>thisExpiration) {
                    lowerBound = midpoint+1;
                } else { // midpointExpiration<thisExpiration
                    upperBound = midpoint-1;
                } // if
            } // while
            return 0;
        } // findInsertionIndex(LinkedList)

        /**
         * Return the expiration time of the LinkedList object
         * at the nth index in expirations.
         */
        private long getExpiration(int n) {
            LinkedList node = (LinkedList)expirations.get(n);
            return node.expirationTime;
        } // getExpiration(int)

        /**
         * Top level logic for removing histories from the
         * cache.
         */
        public synchronized void run() {
            long now;

            try {
                while(!isInterrupted()) {
                    while (expirations.size()==0) {
                        now = System.currentTimeMillis();
                        long nextExpiration = getExpiration(0);
                        if (now < nextExpiration) {
                            wait(nextExpiration - now);
                        } // if
                    } // while 0
                    remove((LinkedList)expirations.get(0));
                    expirations.remove(0);
                } // while !isInterrupted
            } catch (InterruptedException e) {
            } // try
        } // run
    } // class HistoryDeletionScheduler
} // class TransactionHistoryCache()
```

RELATED PATTERNS

Cache Management.   The Ephemeral Cache Item pattern is a
refinement of the Cache Management pattern described in

Volume 1. That discussion includes a much more detailed discussion of caching.

Scheduler. The Ephemeral Cache Item pattern uses the Scheduler pattern (described in *Volume 1*).

Heavyweight/LightWeight. Application clients may use the Ephemeral Cache Item pattern with the Heavyweight/Lightweight pattern to manage lightweight objects.

Transaction State Stack

SYNOPSIS

Implement the ability to restore the original state of objects altered by nested atomic transactions by saving the original state of an object on a stack. This technique is most commonly used for transactions that only alter local objects or objects that are otherwise cheap to access.

CONTEXT

You are part of a team designing a point-of-sale system* for convenience stores. The system architecture will be based on multiple terminals (cash registers) connected to a central processor that performs such services as recording transactions, supplying pricing information to the terminals, and tracking inventory levels. Because convenience stores vary greatly in their budget, you have been given some hard constraints on the hardware resources that can be devoted to the central processor. You find that your central processor software needs some of the services that a database manager would provide, but you are unable to find an off-the-shelf database manager that has all of the features you need that will also fit within your hardware constraints.

You decide to implement your own minimal database manager in order to satisfy all of your requirements. One of those requirements is to support nested transactions. To support nested transactions, you must be able to restore the state of all of the objects that a transaction has modified if the transaction is aborted.

FORCES

☺ You have a requirement to support atomic transactions. This means that if a transaction is aborted, all of the objects it modified must be restored to their original state.

☺ You have a requirement to support nested transactions.

☺ You may not know all of the objects that a transaction will modify until the transaction is complete.

---

* A point-of-sale system is a high-tech cash register.

☻ In some environments, it is important to allow multiple transactions to run concurrently while ensuring that they are isolated from each other, so that each transaction runs as if it is the only one running at that time. To make this happen, it is necessary for transactions that only need read access to an object's state to see the object's original state while there is another uncommitted transaction that has modified the object. You will want to implement this in a way that minimizes the time penalty for transactions that need to find an older version of an object's state.

SOLUTION

Use a stack to organize information for restoring the state of objects modified by a transaction. When a transaction begins, save the position of the top of the stack so it can be restored to its previous position at the end of the transaction. Each time the transaction modifies an object it has not modified before, capture the object's current state and push the captured state onto the stack.

Figure 7.8 shows the roles of classes and interfaces that participate in the Transaction State Stack pattern. Here are descriptions of the roles that classes and interfaces play in the transaction state stack:

TransactionManager.   Classes in this role provide the top-level logic for managing transactions.

TransactionParticipantIF.   This is an interface that must be implemented by all classes that participate in a transaction. Interfaces in this role declare methods for such purposes as getting a lock on an object and saving or restoring its state.

TransationParticipant.   Classes in this role implement the `TransactionparticipantIF` interface with logic that includes ways for them to participate in locks and to save and restore the state of an object. In some cases, the stateful object in question may directly implement the `TransactionparticipantIF` interface. In most cases, the logic to implement the `TransactionparticipantIF` interface comes from a decorator object that wraps the stateful object being manipulated.

StateSavingClass.   Methods of a `TransactionparticipantIF` interface that save an object's state return an object that encapsulates the object's current state. The role of these state-encapsulating objects' class is `StateSavingClass`.

This role is unusual in that classes can fill this role without sharing any common superclasses or interfaces. The only

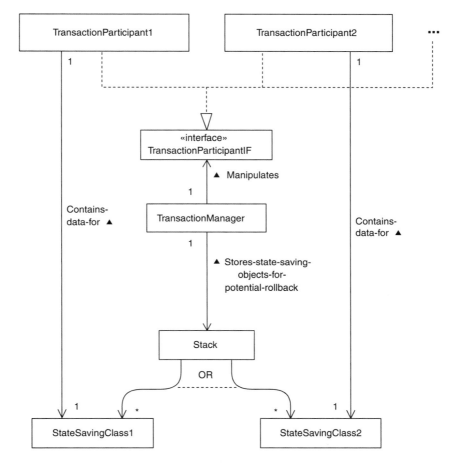

FIGURE 7.8 Transaction state stack.

requirement for classes that fill the StateSavingClass role is that they declare at least two methods. One method must capture an object's state and return the state encapsulated in an object. The other method must take an argument that is an object returned by the first method and use the information it encapsulates to restore the state of the stateful object.

Classes in the StateSavingClass role are usually specialized to work with a specific TransactionParticipant class.

Stack.   Classes in this role implement a Stack data structure.

The collaboration diagram in Figure 7.9 shows the interactions between the classes and interfaces that participate in the Transaction State Stack pattern.

1. This signals the start of a transaction to the `TransactionManager` object. This causes some bookkeeping to happen, including setting the number of objects participating in this transaction to zero.

2. Add the object `p1` to the transaction as read-only participant.

2.1. The `TransactionManager` object gets a lock on `p1` and gets an object that encapsulates the current state of `p1`.

2.2. The `TransactionManager` object pushes the current state of `p1` on the stack.

3. Add the object `p2` to the transaction as writable participant.

3.1. The `TransactionManager` object gets a lock on `p2` and gets an object that encapsulates the current state of `p2`.

3.2. The `TransactionManager` object pushes the current state of `p2` on the stack.

4. The transaction is aborted.

4.1. Pop the saved state of `p2` off the stack.

4.2. Restore the state of `p2` to its saved state.

4.3. Release the lock on `p2`.

4.4. Pop the saved state of `p1` off the stack.

4.5. Restore the state of `p1` to its saved state.

4.6. Release the lock on `p1`.

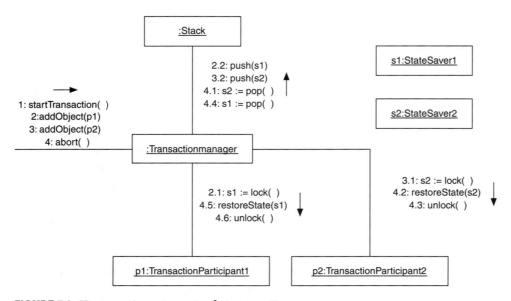

FIGURE 7.9 Transaction state stack interactions.

CONSEQUENCES

- ☺ The Transaction State Stack pattern makes it possible for the objects modified by a transaction to be restored to the state they were in when the transaction started, even if the transaction is nested in another transaction.
- ☹ The Transaction State Stack pattern does not directly include a way to cache the current state of objects modified by a transaction. If it is expensive to fetch or store the current state of an object, then the pattern can be extended to include a caching mechanism at the expense of complicating its implementation.
- ● You can use the Transaction State Stack pattern to ensure that transactions are atomic. However, the Transaction State Stack pattern does nothing to ensure that transactions have any of the other ACID properties.

IMPLEMENTATION

When it is known that a transaction may modify an object, you must lock the object so that concurrent transactions will not modify it. Immediately after the transaction acquires a lock on an object is the earliest time that you can usefully save the object's state on a stack.

The simplest way to decide when to save an object's state is to save it as soon as a transaction acquires a lock on it. Some transactions acquire locks on objects that they may modify. If they acquire a lock on an object that they don't modify, then saving the object's state is a waste of time. If such transactions may be common, then it is more efficient to postpone saving an object's state until just before the first time it is modified by a transaction.

KNOWN USES

Interpreters for dynamically scoped languages often use the Transaction State Stack pattern to manage the scope of local variables.

Some proprietary applications that edit complex objects use the Transaction State Stack pattern to manage an undo facility.

Database managers use the Transaction State Stack pattern to manage rollback of transactions.

CODE EXAMPLE

This code example is a general-purpose implementation of `Transaction-ParticipantIF` interface and the `TransactionManager` class. Here is a listing of the `TransactionParticipantIF` interface. All objects that participate in a transaction must either directly implement the `Transaction-ParticipantIF` interface or be wrapped by an adapter object that implements the `TransactionParticipantIF` interface.

```
public interface TransactionParticipantIF {
    /**
     * This method does not return until it can associate a
     * lock on the participating object with the current
     * thread.
     */
    public void lock() ;

    /**
     * Return an object that encapsulates the state of the
     * participating object.
     */
    public SnapshotIF captureState() ;

    /**
     * Restore the state of the participating object from the
     * information encapsulated in the given object. The given
     * object must have previously been returned by this
     * object's captureState method.
     */
    public void restoreState(SnapshotIF state) ;

    /**
     * Release a previously obtained lock.
     */
    public void unlock() ;
} // interface TransactionParticipantIF
```

Here is a listing of the `TransactionManager` class. An interesting thing about the `TransactionManager` class is that it delegates most of its work to a private inner class called `Transaction`. When a transaction is started, a `TransactionManager` object creates and associates a `Transaction` object with the current thread. This organization is based on the assumption that transactions are single-threaded. Every time a `TransactionManager` object is asked to do something, it uses the `Transaction` object that it previously created for the current thread.

```
public class TransactionManager {
    private ThreadLocal myStack;
    private ThreadLocal currentTransaction;
```

The `myStack` instance variable associates a `Stack` object with the current thread. The stack is used to save the values of objects when they are locked.

The `currentTransaction` instance variable associates the current transaction a thread is working on with that thread. If the transaction is nested in another transaction, its enclosing transaction is saved on the stack. The `TransactionManager` class's constructor initializes these variables.

```
public TransactionManager() {
    myStack = new ThreadLocal();
    myStack.set(new Stack());
    currentTransaction = new ThreadLocal();
} // TransactionManager()

/**
 * Start a new transaction. If there is a transaction in
 * progress, the transactions nest.
 */
public void startTransaction() {
    getStack().push(getCurrentTransaction());
    setCurrentTransaction(new Transaction());
} // startTransaction()
```

A `TransactionManager` object delegates most of the work of its other operations to the current thread's current `Transaction` object.

```
/**
 * Add an object to the current transaction.
 */
public void enroll(TransactionParticipantIF obj) {
    checkCurrentTransaction();
    getCurrentTransaction().enroll(obj);
} // enroll(TransactionParticipantIF)

/**
 * Commit the current transaction.
 */
public void commit() {
    checkCurrentTransaction();
    getCurrentTransaction().commit();
} // commit()

/**
 * Abort the current transaction.
 */
public void abort() {
    checkCurrentTransaction();
    getCurrentTransaction().abort();
} // abort()
```

Here are helper methods that are used by the preceding public methods.

```
/**
 * Throw an <code>IllegalStateException</code> if there is
 * no current transaction.
 */
private void checkCurrentTransaction() {
    if (getCurrentTransaction()==null) {
        throw new IllegalStateException("No transaction");
```

```
        } //if
    } // checkCurrentTransaction()

    /**
     * Return the transaction manager stack associated with the
     * current thread.
     */
    private Stack getStack() {
        return (Stack)myStack.get();
    } // getStack()

    /**
     * Return the current Transaction object.
     */
    private Transaction getCurrentTransaction() {
        return (Transaction)currentTransaction.get();
    } // getCurrentTransaction()

    /**
     * Set the current Transaction object.
     */
    private void setCurrentTransaction(Transaction t) {
    currentTransaction.set(t);
} //setCurrentTransaction(Transaction)
```

Transactions are represented as instances of this private class:

```
private class Transaction {
    // Collection of TransactionParticipantIF objects.
    private ArrayList participants = new ArrayList();

    /**
     * Add the given object to this transaction to be
     * modified.
     */
    void enroll(TransactionParticipantIF obj) {
        obj.lock();
        getStack().push(obj.captureState());
        participants.add(obj);
    } // enroll(TransactionParticipantIF)

    /**
     * commit this transaction.
     */
    void commit() {
        int count;
        count = participants.size();
        for (int i=count-1; i>=0; i--) {
            TransactionParticipantIF p;
            p = (TransactionParticipantIF)
                participants.get(i);
            p.unlock();
            getStack().pop();
```

```
        } // for
        Transaction prevTransaction;
        prevTransaction = (Transaction)getStack().pop();
        setCurrentTransaction(prevTransaction);
    } // commit()

    ...

    /**
     * Abort this transaction.
     */
    void abort() {
        int count;
        count = participants.size();
        for (int i=count-1; i>=0; i--) {
            SnapshotIF state;
            state = (SnapshotIF)getStack().pop();
            TransactionParticipantIF participant
              =(TransactionParticipantIF)participants.get(i);
            participant.restoreState(state);
            participant.unlock();
        } // for
            setCurrentTransaction((Transaction)getStack().pop());
        } // abort()
    } // class Transaction
} // class TransactionManager
```

RELATED PATTERNS

ACID Transaction.   The ACID Transaction pattern contains more information about the atomic and isolated properties of transactions.

Decorator.   The logic for a `TransactionParticipantIF` interface for a class that participates in a transaction is often implemented using the Decorator pattern (described in *Volume 1*).

Snapshot.   The Transaction State Stack pattern uses the Snapshot pattern (described in *Volume 1*) to encapsulate the current state of an object in a way suitable for being put on a stack and possibly being restored later.

8

Temporal Patterns

The patterns in this chapter describe ways that applications manage time-related data. There are only a few patterns in this chapter. That should not be taken to mean that handling time is a simple matter. Issues related to handling and modeling time can be very complex. The small number of patterns is a symptom that the state of the art related to time is less well developed than other areas.

Time Server

This pattern was previously described in [Lange98].

SYNOPSIS

In order for some distributed applications to function correctly, the clocks on the computers they run on must be synchronized. Ensure that clocks on multiple computers are synchronized by synchronizing them with a common clock.

CONTEXT

You are designing an employee timekeeping system. The system architecture will include multiple timekeeping terminals. Employees will use the timekeeping terminals to indicate when they begin working a shift, are done working, and other timekeeping events. The terminals report timekeeping events to a server that collects the events in a database.

Employees may use different timekeeping terminals to indicate the beginning of a shift and the end of a shift. When a timekeeping terminal reports a timekeeping event, the time of the event is determined by the timekeeping terminal's own clock. If the clocks on the different terminals are not synchronized, the duration of the employee's shift will appear to be longer or shorter than it actually was.

FORCES

- ☺ An application is distributed over multiple computers.
- ☺ A distributed application is required to do things at predetermined times, to ensure the relative order of its actions. If the clocks on the computers an application is running on are not synchronized, their differences can cause the application to perform its actions in the wrong relative order.
- ☺ A distributed application records events it receives on different computers. It is important to accurately determine the elapsed time

between events, even if the events are received on different computers.

☺ Relying on the continuous availability of a single central clock to determine the time that an event occurs can reduce the availability of an application, since the application will be unable to function if the clock becomes unavailable. Relying on a single central clock can also limit the performance of a distributed application, since relying on a central clock or any other central resource can result in that resource's becoming a bottleneck.

☹ Relying on a remote clock can introduce inaccuracies into the determination of the time if the network delays encountered in communicating with the clock vary in an unpredictable way.

SOLUTION

Have each computer that hosts part of a distributed application periodically set its own clock from the clock of a remote computer that functions as a time server.

The frequency with which a host synchronizes its clock with the time server should be often enough that the clocks do not noticeably diverge. Typically, this is once every hour or two. Though this is more frequent than may be required to keep clocks synchronized, it serves to minimize the consequences of the time server's being unavailable when another computer wants to synchronize its clock with the time server's.

Communication between a computer requesting the current time and a time server takes some amount of time. There is no way to know in advance exactly how long it will take. After a computer has requested the current time from a time server and it has received the time, it knows the total elapsed time that the request took. It does not know how long the request took to reach the time server and it does not know how long the response took to get from the server to the requesting computer. The elapsed time between when a request reaches a server and when the response leaves the server is usually very small. For practical purposes, the time that it takes for the response to travel from the server to the requesting computer is the inaccuracy of the response when it reaches the requesting computer. A reasonable way to estimate this time is to assume that the time it takes the request to travel from the requesting computer to the server is equal to the time it takes the response to travel from the server to the requesting computer. This makes our estimate of the time it takes for the response to get to the requesting computer one half of the elapsed time between when the request was issued and the response was received.

When the requesting computer receives the current time from a time server, it adds one half of the elapsed time to the time it receives and uses that as the actual current time.

CONSEQUENCES

☺ Given events recorded by different computers, the Time Server pattern allows the times at which those events occurred to be accurately compared.

☹ If the time server becomes unavailable for a long period of time, a distributed application that relies on the clocks of multiple computers being synchronized may fail. This situation can generally be avoided by using multiple time servers, as is discussed under the following "Implementation" heading.

IMPLEMENTATION

The Time Server pattern is most often implemented at the system level rather than at the application level. If the computers in question are general-purpose computers that run multiple applications, then implementing the Time Server pattern at the system level allows all applications that run on the computer to share the benefits of a single implementation of the Time Server pattern.

In some cases, it is not possible for a distributed application to assume that the time clocks of the computers it runs on are synchronized. In that case, the application must have an application-level implementation of the Time Server pattern.

By using multiple time servers, you can minimize the effects of erratic network speeds and greatly increase the availability of the current time service. Computing the current time by averaging the adjusted results from multiple time servers minimizes the effects of erratic network speeds. Using multiple time servers ensures that the failure of a single time server does not make the current time unavailable.

If the Time Server pattern is implemented at the application level, it will generally not be possible for the class that implements the pattern to set the system clock. Instead, the class can keep track of the difference between the local system time and the time server's time. By making the time client class the source of the current time for the rest of the application, the time client class can achieve the same effect by applying the difference between the local and server time to the system time before returning it. The shortcoming to this approach is that if the local clock is set to another time, the time client class will be applying the wrong difference to the time until it next consults the server.

KNOWN USES

The author is aware of a proprietary employee timekeeping application that uses the Time Server pattern to synchronize the time on multiple timekeeping terminals.

The Time Server pattern is used in some point-of-sale systems to synchronize the time in cash registers.

The Time Server pattern is also used in the HP TraceVue Series 50 product. This is used during the birth of a child to track its vital signs.

CODE EXAMPLE

This code example consists of just a simple time server and time client class. The server implements this interface:

```
public interface TimeServerIF extends Remote {
    // The name of all time servers
    public static final String TIME_SERVER_NAME = "time";

    /**
     * Return the current time
     */
    public Calendar currentTime() throws RemoteException;
} // interface TimeServerIF
```

Here is the time server class that implements the interface:

```
public class TimeServer implements TimeServerIF {
    /**
     * Constructor
     */
    public TimeServer() throws RemoteException,
                               MalformedURLException,
                               UnknownHostException {
        // Note that the name TIME_SERVER_NAME is hard-coded,
        // which means that only one TimeServer object can
        // exist on each host machine.
        Naming.rebind(TIME_SERVER_NAME, this);
    } // constructor()
    /**
     * Return the current time
     */
    public Calendar currentTime() {
        return Calendar.getInstance();
```

```
        } // currentTime()
} // class TimeServer
```

Finally, here is the class that is the server's client:

```java
public class TimeClient {
    private static final long UPDATE_PERIOD
        = 1000*60*60;              // 1 hour

    // difference between the local and server time
    private int timeDifference;

    private TimeServerIF theTimeServer;

    /**
     * constructor
     */
    public TimeClient(String timeHost)
                                throws RemoteException,
                                       UnknownHostException,
                                       NotBoundException,
                                       MalformedURLException {
        String urlName = "//" + timeHost
            + "/" + TimeServerIF.TIME_SERVER_NAME;
        theTimeServer = (TimeServerIF)Naming.lookup(urlName);
        new DifferenceUpdater();
    } // constructor()

    public Calendar currentTime() {
        Calendar now = Calendar.getInstance();
        now.add(Calendar.MILLISECOND, -timeDifference);
        return now;
    } // currentTimeMillis()

     private class DifferenceUpdater extends Thread {
        public void run() {
            try {
                while (!isInterrupted()) {
                    try {
                        long startTime =
                          System.currentTimeMillis();
                        Calendar serverTime =
                          theTimeServer.currentTime();
                        long endTime =
                          System.currentTimeMillis();
                        long latency = (endTime-startTime)/2;
                        long adjustedTime
                          = serverTime.getTime().getTime()+latency;
                        timeDifference = (int)(endTime-adjustedTime);
                    } catch (RemoteException e) {
                        // Nothing to do but keep trying.
                    } // try
                    sleep(UPDATE_PERIOD);
```

```
                    } // while
                } catch (InterruptedException e) {
                    // It's all over
                } // try
            } // run()
        } // class DifferenceUpdater
} // class TimeClient
```

RELATED PATTERNS

Versioned Object.   Distributed applications that use the Versioned Object pattern are likely to also use the Time Server pattern.

Temporal Property.   Distributed applications that use the Temporal Property pattern are likely to also use the Time Server pattern.

Versioned Object

This pattern was previously described in [Lange98].

SYNOPSIS

You may need to access previous or future states of an object. When an object gets a new state, keep both its new and its previous states. Identify the states by a timestamp or a version number. Allow access to a specific state of an object by identifying its timestamp or version number.

CONTEXT

You are designing an inventory management system. The purpose of this system is to manage information about items that a business uses and sells. Over time, the information for a given item may change. For example, a business may get an item from a different vendor. When that happens, some of the item's attributes may be different. In addition to the vendor, the dimensions, the exact description, and perhaps the weight of the item also change

The system you design must be able to use an item's new and old information at the same time. It must be able to simultaneously describe the attributes of an item that a business used last week, a newer version of the item that is sitting on the warehouse shelves now, and the newest version of the item that is on order.

As you design the classes for the inventory management system, you include an `ItemDescription` class in the design. The nature of the system requires that when an `Item` object's description or state changes, both the new and old states are kept. The different states of an `Item` object are distinguished by the time interval for which the state is valid. When getting an item's weight, textual description, or other information from an `Item` object, it is necessary to specify a point in time so that the object can know which of its states to consult. Figure 8.1 is a class diagram that shows a design that supports this.

In this design, `ItemDescription` objects do not contain their own state. Instead, they keep their states in a collection of `ItemDescriptionVersion` objects that is keyed to the time interval for which each state is valid.

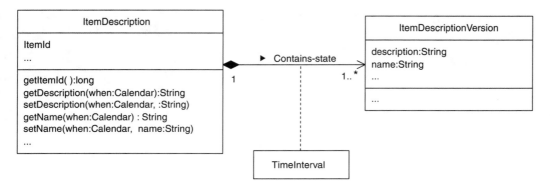

FIGURE 8.1 Item class design.

FORCES

☺ The state of an object may change.

☺ When the state of an object changes, the change usually involves more than one of the object's attributes.

☺ In addition to accessing the current state of an object, you need to access other states that it had or will have at given points in time.

☺ Objects are stored in a database that does not incorporate the concept of time-based versioning in its data model.

☹ If an existing application was designed to only keep the current state of an object, retrofitting it to keep the object's different states over time may involve a very large effort.

SOLUTION

When the state of a business object changes, do not discard the previous state. Instead, keep the new state and the previous state, distinguishing between them by the time intervals when each state is valid. Every time the state of a business object is fetched, it must happen in the context of a point in time. Figure 8.2 shows this design.

In this design, the state of a `BusinessObject` is extrinsic. Its state does not reside in the `BusinessObject` instance itself, but in associated instances of `BusinessObjectState`. The only attributes of `BusinessObject` that are intrinsic (reside within instances of the class) are those that are immutable. If the value of an attribute of a `BusinessObject` instance can change, then it is part of its state and must be kept in a `BusinessObjectState` instance.

Instances of `BusinessObjectState` are associated with instances of `BusinessObject` through disjoint time intervals. When the `get` method for a `BusinessObject` attribute is passed a point in time, that point in

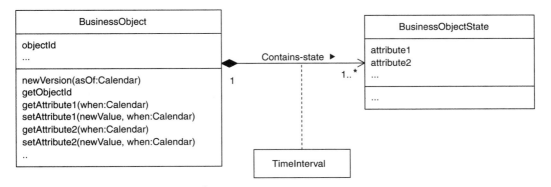

FIGURE 8.2 Versioned Object pattern.

time is contained by either zero or one of the time intervals. If it is contained by one of the time intervals, then the `get` method returns the value that corresponds to the time interval.

When an instance of `BusinessObject` is first created, an instance of `BusinessObjectState` is also created. This instance of `BusinessObjectState` contains the initial state of the `BusinessObject` instance. The time interval for which the state in this `BusinessObjectState` applies to the `BusinessObject` instance is the entire time it correctly describes the real-world entity that the `BusinessObject` represents. In practice, this is often not known. In absence of this information, an interval stretching from the beginning to the end of time is usually a good enough approximation.

When something changes about the real-world entity a `Business-Object` represents, the usual consequence is that the `BusinessObject` needs to be given a new state. This is a two-part process. First the `BusinessObject` instance's `newVersion` method is called to indicate that a new state is being created. The `newVersion` method is passed the effective time of the change. Initially the new state is a copy of the state that preceded it. Then the appropriate set methods of the `BusinessObjectState` instance are called to change the information in the new state to match the real world.

The time interval for the new state is from the effective time to the end of the interval of the previously latest state. When a new state is created, the end time of the interval associated with the previously latest state changes. The end of the interval becomes the moment in time just before the effective time of the new state.

Implementations of the Versioned Object pattern involve another class that has not been discussed yet. This class implements the data structure responsible for associating `BusinessObjectState` instances with an interval of time and finding the appropriate `BusinessObjectState` instance for a given point in time. The details of this class are discussed under the following "Implementation" heading.

CONSEQUENCES

☺ The Versioned Object pattern allows an application to recognize that real-world entities change over time.

☹ The Versioned Object pattern requires that all access to an object's state be in the context of a point in time. It generally becomes the responsibility of clients of a versioned object to provide the context. Some designs avoid burdening client objects in that way by offering calls that assume either the last context or the context corresponding to the current time. These assumptions can sometimes be a source of bugs or confusion.

☹ The Versioned Object pattern increases the amount of memory needed to store objects. In particular, even if only one attribute changes, all of the object's attributes that are stored in a `BusinessObjectState` instance must be copied. It also makes the details of persisting an object more complicated.

IMPLEMENTATION

Data Structure

To implement the Versioned Object pattern, you must include a data structure in your design that associates an interval of time with each `BusinessObjectState` instance. It must also be able to find and fetch the `BusinessObjectState` instance associated with an interval that includes a given point in time.

A class that implements this data structure must ensure it does not contain any intervals that overlap. If it is presented with an interval that overlaps any intervals already in the data structure, the conflict should be resolved in favor of the new interval.

The choice of data structure should be based on the number of states that the average object is expected to have. If it is just a few, then a simple data structure based on an array or linked list is generally best. If the number of versions is expected to be large, some sort of tree-based structure may be best. The `IntervalMap` class shown under the "Code Example" heading is an example of this sort of data structure. It is based on an array.

Loading from Persistent Storage

Another implementation issue comes up when versioned objects are fetched from a persistent store. This issue is based on the observation that usually only one or sometimes two states of a versioned object are of interest in one session. Because of this, loading all the states of a `BusinessObject` instance is something that you will usually want to avoid. It wastes the time that it takes to load states that will never be used. It is also wastes memory.

A way to avoid loading states is to create a virtual proxy for each state that is not loaded.* When the content of a state is actually needed, the proxy for a state causes the state to be loaded. If you expect that at least one state will be used and there is a good and simple heuristic for guessing which state will be used, then it may be a more efficient use of time to load that one state along with the `BusinessObject` instance. Most often, that heuristic will be to load the current state of the `BusinessObjectState` instance or its last state.

Saving to Persistent Storage

A different implementation issue comes up when storing an item to persistent storage. It is unusual for more than one or two states of a `BusinessObject` instance to be new or modified since the `BusinessObject` instance was loaded from persistent storage. To avoid the overhead of saving states that do not need to be saved, it is common for `BusinessObjectState` classes to have a method that returns true for a `BusinessObject` instance that needs to be saved to persistent storage. This method is often called `isDirty`.

KNOWN USES

The Versioned Object pattern is used in many applications that have to model real-world entities.

- It is used in manufacturing software.
- It is used in application frameworks.
- It is used in some database engines.

CODE EXAMPLE

The code example for Versioned Object is a class that describes an item used by a business. Before we look at that class, we will begin by looking at some support classes. The first class is a class to represent a time interval.

---

* The Virtual Proxy pattern is described in *Volume 1*.

```java
public class Interval {
    // The number of milliseconds difference between daylight
    // savings and standard time.
    private static final long DAYLIGHT_SAVINGS_OFFSET
      = 60*60*1000;

    /**
     * An interval that spans all of time.
     */
    public static Interval ETERNITY
      = new Interval(Long.MIN_VALUE, Long.MAX_VALUE);

    // The start time of this interval, expressed as the number
    // of seconds since midnight, January 1, 1970, UTC
    private long start;

    // The end time of this interval, expressed as the number
    // of seconds since midnight, January 1, 1970, UTC
    private long end;

    /**
     * Construct an interval with the given start and end time.
     * @param start The start of the interval or null if the
     *              interval starts at the beginning of time.
     * @param end The end of the interval or null if the
     *              interval ends at the end of time.
     */
    public Interval(Calendar start, Calendar end) {
        long myStart;
        if (start==null) {
          myStart = Long.MIN_VALUE;
        } else {
            myStart = start.getTime().getTime();
        } // if
        long myEnd;
        if (end==null) {
            myEnd = Long.MAX_VALUE;
        } else {
            myEnd = end.getTime().getTime();
        } // if
        init(myStart, myEnd);
    } // constructor(Calendar, Calendar)
    ...
    /**
     * constructor
     * @param start
     *          The start time of this interval, expressed as the
     *          number of seconds since midnight,
     *          January 1, 1970, UTC.
     * @param end
     *          The end time of this interval, expressed as the
     *          number of seconds since midnight,
     *          January 1, 1970, UTC.
     */
```

```
Interval(long start, long end) {
    init(start, end);
} // constructor(long, long)


/**
 * Common initialization logic
 */
private void init(long start, long end) {
    if (end<start) {
        String msg = "Ends before it starts";
        throw new IllegalArgumentException(msg);
    } // if
    this.start = start;
    this.end = end;
} // init(long, long)
```
...
```
/**
 * Return true if the given time is contained in this
 * interval. More precisely, this method returns true if
 * the given time is greater than or equal to the start of
 * this interval and less than or equal to the end of this
 * interval.
 */
public boolean contains(Calendar time) {
    long tm = time.getTime().getTime();
    return tm>=start && tm<=end;
} // contains(Calendar)


/**
 * Return true if the given interval is completely
 * contained in this interval.
 */
public boolean contains(Interval that) {
    return this.start<=that.start && this.end>=that.end;
} // contains(Interval)
```
...
```
/**
 * Return true if this interval and the given interval
 * share any points in time.
 */
public boolean overlaps(Interval that) {
    return this.start<=that.end && this.end>=that.start;
} // overlaps(Interval)

/**
 * Return true if this interval ends after the given
 * interval.
 */
public boolean endsAfter(Interval that) {
    return this.end > that.end;
} // endsAfter(Interval)
```

```java
/**
 * Return the start time of this interval, expressed as the
 * number of seconds since midnight, January 1, 1970, UTC.
 */
long getStart() { return start; }

/**
 * Return the end time of this interval, expressed as the
 * number of seconds since midnight, January 1, 1970, UTC.
 */
long getEnd() { return end; }

/**
 * Return true if the given object is an
 * Interval object with the same start and end.
 */
public boolean equals(Object obj) {
    if (obj instanceof Interval) {
        Interval that = (Interval)obj;
        return (this.start==that.start
                && this.end==that.end);
    } //if
    return false;
} // equals(Object)
...
} // class Interval
```

The `IntervalMap` class implements a data structure that associates an `Interval` object with another object. It also finds the object associated with an interval that contains a given point in time.

```java
public class IntervalMap implements Serializable {
    private static final int GROWTH=2;

    // This implementation is based on two parallel arrays.
    // The order of their contents is self-adjusting. This
    // structure is optimized for lookup operations, not
    // adding.
    private Interval[] intervals;
    private Object[] values;

    private int length;

    /**
     * Constructor for an interval map with a default initial
     * size for internal data structure.
     */
    public IntervalMap() {
        this(1);
    } // constructor()

    /**
     * Constructor for interval map with at least the specified
```

```
 * internal size for its internal data structure.
 */
public IntervalMap(int capacity) {
    capacity += GROWTH;      // leave room to grow
    intervals = new Interval[capacity];
    values = new Object[capacity];
} // constructor(int)

/**
 * Convenience method to create an IntervalMap
 * that maps all of time to the given object.
 */
public static IntervalMap createEternalMap(Object obj) {
    IntervalMap im = new IntervalMap();
    im.add(Interval.ETERNITY, obj);
    return im;
} // createEternalMap(Object)

/**
 * Return the number of intervals in this IntervalMap
 * object.
 */
public int size() {
    return length;
} // size()

/**
 * Add an interval to this map. If the given interval
 * equals an interval already in this map, the given value
 * replaces the old value. If the given interval overlaps
 * an interval already in the map, then the overlapped
 * interval is replaced with one or two smaller intervals
 * with the same value as the original interval.
 */
public synchronized void add(Interval interval,
                             Object value) {
    long theStart = interval.getStart();
    long theEnd = interval.getEnd();
    for (int i=0; i<length && intervals[i]!=null; i++) {
        if (interval.overlaps(intervals[i])) {
            long thisStart = intervals[i].getStart();
            long thisEnd = intervals[i].getEnd();
            if (thisStart < theStart) {
                if (thisEnd > theEnd) {
                    // divide overlapped interval into 3
                    intervals[i] = new Interval(theEnd+1,
                                                thisEnd);
                    add(new Interval(thisStart,
                                     theStart-1),
                        values[i]);
                } else {
                    intervals[i]
                      = new Interval(thisStart,
                                     theStart-1);
```

```
                    } // if
                } else if (thisEnd>theEnd) {
                    intervals[i] = new Interval(theEnd+1,
                                                thisEnd);
                } // if
            } // if overlaps
        } // for
        ensureCapacity(length+1);
        intervals[length] = interval;
        values[length] = value;
        length++;
    } // add(Interval, Object)

    /**
     * Ensure that the capacity of the data structures is
     * at least the given size.
     */
    private void ensureCapacity(int capacity) {
        if (length < capacity) {
            Interval[] newIntervals;
            newIntervals = new Interval[capacity+GROWTH];
            System.arraycopy(intervals,
                             0, newIntervals,
                             0, length);
            intervals = newIntervals;
            Object[] newValues = new Object[capacity+GROWTH];
            System.arraycopy(values, 0, newValues, 0, length);
            values = newValues;
        } // if
    } // ensureCapacity(int)

    /**
     * Map the given point in time to an object.
     * @return This map maps the given point in time to an
     *         object using the Interval objects in this map.
     *         This method returns the mapped object.
     * @exception NotFoundException
     *         If then given point in time is outside of all
     *         the intervals in this map.
     */
    public synchronized Object get(Calendar when)
                                    throws NotFoundException {
        for (int i=0; i<length; i++) {
            if (intervals[i].contains(when)) {
                Object value = values[i];
                adjust(i);
                return value;
            } // if intervals
        } // for
        throw new NotFoundException(when.toString());
    } // get(Calendar)

    /**
     * Return the object associated with the given interval.
```

```
 * If there is an interval that equals the given interval
 * in this map, the corresponding value object is returned.
 * If there is no such interval, this method returns null.
 */
public synchronized
  Object getMatching(Interval thatInterval) {
    for (int i=0; i<length; i++) {
        if (intervals[i].equals(thatInterval)) {
            return values[i];
        } // if intervals
    } // for
    return null;
} // getMatching(Interval)

/**
 * Adjust the position of the interval and value at the
 * given index one up towards the beginning.
 */
private void adjust(int i) {
    if (i>0) {
        // Adjust position in array
        Interval tmpInterval = intervals[i];
        intervals[i] = intervals[i-1];
        intervals[i-1] = tmpInterval;
        Object tmpValue = values[i];
        values[i] = values[i-1];
        values[i-1] = tmpValue;
    } // if i
} // adjust(int)

/**
 * Return the object associated with the latest interval.
 * @exception NoSuchElementException
 *             If no intervals are in this IntervalMap.
 */
public synchronized Object getLatestValue() {
    return values[getLatestIndex()];
} // getLatestValue()

/**
 * Return an iterator over the Interval
 * objects in this IntervalMap.
 */
public Iterator intervals() {
    return new ArrayIterator(intervals);
} // intervals()

/**
 * Return an Iterator over the value object in
 * this IntervalMap.
 */
public Iterator values() {
    return new ArrayIterator(values);
} // values()
```

```
/**
 * Return the index of the latest interval.
 * @exception NoSuchElementException
 *            if there are no intervals in this IntervalMap.
 */
private int getLatestIndex() {
    if (length==0) {
        throw new NoSuchElementException();
    } // if
    int latestIndex = 0;
    Interval latestInterval = intervals[latestIndex];
    for (int i=1; i<length; i++) {
        if (intervals[i].endsAfter(latestInterval)) {
            latestIndex = i;
            latestInterval = intervals[i];
        } // if
    } // for
    return latestIndex;
} // getLatestIndex(int)
} // class IntervalMap
```

Here is the class promised at the beginning of this section that is used to describe items that are used by a business.

```
public class ItemDescription {
    private long id;              // a unique id

    /**
     * This object is used to map this object to its states
     * over time.
     */
    private IntervalMap versions;

    /**
     * This is true if the intervals in the versions
     * IntervalMap have changed.
     */
    private boolean versionsDirty = false;

    /**
     * Constructor for creating an ItemDescription for an
     * existing item.
     * @param id A unique identifying number.
     * @param im An IntervalMap that contains the
     *           ItemDescriptionVersion objects for this
     *           ItemDescription.
     */
    public ItemDescription(long id, IntervalMap im) {
        this.id = id;
        versions = im;
    } // constructor(long)

    /**
     * Create a new version of this item that will be
```

```
 * effective as of the given point in time. Changes made
 * with an effective date at or after this point in time
 * will have no effect on item attributes that were
 * effective for previous versions. Similarly, changes to
 * previous versions of the item will have no effect on
 * other versions.
 *
 * The initial values for the attributes of the new
 * version will be the same as the attributes that were
 * previously effective at the given effective date.
 */
public void addVersionDate(Calendar effectiveDate) {
    ItemDescriptionVersion newVersion;
    newVersion = getVersion(effectiveDate);
    newVersion
      = (ItemDescriptionVersion)newVersion.clone();
    versions.add(new Interval(effectiveDate, null),
               newVersion);
    versionsDirty = true;
} // addVersionDate(Calendar)


/**
 * Return the ItemDescriptionVersion effective at the
 * given point in time.
 */
private ItemDescriptionVersion getVersion(Calendar when) {
    try {
        return (ItemDescriptionVersion)versions.get(when);
    } catch (NotFoundException e) {
        String msg;
        msg = "No version of this item found for " + when;
        throw new IllegalStateException(msg);
    } // try
} // getVersion(Calendar)


/**
 * Return the IntervalMapover this object's
 * ItemDescriptionVersion objects. This is intended for
 * use by classes responsible for persisting instances of
 * this class.
 */
IntervalMap getVersionMap() {
    return versions;
} // getVersionMap()


/**
 * Return true if the set of intervals in the version's
 * IntervalMap may not match what is persisted.
 */
boolean isVersionsDirty() {
    return versionsDirty;
} // isVersionsDirty()
```

```
/**
 * Clear the flag that indicates that the intervals in
 * the version's IntervalMap may not match what is
 * persisted.
 */
void clearVersionsDirty() {
    versionsDirty = false;
} // clearVersionsDirty()


/**
 * Set the dirty flags of all of this object's versions.
 */
void setDirty() {
    Iterator iter = versions.values();
    while (iter.hasNext()) {
        ((ItemDescriptionVersion)iter.next()).setDirty();
    } // while
} // setDirty()


/**
 * Clear the dirty flags of all of this object's versions.
 */
void clearDirty() {
    Iterator iter = versions.values();
    while (iter.hasNext()) {
        ((ItemDescriptionVersion)iter.next()).clearDirty();
    } // while
} // clearDirty()


/**
 * Set the textual description for this item.
 * @param textualDescription The new description.
 * @param when A point in time that the description
 *             applies to. This method only sets this
 *             attribute for the item description version
 *             that is effective at this point in time.
 */
public void setTextualDescription(String textualDescription,
                                  Calendar when) {
    getVersion(when).setTextualDescription(textualDescription);
} // setTextualDescription(String)


/**
 * Return the textual description for this item.
 * @param when A point in time that the description
 *             applies to. This method only sets this
 *             attribute for the item description version
 *             that is effective at this point in time.
 */
public String getTextualDescription(Calendar when){
    return getVersion(when).getTextualDescription();
} // getTextualDescription()
```

```
/**
 * Return a number that uniquely identifies this item.
 */
public long getId(){ return id; }


/**
 * Return the name of this item.
 * @param when A point in time that the description
 *              applies to. This method only gets this
 *              attribute for the item description version
 *              that is effective at this point in time.
 */
public String getName(Calendar when){
    return getVersion(when).getName();
} // getName()


/**
 * Set the name of this item.
 * @param name The new name for this item.
 * @param when A point in time that the description
 *              applies to. This method only sets this
 *              attribute for the item description version
 *              that is effective at this point in time.
 */
public void setName(String name, Calendar when) {
    getVersion(when).setName(name);
} // setName(String)
...
} // class ItemDescription
```

Finally, here is the class that is responsible for encapsulating states of ItemDescription objects.

```
class ItemDescriptionVersion implements Cloneable {
    private String textualDescription;
    private String name;

    /**
     * This will be true if the attributes of this object are
     * known not to match their persisted values.
     */
    private boolean dirty = false;
...
    void setTextualDescription(String textualDescription){
        this.textualDescription = textualDescription;
        dirty = true;
    } // setTextualDescription(String)


    String getTextualDescription(){
        return textualDescription;
    } // getTextualDescription()
```

```
        String getName(){
            return name;
        } // getName()

        void setName(String name){
            this.name = name;
            dirty = true;
        } // setName(String)


        /**
         * Returns a clone of this object.
         */
        public Object clone() {
            try {
                ItemDescriptionVersion theClone;
                theClone = (ItemDescriptionVersion)super.clone();
                theClone.dirty = true;
                return theClone;
            } catch (CloneNotSupportedException e) {
                // this shouldn't happen, since we are Cloneable
                throw new InternalError();
            } // try
        } // clone()
...
        /**
         * Return true if this object's attributes may not match
         * their persisted values.
         */
        boolean isDirty() { return dirty; }


        /**
         * Clear the flags the indicate that the attributes of
         * this object may not match what is persisted.
         *
         * This is intended for use only by instances of classes
         * the implement ItemDescriptionPersisterIF that are
         * responsible for persisting ItemDescription
         * objects.
         */
        void clearDirty() {
            dirty = false;
        } // clearDirty()


        /**
         * Force the dirty flags to indicate that the attributes
         * of this object may not match what is persisted.
         */
        void setDirty() {
            dirty = true;
        } // setDirty()
    } // class ItemDescriptionVersion
```

RELATED PATTERNS

Time Server.　The Versioned Object pattern is often used in conjunction with the Time Server pattern to ensure consistent timestamping of object versions.

Virtual Proxy.　The Virtual Proxy pattern (described in *Volume 1*) is sometimes used with the Versioned Object pattern to avoid having to load all the states of an object from a persistent store.

Temporal Property.　The Temporal Property pattern provides an alternate way of organizing changes in an object's state over time. It is more appropriate for classes whose state changes tend to involve only one attribute at a time.

Lazy Retrieval.　In many applications, past and future versions of an object's state are used less often than its present state. To minimize the amount of time spent retrieving state information that will not be needed, the Lazy Retrieval pattern is often used to design classes responsible for retrieving versioned objects.

Temporal Property

The implementation of this pattern is similar to the Versioned Object pattern. It uses the same underlying class to create a different organization. This pattern was previously described in [CEF98].

SYNOPSIS

The values of an object's attributes may change over time. They usually change independently of each other. Keep historical values of attributes in a way that allows clients to get the effective value of a particular attribute as of a particular time.

CONTEXT

You are designing a human resource management system. The purpose of this system is to manage information about a business's employees. Over time, the information for a given employee may change. For example, over time an employee may hold different positions within a business. When an employee is assigned to a new position, the assignment may not be effective immediately, but instead be effective a few weeks after the assignment is made.

The system you are designing must be able to display an employee's current information, even if the employee is scheduled to take a new position in the near future. It must be able to show the position an employee holds or held at any point in time. It must also be able to handle changes that happen to an employee's other attributes that change independently, such as marital status, benefit elections, and work phone number.

As you design the classes for the human resources management system, you include an `Employee` class in the design. The nature of the system requires that when an attribute value of an `Employee` object changes, both the new and old values are kept. The different values of an attribute are distinguished by the time interval for which they are valid. When getting an employee's position, marital status, or other information from an employee object, it is necessary to specify a point in time so that the object can know which of an attribute's values to use. Figure 8.3 is a class diagram that shows a design that supports this.

In this design, `Employee` objects do not contain the values of their own attributes. Instead, they keep their attributes in a collection of objects

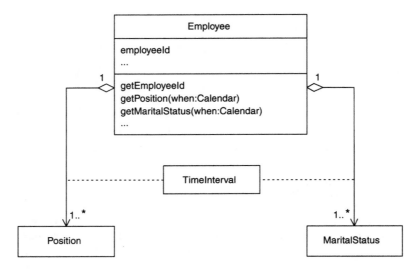

FIGURE 8.3 Employee class design.

keyed to the time interval for which each value is valid. The exception to this organization is immutable attributes. The value of attributes whose values do not change can be stored directly in instance variables

FORCES

- ☺ The state of an object may change.
- ☺ An object's state changes usually involve just one of the object's attributes.
- ☺ In addition to accessing the current values of an object's attributes, you may access other values that it had or will have at given points in time.
- ☹ If an existing application was designed to only keep the current values of an object's attributes, retrofitting it to keep the attribute's different values over time may involve a very large effort.

SOLUTION

When the value of one of an object's attributes changes, do not discard the previous value. Instead, keep the new and the previous values, distinguishing between them by the time intervals when each value is valid. Doing this implies that each time the business object fetches the value of one of its attributes, it must do so in the context of some point in time. Figure 8.4 shows this design.

In this design, the values of most attributes of a `BusinessObject` are separate objects associated with the `BusinessObject` through a time interval. An attribute may have multiple values. However, the time intervals for each value of an attribute are disjoint. This means that when the `get` method for an attribute is passed a point in time, that point in time will be contained in either zero or one of the time intervals. If it is contained in one of the time intervals, then the `get` method returns the value that corresponds to the time interval.

The only attributes of `BusinessObject` contained directly within instances of the class are those that are immutable. If the value of an attribute of a `BusinessObject` instance can change, then it must be associated with the `BusinessObject` through a time interval.

When an instance of `BusinessObject` is first created, the time interval for which the initial values apply to the `BusinessObject` instance is the entire time they correctly describe the real-world entity that the `BusinessObject` represents. In practice, this is often not known. In the absence of this information, an interval stretching from the beginning to the end of time is usually a good enough approximation.

When something changes about the real-world entity a `BusinessObject` object represents, the value of a `BusinessObject` object's corresponding attributes changes. The set methods of the

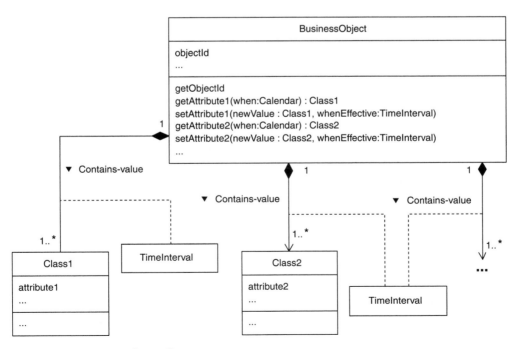

FIGURE 8.4 Temporal Attribute pattern.

`BusinessObject` classes generally take two arguments. One argument is the new value for the attribute. The other argument is the time interval that the value applies to. This is often from the current time through the end of time.

When a new value is provided for an attribute of a `BusinessObject`, the time interval it applies to may overlap the time intervals of previously provided values. The new value takes precedence and the older values are no longer associated with the attribute during the interval for the new value.

Implementations of the Temporal Attribute pattern involve another class that has not been discussed yet. This class implements the data structure responsible for associating instances with an interval of time and finding the appropriate value object for a given point in time. The details of this class are discussed under the "Implementation" heading.

CONSEQUENCES

☺ The Temporal Attribute pattern allows an application to recognize that real-world entities change over time in different ways. It gracefully handles situations where the different ways an entity changes happen asynchronously.

☹ The Temporal Attribute pattern requires that all fetches of an object's attribute values be in the context of a point in time. It also requires that, when an object's attribute value is set, the operation is done in the context of a time interval. It generally becomes the responsibility of clients of a versioned object to provide the contexts.

Some designs avoid burdening client objects in this way by offering calls that assume the context corresponding to the current time. These assumptions can sometimes be a source of bugs or confusion.

☹ The Temporal Attribute pattern increases the amount of memory needed to store objects. The more mutable attributes objects have, the greater the overhead of the pattern. It also makes the details of persisting an object more complicated.

IMPLEMENTATION

Data Structure

To implement the Temporal Attribute pattern, you must include a data structure in your design that associates an interval of time with each attribute value. It must also be able to find and fetch the attribute value that is associated with an interval that includes a given point in time.

An invariant this data structure must implement is that it must not contain any overlapping intervals. If it is presented with an interval that overlaps any intervals already in the data structure, the conflict should be resolved in favor of the new interval.

The choice of data structure should be based on the expected number of values the average attribute is expected to have over time. If it is just a few, then a simple data structure based on an array or linked list is generally best. If the number of versions is expected to be large, some sort of tree-based structure may be best.

The `IntervalMap` class shown under the "Code Example" heading is an example of this sort of data structure. It is based on an array. Note that this is the same data structure used by the Versioned Object pattern.

Loading from Persistent Storage

Another implementation issue comes up when objects organized using the Temporal Attribute pattern are fetched from a persistent store. This issue is based on the observation that usually no more than one or sometimes two values of an attribute are of interest in a given session. Because of this, loading all the values of all of a `BusinessObject` instance's attributes is something that you may want to avoid if the values are of a significant size.

KNOWN USES

The Temporal Attribute pattern is used in many applications that have to model real-world entities.

- It is used in human resource management software.
- It is used in inventory management software.
- It is used in application frameworks.

CODE EXAMPLE

The code example for the Temporal Property pattern is a class used to encapsulate information about people.

```
public class Person {
    private String mothersMaidenName;
```

Because a person's mother's maiden name is an attribute that never changes, this information is stored directly in an instance variable.

However, a person's own name or phone number may change. For that reason, the `Person` class does not store the values of these attributes in instance variables. Instead, it uses a class called `IntervalMap` to organize the values of these attributes.

Instances of the `IntervalMap` class encapsulate a data structure that associates values with the time interval that each value is valid. When asked for the value that is valid at a given point in time, an `IntervalMap` object returns the value associated with the time interval that contains the given point in time.

```
private IntervalMap nameIntervalMap;
private IntervalMap phoneIntervalMap;

...
/**
 * Constructor
 * @param name A PersonName object that encapsulates this person's
 *             name information.
 */
public Person(PersonName nameInfo) {
    nameIntervalMap =
IntervalMap.createEternalMap(nameInfo);
    phoneIntervalMap = new IntervalMap();
} // constructor(PersonName)

/**
 * Return the PersonName object that contains this
 * person's name information that is effective at that
 * given point in time.
 * @param when The point in time that the returned value
 *             should be effective.
 */
public PersonName getName(Calendar when) throws
NotFoundException {
    return (PersonName)nameIntervalMap.get(when);
} // getName(Calendar)

/**
 * Set this person's name information, effective for the given interval.
 * @param nameInfo The name information.
 * @param effective The interval for which the name
 *                  information will be effective.
 */
public void setName(PersonName nameInfo, Interval effective){
    nameIntervalMap.add(effective, nameInfo);
} // setName(PersonName, Interval)

/**
 * Return this person's phone number that is effective at
 * the given point in time.
 * @param when The point in time that the returned value
```

```
*             should be effective.
 * @exception NotFoundException
 *             if there is no phone number for the given point in time.
 */
public String getPhoneNumber(Calendar when) throws NotFoundException {
    return (String)phoneIntervalMap.get(when);
} // getPhoneNumber(Calendar)

/**
 * Set this person's phone number.
 * @param phone The phone number.
 * @param effective The interval for which the phone number will
 *                  be effective.
 */
public void setPhoneNumber(String phone, Interval effective) {
    phoneIntervalMap.add(effective, phone);
} // setPhoneNumber(String, Interval)

/**
 * Return this person's mother's maiden name.
 */
public String getMothersMaidenName(){ return mothersMaidenName; }

/*
 * Set this person's mother's maiden name.
 */
public void setMothersMaidenName(String mothersMaidenName){
    this.mothersMaidenName = mothersMaidenName;
} // setMothersMaidenName(String
...
} // class Person
```

The `IntervalMap` and `Interval` classes that the `Person` class uses are the same as for the Versioned Object pattern. The listing is repeated here for the benefit of readers who are not reading this book in sequence.

The `Interval` class is used to represent a time interval.

```
public class Interval {
    // The number of milliseconds difference between daylight
    // savings and standard time.
    private static final long DAYLIGHT_SAVINGS_OFFSET
      = 60*60*1000;

    /**
     * An interval that spans all of time.
     */
    public static Interval ETERNITY
      = new Interval(Long.MIN_VALUE, Long.MAX_VALUE);

    // The start time of this interval, expressed as the number
    // of seconds since midnight, January 1, 1970, UTC
    private long start;
```

```
// The end time of this interval, expressed as the number
// of seconds since midnight, January 1, 1970, UTC
private long end;

/**
 * Construct an interval with the given start and end time.
 * @param start The start of the interval or null if the
 *              interval starts at the beginning of time.
 * @param end The end of the interval or null if the
 *              interval ends at the end of time.
 */
public Interval(Calendar start, Calendar end) {
    long myStart;
    if (start==null) {
      myStart = Long.MIN_VALUE;
    } else {
        myStart = start.getTime().getTime();
    } // if
    long myEnd;
    if (end==null) {
        myEnd = Long.MAX_VALUE;
    } else {
        myEnd = end.getTime().getTime();
    } // if
    init(myStart, myEnd);
} // constructor(Calendar, Calendar)
...
/**
 * constructor
 * @param start
 *        The start time of this interval, expressed as the
 *        number of seconds since midnight,
 *        January 1, 1970, UTC.
 * @param end
 *        The end time of this interval, expressed as the
 *        number of seconds since midnight,
 *        January 1, 1970, UTC.
 */
Interval(long start, long end) {
    init(start, end);
} // constructor(long, long)

/**
 * Common initialization logic
 */
private void init(long start, long end) {
    if (end<start) {
        String msg = "Ends before it starts";
        throw new IllegalArgumentException(msg);
    } // if
    this.start = start;
    this.end = end;
} // init(long, long)
```

```
...
    /**
     * Return true if the given time is contained in this
     * interval. More precisely, this method returns true if
     * the given time is greater than or equal to the start of
     * this interval and less than or equal to the end of this
     * interval.
     */
    public boolean contains(Calendar time) {
        long tm = time.getTime().getTime();
        return tm>=start && tm<=end;
    } // contains(Calendar)

    /**
     * Return true if the given interval is completely
     * contained in this interval.
     */
    public boolean contains(Interval that) {
        return this.start<=that.start && this.end>=that.end;
    } // contains(Interval)

...

    /**
     * Return true if this interval and the given interval
     * share any points in time.
     */
    public boolean overlaps(Interval that) {
        return this.start<=that.end && this.end>=that.start;
    } // overlaps(Interval)

    /**
     * Return true if this interval ends after the given
     * interval.
     */
    public boolean endsAfter(Interval that) {
        return this.end > that.end;
    } // endsAfter(Interval)

    /**
     * Return the start time of this interval, expressed as the
     * number of seconds since midnight, January 1, 1970, UTC.
     */
    long getStart() { return start; }
    /**
     * Return the end time of this interval, expressed as the
     * number of seconds since midnight, January 1, 1970, UTC.
     */
    long getEnd() { return end; }

    /**
     * Return true if the given object is an
     * Interval object with the same start and end.
```

```
                */
           public boolean equals(Object obj) {
               if (obj instanceof Interval) {
                   Interval that = (Interval)obj;
                   return (this.start==that.start
                           && this.end==that.end);
               } //if
               return false;
           } // equals(Object)
...
} // class Interval
```

The `IntervalMap` class implements a data structure that associates an `Interval` object with another object and finds the object associated with an interval that contains a given point in time.

```
public class IntervalMap implements Serializable {
    private static final int GROWTH=2;

    // This implementation is based on two parallel arrays.
    // The order of their contents is self-adjusting. This
    // structure is optimized for lookup operations, not
    // for adding.
    private Interval[] intervals;
    private Object[] values;

    private int length;

    /**
     * Constructor for an interval map with a default initial
     * size for internal data structure.
     */
    public IntervalMap() {
        this(1);
    } // constructor()

    /**
     * Constructor for interval map with at least the specified
     * internal size for its internal data structure.
     */
    public IntervalMap(int capacity) {
        capacity += GROWTH; // leave room to grow
        intervals = new Interval[capacity];
        values = new Object[capacity];
    } // constructor(int)

    /**
     * Convenience method to create an IntervalMap
     * that maps all of time to the given object.
     */
    public static IntervalMap createEternalMap(Object obj) {
        IntervalMap im = new IntervalMap();
        im.add(Interval.ETERNITY, obj);
        return im;
    } // createEternalMap(Object)
```

```
/**
 * Return the number of intervals in this IntervalMap
 * object.
 */
public int size() {
    return length;
} // size()


/**
 * Add an interval to this map. If the given interval
 * equals an interval already in this map, the given value
 * replaces the old value. If the given interval overlaps
 * an interval already in the map, then the overlapped
 * interval is replaced with one or two smaller intervals
 * with the same value as the original interval.
 */
public synchronized void add(Interval interval,
                             Object value) {
    long theStart = interval.getStart();
    long theEnd = interval.getEnd();
    for (int i=0; i<length && intervals[i]!=null; i++) {
        if (interval.overlaps(intervals[i])) {
            long thisStart = intervals[i].getStart();
            long thisEnd = intervals[i].getEnd();
            if (thisStart < theStart) {
                if (thisEnd > theEnd) {
                    // divide overlapped interval into 3
                    intervals[i] = new Interval(theEnd+1,
                                                thisEnd);
                    add(new Interval(thisStart,
                                     theStart-1),
                        values[i]);
                } else {
                    intervals[i]
                      = new Interval(thisStart,
                                     theStart-1);
                } // if
            } else if (thisEnd>theEnd) {
                intervals[i] = new Interval(theEnd+1,
                                            thisEnd);
            } // if
        } // if overlaps
    } // for
    ensureCapacity(length+1);
    intervals[length] = interval;
    values[length] = value;
    length++;
} // add(Interval, Object)


/**
 * Ensure that the capacity of the data structures is
 * at least the given size.
 */
private void ensureCapacity(int capacity) {
```

```
        if (length < capacity) {
            Interval[] newIntervals;
            newIntervals = new Interval[capacity+GROWTH];
            System.arraycopy(intervals,
                             0, newIntervals,
                             0, length);
            intervals = newIntervals;
            Object[] newValues = new Object[capacity+GROWTH];
            System.arraycopy(values, 0, newValues, 0, length);
            values = newValues;
        } // if
    } // ensureCapacity(int)

    /**
     * Map the given point in time to an object.
     * @return This map maps the given point in time to an
     *         object using the Interval objects in this map.
     *         This method returns the mapped object.
     * @exception NotFoundException
     *             If then given point in time is outside of all
     *             the intervals in this map.
     */
    public synchronized Object get(Calendar when)
                                        throws NotFoundException {
        for (int i=0; i<length; i++) {
            if (intervals[i].contains(when)) {
                Object value = values[i];
                adjust(i);
                return value;
            } // if intervals
        } // for
        throw new NotFoundException(when.toString());
    } // get(Calendar)

    /**
     * Return the object associated with the given interval.
     * If there is an interval that equals the given interval
     * in this map, the corresponding value object is returned.
     * If there is no such interval, this method returns null.
     */
    public synchronized
      Object getMatching(Interval thatInterval) {
        for (int i=0; i<length; i++) {
            if (intervals[i].equals(thatInterval)) {
                return values[i];
            } // if intervals
        } // for
        return null;
    } // getMatching(Interval)

    /**
     * Adjust the position of the interval and value at the
     * given index one up towards the beginning.
```

```
    */
private void adjust(int i) {
    if (i>0) {
        // Adjust position in array
        Interval tmpInterval = intervals[i];
        intervals[i] = intervals[i-1];
        intervals[i-1] = tmpInterval;
        Object tmpValue = values[i];
        values[i] = values[i-1];
        values[i-1] = tmpValue;
    } // if i
} // adjust(int)

/**
 * Return the object associated with the latest interval.
 * @exception NoSuchElementException
 *             If no intervals are in this IntervalMap.
 */
public synchronized Object getLatestValue() {
    return values[getLatestIndex()];
} // getLatestValue()

/**
 * Return an iterator over the Interval
 * objects in this IntervalMap.
 */
public Iterator intervals() {
    return new ArrayIterator(intervals);
} // intervals()

/**
 * Return an Iterator over the value object in
 * this IntervalMap.
 */
public Iterator values() {
    return new ArrayIterator(values);
} // values()

/**
 * Return the index of the latest interval.
 * @exception NoSuchElementException
 *             if there are no intervals in this IntervalMap.
 */
private int getLatestIndex() {
    if (length==0) {
        throw new NoSuchElementException();
    } // if
    int latestIndex = 0;
    Interval latestInterval = intervals[latestIndex];
    for (int i=1; i<length; i++) {
        if (intervals[i].endsAfter(latestInterval)) {
            latestIndex = i;
            latestInterval = intervals[i];
```

```
            } // if
        } // for
        return latestIndex;
    } // getLatestIndex(int)
} // class IntervalMap
```

RELATED PATTERNS

Time Server.   The Temporal Property pattern is often used in conjunction with the Time Server pattern to ensure consistent timestamping of property values.

Versioned Object.   The Versioned Object pattern provides an alternate way of organizing changes in an object's state over time. It is more appropriate for classes whose state changes tend to involve changes to multiple attributes.

Database Patterns

The patterns in this chapter describe techniques you can use to store objects in a database. These patterns can be adapted to work with objects kept in any kind of persistent storage. However, since a database is the most common sort of persistent storage used for objects, these patterns are written with the assumption that objects are stored in a database.

The patterns in this chapter are interrelated. Figure 9.1 shows the patterns in this chapter and their relationships.

The Persistence Layer pattern describes how to keep the classes of persisted objects and the classes that use persisted objects independent of the persistence mechanism being used.

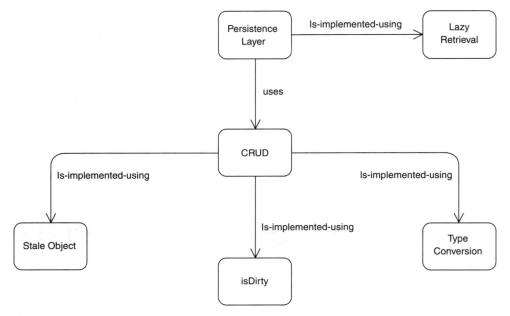

FIGURE 9.1 Relationships between the database patterns.

The CRUD pattern describes how to design the interface methods of an implementation of the Persistence Layer pattern.

The Stale Object pattern describes how to make update methods designed using the CRUD pattern more robust.

The Type Conversion pattern describes how to manage differences in the way a runtime environment and database represent data.

The Dirty pattern is used in the implementation of the CRUD pattern to avoid unnecessary updates to persisted objects.

The Lazy Retrieval pattern describes an optimization to the Persistence Layer pattern that avoids retrieving objects from a database that are not needed.

Persistence Layer

This pattern was previously described in [Yoder98]. It is also the most complicated pattern in this book. If you do not understand it on the first reading, try reading the related design patterns and then read this pattern again.

SYNOPSIS

Keep the details of persisting objects and dependencies on a specific kind of database out of application-specific classes. Do this by organizing persistence-related details into classes that make up a persistence layer. Design application classes to perform all persistence operations through the persistence layer.

CONTEXT

You are designing a system that allows people to barter goods and services. It must accommodate different kinds of transactions. The business logic for each kind of transaction will fetch or store objects from a database.

The system has been specified to work with a relational database. However, you anticipate that the system will eventually migrate to work with an object-oriented database.

FORCES

- ☺ You want to organize business logic into classes that will be reusable and easily maintained.
- ☺ Mixing the logic of an application and the logic of object persistence in the same classes makes maintaining them more difficult.
- ☺ Writing SQL and persistence-related logic requires different skills than writing good business logic. People with both skills sets are rare.
- ☺ Creating a common superclass for classes responsible for persisting specific kinds of objects promotes code reuse.
- ☺ During the life of an application, the data model it uses and the mechanism it uses for persistent storage may change.

⊗ Using a single interface to persist each kind of object can lead to using the lowest-common-denominator actions to manage their persistence. This may result in less than optimal ways of organizing transactions that involve more than one kind of persistent object.

SOLUTION

Organize an application's design so there is a set of classes and interfaces that encapsulate the entire responsibility for persisted form of the application's persistent objects. We call this set of classes and interfaces the application's *persistence layer*. The rest of the application uses interfaces that the persistence layer provides to persist objects and access already persisted objects.

The operations a persistence layer provides for each kind of object are usually organized using the CRUD pattern. For each kind of persisted object, there may be operations to **c**reate its persisted form, **r**etrieve the persisted form, **u**pdate the persisted form, or **d**elete the persisted form.

The persistence layer will need to know how to fetch and store each kind of persistent or data object that the application uses. An exception to this involving Java's serialization mechanism is discussed under the following "Implementation" heading.

There are three common ways to organize a persistence layer.

A tool-based approach.   This generally involves the purchase of a commercial tool that is expensive and may involve a significant learning curve. However, this approach is generally the most scalable and involves the least maintenance effort over the lifetime of an application.

An organization based on the application's object model.   In this organization, there is typically an interface defined for persisting each type of data object that the application uses. If the contents of the persisted form of an object are split over multiple tables or multiple persistent stores, such details are generally hidden. The application's classes can be designed without having to take into account the organization of the persistent store.

This approach generally has a small impact on the design of application classes. The impact is usually just a requirement that the class of each kind of data object to be persisted implements an interface. The interface is independent of the underlying persistence mechanism. It serves as a way for the persistence mechanism to access information about objects it is asked to persist.

An organization based on the schema for the persistent storage that the application will use. This approach usually results in the simplest persistence layer. However, it tends to force the organization of an application's classes to resemble the organization of the persistent store. This results in a class design that is harder to implement and maintain because part of the complexity of persistence must be in the application's classes.

When using a tool-based approach, the organization of the persistence layer is determined primarily by the tool and its associated infrastructure. For this reason, there will be no further discussion of what a design based on this approach looks like.

The diagrams and examples for the Persistence Layer pattern focus on the second choice, an organization based on the application's object model. The typical roles that classes and interfaces play in such an organization are shown in Figure 9.2.

Here are descriptions of the roles that the classes and interfaces shown in Figure 9.2 play in the Persistence Layer pattern.

BusinessClass1, BusinessClass2, . . . Instances of classes in this role are an application's business objects that are stored in and fetched from persistent storage by a persistence layer.

BusinessClass1PersisterIF, BusinessClass2PersisterIF, . . . Interfaces in this role declare methods used to persist instances of a corresponding business class. The names and signatures of the methods declared in these interfaces vary, but generally follow the CRUD pattern.

PersistableIF. Classes whose instances are to be persisted by the persistence layer are generally required to implement an interface that is in this role. This interface may simply be a Marker Interface* or it may declare methods that allow the persistence layer to determine things about objects to persist. For example, an interface in this role may declare a method that returns an object's object identifier.

BusinessClass1PersisterImpl, BusinessClass2PersisterImpl, . . . Classes in this role implement the interfaces for managing persistence. There may be a one-to-one correspondence between the interfaces and classes in this role. When the code that implements the persistence logic is manually generated, you will typically see

---

* A marker interface does not declare any members. It is used to determine a Boolean property of the classes that implement it. If a class implements the interface, the property is true. Marker Interface is described as a pattern in *Volume 1*.

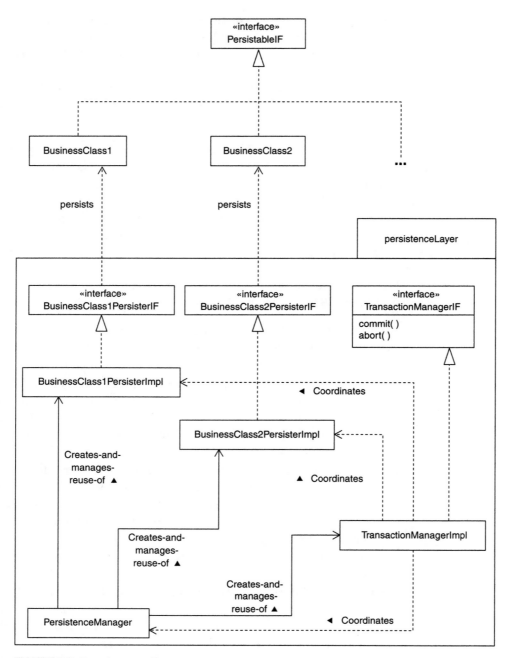

FIGURE 9.2 Persistence Layer pattern.

this one-to-one relationship. Alternatively, there may be one or a small number of classes in the role that implement multiple interfaces and so are responsible for managing the persistence of instances of multiple classes. You usually see this organization when the code that implements the persistence logic is generated at runtime by a code generator. Using a code generator to generate the persistence code can be a big savings in programmer time. However, automatically generated code tends not to be as well optimized as code written by a skilled programmer.

TransactionManagerIF. Interfaces in this role declare methods that are used to commit or abort transactions.

TransactionManagerImpl. Classes in this role implement the `TransactionManagerIF` interface.

PersistenceManager. Classes in this role define methods that are responsible for creating and returning objects that implement the `BusinessClass1PersisterImpl`, `BusinessClass2Persister-Impl, ...,` and `TransactionManagerIF` interfaces. If more than one type of persistent storage is supported, then the classes' methods are also responsible for ensuring that the objects they return are appropriate for the type of persistent storage being used.

CONSEQUENCES

☺ If the underlying technology used to persist an application changes, then only the persistence layer needs to change. For example, an application that is initially developed to use a relational database may be changed to use an object-oriented database or a data cube.

☺ The underlying persistence schema can be changed without modifying any part of an application outside of its persistence layer.

☺ The logical complexities of working with the underlying database are hidden by the persistence layer from the rest of the application. For example, most databases require a different call or command to store a new object than to update the contents of an existing object.

☹ Some operations that are easy to do in SQL, OQL, or another query language may be difficult to do through a persistence layer. For example, determining the number of customers that live in a particular zip code may be a simple query in SQL. However, working through a persistence layer that does not have a method specifically for that query generally involves writing a loop with procedural code to get each customer's zip code, and if it matches the zip code in question, increment a count.

☹ If a persistence layer is not carefully tuned for a specific application, it will generally be difficult or impossible to optimize access to the application's persistent store at the application level.

IMPLEMENTATION

Transactions

The Persistence Layer pattern is usually implemented on top of one or more databases or external persistent storage managers. Each of these databases will have a unique set of strategies for managing locks on behalf of transactions. Two transactions may run concurrently on top of one database. The same two transactions may be forced to run serially or even deadlock when run on top of another database.

For example, suppose that you have two transactions that are running on top of a relational database manager. One transaction fetches rows from a table. The other transaction updates individual rows in the same table. Under one database manager, this works perfectly well, because the database manager is sophisticated enough to do row-level locking and a shadow write* to the row being updated.

A less sophisticated database manager sees that the fetch of the rows will involve most of the rows in the table and so it tries to be efficient by doing a tablelock instead of a rowlock. The transaction to update a row is now unable to get its rowlock, because the whole table is locked and the database manager does not do shadow writes. Because these are being used in a loop where the fetched rows are being used to drive the updates, the loop hangs since the first update waits forever to get its lock.[†]

For this reason, to remain as independent of the underlying storage manager as possible, the application should organize all related actions into the same transaction. The persistence layer cannot enforce such an organization, but it can be designed to facilitate it:

- The persistence layer should be designed to allow any sequence of operations on the persistent store to be included in the same transaction.
- The persistence layer should be designed so that every operation in the persistent store is part of an explicit transaction. If an operation

---

* A shadow write is a write that is visible only to the transaction that wrote it and to subsequent transactions.

[†] This actually happened to the author with two different database managers. The names of the database managers are not stated because this behavior is not unique to these database managers.

is not part of an explicit transaction, database managers and the like will treat it as being part of its own implicit transaction.

- To ensure consistent behavior across different persistent stores, the persistence layer should either prohibit nested transactions* or simulate the feature when it runs over a persistent storage manager that does not support it.

The first item, allowing any sequence of operations on the persistent store to be included in the same transaction, is generally just a matter of avoiding anything in the design that prevents it.

The second item is almost as simple. To ensure that every operation is part of an explicit transaction simply requires a way of putting operations in the context of an explicit transaction and the appropriate checks being made to ensure that each operation is in the context of a transaction.

The third item is complicated. The simplest way to resolve it is to prohibit nested transactions. The reason to resolve the issue this way is that some popular database engines, such as Oracle, do not support nested transactions and simulating nested transactions at the persistence layer is complicated. However, support for nested transactions has the benefit of increasing reuse of code, which also results in less maintenance effort. If nested transactions are supported, method A can call method B without having to be concerned whether method B will perform its own transaction. If a persistence layer does *not* support nested transactions, then special arrangements will have to be made for method B to be aware of its caller's transaction and to use it.

Clearly, support for nested transactions is desirable. The problem is that some persistent stores do not support nested transactions. In some cases, it may be possible for a persistence layer to simulate support for nested transactions. However, with some database managers, it is impossible to run an application that relies on nested transactions.

Complex Objects

Retrieving a complex object may involve retrieving a number of related objects. If the related objects are not always used, defer loading them by using the Lazy Retrieval pattern. This means that the methods of the complex object's class need to assume that links to the appropriate related

---

* If transactions are allowed to nest, that means that within the same thread, a shorter transaction can begin and end while a longer transaction is pending and the following will be true: If the shorter transaction is committed, it only commits changes that occur after the shorter transaction started. If the longer transaction is aborted, the changes made during the shorter transactions are undone, even if the short transaction was committed.

objects may be null and to call the persistence layer to retrieve those objects if they are needed.

Caching

For performance reasons, it is often advantageous for classes in the `BusinessClassPersisterImpl` role to cache objects they retrieve from the database. Using a cache benefits performance in two ways.

- Caching saves time. If a requested object is in the cache, there is no need to spend the time it takes to retrieve the object from the database.
- Caching may save memory. Some complex objects may share the same related objects. Using a cache may allow them to share the same copy of the object by avoiding a situation where a different copy of the related object is loaded for each complex object that refers to it.

The technique of object caching is discussed in detail in the discussion of the Cache Management pattern in *Volume 1*.

There are some constraints on the use of caching in a persistence layer. The problem is that objects in the cache cease to be identical to the objects in the database if another database client updates those objects. Many database engines do not have a way for the database engine to notify its clients in real time when an object is modified. Even if a database engine does allow real-time notifications, if the database has many clients, notifying all of them may introduce an unacceptable performance problem. This difficulty does not prevent the use of caching in all cases. There are two situations in which caching is a useful optimization.

Caching works well for objects that are not expected to always be up-to-date. For example, objects that summarize real-time data, such as a business's gross sales for the current day, may be satisfactory if they are guaranteed not to be more than ten minutes behind reality. Some objects have no specific requirement for being up-to-date. For example, in an airline reservation system, there is no expectation that just because a particular seat appears to be available it will actually be available when someone tries to assign the seat to a passenger. Management of cached objects that may not be up-to-date is described in more detail by the Cache Consistency pattern.

The other situation in which caching is a good optimization is when you can be sure that the state of a persisted object will never change while a copy of it is in a cache. There are two common cases of this. One case is if the object in question will never change. An example of this is an object that describes an event that happened in the past. The other case is when you have a lock on a persisted object. This will generally be the case while you are updating its contents. To update a persisted object, you will tell a persistence layer to retrieve the object for update. The persistence layer should then ensure that you have a lock on the object at least until you update it or the current transaction ends.

While there is a lock on a persisted object retrieved for update, it is safe to cache the object. Caching the object in this circumstance is generally not an effective optimization technique, since applications will generally not retrieve the object again while they have a lock on it. However, it does allow the persistence layer to detect a relatively common sort of bug. Sometimes an application will try to update the contents of an object using an old version of the object. This can result in some of the object's contents unintentionally reverting to old values. This is discussed in more detail in the Stale Object pattern.

Serialization

If there will be no need to do ad hoc queries on a kind of object, it may be possible to simplify the details of its persistence by using serialization.

Single Instances

There is generally no need to have more than one instance of the `PersistenceManager` class or each `BusinessClass1PersisterImpl` class. Having only one instance of each `BusinessClass1PersisterImpl` class makes updates easier by simplifying the implementation of the Stale Object pattern. Managing classes so that they have only one instance is done using the Singleton pattern, described in *Volume 1*.

KNOWN USES

The author has seen many applications that are designed with a persistence layer. There are also a number of commercial tools, such as CoCoBase, to help create one.

In addition, entity beans, a form of Enterprise JavaBean, provide a limited implementation of the Persistence Layer pattern. The Enterprise JavaBean specification* allows entity beans to have *container managed persistence*, which relieves the programmer of the burden of manually generating persistence code. However, this mechanism only works well for

---

* At the time of this writing, the current version of the Enterprise JavaBean specification is 1.1.

mapping rows of a table into an object. It is not very helpful for managing the persistence of complex objects that may be stored in multiple tables, such as a customer object that may have multiple addresses, phone numbers, purchase history, and demographic information associated with it. It is particularly inappropriate for complex objects that have a one-to-many relationship with some of their associated objects.

Object-oriented databases such as GemStone provide a persistence layer.

DESIGN EXAMPLE

The design example for the Persistence Layer pattern is a persistence framework that is part of a larger open source framework called ClickBlocks.* This framework comes with classes that support object persistence in relational databases through the JDBC API. Because this example is relatively complex, the class diagrams showing its organization are split into multiple figures. To help in understanding the persistence framework, Appendix A contains an introduction to the use of the persistence framework. The source code is on the CD distributed with this book.

Figure 9.3 shows some interfaces that are used by the persistence framework. The rest the persistence framework is shown in Figure 9.4. Here are descriptions of the interfaces shown in Figure 9.3:

> **PersistableIF.** Every class whose instances are to be persisted must implement this interface. The interface is a convenient way for the persistence package to declare references to

---

* The current version of the persistence package should be available at www.clickblocks.org as the package `org.clickblocks.persistence`.

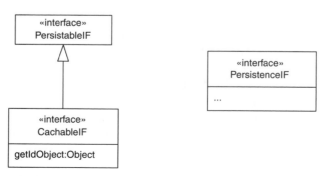

FIGURE 9.3 Interfaces.

objects it persists. The interface also defines a method named `getPersistenceInterface` that is useful to development environments and tools that are aware of the persistence framework.

The `getPersistenceInterface` method returns a `Class` object that encapsulates an interface. The interface it encapsulates is the interface responsible for managing the persistence of instances of the class that implements the `PersistableIF` interface. For example, consider a class named `Foo` that implements the `PersistableIF` interface. If the `Foo` class's implementation of the `getPersistenceInterface` method returns a `Class` object that encapsulates an interface named `FooPersisterIF`, then any class responsible for managing the persistence of `Foo` objects must implement the `FooPersisterIF` interface.

CachableIF.   This interface extends the `PersistableIF` interface. This interface must be implemented by classes whose instances the persistence layer will be expected to cache.

The `CachableIF` interface defines a method named `getIdObject`, which is expected to return the object's unique object ID encapsulated in an object. The object it returns is used as a key in a `HashMap`, so the object's class must have implementations of the `hashCode` and equals methods that reflect the value of the object ID it encapsulates. The motivations for this are discussed under the "Implementation" heading of the CRUD pattern.

PersistenceIF.   Every class that is responsible for persisting objects must implement this interface.

Figure 9.4 shows the static organization of most of the rest of the persistence package. The complete persistence framework is on the CD that accompanies this book. Here are descriptions of the classes and interfaces that appear in Figure 9.4:

PersistenceManagerFactory.   Instances of classes in the `PersistenceManager` role are responsible for creating objects responsible for managing the persistence of other objects. In this example, all such classes must implement the `PersistencemanagerIF` interface. Each concrete class that implements the `PersistencemanagerIF` interface creates `PersistenceManager` objects that manage the persistence of objects using one particular kind of database.

The `PersistenceManagerFactory` class allows the persistence framework to support multiple types of databases. The `PersistenceManagerFactory` class is responsible for

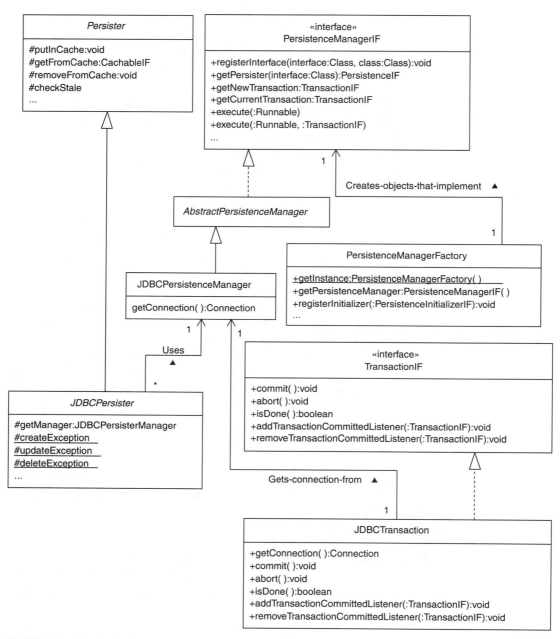

FIGURE 9.4 ClickBlocks persistence package.

creating instances of a class that implements the `PersistencemanagerIF` interface and supports the type of database being used.

Here are descriptions of the `PersistenceManagerFactory` class's methods:

getInstance.   This method is static and returns the single instance of the `PersistenceManagerFactory` class.

getPersistenceManager.   This method returns the `PersistenceManagerIF` object that will be responsible for creating objects that know how to persist objects to the desired type of persistent store.

registerInitializer.   This persistence package does not contain any classes that know how to persist a specific business class. The application that uses this persistence package is expected to provide those classes. The application is also expected to register those classes with the persistence package.

The application arranges to register its classes to persist business objects by passing a `PersistenceInitializerIF` object to this method before its first call to the `getPersistenceManager` method. During the first call to the `getPersistenceManager` method, it passes the freshly created `PersistenceManagerIF` object to the `initialize` method of every `PersistenceInitializerIF` object that was passed to this method. Those initialize methods are expect to register classes to persist business objects at that time by calling the `PersistenceManagerIF` object's `registerInterface` method.

PersistenceManagerIF.   Classes in the `PersistenceManager` role must implement the `PersistenceManagerIF` interface. The `PersistenceManagerIF` interface defines methods to get/create objects to persist business objects and to support transaction management. Classes that implement this interface are usually specific to one kind of database. Here are descriptions of its methods.

getPersister.   This method returns a `PersisterIF` object that implements a given subinterface of the `PersisterIF` interface. The argument should be a `Class` object that encapsulates the interface responsible for the persistence of a particular class of object. The object this method returns is an instance of a class that knows how to persist objects to the database manager being used.

For example, suppose there is an interface named `FooPersisterIF` and that classes responsible for persisting instances of a class named `Foo` must implement the `FooPersisterIF` interface. Also, suppose there is a class that implements the `PersistenceManagerIF` interface for persisting objects to a persistence store using the JDBC API. If its `getPersister` method is passed a `Class` object that encapsulates the `FooPersisterIF` interface, the method will return an object that implements the `FooPersisterIF` interface and knows how to persist `Foo` objects using the JDBC API.

registerInterface. The `getPersister` method knows what class it should return an instance of for a given interface. It gets this knowledge from a previous call to the `RegisterInterface` method. Applications call the `RegisterInterface` method to register interfaces for persisting application-specific objects and the classes that implement the interfaces.

The arguments to the `RegisterInterface` method are two `Class` objects. The first `Class` object must encapsulate an interface that is a subinterface of `PersistenceIF`. The second `Class` object is expected to encapsulate a class that implements `PersistenceIF` and has a constructor that takes a single argument. The class of the constructor's argument must be the same as the concrete class that implements the `PersistenceManagerIF` interface.

Implementations of the `PersistenceManagerIF` interface are expected to be specific to a particular kind of database. For this reason, calls to an implementation of this method are allowed to ignore classes that implement the `PersistenceIF` interface but are not intended to be used with a different kind of database than the one the implementation of the `PersistenceManagerIF` interface is intended for.

execute. This method is overloaded. There are two forms of the method. The simpler version of this method takes one argument, which is an object that implements the `java.lang.Runnable` interface. This method creates a transaction and calls the `Runnable` object's `run` method. The transaction provides a context for the operations that are performed by the `run` method. When the `run` method returns, the `execute` method commits the transaction. If the `run` method throws an exception, the `execute` method aborts the transaction. The transaction this method creates is independent of any transaction in the current context. That is to say that it will make no difference to either transaction what the outcome of the other is.

Applications usually use the one-argument version of the `execute` method to provide a transaction context for operations. Sometimes, the one-argument version of `execute` is not appropriate because the application must interleave operations that are part of different transactions. If an application must interleave operations that are part of different transactions, then it can use the two-argument flavor of the `execute` method.

The second argument of the two-argument flavor of the `execute` method is an object that implements the `TransactionIF` interface. This flavor of the `execute` method is useful for methods that need to alternate between transactions. This flavor of the `execute` method does not commit or abort transactions. It just establishes the given transaction as the context while the `run` method of the given `Runnable` object is running. You can get a `TransactionIF` object by calling the `getNewTransaction` method.

getCurrentTransaction. Classes responsible for persisting objects call this method to get the current transaction object. This transaction object will allow them to work with the persistent store in the contexts of the current transaction.

getNewTransaction. Classes that use the two-argument version of the `execute` method call this method to get a new transaction to use with that method.

AbstractPersistenceManager. This class provides default implementations for methods declared by the `Persistence-ManagerIF` interface.

JDBCPersistenceManager. This class is a concrete subclass of `AbstractPersistenceManager`. It is responsible for creating objects that know how to manage the persistence of objects using JDBC. Its implementation of the `registerInterface` method ignores classes that are intended to manage persistence using some other mechanism.

The `JDBCPersistenceManager` class has a method called `getConnection` that is called by the objects it creates to get a JDBC connection to use for database operations.

Persister. All classes responsible for persisting objects should be a subclass of this abstract class. It has methods related to caching objects in memory that are used in implementing the Stale Object pattern. Concrete subclasses of this class define appropriate methods to persist instances of a particular class.

JDBCPersister. This is the abstract superclass of classes that persist objects using JDBC. It defines protected methods that are useful in writing concrete subclasses of JDBCPersister that persist instances of specific classes. It defines a method named getManager that returns the JDBCPersistenceManager object that created the JDBCPersister instance. It also defines methods to classify return codes produced by JDBC operations and convert them to an exception, if appropriate.

TransactionIF. Classes that are responsible for encapsulating transactions implement this interface. Here are descriptions of its methods.

commit. This method commits all of the operations that have been performed in the context of an object that implements this object. It also ends the transaction.

abort. This method rolls back the effects of all operations that have been performed in the context of an object that implements this object. It also ends the transaction.

isDone. This method returns true if the object's commit or abort methods have been called.

addTransactionCommittedListener. Sometimes it is necessary to do something after a transaction is committed. For example, after a retail purchase transaction is committed you may want to send an e-mail confirmation to the customer. This method allows objects that implement the TransactionListener interface to register to receive an event that notifies them when the transaction encapsulated in a TransactionIF object is committed.

removeTransactionCommittedListener. This method unregisters objects previously registered by a call to AddTransactionCommittedListener.

JDBCTransaction. This class implements the TransactionIF interface for transactions that work through JDBC.

To round out this description of the ClickBlocks persistence package, Figure 9.5 is a class diagram that shows an application of the persistence package. An application that works with persisted Item objects might use the classes shown in Figure 9.5 as follows:

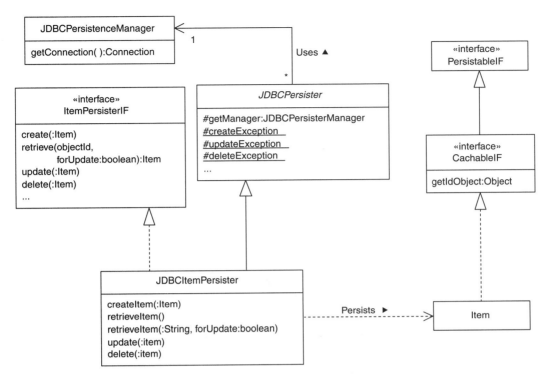

FIGURE 9.5 Application of the persistence package.

- Register a `PersistenceInitializer` object with the `PersistenceManagerFactory` class by calling its `registerInstance` method. At a later time, the `PersistenceManagerFactory` class calls a method of the `PersistenceInitializer` object to give it a chance to register the classes that will be responsible for persisting the specific classes of interest to the application.
- Call the `PersistenceManagerFactory` class's `getInstance` method to get the singleton instance of that class.
- Using the object returned by the `getInstance` method, call its `getPersistenceManager` to get the object that will be used to manage objects responsible for persisting specific types of objects. In this example, the persistence mechanism being used is JDBC-based, so the object returned is an instance of `JDBCPersistenceManager`.
- The `ItemPersisterIF` interface declares the methods that applications will use to persist `Item` objects.
- Pass the `Class` object that encapsulates the `ItemPersisterIF` interface to the `JDBCPersistenceManager` object's `getPersister` method. Because `JDBCItemPersister` was previously registered, it

knows the class is responsible for persisting `Item` objects. Because the class extends `JDBCPersister`, it knows that the class uses JDBC as its persistence mechanism. For these reasons, the call returns a `JDBCItemPersister` object.

● When the application wants to perform persistence-related operations on `Item` objects, it uses the `JDBCItemPersister` object.

RELATED PATTERNS

Layers.   The Persistence Layer pattern is an application of the Layers patterns described in [Buschman96].

CRUD.   The CRUD pattern is used to design the operations declared by `BusinessClassPersisterIF` interfaces for the Persistence pattern.

Stale Object.   The Stale Object pattern is used with the Persistence Layer pattern to ensure the consistency of updates.

Object Identifier.   The Object Identifier pattern is used with the Persistence Layer pattern to generate object IDs that will be unique across all domains that an object will be used in.

Abstract Factory.   The Persistence Layer pattern uses the Abstract Factory pattern, described in *Volume 1*, to encapsulate the selection of a database and to ensure that the application used persister objects for the correct type of database.

Cache Management.   The Cache Management pattern (described in *Volume 1*) is used with the Persistence Layer pattern to avoid unnecessary fetches from the database.

Cache Consistency.   The Cache Consistency pattern may be used by a persistence layer to implement guarantees on how current the objects in a cache are.

Singleton.   The Persistence Layer pattern uses the Singleton pattern (described in *Volume 1*) to manage instances of classes.

Marker Interface.   The Persistence Layer pattern uses the Marker Interface pattern, described in *Volume 1*, to recognize instances of classes that it may persist.

CRUD

This pattern was previously described in [Yoder98].

SYNOPSIS

Organize the persistence operations of an application into Create, Retrieve, Update, and Delete operations that are implemented by a persistence layer.

CONTEXT

You are designing the methods of an interface that programs will use to manage persistent information about items in a company's inventory. You know that objects used to represent inventory items will be used in a great variety of transactions. However, the exact nature of most of the transactions that will involve inventory items is not yet known. To minimize development time and produce a reusable interface, you want to design an interface that declares only a small number of persistence operations and places few limits on the kinds of transactions they support. Given these concerns, you decide on the design shown in Figure 9.6.

You decide that the interface will have methods to create, update, and delete Item objects in a database. It will also have methods to retrieve Item objects from a database.

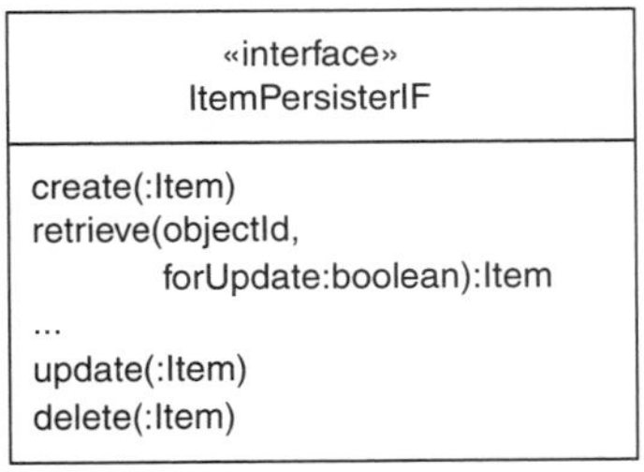

```
          «interface»
         ItemPersisterIF

create(:Item)
retrieve(objectId,
        forUpdate:boolean):Item
...
update(:Item)
delete(:Item)
```

FIGURE 9.6 ItemPersisterIF.

FORCES

- ☺ You want to define operations to manage the persistence of a class of objects in a way that will allow all possible transactions to be performed.
- ☺ It is possible to compose complex transactions from simple operations in a straightforward way.
- ☺ Organizing operations to persist a class of objects into a single interface results in a highly cohesive design.
- ☹ Managing the persistence of objects using only simple operations may place a greater burden on the programmer writing complex transactions than using more complex and specialized operations would.
- ☹ Composing complex persistence operations from simple ones sometimes results in a performance penalty.

SOLUTION

Define a single interface that declares all the persistence operations for instances of a class. Provide simple operations that are a form of one of the following:

Create an object in the persistent store.

Retrieve an object or objects from a persistent store.

Update the state of an object in a persistent store.

Delete an object from a persistent store.

There are a number of reasons why it may be desirable to add more operations to an interface. The CRUD operations form a good foundation that is sufficient in many cases.

CONSEQUENCES

- ☺ By using the CRUD pattern, you limit the programming effort for the infrastructure for persisting instances of a class to supporting a few simple operations.
- ● Arbitrarily complex transactions can be composed from simple CRUD operations. However, if a transaction involves a large number of objects, then building it from the simplest possible operations can create a performance problem.

    For example, suppose that you have a database that contains information about students in a school. You want to retrieve the students who have the best average grade in each class. It will generally result in faster transactions to allow a database engine to sift through the students and return just those that fit the criteria, rather than pass all of the student and class objects from the database to the application and let the application sort it out.

If an application must work through a CRUD interface that supports only simple operations, it is forced to retrieve all of the student and class objects. An interface that allows the application to present the entire request to the database will avoid the overhead of the database engine's retrieving many objects that are not wanted.

IMPLEMENTATION

The Basic CRUD Methods

The `create` method of a CRUD interface generally looks something like this:

```
public void create(BusinessObject theObject) throws ...
```

This `create` method is responsible for creating a copy of the given object in the database. It will generally be declared to throw at least three different kinds of exceptions.

- It will throw an exception to indicate that there is already an object with the same object ID in the database.
- It will throw an exception to indicate that something about the object violates a business rule.
- It will throw at least one other kind of exception to indicate that some other kind of problem was detected.

A `retrieve` method can have a variety of forms. It is quite common for a CRUD interface to include multiple forms of `retrieve` method. There are two basic varieties of `retrieve` methods. One variety always returns a single object. The other variety can return any number of objects. A `retrieve` method that returns exactly one object tends to have more complicated signatures than a `retrieve` method that returns multiple objects. This is because its parameters must specify enough information to select a single object. Here is an example of a `retrieve` method that returns any number of objects:

```
public Iterator retrieve() throws ...
```

This form of `retrieve` method returns all persisted instances of the class for which the interface is responsible. Usually, the only sort of exception this form of `retrieve` method is declared to throw is to reflect a problem in the underlying database.

Here is an example of a `retrieve` method that returns a single object. Its argument specifies a key value that should match only one object:

```
public BusinessObject retrieve(String key, boolean forUpdate)
throws ...
```

The first parameter identifies the object to retrieve. The second parameter, `forUpdate`, indicates if the object retrieved by the method may be the object of a subsequent update or delete operation. If `forUpdate` is true, the underlying database engine or persistent storage manager must be told to lock the retrieved object so that it is not modified by any other process between the time the object is retrieved and the time the update occurs. Though it is less common, some applications define the form of `retrieve` method that returns all objects to have a parameter to indicate the retrieved objects may be updated.

In addition to throwing exceptions to indicate problems in the underlying database, if a `retrieve` method has parameters to identify the object to retrieve, it should also throw an exception if no objects match a given parameter. `retrieve` methods that return an iterator over the objects they return do not need to throw such an exception, since callers will recognize iterators that contain no objects.

The `update` method of a CRUD interface generally looks like this:

```
public void update(Organization theOrganization) throws ...
```

This method uses the ID of the in-memory object passed to it to identify a persisted object in the database. It used the data in the in-memory object to update the data in the persisted object. It will generally be declared to throw at least four different kinds of exceptions.

● It will throw an exception to indicate that there is no object in the database with the same object ID as the given object.
● It will throw an exception to indicate that something about the new version of the object violates a business rule.
● It will throw an exception to indicate that the given object is stale or is based on an old copy of the object. The Stale Object pattern explains this in more detail.
● It will throw at least one other kind of exception to indicate that some other kind of problem was detected.

The `delete` method of a CRUD interface generally looks like this:

```
public void delete(Organization theOrganization) throws ...
```

This method removes the object in the database that has the same object ID as the given object. It will generally be declared to throw at least two different kinds of exceptions.

- It will throw an exception to indicate something about removing the object that would violate a business rule.
- It will throw at least one other kind of exception to indicate that some other kind of problem was detected.

Additional Operations

As an optimization, interfaces may define additional methods that are more complex. For example, you may have a transaction that calls for multiple objects to be updated. In the case of a student records system for a middle school, you may want to have a transaction that promotes all students with a minimum average to the next grade. Retrieving each student from the database and then updating the student, if appropriate, is generally a lot less efficient than asking the underlying database engine to perform the entire transaction. Given such a transaction, it will generally make sense to add a specialized method in the CRUD interface to perform the transaction.

Responsibility for Implementing the CRUD Interface

The responsibility for implementing a CRUD interface should be assigned to a class other than the class whose instances are being persisted. There are good reasons for a class with persisted instances not to implement its own CRUD interface.

- If a class is responsible for its own persistence, there is a natural tendency for the internal logic of the class to depend on the particular way that the object is being persisted at the time the internal logic is written. Such dependencies can significantly increase the cost of maintenance when the organization of the database is changed.
- If a class implements its own persistence, it is closely coupled with the persistence mechanism in its implementation. If you ever need it to work with different persistence mechanisms, it is a lot easier to have a separate class that implements the CRUD interface.

Object IDs

In order to implement a CRUD interface, there must be a consistent way to identify an object in a database and in memory. Object IDs (described in the Object Identifier pattern) are the usual way of doing this.

Implementations of CRUD pattern need to have a way to determine the Object ID of the objects they work with. If the class responsible for implementing a CRUD interface is not the class of the objects it is responsible for persisting, then it will need to be able to call one of the objects' methods to get the object ID.

To make an implementation that is reusable in the sense of knowing how to get the object ID from an open-ended set of classes, the objects to be persisted must implement a common interface that defines a method that returns the object ID. You can find an example of such an interface under the "Design Example" heading of the Persistence Layer pattern. The name of the interface is CachableIF.

In order for an object to have a unique ID at all times, it must be assigned a unique ID when it is constructed. The unique ID for an object can be assigned using the Object ID pattern.

KNOWN USES

The author has seen the CRUD pattern in many independently developed proprietary applications.

DESIGN EXAMPLE

Given a class named Organization that is responsible for representing organizations, the design for an interface to persist instances of Organization might look like the one shown in Figure 9.7.

RELATED PATTERNS

Object Identifier.   Implementations of CRUD interfaces use the Object Identifier pattern to identify objects in memory and in databases.

Persistence Layer.   The CRUD pattern is used by the Persistence Layer pattern.

Stale Object.   The Stale Object pattern is used when implementing the CRUD pattern to ensure the consistency of updates.

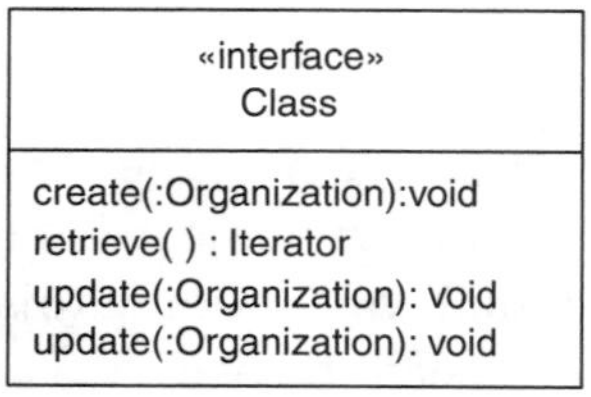

«interface»
Class
create(:Organization):void retrieve( ) : Iterator update(:Organization): void update(:Organization): void

FIGURE 9.7 Organization persister.

Stale Object

SYNOPSIS

A program may have multiple in-memory copies of a persisted object. These copies may have been retrieved from the database at different times and reflect different states of the object. A relatively common yet difficult-to-diagnose bug is to update the persisted object using an obsolete copy of the object. Use cached information about the most recently retrieved version of an object to ensure that updates to it are based on the current version of the object.

CONTEXT

The experience that led to the author's own discovery of the Stale Object pattern involved a bug in an application that displayed a list of organizations. It allowed the user to select an organization and then edit some information about the organization. After the user selected an organization, the application would retrieve the organization object a second time from the database to get a lock on the object. After it had the lock, the application modified the version of the object that it retrieved to display the list and used that object to update the database. Unfortunately, between the time the object was fetched and the application got the lock, the object had been changed in the database. The update produced the wrong result because it was based on a stale version of the object.

FORCES

- ☺ Clients of a database have no direct knowledge of what locks the database holds. At best, they can infer some locks.
- ☺ When an object is retrieved from a database in a way that tells the database manager that its client intends to update the object, the database client can infer that there is a lock on the object.
- ☺ A relatively common bug is to try to update the contents of a persisted object using an in-memory copy of the object that is not the most recently fetched copy. This creates the possibility of changing some values that the update is not intended to change.
- ☹ It is possible to keep an in-memory record of which the in-memory object is the most recently retrieved copy of a persisted object. If an

application is engaged in a large number of concurrent transactions, the amount of memory required to keep track of this can be considerable.

SOLUTION

The persistence layer should cache objects that are retrieved for update. It should do so in a way that associates them with the combination of their object ID and the transaction under which the object was retrieved. The reason for the association with the transaction is that later on it will be important to know that the `retrieve` object was retrieved under the particular transaction and not some other concurrent transaction.

When an in-memory object is presented to a persistence layer to update a persisted object, the persistence layer checks its cache for a copy of the persisted object to be updated. If the cache contains a copy of the persisted object (it usually will), then that object will be the most recently retrieved copy. If that copy is not the same in-memory object that was passed in to update the persistent object, then the persistence layer should throw an exception, indicating that the object passed for update is stale.

It is very easy to implement this behavior for a persistence layer if the persistence layer is implemented on top of an object-oriented database that provides the behavior as one of its features. However, when implementing a persistence layer over a relational database, the persistence layer must take responsibility for the behavior since a relational database cannot. Figure 9.8 shows the structure of classes within a persistence layer to support the Stale Object pattern.

Here are the roles that the classes and interfaces shown in Figure 9.8 play in the Stale Object pattern:

PersistenceManager. Classes in this role are responsible for providing an instance of a class that implements the `TransactionIF` interface and encapsulates the current transaction. It implements this responsibility in its `getCurrentTransaction` method. The objects that the `getCurrentTransaction` method returns are instances of a class that is specific to the persistence engine being used.

TransactionIF. Interfaces in this role declare essential and generic methods that are needed to manage transactions.

EngineSpecificTransaction. Classes in this role are specific to the persistence engine being used. They encapsulate the mechanism being used to manage transactions with the persistence engine.

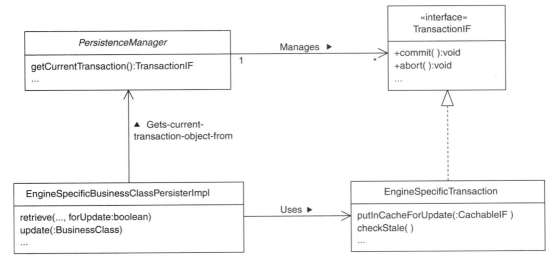

FIGURE 9.8 Stale Object pattern.

With respect to this pattern, if the underlying persistence engine detects when a stale in-memory copy of a persisted object is being used to update a persisted object and throws an exception, then the class in this role does not need to add any methods to those declared by the `TransactionIF` interface that it implements. However, if the underlying persistence engine does not detect this situation, then the class in this role should define two methods not declared by the `TransactionIF` interface.

- It should declare a method named `putInCacheForUpdate` that puts the object passed to it in a cache associated with the `EngineSpecificTransaction` object.
- It should define a method named `checkStale` that throws an exception if the object passed to it was not previously put in the `EngineSpecificTransaction` object's cache by a call to the `putInCacheForUpdate` method.

EngineSpecificBusinessClassPersisterImpl. Classes in this role implement methods to create, retrieve, update, and delete instances of a particular class in a database. Classes in this role are specific to a particular persistence engine. If the `EngineSpecificTransaction` class for a persistence engine has `putInCacheForUpdate` and `checkStale` methods, then the `EngineSpecificBusinessClassPersisterImpl` classes for the persistence engine should make use of those methods.

The way that an `EngineSpecificBusinessClassPersisterImpl` object makes use of an `EngineSpecificTransaction` object's `checkStale` and `putInCacheForUpdate` methods is shown in Figure 9.9.

Here are descriptions of the interactions shown in Figure 9.9:

1. Call the `EngineSpecificBusinessClassPersisterImpl` object's `retrieve` method, telling it that you want to retrieve an object for the purpose of updating the object.

1.1. Get the transaction object responsible for managing the current transaction.

1.2. Put the freshly retrieved business object in the transaction's update cache.

2. After making changes to the in-memory business object, call the `EngineSpecificBusinessClassPersisterImpl` object's `retrieve` method, passing it the modified business object.

2.1. Get the transaction object responsible for managing the current transaction.

2.2. Check if the object passed into the `update` method is in the transaction's update cache. If it is not, then the object must not be the one most recently returned by the `retrieve` method for update during this transaction. If it is not, the `checkStale` method throws a `StaleObjectException`. Otherwise, if the object is in the cache, then the `checkStale` method just returns.

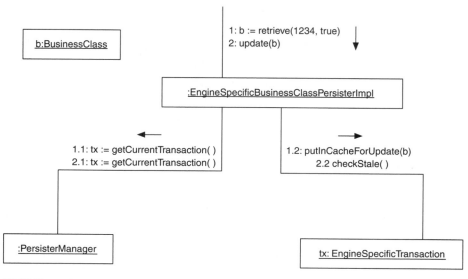

FIGURE 9.9 Interactions for stale object checking.

CONSEQUENCES

☺ Using the Stale Object pattern makes it unlikely that the bug of passing the wrong object to an `update` method will go undetected.

The Stale Object pattern does allow the wrong object to be passed to an `update` method in some unusual cases. If more than one of the same type of object is retrieved for update as part of the same transaction, then if the wrong one of those objects is passed to an `update` method it will go undetected by the Stale Object pattern.

☹ The Stale Object pattern adds complexity to the code that implements a persistence layer.

IMPLEMENTATION

Optimization

A sometimes worthwhile optimization is to have the `retrieve` method attempt to fetch an object being retrieved for update from the update cache. This can be useful if it is likely that the same object may be fetched for update more than once during a transaction.

Removal from Update Cache

Many implementations of a cache provide mechanisms that automatically remove objects from the cache. Examples of such mechanisms are the following:

● Removing objects from a cache to limit the size of the cache.
● Removing objects from a cache after they have been in the cache more than a certain amount of time.

A cache that is used to implement the Stale Object pattern must not incorporate any mechanism that removes objects from the cache before the transaction that uses the cache has completed. A simple `java.util.HashMap` object is usually adequate for this purpose.

Undo

Some applications may need the ability to undo changes that were made to an in-memory object after it was retrieved for update. The Snapshot pattern described in *Volume 1* describes how to do this by saving the necessary information. If you are using this technique, it may be convenient for the update cache to contain the information needed to restore an object's internal state in addition to the object itself.

KNOWN USES

The ClickBlocks persistence framework* provides support for the Stale Object pattern by providing an update cache as a feature of its transaction classes.

A number of object-oriented databases use the Stale Object pattern.

CODE EXAMPLE

The code example for this pattern is taken from the same body of code as the example for the Persistence Layer pattern. You will find the code for this pattern on the CD-ROM that accompanies this book under the code for the Persistence Layer pattern.

Here is a `retrieve` method from an `EngineSpecificBusiness-ClassPersisterImpl` class that participates in the Stale Object pattern.

```
public Restaurant retrieve(long restaurantId,
                          boolean forUpdate) throws CBSystemException {
   Long thisId = new Long(restaurantId);
   Restaurant restaurant;
   ...
   JDBCTransaction tx
     = (JDBCTransaction)getManager().getCurrentTransaction();
   Connection myConnection = ((JDBCTransaction)tx).getConnection();
   String query = null;
   Statement myStatement = null;
   try {
      myStatement = myConnection.createStatement();
      query
        = "SELECT a.entity_id, a.name, a.cuisine, a.price_min,"
        +         " a.price_max, a.rating,"
        ...
      if (forUpdate) {
         query += " FOR UPDATE";
      } // if
      ResultSet rs = myStatement.executeQuery(query);
      restaurant = (Restaurant)instantiate(rs);
      if (forUpdate) {
         tx.putInCacheForUpdate(restaurant);
         ...
      }// if forUpdate
      return restaurant;
   } catch (SQLException e) {
      retrieveException(e, query);
   } finally {
```

---

* You can find the ClickBlocks persistence framework on the CD accompanying this book or at www.clickblocks.org.

```
        JDBCUtil.close(myStatement);
    } // try
    return null;
} // retrieve(long, boolean)
```

Notice, in the `retrieve` method, that after it instantiates an in-memory copy of the restaurant whose data it just retrieved, it checks to see if `forUpdate` is true. If `forUpdate` is true, then the method puts the `Restaurant` object in the transaction object's update cache.

The next listing is from the update method in the same class:

```
public void update(Restaurant restaurant)
                        throws NotFoundException,
                               CBSystemException,
                               StaleObjectException,
                               BusinessRuleException {
    JDBCTransaction tx
      = (JDBCTransaction)
        getManager().getCurrentTransaction();
    tx.checkStale(restaurant);
    ...
} // update(Restaurant)
```

The main thing to notice about the `update` method is that it begins by getting the transaction object for the current transaction and calling its `checkStale` method. It passes the object that contains the values to update the database to the `checkStale` method. If the object is *not* in the transaction's update cache, then the `checkStale` method throws a `StaleObject` exception. Otherwise, if the object is in the update cache, the `checkStale` method simply returns and the `update` method proceeds with the update.

Here is a listing that shows the relevant portions of the `JDBCTransaction` class:

```
public class JDBCTransaction implements TransactionIF {
...
    /**
     * A HashMap to cache objects retrieved in the context of
     * this transaction for update. Attempts to update the
     * database using objects not in this cache are presumed
     * to be using a stale object.
     */
    private HashMap cache = null;
...
    /**
     * Put the given object in the cache associated with this
     * transaction. This is intended to be called by retrieve
     * methods that are retrieving an object for update.
     *
```

```
 *  @param obj
 *          The object to be cached.
 */
public void putInCacheForUpdate(CachableIF obj) {
    if (cache==null) {
        cache = new HashMap();
    } // if
    cache.put(obj.getIdObject(), obj);
} // putInCacheForUpdate(CachableIF)


/**
 * Return the object associated with the given ID object
 * in the cache associated with this transaction or null
 * if there is no such object.
 *
 * @param idObject
 *          The object id to retrieve a profile for.
 */
public Object getFromCacheForUpdate(Object idObject) {
    if (cache==null) {
        return null;
    } // if
    return cache.get(idObject);
} // getFromCacheForUpdate(Object)


/**
 * Throw a StaleObjectException if there is an object in
 * the cache identified by the given key that is a
 * different object (!=) than the given object. If this
 * is the case, it indicates that the object is not the
 * one retrieved by the last retrieve for update
 * operation.
 *
 * @param obj
 *          The object to compare to one in the cache.
 */
public void checkStale(CachableIF obj)
                              throws StaleObjectException {
    if (cache!=null) {
        Object cachedObject = cache.get(obj);
        if (cachedObject!=null && obj!=cachedObject) {
            throw new StaleObjectException(toString(),
                                           obj.toString());
        } // if cachedObject
    } // if cache
} // isStale()
...
} // class JDBCTransaction
```

The methods shown in the listing are able to determine the object ID of the object passed to them because the objects are required to implement the `CachableIF` interface. Here is a listing of the `CachableIF` interface:

```
public interface CachableIF extends PersistableIF {
    /**
     * Return an object that encapsulates the object id for
     * this object. Whatever the class of the object is, it
     * must be the case that if two objects named obj1 and
     * obj2 encapsulate the object id of the same object then
     *     obj1.equals(obj2)
     * is true and
     *     obj1.hashCode()==obj2.hashCode()
     * is also true.
     */
    public Object getIdObject() ;
} // interface CachableIF
```

RELATED PATTERNS

Persistence Layer.   The Stale Object design pattern is used in designing the implementation of the Persistence Layer pattern.

CRUD.   The Stale Object pattern is used with the CRUD pattern in designing classes responsible for persisting specific kinds of objects for an application.

Type Conversion

This pattern is also known as the Data Conversion pattern and as the Type Translation pattern. This pattern was previously described in [Yoder98].

SYNOPSIS

If the values in a persisted object in a database are represented differently than the values in in-memory objects, then some type conversions will need to be done. Organize the methods that perform the conversions into type conversion classes.

CONTEXT

When storing objects in a database, a common problem is that some values are represented differently in the database than in the in-memory objects. For example:

- True and false may be directly represented in Java-based objects using Java's `boolean` data type. However, many databases do not have a direct representation of true and false, so they may be represented in the database as `'T'` and `'F'`.
- Male and female may be represented as instances of Java classes that implement a common interface with different implementations of the interface's methods. If a database is not able to directly represent Java classes, then male and female may be represented in the database as `'M'` and `'F'`.
- The representation of monetary amounts in a database may be as a simple numeric value but in memory as an object that includes a numeric amount and a unit of currency.

In all of these cases, a conversion must be performed between different representations of the data.

FORCES

☺ Values are represented in memory and in a database using different data types or systems of representation. For example, distinctions that are represented in memory as different objects may be represented in the database as different values; an in-memory object may represent a measurement in centimeters and the database may represent the same measurement in meters.

☺ The representation of data in a database and its overall structure may be constrained by the need to support multiple applications.

☺ Forcing applications that use a database to use the same data representations as the database may be more work to implement and less efficient if the application platform does not provide good support for the types used in the database.

☹ Putting the code to convert between the in-memory and database representations of data directly in the method responsible for a CRUD* operation can make the code more readable if the conversion is very simple.

SOLUTION

Organize the code to convert data between its database representation and its in-memory representation into methods that are part of a utility class. These type conversion utility classes can then be shared by a persistence layer's classes responsible for persisting specific kinds of objects. Figure 9.10 shows the relationship between these classes that is the essential organization of the Type Conversion pattern.

The class diagram in Figure 9.10 shows classes in a `BusinessClass-PersisterImpl` role that need to convert data between its database form and its in-memory object form. They delegate this set of responsibilities to classes in the `TypeConversion` role.

The methods of classes in the `TypeConversion` role vary. However, they generally do one or more of the following things:

Formatting.   It may be necessary to format the string that represents a piece of data in a particular way. For example, if a date needs to be expressed in an SQL expression, the simplest way to do so may be to use the ANSI standard syntax for a date in SQL. Dates in this format look like this:

```
DATE'2001-12-25'
```

Computational transformation.   It may be necessary to compute a different representation of data as represented in a database and in an in-memory object. For example, geographical distances in a

---

* See the CRUD pattern for an explanation.

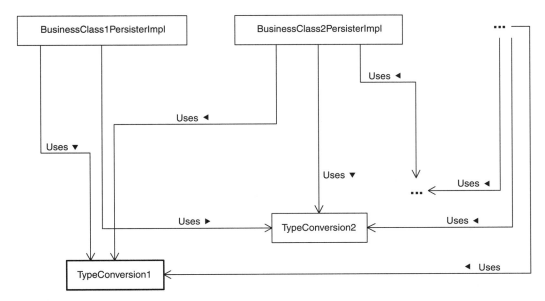

FIGURE 9.10 Type Conversion pattern.

database may be expressed in kilometers, but in a particular application's objects, the same distances may be expressed in miles.

Supply missing data. In some cases, the database or in-memory object representation of some information may be missing some data that the other needs. A type conversion method may be able to supply the additional information by consulting an additional source of information or just assuming the value(s) for the data. For example, an application framework may contain a class named MonetaryAmount that represents monetary amounts as a combination of a numeric value and a unit of currency. If the MonetaryAmount class is used with a database that stores monetary amounts as just a numeric value, then the type conversion will need to assume the missing unit of currency when it creates MonetaryAmount objects from database values.

CONSEQUENCES

☺ A type conversion class provides a single place to handle mismatches between the way data is represented in in-memory objects and in a database. This helps ensure that the conversion between in-memory and database representations of data happens in a consistent way.

☺ If the database or in-memory representation of a piece of data changes, having a type conversion class limits the number of places that have to change as a result of the data representation change. This generally results in applications and databases that are more reliable.

For multiple persistence engines, you may need multiple sets of type conversion utility classes.

IMPLEMENTATION

There are no noteworthy issues in implementing the Type Conversion pattern.

KNOWN USES

The ClickBlocks persistence framework includes a type conversion class for use with common Java types and relational databases.

Some object-oriented databases include a mechanism to import and export data to or from relational databases. Such mechanisms generally include some support for the Type Conversion pattern.

The author of this book is aware of numerous proprietary applications that use the Type Conversion pattern.

CODE EXAMPLE

You will find the code examples for this pattern on the accompanying CD-ROM under the code for the Persistence Layer pattern.

The ClickBlocks persistence framework includes a utility class called JDBCUtil. Most of the methods in JDBCUtil are type conversion methods that are used for working with the basic types that Java provides.

```java
public class JDBCUtil {
    /**
     * Format a Date object as a pure date in ANSI format.
     */
    public static String format(Date dt) {
        if (dt==null) {
            return "NULL";
        } // if
        long time = dt.getTime();
        if (time==Long.MIN_VALUE) {
            return "DATE'1000-1-1'";
```

```
            } // if MIN_VALUE
            if (time==Long.MAX_VALUE) {
                return "DATE'9999-12-31'";
            } // if
            StringBuffer buf = new StringBuffer(16);
            buf.append("DATE'").append(dt.getYear()+1900);
            buf.append('-').append(dt.getMonth()+1).append('-');
            buf.append(dt.getDate()).append('\'');
            return buf.toString();
        } // format(Date)

        /**
         * Format a String object by enclosing it in single quotes and
         * doubling any internal single quotes.
         */
        public static String format(String s) {
            if (s==null) {
                return " NULL ";
            } // if

            int slength = s.length();

            // Size the new StringBuffer for external single quotes
            // and two doubled internal single quotes.
            StringBuffer buf = new StringBuffer(slength+4);
            buf.append('\'');
            for (int i=0; i<slength; i++) {
                char c = s.charAt(i);
                buf.append(c);
                if (c=='\'') {
                    buf.append('\'');
                } // if
            } // for
            buf.append('\'');
            return buf.toString();
        } // format(String)
    ...
        /**
         * Format a boolean value.
         */
        public static String format(boolean b) {
            return b ? "'T'" : "'F'";
        } // format(boolean)

        /**
         * Format an arbitrary object
         */
        public static String format(Object obj) {
            if (obj==null) {
                return " NULL ";
            } // if
            return format(obj.toString());
        } // format(Object)
```

The preceding `format` methods are used to ensure that values concatenated into an SQL string are formatted in a way that obeys the rules for SQL syntax. Rather than force programmers to remember which Java types require the use of the `format` method and which do not, the JDBCUtil class provides `format` methods for types that do not need a `format` method. These format methods simply format their arguments the same way that concatenation would.

```
/**
 * Format an <code>int</code>
 */
public static String format(int x) {
    return Integer.toString(x);
} // format(int)

/**
 * Format a <code>long</code>
 */
public static String format(long x) {
    return Long.toString(x);
} // format(long)

/**
 * Format a <code>char</code>.
 */
public static String format(char c) {
    return format(new String( new char[]{c} ));
} // format(char)
```

Because the `format` method handles boolean values by translating them into `'T'` or `'F'`, a method is needed to perform the reverse conversion.

```
/**
 * Return the boolean value that corresponds to one of the
 * strings "T", "t", "F" or "f".
 *
 * @exception IllegalArgumentException
 *             If the argument is any other string.
 */
public static boolean toBoolean(String s) {
    if (s.length()==1) {
        char c = s.charAt(0);
        if (c == 'T' || c == 't') {
            return true;
        } // if t
        if (c == 'F' || c == 'f') {
            return false;
        } // if f
    } // if length
    throw new IllegalArgumentException(s);
```

```
        } // toBoolean(String)
...
} // class JDBCUtil
```

Here is some code that uses methods from the `JDBCUtil` class:

```
query = "INSERT INTO 1fx_restaurant_tb"
   +        " (cuisine, price_min, price_max,"
   +         " rating, delivery_available,"
   +         " take_out_available,"
   +         " sit_down_available, entity_id,"
   +         " govt_identifier)"
   +        " VALUES ("+JDBCUtil.format(restaurant.getCuisine())
   +        ","+minPriceString
   +        ","+maxPriceString
   +","+JDBCUtil.format(restaurant.getStarRating())
   +","+JDBCUtil.format(restaurant.isDeliveryAvailable())
   +","+JDBCUtil.format(restaurant.isTakeOutAvailable())
   +","+JDBCUtil.format(restaurant.isSitDownAvailable())
   +        ","+restaurantID
   +","+JDBCUtil.format(restaurant.getGovtIdentifier())

   +        ")";
```

Finally, here is an example of a type conversion class for an application class:

```
public class JDBCMonetaryAmountUtil {
    /**
     * Return a MonetaryAmount object that represents the given
     * amount of U.S. Dollars. If the given amount is null
     * then return null.
     */
    public static
      MonetaryAmount dollarAmount(BigDecimal amount) {
        if (amount==null) {
            return null;
        } // if
        return new MonetaryAmount(Currency.USD, amount);
    } // dollarAmount(BigDecimal)

    /**
     * Format a MonetaryAmount object as a string suitable
     * for use in an SQL query as a purely numeric value
     * with no unit of currency specified.
     */
    public static String format(MonetaryAmount amt) {
        if (amt==null) {
            return "NULL";
        } else {
            return JDBCUtil.format(amt.getAmount());
        } // if
    } // format(MonetaryAmount)
} // class JDBCMonetaryAmountUtil
```

RELATED PATTERNS

CRUD. The Type Conversion design pattern is used in designing implementations of the CRUD architectural pattern.

Intention Revealing Method. The Type Conversion pattern is often an application of the Intention Revealing Method described in *Volume 2*.

isDirty

This pattern is also known as the hasChanged pattern. This pattern was previously described in [Yoder98].

SYNOPSIS

Avoid the expense of updating database objects that don't need to be updated by keeping track of whether they actually do need to be updated.

CONTEXT

Suppose you are designing a package to be used with Web sites that sell merchandise. The purpose of the package is to customize the presentation of an on-line merchandise catalog based on a customer's known preferences. As the customer peruses the catalog, the customer should see varieties of merchandise that are most likely to be of interest to the particular customer. As the customer selects items to buy, the customer should see related and alternative selections.

In order for your package to accomplish all this, it will need to retrieve a variety of information about the customer from a database. It uses objects that encapsulate the information to model and predict customer behavior. As the package learns things about a customer's preferences, it will add to and modify these objects so that the model includes what can be learned from the customer's current behavior.

When a customer has completed a purchase, the package needs to update the database with the new and improved information in the model. Updating the database with every object in the model would work, but it would be inefficient because most of the updates would probably be unnecessary.

FORCES

☺ Objects retrieved from a database are not necessarily updated, even if the retrieve operation was flagged as being for update. This is especially the case for complex objects, where the retrieval of one object may imply the retrieval of associated objects. When updating a complex object, it is often the case that only a small fraction of its associated objects are actually updated.

☺ Updating objects in a database with objects that have not changed is a waste of time.

☺ Updating objects in a database that have not changed can make an audit trail more difficult to analyze or even misleading. This problem can be solved by having the audit trail mechanism detect unnecessary updates, but that makes the unnecessary updates an even bigger waste of time. It also adds complexity to the audit trail mechanism.

☹ Mechanisms to detect unnecessary updates before they happen can also waste time and add complexity.

SOLUTION

Design a class whose instances are to be persisted so that they have a method that can be called to find out if the contents of an instance have changed. This method is typically called `isDirty` or `hasChanged`. To avoid wasting time making unnecessary updates, call an instance's `update` method before persisting it. If you are using the Persistence Layer pattern, the `update` methods of classes that are responsible for persisting instances of other classes should call an object's `isDirty` method before proceeding with an update. Figure 9.11 shows this class structure.

The responsibilities of the `BusinessClassPersister` class shown in Figure 9.11 include retrieving instances of `BusinessClass` from a database and using the contents of in-memory instances of `BusinessClass` to update the persisted version of its instances. When a `BusinessClassPersister` object instantiates a `BusinessClass` object, it ensures that its `isDirty` method returns false by calling its `makeClean` method. The `makeClean` method sets the value of a `BusinessClass` object's `dirty` variable to `true`.

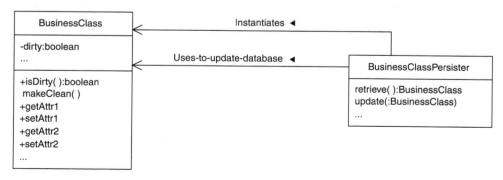

FIGURE 9.11 IsDirty pattern.

The value of the `dirty` variable is not included in the persisted form of the object. All the methods of a `BusinessClass` object that modify the persistent portion of its contents, set its `dirty` variable to `true`.

When a `BusinessClassPersister` object's `update` method is called, it calls the `isDirty` method of the `BusinessClass` object passed to it. If the `isDirty` method returns false, then the `update` method just returns without performing any database operation.

At the conclusion of a retrieve operation, a `BusinessClass-Persister` object's `retrieve` method calls the `makeClean` method of the `BusinessClass` object it just instantiated. It calls its `makeClean` method, because at the conclusion of a `retrieve` method the contents of the `BusinessClass` object match the contents of the database. For the same reason, at the conclusion of an update or create operation, the `BusinessClassPersister` object's `update` or `create` method calls the `makeClean` method of the `BusinessClass` object.

CONSEQUENCES

☺ Using the isDirty pattern is a way of avoiding unnecessary database update operations.

☹ The isDirty pattern adds complexity to classes. Mistakes in implementing the pattern can cause the bug of database objects not being updated when they should.

IMPLEMENTATION

The implementation of the isDirty pattern is usually very straightforward. However, if there is a lot of data associated with the instances of a class, a slightly more complicated approach may be justified. Under some circumstances, it may be advantageous to have multiple `dirty` flags.

Some objects have a complex structure that tightly couples them to other objects. Updating the persisted version of such an object in a database can involve the equivalent of updating multiple objects.

In the class diagram shown in Figure 9.12, a `Traveler` object can have multiple `PhoneNumber` and `Preference` objects associated with it. If we change one of a traveler's phone numbers, we want an update operation to update just that phone number. We do not want it to update all of the traveler's other phone numbers and the traveler's accommodation preferences. To accomplish this we would design these classes so that each instance of `Traveler`, `PhoneNumber`, and `Preference` has its own `dirty` flag.

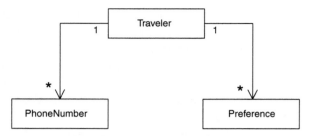

FIGURE 9.12 Complex object.

KNOWN USES

The author has been involved with e-commerce sites where the isDirty pattern has been used to avoid unnecessary database updates of customer-supplied information.

Most word processors and spreadsheets use the isDirty pattern to keep track of whether a document needs to be saved.

CODE EXAMPLE

The code example for this pattern is taken from a class that represents information about a restaurant and a class that is responsible for persisting restaurant objects in a database. Here is the `Restaurant` class:

```
public class Restaurant extends Organization
                        implements PersistableIF {
    private String cuisine;
    private MonetaryAmount minPrice;
...
    private boolean dirty;
...
    /**
     * Set the name of the cuisine that this restaurant serves.
     */
    public void setCuisine(String cuisine){
        if (isModification(this.cuisine, cuisine)) {
            this.cuisine = cuisine;
            dirty = true;
        } // if
    } // setCuisine(String)
...
```

Set methods that simply modify an instance variable whose value is an object generally follow the same logic, so there is a private method to see whether the new value is different from the old value and set the dirty flag to true.

```
   /**
    * Return true if neither of the objects are null and
    * their equals method returns false. If this method
    * returns true, it also sets dirty to true.
    */
   private boolean isModification(Object o1, Object o2) {
       if ((o1!=null && !o1.equals(o2))
           || (o1==null && o2!=null)) {
           dirty = true;
           return true;
       } // if
       return false;
   } // isModification(Object, Object)
...
```

The logic of methods that set the value of an instance variable whose value is a primitive type does not need to check for null. This makes it simple enough that it may not be worth calling another method.

```
   /**
    * Set the star rating for this restaurant.
    */
   public void setStarRating(Integer starRating){
       if (this.starRating != starRating) {
           this.starRating = starRating;
           dirty = true;
       } // if
   } // setStarRating(Integer)
...

   /**
    * Return true if the information is this object has been
    * modified.
    */
   public boolean isDirty() { return dirty; }

   /**
    * Set this object's dirty flag to false.
    *
    * This method is package private because it is indented
    * to be called only by persister objects that retrieve or
    * update this object.
    */
   void makeClean() { dirty = false; }
} // class Restaurant
```

Here are selected portions of the class responsible for persisting Restaurant objects:

```
public class JDBCRestaurantPersister extends JDBCPersister
                                implements RestaurantPersisterIF {
...
   /**
```

```
         * Persist the given restaurant.
         * ...
         */
        public void create(Restaurant restaurant)
                                  throws DuplicateException,
                                         CBSystemException,
                                         BusinessRuleException {
    ...
            try {
                Connection myConnection = tx.getConnection();
    ...
                myStatement = myConnection.createStatement();
                myStatement.executeUpdate(query);
    ...
                restaurant.makeClean();
    ...
            } catch (SQLException e) {
                createException(e, query);
            } finally {
                JDBCUtil.close(myStatement);
            } // try
        } // create(Restaurant)
    ...
```

After the `create` method creates the given `Restaurant` object in the database, it calls the `Restaurant` object's `makeClean` method.

Here is the `Restaurant` class's `retrieve` method:

```
public Restaurant retrieve(long restaurantId,
                           boolean forUpdate) throws CBSystemException {
    ...
        try {
            ...
            ResultSet rs = myStatement.executeQuery(query);
            restaurant = (Restaurant)instantiate(rs);
            ...
            return restaurant;
        } catch (SQLException e) {
            retrieveException(e, query);
        } finally {
            JDBCUtil.close(myStatement);
        } // try
        return null;
    } // retrieve(long, boolean)
```

After the `retrieve` method's database query returns, it calls the `instantiate` method to instantiate a `Restaurant` object from the result of the query.

```
    /**
     * Instantiate a Restaurant object from the
     * current row data in a ResultSet.
     */
```

```
protected Object instantiate(ResultSet rs) {
    try {
        long id = rs.getLong(1);
        ...
        String name = rs.getString(2);
        String cuisine = rs.getString(3);
        ...
        // Create the <code>Restaurant</code> object.
        thisRestaurant = new Restaurant(id);
        thisRestaurant.setCuisine(cuisine);
        thisRestaurant.setMinPrice(minDollarAmt);
        ...
        thisRestaurant.makeClean();
        ...
        return thisRestaurant;
    } catch (SQLException e) {
        String msg = "Error occurred retrieving restaurant data";
        throw new CBInternalException(toString(), msg, e);
    } // try
} // instantiate(ResultSet)
```

The `update` method is the one that actually cares about the current setting of a `restaurant`'s dirty flag.

```
public void update(Restaurant restaurant)
                            throws NotFoundException,
                                   CBSystemException,
                                   StaleObjectException,
                                   BusinessRuleException {

    ...
    try {
        myStatement = myConnection.createStatement();
        if (restaurant.isDirty()) {
            long restaurantID = restaurant.getId();
            String cuisineString
                = JDBCUtil.format(restaurant.getCuisine());
            ...
            query
                = "UPDATE lfx_restaurant_tb"
                + " SET cuisine=" + cuisineString
                ...
                + " WHERE entity_id="+restaurantID;
            int count = myStatement.executeUpdate(query);
            ...
        } // if !isDirty
        ...
        restaurant.makeClean();
        tx.addTransactionCommittedListener(restaurant);
    } catch (SQLException e) {
        updateException(e, query);
    } finally {
        JDBCUtil.close(myStatement);
    } // try
```

```
        } // update(Restaurant)
...
} // class JDBCRestaurantPersister
```

RELATED PATTERNS

Persistence Layer.   The isDirty pattern can be used with the
Persistence Layer pattern.

CRUD.   The isDirty pattern is used to design the implementation of
method identified by the CRUD pattern.

Lazy Retrieval.   The Lazy Retrieval pattern is used to avoid unnecessary retrieval operations on a complex object's associated
objects.

Lazy Retrieval

This pattern is also known as Fault.

SYNOPSIS

If the design of a program involves persisted complex objects, you may find a persistence layer having to move large numbers of related objects in and out of a database all at once. If they are not all needed at once, then delay the retrieval of portions of complex objects until they are needed.

CONTEXT

Suppose you are designing a program to fill the human resources management needs of a company. In your design, you find that the class that represents an employee is associated with a number of other classes. Figure 9.13 shows part of this design.

As you can see, an `Employee` object owns other kinds of objects. Each of those objects may own other objects. Most operations relating to an `Employee` object use only one or two of the other objects. Retrieving all objects an `Employee` object owns when you retrieve the `Employee` object is a waste of time. To avoid wasting time this way, do not retrieve an object that the `Employee` object owns until there is a need for the object.

FORCES

- ☺ Complex objects may refer to a number of associated objects.
- ☺ Operations on a complex object may only involve a fraction of its associated objects.
- ☺ Retrieving a complex object and all of its associated objects from a database takes more time and memory than retrieving a complex object and just a fraction of its associated objects.
- ☺ If an application does not use all of a complex object's associated objects, then the time and memory spent retrieving the unused associated objects are wasted.
- ☺ At the time a complex object is retrieved, it may not be possible to predict which of its associated objects will be used.

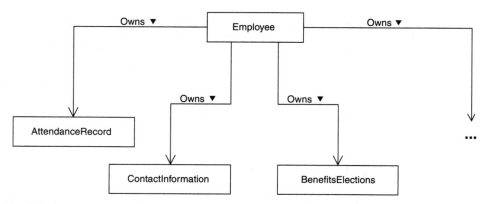

FIGURE 9.13 HRMS design.

☹ It generally takes less time to retrieve all of a complex object's associated objects all at once than it does to retrieve them individually. If it is likely that an operation will use all or even most of a complex object's associated objects, then it may be most efficient to retrieve them all at once.

SOLUTION

Unless it is likely that all of a complex object's associated objects will be used, design the persistence layer to retrieve only the complex object itself. Design the complex object to retrieve its associated objects through the persistence layer when they are first needed. This organization is shown in Figure 9.14.

Here are descriptions of the interactions shown in Figure 9.14:

1. An object responsible for persisting some complex objects is asked to retrieve one.

1.1. In the course of retrieving a persisted complex object, an in-memory version of the complex object is created without any of its associated objects.

2. A method of the complex object is called that returns some historical information about the complex object.

2.1. To get the requested information, the method must use one of the complex object's associated objects. Since there is no in-memory version of the associated object, the complex object calls the appropriate object's `retrieve` method to retrieve an in-memory version of the associated object.

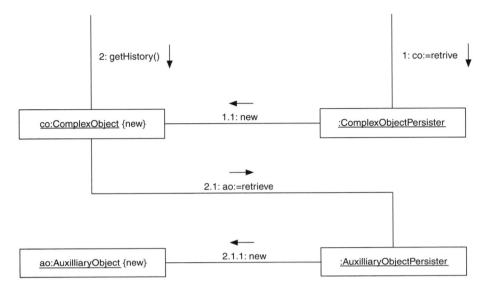

FIGURE 9.14 Lazy Retrieval pattern.

> **2.1.1.** In the course of retrieving a persisted associated object, an in-memory version of the associated object is created.

CONSEQUENCES

- ☺ Using the Lazy Retrieval pattern avoids wasting time and memory retrieving objects that will not be used.
- ☺ Using the Lazy Retrieval pattern causes the overhead of retrieving a complex object's associated objects to be spread out over time.
- ☹ The Lazy Retrieval pattern adds complexity to classes.

IMPLEMENTATION

It is possible for the Lazy Retrieval pattern to be used with multiple layers of complex objects.

KNOWN USES

The author is familiar with numerous proprietary applications that use the Lazy Retrieval pattern.

A Java virtual machine does not fetch all of the classes in an application when the application first starts. It waits until the first time a class is used.

CODE EXAMPLE

The code example for the Lazy Retrieval pattern is a class named `Organization` that is from a framework that uses the class to model real-world business organizations.

```
public class Organization extends PhysicalEntity
                    implements TaxExemptIDOwner,
                               PersistableIF,
                               TransactionCommittedListener {
...
    /**
     * The entity that is responsible for the accounts, items,
     * measurements, etc. that this organization uses.
     */
    private ResponsibleEntity responsibleEntity;
```

This `Organization` class has an attribute called `responsibleEntity`. Its `responsibleEntity` attribute is managed using the Lazy Retrieval pattern. When objects responsible for the persistence of `Organization` objects retrieve an `Organization` object, they do not set its `responsibleEntity` attribute. Instead, they set an `Organization` object's `responsibleEntityId` attribute to the object identifier of the object that is the value of the `Organization` object's `responsibleEntity` attribute.

```
    /**
     * If responsibleEntity is null and idIsSet is true, then
     * use this id to fetch the ResponsibleEntity object that
     * will be its value.
     */
    private long responsibleEntityId;
```

If an attribute of an object is another object, then the natural way to indicate that the value of the attribute has not been set is for its value to be null. Because `responsibleEntityId` is a `long`, there is no natural way to indicate that the value of `responsibleEntityId` has not been set.

One way of indicating that the value of `responsibleEntityId` has not been set is to reserve a value, such as −1, for that purpose. If you have to assume that every possible value of `responsibleEntityId` may be used, then reserving a value is not an acceptable solution. The `Organization` class uses a separate boolean variable called `responsibleIdIsSet` to indicate that the value of `responsibleEntityId` has not been set.

```
    /**
     * true when an ID is passed to the setResponsibleEntity
     * method.
     */
    private boolean responsibleIdIsSet = false;
...
```

```
/**
 * Return the responsible organization that governs this
 * entity or null if there is none.
 */
public ResponsibleEntity getResponsibleEntity() {
    if (responsibleEntity!=null) {
        return responsibleEntity;
    } // if responsibleEntity
    if (responsibleIdIsSet) {
        ...
    } // if
    return responsibleEntity;
} // getResponsibleEntity()
...
} // class Organization
```

RELATED PATTERNS

isDirty. The isDirty pattern is often used with the Lazy Retrieval pattern to avoid unnecessary update operations for a complex object's associated objects.

Lazy Initialization. The Lazy Retrieval pattern is a specialized version of the Lazy initialization pattern described in *Volume 2*.

Object Identifier. An implementation of the Lazy Retrieval pattern may use the Object Identifier pattern to identify an object that is associated with a complex object but not yet retrieved from the database.

Persistence Framework

The persistence framework is in the package com.clickblocks.persistence. The classes it contains provide support for persisting objects in a reusable way. It also supports transactions. It can be extended to work with most persistent stores that support or are compatible with ACID transaction management. This version only comes with support for persistence through the JDBC API.

The persistence framework relies on some classes in the com .clickblocks.util package.

The following sections describe the steps to follow to implement persistence for instances of a given class. The remainder of this section is a brief description of the classes and interfaces that you will need to be aware of in the persistence framework. This is provided to give the interested reader a big picture of what the steps that follow accomplish. If you are not interested, you can skip this section. All of the classes listed in Table A.1 can be found in the com.clickblocks .persistence package.

TABLE A.1 Classes Found in the com.clickblocks.persistence Package

PersistenceManagerFactory	This class is responsible for creating an instance of a class that is responsible for creating objects that manage the persistence of other objects. This implementation always creates an instance of the same class. The class it instantiates will be specific to a single type of persistent store. The class that this release instantiates is specific to JDBC-based persistence. Future releases may relax this restriction.
PersistenceManagerIF	The classes that PersistenceManagerFactory instantiates must implement this interface. Classes that implement this interface have two responsibilities. Given an interface for classes responsible for persisting a kind of object a `PersistenceManagerIF` must provide an object that implements that interface for the appropriate persistent store. Persistence-ManagerIF objects are also responsible for providing TransactionIF objects to manage multioperation transactions against the persistent store the object works with.
PersistenceIF	For each class whose instances you want to persist, there must be a corresponding interface. This interface should extend PersistenceIF. The name of the interface for persisting instances of a class should have the form *Classname*-PersisterIF. For example, if the name of the class whose instances are to be persisted is Role, then the name of the interface for classes that will be responsible for persisting Role objects should be RolePersisterIF. Such interfaces should be part of the same package as the class they are responsible for persisting.
PersistableIF	Classes should implement PersistableIF or CachableIF if their instances are to be persisted. Classes whose instances *do not* have a unique object ID should implement PersistableIF.
CachableIF	Classes should implement PersistableIF or CachableIF if their instances are to be persisted. Classes whose instances *do* have a unique object ID should implement CachableIF. The name of this class comes from the principle that if a persisted object has a unique object ID, then it should be represented in a JVM by at most one object. That is achieved by caching CachableIF objects.

JDBCPersister	Classes that implement the PersistableIF or CachableIF interface by persisting objects through the JDBC API must extend this abstract class.
TransactionIF	TransactionIF objects are responsible for encapsulating transactions on behalf of an underlying persistent store. PersistenceManagerIF objects are responsible for creating TransactionIF objects. Methods of PersistableIF interfaces that perform operations in the context of a transaction take an argument of this type. TransactionIF classes have methods for committing or aborting the transaction that they encapsulate.
TransactionCommittedListener TransactionCommittedEvent	Some objects are complex in the sense that fully representing them in a persistent store requires the persisting of multiple related objects. To avoid wasted effort when updating the persisted form of an object, classes of complex objects will generally have one or more dirty attributes to determine if all or some parts of a complex object may not match the contents of the persistent store. When such an object is involved in an insert or update operation that is part of a transaction, its dirty flags should not be cleared until the transaction is committed. For that reason, classes of complex objects should implement the TransactionCommittedListener interface. Objects that implement the TransactionCommittedListener interface can be registered with a TransactionIF object by the code that implements create and update operations. When a TransactionIF object commits its underlying transaction, it sends a TransactionCommittedEvent to all objects that have registered to receive the event. When an object receives a TransactionCommittedEvent, it should clear all of its dirty flags.

Define the Persister Interface

The first step in extending the persistence framework to persist instances of a particular class is to define a public interface that extends PersistenceIF. The purpose of this interface is to declare the methods that all classes responsible for persisting the class in question must implement. This interface should be in the same package as the class to be persisted.

The name of the interface for persisting instances of a class should have the form *Classname*PersisterIF. For example, if the name of the class whose instances are to be persisted is Role, then the name of the interface for classes that will be responsible for persisting Role objects should be RolePersisterIF.

The methods defined in the interface will typically have the names create, retrieve, update, and delete, with varying signatures. More detailed descriptions of these methods follow.

create

The purpose of methods named create is to create a persisted version of an object. All create methods should take at least one parameter which is the object to be persisted.

Most persister interfaces will have a create method that takes one argument which is the object to be persisted.

```
/**
 * Persist the given item description.
 *
 * @param theItem
 *          The ItemDescription object to be persisted.
 * @exception DuplicateException
 *              If an ItemDescription with the same object
 *              ID as the given ItemDescription has already
 *              been persisted.
 * @exception CBSystemException
 *              If there is a problem that this method
 *              cannot otherwise classify, it wraps the
 *              exception in a CBSystemException.
 * @exception BusinessRuleException
 *              If the operation violates a constraint in the
 *              database that appears to reflect a business
 *              rule.
 */
public void create(ItemDescription theItem)
    throws DuplicateException,
           CBSystemException,
           BusinessRuleException ;
```

retrieve

The purpose of methods named retrieve is to retrieve persisted objects and create in-memory Java versions of the persisted objects. The return type of retrieve methods should either be the class of the objects it will retrieve or Iterator.

There is no specific pattern for the parameters of retrieve methods. If the return type of a retrieve method is the class of the objects it retrieves, then the method's parameters should be sufficient to select a single object. If the objects in question have a unique object identifier, the interface should include a `retrieve` method that takes an object identifier as a parameter.

If the objects being retrieved may be retrieved for the purpose of updating their contents, then the `retrieve` method should have a boolean parameter. This parameter is typically called `forUpdate`. If `forUpdate` is true, then the transaction that the retrieve operation is associated with should get a lock on the object in anticipation of its being updated or deleted. Transactions are discussed later on.

Here is an example of the sort of `retrieve` method we have been discussing:

```
/**
 * Return the persisted version of the ItemDescription
 * object with the given id.
 *
 * @param itemId
 *        The persisted ItemDescription object.
 * @param forUpdate
 *        If this is true, then the persisted
 *        itemDescription information is write locked in
 *        the expectation that it will be updated by a
 *        future operation with the same transaction.
 * @exception NotFoundException
 *            If there is no persisted ItemDescription
 *            object with the given id.
 * @exception CBSystemException
 *            If there is a problem that this method cannot
 *            otherwise classify, it wraps the exception in a
 *            CBSystemException.
 */
public ItemDescription retrieve(long itemId ,
                                boolean forUpdate)
    throws CBSystemException, NotFoundException;
```

If the return type of a `retrieve` method is Iterator, then the method's parameters need only be sufficient to identify the set of objects to return through the iterator.

```
/**
 * Return an Iterator over all the persisted
 * Organization objects.
 *
 * @exception CBSystemException
 *            If there is a problem that this method
 *            cannot otherwise classify, it wraps the
 *            exception in a CBSystemException.
 */
public Iterator retrieve() throws CBSystemException;
```

update

The purpose of the `update` method is to make the state of the persisted version of an object match the state of a given in-memory version of the same object. `update` methods generally return no result and take one parameter, which is the in-memory object whose contents will be used to update the corresponding persisted object.

```
/**
 * Update the persisted version of the given
 * ItemDescription.
 * @param item
 *          The ItemDescription object to be updated.
 * @exception StaleObjectException
 *              if the ItemDescription object is stale. For
 *              any given object id, the retrieve method or
 *              any iterators that it may create normally
 *              return the same object for any given object
 *              ID. However when an object is retrieved for
 *              update, the object returned may be a
 *              different object than returned previously.
 *              When that happens, objects previously
 *              returned with the same object id are
 *              considered stale.
 * @exception NotFoundException
 *              If there is no persisted ItemDescription
 *              object with the same object ID as the given
 *              object.
 * @exception CBSystemException
 *              If there is a problem that this method
 *              cannot otherwise classify, it wraps the
 *              exception in a CBSystemException.
 */
public void update(ItemDescription org)
throws NotFoundException,
       CBSystemException,
       BusinessRuleException,
       StaleObjectException;
```

delete

The purpose of the `delete` method is to delete the persisted version of an object from the persistent store. `delete` methods generally return no result and take one parameter which is an in-memory object that corresponds to the persisted object to be deleted.

```
/**
 * Delete the persited form of the given
 * ItemDescription object.
 *
 * @param theItem
```

```
*           The ItemDescription object to be deleted.
* @exception BusinessRuleException
*               If the given ItemDescription object cannot
*               be deleted because it is referenced by
*               another object.
* @exception CBSystemException
*               If there is a problem that this method
*               cannot otherwise classify, it wraps the
*               exception in a CBSystemException.
*/
public void delete(ItemDescription theItem)
                              throws BusinessRuleException,
                                     CBSystemException;
```

Modify the Class to Cooperate with the Framework

To persist an object's entire state, it may be necessary to access a portion of the object's state information that is not public. To facilitate that, you should add package private methods to the object's class that will allow persister classes to get and set the object's nonpublic state.

Classes that are to be persisted should implement either the PersistableIF interface or the CachableIF interface. Classes that *do not* have a unique object identifier for their instances should implement the PersistableIF interface.

The PersistableIF interface declares one method called getPersistence-Interface. The purpose of this method is so that, given an arbitrary object that implements the PersistableIF interface, you can determine the interface you will need to use to persist it.

```
public interface PersistableIF {
    /**
     * Return a class object that represents the sub-interface
     * of PersistenceIF that should be used to manage the
     * persistence of this class.
     */
    public Class getPersistenceInterface();
} // interface PersistableIF
```

A typical implementation of getPersistenceInterface looks like this;

```
    /**
     * Return a class object that represents the
     * sub-interface of PersistenceIF that should be used to
     * manage the persistence of this class.
     */
    public Class getPersistenceInterface(){
        return ItemDescriptionPersisterIF.class;
    } // getPersistenceInterface()
```

Classes that *do* have a unique object identifier for their instances should implement the CachableIF interface. The CachableIF interface extends the PersistableIF interface. It inherits the getPersistenceInterface method and adds another method called getIdObject. The getIdObject method returns the object's object ID as an object. If the object ID is a primitive value such as a `long`, then the method should encapsulate it in the appropriate class such as Long. The object that it returns must be suitable for use as a key in a hash table.

```
/**
 * Return an object that encapsulates the object id for
 * this object. Whatever the class of the object is, it
 * must be the case that if two objects obj1 and obj2
 * encapsulate the object id of the same object then
 *     obj1.equals(obj2)
 * is true and
 *     obj1.hashCode()==obj2.hashCode()
 * is also true.
 */
public Object getIdObject() ;
```

A typical implementation of the getIdObject method looks like this:

```
private long id;                  // a unique id

/**
 * This object when instantiated will encapsulate id.
 */
private Long idObject = null;

...

/**
 * Return an object that encapsulates this object's
 * object id.
 */
public final Object getIdObject() {
    if (idObject==null) {
        synchronized (this) {
            if (idObject==null) {
                idObject = new Long(id);
            } // if
        } // synchronized
    } // if
    return idObject;
} // getIdObject()
```

Define a Persister Class

The next step is to define a class that will do the actual work of persisting objects of a given type to the intended type of persistent store. This first release of the persistence framework comes only with support for JDBC-based persistence; that is the only type of persistent store that we consider here.

The name of a persister class intended to persist instances of a particular class using JDBC should be of the form JDBC*Classname*Persister. For example, a persister class intended to persist instances of a class named Foo using JDBC would be named JDBCFooPersister. Persister classes should have package scope and be part of the same package as the class they are designed to persist.

We explain the details of defining a JDBC-based persister class through examples.

```
/**
 * Manage the persistence of ItemDescription objects.
 */
public class JDBCItemDescriptionPersister
                     extends JDBCPersister
                     implements ItemDescriptionPersisterIF {
```

Persister classes must implement the appropriate persister interface. In this example, we see that the class JDBCItemDescriptionPersister implements the ItemDescriptionPersisterIF interface.

JDBC-based persister classes must also extend the class JDBCPersister. This allows them to inherit methods that encapsulate common logic for JDBC-based persister classes.

```
    private ResponsibleEntityPersisterIF
      responsibleEntityPersister;
```

Persister classes that are intended to persist complex objects will generally delegate the persistence of objects referenced by the complex object to other persister classes. As an optimization, such persister objects usually have instance variables that they use to cache a reference to the other persister objects that they use. This is the purpose of the preceding declaration.

The type of the instance variable should be the persister interface and not a persister class. Observing this rule ensures that code based on the current release of the persistence framework will continue to work when the persistence framework supports using multiple types of persistent stores at the same time.

```
    /**
     * constructor
     * @param myManager
     *         The JDBCPersistenceManager this object will work
     *         with.
     */
    public JDBCItemDescriptionPersister(JDBCPersistenceManager
```

```
                                                    myManager) {
      super(myManager);
      Class persisterClass
        = ResponsibleEntityPersisterIF.class;
      try {
          responsibleEntityPersister
            = (ResponsibleEntityPersisterIF)
            myManager.getPersister(persisterClass);
      } catch (NotFoundException e) {
          String msg
            = persisterClass.getName()
            + " not registered with persistence manager.";
          throw new CBInternalException("", msg, e);
      } // try
} // constructor(JDBCPersistenceManager)
```

Every JDBC-based persister class must have a public constructor that takes a single argument that is a JDBCPersistenceManager object. All it is expected to do with the JDBCPersistenceManager argument is pass it to the superclass's constructor.

The purpose of the rest of the body of the constructor is to get the persister object it will use to persist ResponsibleEntity objects. The details of this are explained in the section of this document titled "Using the Persister Framework."

The following listing shows a typical implementation of a create method. There are portions of the listing that are highly reusable. These sections are shown in bold. You can probably paste the bold portion of the create method into your persister class and only change the type of the item to be persisted.

There are also large chunks of code that are not in bold. Those chunks of code are less likely to be reusable.

```
/**
 * Persist the given item description.
 * @param theItem
 *          The ItemDescription object to be persisted.
 * @exception DuplicateException
 *              If an ItemDescription with the same object
 *              ID as the given ItemDescription has already
 *              been persisted.
 * @exception CBSystemException
 *              If there is a problem that this method cannot
 *              otherwise classify, it wraps the exception in a
 *              CBSystemException.
 * @exception BusinessRuleException
 *              If the operation violates a constraint in the
 *              database that appears to reflect a business
 *              rule.
 */
public void create(ItemDescription theItem)
```

```
                              throws DuplicateException,
                                     CBSystemException,
                                     BusinessRuleException {
Statement myStatement = null;
PreparedStatement pstmt = null;
String query = null;
long itemId = theItem.getId();
IntervalMap versions = theItem.getVersionMap();
Iterator versionIterator = versions.intervals();
JDBCTransaction tx
  = (JDBCTransaction)
    getManager().getCurrentTransaction();
try {
    Connection myConnection = tx.getConnection();
    myStatement = myConnection.createStatement();
    while (versionIterator.hasNext()) {
        Interval myInterval
          = (Interval)versionIterator.next();
        ItemDescriptionVersion myVersion
          = (ItemDescriptionVersion)
              versions.getMatching(myInterval);
        ResponsibleEntity myResponsibleEntity
          = myVersion.getResponsibleEntity();
        String responsibleEntityString
          = myResponsibleEntity.toString();
        Date startDate = myInterval.getStartDate();
        String startDateString;
        startDateString = JDBCUtil.format(startDate);
        Date endDate = myInterval.getEndDate();
        String endDateString;
        endDateString = JDBCUtil.format(endDate);
        String nameString
          = JDBCUtil.format(myVersion.getName());
        String description
          = myVersion.getTextualDescription();
        String descriptionString
          = JDBCUtil.format(description);
        String unit
          = myVersion.getMeasurementUnit().getName();
        String unitString = JDBCUtil.format(unit);
        String dimension
          = myVersion.getMeasurementDimension()
                                          .getName();
        String dimensionString;
        dimensionString = JDBCUtil.format(dimension);
        String inventoryFlagString
          = JDBCUtil.format(myVersion.isInventory());
        query = "INSERT INTO itm_item_version_tb"
            +      "(item_id,"
            +      "responsible_organization_id,"
            +      "effective_begin,"
            +      "effective_end, item_name,"
            +      "item_description,"
```

```
            +           "measurement_unit,"
            +           "dimension_name, inventory_item)"
            +           "VALUES ("+ itemId + ","
            +                   responsibleEntityString+","
            +                   startDateString + ","
            +                   endDateString + ","
            +                   nameString + ","
            +                   descriptionString + ","
            +                   unitString + ","
            +                   dimensionString + ","
            +                   inventoryFlagString
            +               ")";
        myStatement.executeUpdate(query);
        ...
      } // while versionIterator
      putInCache(theItem);
    } catch (SQLException e) {
      createException(e, query);
    } finally {
      JDBCUtil.close(myStatement);
      JDBCUtil.close(pstmt);
    } // try
} // create(ItemDescription)
```

At the beginning of the method are declarations of the variables for the statement and the query. These need to be declared outside of the try statement because they are used in more than one part of the try statement.

All persistence operations performed by the persistence framework are performed in the context of a transaction. The PersistenceManagerIF object that creates a persister object is responsible for maintaining the transaction context for the persister object's operations. The `create` method gets the TransactionIF object that encapsulates its transaction context by getting the PersistenceManagerIF object and calling its getCurrentTransaction method. A TransactionIF object can be used to explicitly commit or abort a transaction. However, the `create` method does not use it for that purpose.

Because the `create` method is part of a class that is specific to JDBC, it can assume that the class of the object that implements TransactionIF is also specific to JDBC. The class that implements TransactionIF for JDBC is JDBCTransaction. The JDBCTransaction class is responsible for the JDBC connection that all JDBC operations in a transaction's context should use. To perform any database operation through JDBC, the `create` method needs to have a connection to the database. The `create` method gets a JDBC connection by first assuming that the class of the TransactionIF object is JDBCTransaction. It then calls the JDBCTransaction object's getConnection method, which returns the needed connection.

Values concatenated into an SQL query should be formatted using the JDBCUtil.format method. This method does the necessary formatting to represent Java types as strings that conform to SQL syntax.

The main block of the try statement ends with a call to the
`putInCache` method. It puts the freshly persisted object in a cache. When
there is an attempt to retrieve the persisted object, it can be fetched from
the cache rather than from the database. Caching objects in this way is
useful in two situations. One is when you know the persisted object will
not be modified. The other is when it is better to access an old version of a
persisted object quickly than to access the current version of the object
slowly. The cache discards objects after a predetermined amount of time.
If an object in the cache no longer matches the corresponding object in the
database, there is a limit on how old the object can be.

The try statement has a catch clause that catches any `SQLException`
thrown from within the main body of the try statement. It handles the
`SQLException` by calling the `createException` method. It passes the
`createException` method the exception and the query string. The `create-
Exception` method analyzes the exception and throws an appropriate
`DuplicateException`, `CBSystemException`, or `BusinessRuleException`.

The try statement has a finally clause that closes the statement
object(s) used in the main block of the try statement. It closes them using
the `JDBCUtil.close` method. That method handles any exceptions that
may be thrown out of the close operation.

A persister class's `retrieve` methods follow a pattern similar to the
`create` methods.

```
/**
 * Return the persisted version of the
 * <code>ItemDescription</code> object with the given id.
 *
 * @param itemId
 *         The persisted <code>ItemDescription</code>
 *         object.
 * @param forUpdate
 *         If this is true, then the persisted
 *         <code>ItemDescription</code> information is write
 *         locked in the expectation that it will be updated
 *         by a future operation with the same transaction.
 * @exception NotFoundException
 *             If there is no persisted
 *             <code>ItemDescription</code> object with the
 *             given id.
 * @exception CBSystemException
 *             If there is a problem that this method
 *             cannot otherwise classify, it wraps the
 *             exception in a CBSystemException.
 */
public ItemDescription retrieve(long itemId,
                        boolean forUpdate)
                            throws CBSystemException,
                                NotFoundException {
    Long thisId = new Long(itemId);
```

```
ItemDescription theItem;
if (!forUpdate) {
    theItem = (ItemDescription)getFromCache(thisId);
    if (theItem!=null) {
        return theItem;
    } // if theItem
} // if !forUpdate
Statement myStatement = null;
String query = null;
JDBCTransaction tx
  = (JDBCTransaction)
    getManager().getCurrentTransaction();
try {
    Connection myConnection = tx.getConnection();
    myStatement = myConnection.createStatement();
    query
    = "SELECT a.item_id,"
    +       " a.responsible_organization_id,"
    +       " a.effective_begin, a.effective_end,"
    +       " a.item_name, a.item_description,"
    +       " a.measurement_unit, a.dimension_name,"
    +       " a.inventory_item,"
    +       " b.property_name, b.property_value"
    + " FROM itm_item_version_tb a,"
    +       " itm_item_property_tb b"
    + " WHERE a.item_id=" + JDBCUtil.format(itemId)
    +       " AND a.item_id(+)=b.item_id"
    +       " AND a.effective_begin(+)"
    +                       "=b.effective_begin"
    +       " AND a.effective_end(+)=b.effective_end";
    if (forUpdate) {
        query += " FOR UPDATE";
    } // if
    ResultSet rs = myStatement.executeQuery(query);
    if (rs.next()) {
        ItemDescription thisItem
          = (ItemDescription)
            instantiateItemDescription(rs);
        if (forUpdate) {
            tx.putInCacheForUpdate(thisItem);
        } else {
            putInCache(thisItem);
        } // if
        return thisItem;
    } else {
        String msg = Long.toString(itemId);
        throw new NotFoundException(toString(),msg);
    } // if
} catch (SQLException e) {
    retrieveException(e, query);
    return null;
} finally {
    JDBCUtil.close(myStatement);
```

```
        } // try
    } // retrieve(long, boolean)
```

The first thing this `retrieve` method does, if the retrieval is not for update, is to try to get the requested object out of the cache. This has the effect of speeding up the operation by avoiding a database access when the object is in the cache. Note that if a `retrieve` method must guarantee that it always retrieves the current version of a persisted object, it should not use the cache. However, this is not the most important reason for checking the cache first. The persistence framework guarantees there will be at most one object in memory that corresponds to a persisted object. By using a cache in this way, the `retrieve` method ensures that when it is asked to retrieve a particular persisted object that is not for update, it will always return the same object. This is the reason that when the retrieval is being done for update, the method does not look in the cache. It does not look in the cache because performing an update on the object implies getting a lock on the object. The only way it can get a lock on an object is to query the database. Also, the only way to be sure that the update is done correctly is to begin by retrieving the current version of the object.

Before the beginning of the try statement are declarations of the variables for the statement and the query. These need to be declared outside of the try statement because they are used in more than one part of the try statement.

The main block of the try statement queries the database. If the query finds the object's data in the database, it calls another method to instantiate the Java object from the data. It then updates the cache with the object and returns the object.

After a `retrieve` method has retrieved an object, it may put the object in a cache. Each Persister object has two caches that are available to it: a retrieve cache and an update cache. The purpose of the retrieve cache is to speed up retrieve operations. We have already encountered this cache. As discussed before, the use of this sort of caching is not appropriate for many kinds of persisted objects. A retrieve `method` for a kind of object that is to be cached in a retrieve cache should cache the objects that it retrieves in the retrieve cache when the retrieve is not for update. A `retrieve` method caches an object in the retrieve cache by calling the putInCache method.

When a retrieve operation is for update, the retrieved object must not be put in the retrieve cache. The reason for this is to preserve the isolation property of transactions. If an object to be updated is put in the retrieve cache, then changes made to it by the updating transaction may be visible to others before the updating transaction is committed. Also, the changes made to the object will continue to be visible after the updating transaction is aborted.

The update cache is associated with the JDBCTransaction object that is associated with the update transaction. The purpose of the update cache is to help avoid a hard-to-track-down type of bug. Putting an object retrieved for update in the update cache allows the update method to verify that an update is being done using the most recently retrieved version of an object.

The try statement has a catch clause that catches any SQLException that is thrown from within the main body of the try statement. It handles the SQLException by calling the retrieveException method. It passes the createException method the exception and the query string. The createException method analyzes the exception and throws an appropriate NotFoundException or CBSystemException.

The try statement has a finally clause that closes the statement(s) used in the main block of the try statement. It closes them using the JDBCUtil.close method. That method handles any exceptions that may be thrown out of the close operation.

Another common type of retrieve method is one whose arguments do not specify a single object. Such retrieve methods typically have a return type of Iterator. Here is a listing of such a retrieve method.

```
/**
 * Return an Iterator over the persisted
 * Restaurant objects.
 * @exception CBSystemException
 *             If there is a problem that this method
 *             cannot otherwise classify, it wraps the
 *             exception in a CBSystemException.
 */
public Iterator retrieve() throws CBSystemException {
    JDBCTransaction tx
      = (JDBCTransaction)
        getManager().getCurrentTransaction();
    String query = null;
    Statement myStatement= null;
    Connection myConnection = null;
    try {
        myConnection = tx.getConnection();
        myStatement = myConnection.createStatement();
        query
          = "SELECT a.entity_id, a.name, a.cuisine,"
          +       " a.price_min,"
          +       " a.price_max, a.rating,"
          +       " a.delivery_available,"
          +       " a.take_out_available,"
          +       "a.sit_down_available,"
          +       "a.govt_identifier,"
          +       "b.rel_desc, b.start_date, b.end_date"
          +   " FROM lfx_restaurant_tb a, hw_entity_tb b"
          +   " WHERE a.entity_id=b.entity_id";
```

```
        ResultSet rs = myStatement.executeQuery(query);
        return new JDBCObjectIterator(rs);
    } catch (SQLException e) {
        retrieveException(e, query);
    } finally {
        JDBCUtil.close(myConnection);
    } // try
    return null;
} // retrieve()
```

This `retrieve` method differs from the previous one in that it does not instantiate any persisted object. Instead, it instantiates and returns a `JDBCObjectIterator` which arranges for the persisted objects to be instantiated as Java objects when they are needed by the iterator.

The `JDBCObjectIterator` class is an inner class inherited from the `JDBCPersister` superclass. It provides the skeletal logic for an iterator. It instantiates objects from values in the result set passed to its constructor. It passes the values to the persister object's `instantiate` method. Any JDBC-based persister class that makes use of the `JDBCObjectIterator` class must override the `instantiate` method with one that contains the necessary logic to instantiate an object from a set of values in a result set.

Attempting to use the `JDBCObjectIterator` class without overriding the `instantiate` method is an error that is caught by the framework. The `instantiate` method inherited from the `JDBCPersister` class throws an UnimplementedMethodException when it is called.

Here is an example of an `instantiate` method:

```
/**
 * Instantiate a Restaurant object from the
 * current row data in a ResultSet
 */
protected Object instantiate(ResultSet rs) {
    try {
        long id = rs.getLong(1);
        Long thisId = new Long(id);
        Restaurant thisRestaurant;
        thisRestaurant = (Restaurant)getFromCache(thisId);
        if (thisRestaurant!=null) {
            return thisRestaurant;
        } // if
        String name = rs.getString(2);
        String cuisine = rs.getString(3);
...
        int rating = rs.getInt(6);
        Integer starRating
            = (rating>=1 ? new Integer(rating): null);
        boolean deliveryAvailable
            = "T".equals(rs.getString(7));
...
        // Create the <code>Restaurant</code> object.
```

```
        thisRestaurant = new Restaurant(id);
        thisRestaurant.setCuisine(cuisine);
        thisRestaurant.setMinPrice(dollarAmount(minAmt));
        thisRestaurant.setMaxPrice(dollarAmount(maxAmt));
        thisRestaurant.setStarRating(starRating);
...
        putInCache(thisRestaurant);
        return thisRestaurant;
    } catch (SQLException e) {
      String msg
        = "Error occurred retrieving restaurant data";
      throw new CBInternalException(toString(), msg, e);
    } // try
  } // instantiate(ResultSet)
```

This `instantiate` method contains the logic for looking for the object in the cache and adding any object it instantiates to the cache. An `instantiate` method such as this can also be used directly by a `retrieve` method that retrieves individual objects.

There are two basic approaches to implementing an `update` method. Here is a listing that is an example of the simpler approach to implementing an `update` method:

```
/**
 * Update the persisted version of the given SKU.
 * @param theSku
 *         The SKU object to be updated.
 * @exception StaleObjectException
 *            if the SKU object is stale. For any given
 *            object id, the retrieve method or any
 *            iterators that it may create normally
 *            return the same object for any given object
 *            ID. However when an object is retrieved for
 *            update, the object returned may be a
 *            different object than returned previously.
 *            When that happens, objects previously
 *            returned with the same object id are
 *            considered stale.
 * @exception NotFoundException
 *            If there is no persisted SKU object with the
 *            same object ID as the given object.
 * @exception CBSystemException
 *            If there is a problem that this method
 *            cannot otherwise classify, it wraps the
 *            exception in a CBSystemException.
 */
public void update(SKU theSku) throws NotFoundException,
                                      CBSystemException,
                                      BusinessRuleException,
                                      StaleObjectException {
    JDBCTransaction tx
      = (JDBCTransaction)
```

```
        getManager().getCurrentTransaction();
    tx.checkStale(theSku);
    if (theSku.isVersionsDirty() || theSku.isItemsDirty()){
        delete(theSku);
        try {
            create(theSku);
        } catch (DuplicateException e) {
            String msg
               = "Create after delete"
               + " got a duplicate exception";
            throw new CBSystemException(toString(),
                                        msg, e);
        } // try
    } // if
} // update(SKU)
```

The first thing that the update method does is to get its transaction context. Then it calls the checkStale method. All update implementations should call the checkStale method before performing any actual update operations.* The checkStale method throws a StaleObjectException if its argument is not in the update cache. If an object is not in the update cache then it cannot be the most recently retrieved version of that object that was retrieved for update. Using a stale in-memory object for an update operation is a very serious bug that is very difficult to diagnose if the persistence mechanism an application uses does not check for it.

This implementation of the update method goes on to delete the old version of the persisted object and then create a new persisted version. The try statement is in the method to handle an exception that should never be thrown. Because the call to create immediately follows the call to delete, there should never be a reason for it to throw a DuplicateException. This approach to implementing the update method has the advantage of simplicity. However, it is generally inefficient. It requires much more work to delete existing records and create new ones than it does to just update the contents of existing records.

The other approach to implementing the update method is to have it do all of the work itself by doing an actual update of the relevant database rows.

```
/**
 * Update the persisted version of the given Restaurant.
 *
 * @param restaurant
```

---

* The checkStale method is specific to the JDBCTransaction class. Some object-oriented databases have a way of detecting this problem. If an update method is in a Persister class intended to work with a database that detects this problem, then there is no need for the update method to check for stale objects.

```
 *          The restaurant object to use for the update
 *          operation.
 * @exception StaleObjectException
 *              If the Organization object is stale. For
 *              any given object id, the retrieve method or
 *              any iterators that it may create normally
 *              return the same object for any given object
 *              ID. However when an object is retrieved for
 *              update, the object returned may be a
 *              different object than returned previously.
 *              When that happens, objects previously
 *              returned with the same object id are
 *              considered stale.
 * @exception NotFoundException
 *              If there is no persisted Restaurant object
 *              with the same object ID as the given
 *              restaurant object. There is an assumption
 *              that an object's ID never changes.
 * @exception CBSystemException
 *              If there is a problem that this method
 *              cannot otherwise classify, it wraps the
 *              exception in a CBSystemException.
 * @exception BusinessRuleException
 *              If the operation violates a constraint in
 *              the database that appears to reflect a
 *              business rule.
 */
public void update(Restaurant restaurant)
                            throws NotFoundException,
                                   CBSystemException,
                                   StaleObjectException,
                                   BusinessRuleException {
    JDBCTransaction tx
      = (JDBCTransaction)
         getManager().getCurrentTransaction();
    tx.checkStale(restaurant);
    Connection myConnection
      = ((JDBCTransaction)tx).getConnection();
    JDBCRelationshipEntityUtility.update(myConnection,
                                         restaurant);
    Statement myStatement = null;
    String query = null;
    try {
        myStatement = myConnection.createStatement();
        long restaurantID = restaurant.getId();
        String cuisineString
          = JDBCUtil.format(restaurant.getCuisine());
        String govID = restaurant.getGovtIdentifier();
        String minPrice = format(restaurant.getMinPrice());
        String maxPrice = format (restaurant.getMaxPrice());
        ...
        query
          = "UPDATE lfx_restaurant_tb"
```

```
        + " SET cuisine=" + cuisineString
        +    ",govt_identifier=" +JDBCUtil.format(govId)
        ...
        +    " WHERE entity_id="+restaurantID;
    int count = myStatement.executeUpdate(query);
    if (count==0) {
        String msg = "Restaurant to update not found.";
        throw new NotFoundException(toString(), msg);
    } // if
    Class orgPersisterCls
      = OrganizationPersisterIF.class;
    PersistenceIF persister;
    try {
        persister
          = getManager().getPersister(orgPersisterCls);
    } catch (NotFoundException e) {
        String msg;
        msg = "Unable to get OrganizationPersisterIF";
        throw new CBInternalException(toString(),
                                      msg, e);
    } // try
    JDBCOrganizationPersister orgPersister
      = (JDBCOrganizationPersister)persister;
    orgPersister.updateNames(myStatement, restaurant);
    tx.addTransactionCommittedListener(restaurant);
} catch (SQLException e) {
    updateException(e, query);
} finally {
    JDBCUtil.close(myStatement);
} // try
} // update(Restaurant)
```

This implementation of the update method begins with its getting the TransactionIF object that is in charge of the current transaction. Because the implementation is for JDBC, it is able to assume that the class of the TransactionIF object is JDBCTransaction. It then calls the transaction object's checkStale method, as all update method implementations for JDBC should.

Before the beginning of the try statement are declarations of the variables for the statement and the query. These need to be declared outside of the try statement because they are used in more than one part of the try statement.

The main block of the try statement updates the database. After executing an SQL update command, the update method checks the returned count of the number of rows that the update command updated. If the value is 0, indicating that no rows were updated, then it throws a NotFoundException.

Because the update method is updating a complex object, its job is not yet done. The Restaurant objects it is designed to update are complex objects. It proceeds to use another `Persister` object to update other parts of the `Restaurant` object that was passed to it.

The `try` statement has a catch clause that catches any SQLException thrown from within the main body of the try statement. It handles the SQLException by passing the exception and query string to the `updateException` method. The `updateException` method analyzes the exception and throws an appropriate `NotFoundException`, `CBSystem-Exception`, or `BusinessRuleException`.

The `try` statement has a finally clause that closes the statement(s) used in the main block of the `try` statement. It closes them using the `JDBCUtil.close` method. That method handles any exceptions that may be thrown out of the close operation.

Implementing a `delete` method is usually rather straightforward. Here is a listing for a `delete` method.

```java
/**
 * Delete the persisted version of the given
 * <code>Restaurant</code>.
 * @exception BusinessRuleException
 *            If the given restaurant object cannot be
 *            deleted because it is referenced by another
 *            object.
 * @exception CBSystemException
 *            If there is a problem that this method
 *            cannot otherwise classify, it wraps the
 *            exception in a CBSystemException.
 */
public void delete(Restaurant restaurant)
                        throws BusinessRuleException,
                                CBSystemException {
    Statement myStatement = null;
    String query = null;
    JDBCTransaction tx
      = (JDBCTransaction)
        getManager().getCurrentTransaction();
    try {
        Connection myConnection = tx.getConnection();
        myStatement = myConnection.createStatement();
        long restaurantID = restaurant.getId();
        query = "DELETE FROM hw_organization_name_tb"
            +      " WHERE entity_id="+restaurantID;
        myStatement.executeUpdate(query);
        query = "DELETE FROM lfx_restaurant_tb"
            +      " WHERE entity_id="+restaurantID;
        myStatement.executeUpdate(query);
        JDBCRelationshipEntityUtility.delete(tx,
                                        restaurant);
        removeFromCache(restaurant);
    } catch (SQLException e) {
        deleteException(e, query);
```

```
    } finally {
        JDBCUtil.close(myStatement);
    } // try
} // delete(Restaurant)
```

This implementation of the `delete` method follows a pattern similar to the `update` method.

Before the beginning of the `try` statement are declarations of the variables for the statement and the query. These need to be declared outside of the `try` statement because they are used in more than one part of the `try` statement.

The main block of the `try` statement deletes the appropriate records from the database.

The `try` statement has a catch clause that catches any `SQLException` that is thrown from within the main body of the `try` statement. It handles the `SQLException` by calling the `deleteException` method. It passes the `deleteException` method the exception and the query string. The `deleteException` method analyzes the exception and throws an appropriate `CBSystemException` or `BusinessRuleException`.

The `try` statement has a finally clause that closes the statement(s) used in the main block of the `try` statement. It closes them using the `JDBCUtil.close` method. That method handles any exceptions that may be thrown out of the close operation.

Register the Persister Class and Interface

At this point, you have written the necessary persister interfaces and classes to persist the objects you need persisted. However, you are not ready to use them yet.

Clients of persister objects normally get an instance of a persister object by telling a persistence manager that it needs an object that implements a particular persister interface. The only way a persistence manager knows what class goes with what interface is for pairs of persister interfaces and classes to be registered with the persistence manager.

To register pairs of persister interfaces and classes for an application, you define a class that implements the PersistenceInitializerIF interface.

```
public interface PersistenceInitializerIF {
    /**
     * This is called by PersistenceManagerFactory to
     * initialize an appropriate object that implements the
     * PersistenceManagerIF interface. Classes should
     * implement this method with logic that performs
```

```
 * application specific initialization.
 *
 * @param pm
 *         An instance of a class that implements
 *         PersistenceManagerIF that persister interfaces
 *         and classes should be registered with.
 * @exception CBSystemException
 *             if there is a problem
 */
public void initialize(PersistenceManagerIF pm)
                                   throws CBSystemException;


/**
 * Return the Class object that identifies an interface
 * that persistence managers initialized by this object
 * must implement.  I.E., JDBCPersistenceManagerIF.
 */
public Class getInterfaceInitializedByThisObject() ;
} // interface PersistenceInitializerIF
```

Here is an example of a class that implements the PersistenceInitializerIF interface.

```
public class LunchFXInitializer implements PersistenceInitializerIF {
    /**
     * Perform lunchFX specific initializations on the given
     * PersistenceManagerIF object.
     */
    public void initialize(PersistenceManagerIF pm) {
       pm.registerInterface(RestaurantPersisterIF.class,
                            JDBCRestaurantPersister.class);
    } // initialize(PersistenceManagerIF)
    /**
     * Return the Class object that identifies an interface
     * that persistence managers initialized by this object
     * must implement. The implementation returns
     * JDBCPersistenceManagerIF.
     */
    public Class getInterfaceInitializedByThisObject() {
        return JDBCPersistenceManagerIF.class;
    } // getInterfaceInitializedByThisObject()
} // class LunchFXInitializer
```

Implementations of the initialize method generally consist of calls to the registerInterface method of the PersistenceManagerIF object that is passed to it. These method calls register pairs of the application's persister interfaces and classes.

The getInterfaceInitializedByThisObject method simply returns the interface of the Persister classes that it is intended to work with.

The way to arrange for a PersistenceManagerIF object's registerInterface method to be called is shown by the following code listing:

```
PersistenceManagerFactory persistFactory;
persistFactory = PersistenceManagerFactory.getInstance();
persistFactory.registerInitializer(
                        new LunchFXJDBCInitializer());
```

The code above gets a `PersistenceManagerFactory` object and calls its `registerInitializer` method to register the `PersistenceManagerIF` object. Registering it causes its `registerInterface` method to be called at an appropriate time.

Using the Persistence Framework

After the PersistenceInitializerIF objects have been registered, the persistence framework is ready to be used. To use the persistence framework, you get an object that implements the appropriate persister interface and use it.

The first step in getting a persister object is to get an instance of PersistenceManagerFactory like this:

```
PersistenceManagerFactory persistFactory;
persistFactory = PersistenceManagerFactory.getInstance();
```

The next step is to get a PersistenceManager object like this:

```
PersistenceManagerIF persistenceManager;
persistenceManager = persistFactory.getPersistenceManager();
```

The PersistenceManagerFactory's `getInstance` method returns a PersistenceManagerIF object that is responsible for making the persistence framework work the actual database or other persistence mechanism that is being used.

Once you have a PersistenceManagerIF object, you can get an appropriate object that implements a persister interface like this:

```
RestaurantPersisterIF restaurantPersister;
RestaurantPersister
  = (RestaurantPersisterIF)

persistenceManager.getPersister(RestaurantPersisterIF.class);
```

Complex Objects

This step is a common optimization. It is optional in the sense that the persistence will work without it; however, update operations will be faster with this step.

Updating complex objects can be an expensive operation. To avoid taking the time to update an object when it is unnecessary, there must be a way to determine if the Java object's state may be different from the persisted object. The way this is usually accomplished is that the class of the complex objects is given an attribute, typically called "dirty," that will be true if the state of the Java object may be different from the persisted version of the object. If there is a lot of state information associated with an object, then it may be advantageous for its class to have more than one dirty attribute, with each dirty attribute being associated with a different subset of the state information.

The implementation of dirty attributes is generally rather straightforward. Dirty attributes are initialized to false. When any of the class's set methods are called, in addition to setting the value of the attribute implied by the method's name, it also sets a dirty flag to true. There are also methods to query the value of the dirty attribute and to clear and set it. Here is some sample code:

```java
/**
 * This is true if the contents of the items interval map
 * are dirty.
 */
private boolean itemsIsDirty = false;
/**
 * This is true if the contents of the versions interval map
 * are dirty.
 */
private boolean versionsIsDirty = false;
...

public void addVersionDate(Calendar effectiveDate)
                                throws DuplicateException {
    SKUVersion newVersion = getVersion(effectiveDate);
    newVersion = (SKUVersion)newVersion.clone();
    versions.add(new Interval(effectiveDate, null), newVersion);
    versionsIsDirty = true;
} // addVersionDate(Calendar)
...

public void addItemDate(SKUItems newItems, Calendar effectiveDate) {
    items.add(new Interval(effectiveDate, null), newItems);
    itemsIsDirty = true;
} // addItemDate(Calendar)
...

public void addItemDate(SKUItems newItems, Interval when) {
    items.add(when, newItems);
    itemsIsDirty = true;
} // addItemDate(Calendar)
...

/**
 * Return true if the set of intervals in the items interval
 * map may not match the persisted version of this object.
 */
boolean isItemsDirty() {
    return itemsIsDirty;
} // isItemsDirty()
```

```
/**
 * Return true if the set of intervals in the versions
 * interval map may not match the persisted version of this object.
 */
boolean isVersionsDirty() {
    return versionsIsDirty;
} // isVersionsDirty()

/**
 * Clear all of the dirty flags associated with this object.
 */
void clearDirty() {
    Iterator versionIterator = versions.intervals();
    while (versionIterator.hasNext()) {
        Interval thisInterval = (Interval)versionIterator.next();

((SKUVersion)versions.getMatching(thisInterval)).clearDirty();
    } // while versionIterator
    itemsIsDirty = false;
    versionsIsDirty = false;
} // clearDirty()

/**
 * Set all of the dirty flags associated with this object.
 */
void setDirty() {
    Iterator versionIterator = versions.intervals();
    while (versionIterator.hasNext()) {
        Interval thisInterval = (Interval)versionIterator.next();

((SKUVersion)versions.getMatching(thisInterval)).setDirty();
    } // while versionIterator
    itemsIsDirty = true;
    versionsIsDirty = true;
} // setDirty()
...
```

Once you have implemented the dirty attribute for a class to be persisted, the next thing to do is to add code to the corresponding persister classes' methods that use the dirty attribute. There are two ways that the persister classes will use the dirty attribute.

- Their update method will check the value of the dirty attribute before it tries to update anything. This will avoid unnecessary work.
- After each create, retrieve, or update operation, a Java object's dirty attribute should be set to false. After a delete operation, a Java object's dirty attribute should be set to true.

Setting the object's dirty attribute is more complicated than it may seem at first. The difficulty arises out of the fact that these operations are part of a transaction. At the completion of an operation, there is no way to know if the transaction will eventually be committed. When an object is returned by a retrieve operation, you always want its dirty attribute to be false, whether the transaction will be committed or not.

If immediately after a create or update operation the dirty attribute of an object is set to false and the transaction is later aborted, then future update operations on that object will not work correctly. To be sure that we set the dirty attribute to false only when we are sure it is the right thing to do, we want to set it to true immediately after the transaction is committed. If the transaction is never committed, then the dirty attribute is never set to false because of the create or update operation.

The next paragraph describes the mechanism for scheduling an object's dirty attribute to be set to false immediately after a transaction is committed. Before describing that, let us first think about setting the dirty flag to true after a delete operation. If the persistent version of an object is deleted, the dirty attribute of its Java version set to true, and the transaction then aborted, the worst thing that will happen is that an update operation on the object may perform unnecessary work. Since the result is functionally correct, waiting until a transaction is committed to set an object's dirty attribute to true after a delete operation is an optimization, but not a requirement. This release of the persistence framework does not include a way to schedule the dirty attribute of a deleted object to be set to true after the transaction is committed.

The mechanism for setting an object's dirty attribute to false after a transaction is committed is to use an event. The code for a create or update operation registers the object it operates on with the TransactionIF object. When the TransactionIF object's commit method is called, after it successfully commits the transaction it sends a TransactionCommittedEvent to all registered objects.

To be able to receive a TransactionCommittedEvent, an object must implement that TransactionCommittedListener interface.

```
public class SKU implements Serializable,
                            CachableIF,
                            TransactionCommittedListener {

...
    /**
     * A TransactionCommittedEvent object is passed to this
     * method when a transaction commits. This method clears
     * this object's dirty flags.
     */
    public void transactionCommitted(TransactionCommittedEvent evt) {
        clearDirty();
    } // transactionCommitted(TransactionCommittedEvent)
...
```

Here is a `create` method that registers objects to receive TransactionCommittedEvent.

```
public void create(SKU theSku)
                            throws DuplicateException,
                                   EBoxSystemException,
                                   BusinessRuleException {


    ...
    tx.addTransactionCommittedListener(theSku);
} // create(TransactionIF, SKU)
```

BIBLIOGRAPHY

[Brown-Whitenack98] Kyle Brown, Bruce Whitenack "Crossing Chasms: A Pattern Language for Object-RDBMS Integration 'The Static Patterns'".
www.ksccary.com

[Buschman96] Frank Buschmann, Regine Meunier, Hans Rohnert, Peter Sommerlad, Michael Stal. A System of Patterns. John Wiley & Sons, Baffins Lane, Chichester, West Sussex, England, 1996.

[CEF98] Andy Carlson, Sharon Estepp, Martin Fowler. "Temporal Patterns". Paper presented at PLOP'98.
http://jerry.cs.uiuc.edu/~plop/plop98/final_submissions/P09.pdf

[Date94] Chris J. Date. An Introduction to Database Systems. Addison-Wesley, Reading, MA, 1994.

[Doeringer90] Willibald Doeringer, Doug Dykeman, Matthias Kaiserswerth, Bernd Meister and Harry Rudin, Robin Williamson. "A Survey of Light-Weight Transport Protocols for High-Speed Networks". IEEE Transactions on Communication, November, 1990, Volume 38, Number 11, pp. 2025-2039.

[Fægri95] Tor Erlend Fægri, "Replication in Distributed Object Systems".
http://www.dcs.gla.ac.uk/~faegri/replication-summary.html

[GoF95] Erich Gamma, Richard Helm, Ralph Johnson, and John Vlissides. Design Patterns: Elements of Reusable Object-Oriented Software. Addison-Wesley, Reading, MA, 1995.

[Gray-Reuter93] Jim Gray, Andreas Reuter. Transaction Processing: Concepts and Techniques. Morgan Kaufman Publishers, San Mateo, California, 1993.

[Heaney99] Mathew Heaney. "Static Locking Order", http://www.acm.org/archives/wa.cgi?A2=ind9904&L=patterns&F= &S=&P=878.

[Keller98] Wolfgang Keller, Jens Coldewey: Accessing Relational Databases: A Pattern Language, in Robert Martin, Dirk Riehle, Frank Buschmann (Eds.): Pattern Languages of Program Design 3. Addison-Wesley 1998.

[Kendall-Malkoun96] Elizabeth A. Kendall, Margaret T. Malkoun. The Layered Agent Patterns. http://www.cse.rmit.edu.au/~rdsek/papers/ laypattern.ps

[Lange98] Manfred Lange. "Time Patterns". Paper Presented at PLOP'98. http://jerry.cs.uiuc.edu/~plop/plop98/final_submissions/P04.pdf.

[Lea99] Doug Lea. PooledExecutor http://gee.cs.oswego.edu/dl/classes/EDU/oswego/cs/dl/util/concurrent/ PooledExecutor.java

[ODMG97] ODMG. Edited by R.G.G. Cattell, Douglas Barry, Dirk Bartels, Mark Berler, Jeff Eastman, Sophie Gamerman, David Jordan, Adam Springer, Henry Strickland, and Drew Wade. The Object Database Standard: ODMG 2.0. Morgan Kaufman Publishers, San Mateo, California, 1997.

[Schmidt97] Douglas C. Schmidt, Tim Harrison, Irfan Pyarali, Thomas D. Jordan. "Proactor — An Object Behavioral Pattern for Demultiplexing and Dispatching Handlers for Asynchronous Events" http://st-www.cs.uiuc.edu/%7Eplop/plop97/Proceedings/pyarali .proactor.pdf.

[Sommerlad98] Peter Sommerlad and Marcel Rüedi. "Do-it-yourself Reflection patterns". Paper Presented at EuroPLoP'98. http://www.coldewey.com/europlop98/Program/Papers/Sommerlad.ps

[Sternbach97] Efrem J. Sternbach. "Configurable Prototype". ftp://ftp.irmc.com/irmc.com/papers/configurable_prototype.pdf

[Yoder98] Joseph W. Yoder, Ralph E. Johnson, Quince D. Wilson. "Connecting Business Objects to Relational Database". http://jerry.cs.uiuc.edu/~plop/plop98/final_submissions/P51.pdf.

[Yoder-Barcalow98] Joseph W. Yoder, Jeffery Barcalow. "Architectural Patterns for Enabling Application Security". http://www.joeyoder.com/papers/patterns/Security/appsec.pdf

I N D E X

CUSTOMER NOTE: IF THIS BOOK IS ACCOMPANIED BY SOFTWARE, PLEASE READ THE FOLLOWING BEFORE OPENING THE PACKAGE.